The Collected Writings of Walt Whitman

The Collected Writings of Walt Whitman

give us 500 slip impressions of this — plain white paper —

Not to proof reader please follow copy — punctuation. Capitalization &c. (always leave to your own judgment to correct any evident, hasty, or technical error)

Walt Whitman's
style of same indention as here

New Prose Book

Specimen Days (in one line)

& Collect. (in one line)

A full compendium of the author's Prose Writings, old and new. Gives Mr Whitman's early Days on Long Island and your wanderings in New York city — copious War and Army Hospital Memoranda (1862-'65) — outdoor convalescent out door Notes, in the country County (1876-'81) — jaunts visits in Boston — some literary criticisms — Jaunts over the Great Plains — and along the St Lawrence and Saguenay. the Collect includes all his political and critical writings, & youthful sketches.

Page Subtitle &c

The Two display lines will be of course Specimen Days and Leaves of Grass

WALT WHITMAN

Prose Works 1892

VOLUME I, SPECIMEN DAYS

Edited by Floyd Stovall

 NEW YORK UNIVERSITY PRESS 1963

The Collected Writings of Walt Whitman

GENERAL EDITORS

Gay Wilson Allen and Sculley Bradley

ADVISORY EDITORIAL BOARD

Roger Asselineau   *Harold W. Blodgett*

Charles E. Feinberg   *Clarence Gohdes*

Emory Holloway   *Rollo G. Silver*   *Floyd Stovall*

GRATEFUL ACKNOWLEDGMENT IS MADE TO

Mr. Charles E. Feinberg,

WHOSE ASSISTANCE MADE POSSIBLE THE ILLUSTRATIONS
IN THIS VOLUME AND WHO ALSO MADE
AVAILABLE TO THE PUBLISHER THE RESOURCES OF
THE FEINBERG COLLECTION.

Preface

Walt Whitman won his place in the American literary pantheon as the poet of *Leaves of Grass*, and he will surely maintain it, if at all, in the same capacity; nevertheless, his prose writing has a proper place in the canon which cannot be ignored. His purpose in writing it was not merely to promote his fame or to regale the reader with gossip about himself and the minutiae of his daily life, but also to translate the symbols and indirections of his poems into a language more readily understood and therefore more immediately efficacious in the workaday world. Indeed the best commentary on *Leaves of Grass* is Whitman's own prose, not the prefaces only, but also *Democratic Vistas* and *Specimen Days* as well as certain of the critical essays. His prose is an illuminating commentary also on Whitman's two worlds—the actual world about him and the imaginative world of his own creation.

The best of the prose, moreover, has a literary character hardly less original and distinctive than the poetry. Before the period of the Civil War his published prose was written hurriedly, and though clear and often forceful, had the qualities rather of journalism than of literature. After the preface to the 1855 *Leaves of Grass*, *Democratic Vistas* was the first prose publication which he composed with great care. Most of his literary prose was written after his paralysis, between 1875 and 1888, when his poetic genius had spent itself and he had leisure for meditation and deliberate composition. During this period he lived close to nature and seemed to draw from the earth a new strength for body and mind. The observations jotted down at Timber Creek with no other purpose than to express his sensations and reflections of the moment were later revised with an artist's care for the vivid effects, the complex rhythms, and the nice distinctions of thought and feeling that characterize his best prose writing.

Prose Works 1892, Volumes One and Two, of which this volume is the first, perform that function which is suggested by their title among the several volumes which collectively make up this entire edition of Walt Whitman's *Collected Writings*. These two volumes of *Prose Works* contain all (except the juvenilia) of the contents of Whitman's final edition of his *Complete Prose Works* in 1892. In this volume Whitman gave final

publication to all the prose which he had collected from the past or newly
published; it may be assumed that he included what he judged to be his
best prose, and what little besides that he wished to retain for other reasons. A few items which are not intrinsically superior may have been retained as specimens of recent volumes or because the poet wished to put on
record certain personal data. "Pieces in Early Youth," prose and poetry,
may have been included, as he says in a foreword, "to avoid the annoyance
of their surreptitious issue, (as lately announced, from outsiders)." They
are not included in the present *Prose Works 1892*, but the reader will find
them in another volume of the *Collected Writings*.

Much of Whitman's prose represented the combination and revision of
earlier publications. *Democratic Vistas* (1871) consolidated and expanded
two essays that had appeared in the *Galaxy* magazine; *Memoranda During
the War* (1875) incorporated numerous excerpts from a series of articles
entitled " 'Tis But Ten Years Since," published in 1874 in the New York
Weekly Graphic, some of which had previously appeared in articles he
had contributed to the New York *Times* in 1863–65; the prose volume of
the Author's (or Centennial) Edition, *Two Rivulets* (1876), contained
Memoranda During the War, reprinted without change, and *Democratic
Vistas*, reprinted with very minor changes. Whitman's first carefully
edited collection, *Specimen Days & Collect* (1882), contained revised versions of all the prose of *Two Rivulets* and many clippings from earlier
contributions to periodicals not previously collected, with a good deal of
new writing. That volume, after minor revision of the plates, was reprinted
in Glasgow the next year (identified in *Prose Works 1892* as SDC Glasgow), and again in 1888 in *Complete Poems & Prose of Walt Whitman,
1855–1888*. *Specimen Days*, without "Collect," was published in London
in 1887 as *Specimen Days in America*, and parts of "Collect," together
with some essays first published after 1882, were reprinted in London in
1888 as *Democratic Vistas, and Other Papers*. *November Boughs* (1888)
and *Good-Bye My Fancy* (1891) were collections of poetry and prose,
mostly from new periodical publications. The prose of these volumes, with
Specimen Days & Collect and its appendix of "Pieces in Early Youth,"
made up the contents of Whitman's final collection, *Complete Prose
Works* (1892).

The present edition of Whitman's *Prose Works* is printed directly
from the pages of the 1892 edition with no change except the cor-
rection of obvious errors overlooked in that edition. In the present edition
the whole of Volume I is given to "Specimen Days"; Volume II contains
the remainder. Each variation from the honored text is explained in the
notes. In the textual notes and in the Appendix I have recorded, I think,

every variant reading of every earlier printed text which Whitman used, in whole or in part, in the 1892 *Complete Prose*. Passages omitted from that edition, if short and closely related to the preserved text, are quoted in the notes; if long, these passages are incorporated in the Appendix. Cross references are provided in the notes and in the Appendix to enable the reader to follow all the changes that Whitman made in a given passage or article from its first to its final publication. I have examined at first hand or in photostatic copies every book and periodical publication that contributed to the making of Whitman's final text. I have not collated any text published after Whitman's death, nor any for which he was not personally responsible. In a few cases I have quoted or made reference to passages in texts edited after Whitman's death if they are closely related to his text, particularly if I have also included a version in the textual notes or the Appendix.

I have also examined most of the extant manuscripts of importance to this edition. I have relied chiefly on the indispensable collection of Mr. Charles E. Feinberg, but I have also used some manuscripts in the Clifton Waller Barrett Collection at the University of Virginia. I have consulted other collections, such as those in the Library of Congress and at Duke and New York University; but since the purpose of this edition is to record the evolution of the printed texts, it seemed inappropriate to further extend the already voluminous notes by annotating rough drafts and fragmentary manuscripts. Manuscript readings are therefore not noted unless they are drawn from finished manuscripts and appear to have special significance for the study of Whitman's life or literary method. The most important manuscripts are the printer's copy of *Specimen Days & Collect* and the printer's copy of *Good-Bye My Fancy*, both in the Feinberg Collection. These have been made fully available to me, and I have worked with microfilm copies of them constantly at hand. A large part of the printer's copy of *November Boughs* is not available; I do not know where it is, if it still exists. The manuscripts from which *Two Rivulets*, *Memoranda During the War*, and *Democratic Vistas* were printed have not, so far as I know, been preserved.

I am indebted to more individuals and institutions than I can name here. In particular I am obliged to various members of the staff of each of the following libraries for photostats and other valuable services: the Library of Congress, the New York Public Library, the Brooklyn Public Library, the Free Library of Philadelphia, the Public Library of the District of Columbia, the Duke University Library, the Library of the University of Colorado, the Denver Public Library, and the Library of the University of Western Ontario. I am also indebted to Mr. G. W. Spragge,

Archivist of Ontario, for his generous assistance in securing photostats of the London *Advertiser*. To Professor Rollo G. Silver I am grateful for many kindnesses; and I wish to thank him and the editors of *American Literature* for permission to use his article "Walt Whitman Interviews Himself" (*American Literature*, March, 1938) in collating an item by Whitman in the Denver *Tribune* in 1879. To Mr. Emory Holloway I have debts of long standing, but I owe him special thanks for his kind assistance in helping me try to locate the Christmas Number (1874) of the New York *Daily Graphic*, and, when this could not be done, for providing me with the notes he made on Whitman's contribution to it when he was editing the *Uncollected Poetry and Prose*.

To Mr. Charles E. Feinberg I am indebted beyond all hope of adequate expression. He has always been generous, kind, hospitable, and long-suffering in helping to make my work with his collection both the greatest possible success and the greatest pleasure. He has been equally kind, I know, to many another intruding scholar.

To Mr. Clifton Waller Barrett I take this opportunity to express my appreciation and gratitude for the gift of his magnificent collection of American literature to the Library of the University of Virginia, where it has been most convenient and of inestimable value to me.

I wish to thank the members of the Editorial Board of the *Collected Writings*, of which these volumes are a part, for support and encouragement. In particular I am grateful to the General Editors, Professor Gay W. Allen and Professor Sculley Bradley, for their patience, and for their more direct assistance in planning and editing *Prose Works 1892*.

To my friends and colleagues, the staff of Alderman Library, I am, as always, much indebted. To Mr. John C. Wyllie, the Librarian, and Mr. William Runge, Curator of Rare Books, and through them to the entire Library staff, I extend my most sincere thanks. I wish also to thank the secretaries of the English Department, Mrs. Adele Hall and Mrs. Prudence Gilhams, who have assisted me in the tedious work of preparing a final typescript of the textual notes and Appendix.

I am grateful to the Faculty Committee on Research of the University of Virginia for the grant of money which has facilitated my work.

To my wife, my partner as well as my unwearied encourager and sustainer in this and other literary enterprises, I shall not attempt to express my debt. To her I say only: One more job done; now for the next!

FLOYD STOVALL

CONTENTS

PREFACE   *vii*

CONTENTS   *xi*

NOTE ON THE TEXTUAL VARIANTS   *xix*

ABBREVIATIONS   *xxi*

A Happy Hour's Command   1

Answer to an Insisting Friend   3

Genealogy—Van Velsor and Whitman   4

The Old Whitman and Van Velsor Cemeteries   5

The Maternal Homestead   7

Two Old Family Interiors   8

Paumanok, and My Life on It as Child and Young Man   10

My First Reading.—Lafayette   13

Printing Office.—Old Brooklyn   14

Growth—Health—Work   15

My Passion for Ferries   16

Broadway Sights   16

Omnibus Jaunts and Drivers   18

Plays and Operas Too   19

Through Eight Years   21

Sources of Character—Results—1860   22

Opening of the Secession War   23

National Uprising and Volunteering   24

Contemptuous Feeling   25

Battle of Bull Run, July, 1861   26

The Stupor Passes—Something Else Begins   30

Down at the Front   32

After First Fredericksburg   33

Back to Washington   34

Fifty Hours Left Wounded on the Field 36

Hospital Scenes and Persons 38

Patent-Office Hospital 39

The White House by Moonlight 40

An Army Hospital Ward 41

A Connecticut Case 42

Two Brooklyn Boys 43

A Secesh Brave 43

The Wounded from Chancellorsville 44

A Night Battle, Over a Week Since 45

Unnamed Remains the Bravest Soldier 48

Some Specimen Cases 49

My Preparations for Visits 51

Ambulance Processions 52

Bad Wounds—the Young 52

The Most Inspiriting of All War's Shows 53

Battle of Gettysburg 54

A Cavalry Camp 55

A New York Soldier 56

Home-Made Music 57

Abraham Lincoln 59

Heated Term 61

Soldiers and Talks 62

Death of a Wisconsin Officer 64

Hospitals Ensemble 65

A Silent Night Ramble 67

Spiritual Characters among the Soldiers 67

Cattle Droves about Washington 68

Hospital Perplexity 69

Down at the Front 69

Paying the Bounties 70

Rumors, Changes, &c. 71

Virginia 71

Summer of 1864 72

A New Army Organization Fit for America 74

Death of a Hero 75

Hospital Scenes—Incidents 76

A Yankee Soldier 77

Union Prisoners South 78

Deserters 79

A Glimpse of War's Hell-Scenes 79

Gifts—Money—Discrimination | 81
Items from My Note Books | 82
A Case from Second Bull Run | 83
Army Surgeons—Aid Deficiencies | 84
The Blue Everywhere | 85
A Model Hospital | 86
Boys in the Army | 86
Burial of a Lady Nurse | 87
Female Nurses for Soldiers | 88
Southern Escapees | 89
The Capitol by Gas-Light | 91
The Inauguration | 92
Attitude of Foreign Governments During the War | 93
The Weather.—Does It Sympathize with These Times? | 94
Inauguration Ball | 95
Scene at the Capitol | 95
A Yankee Antique | 96
Wounds and Diseases | 97
Death of President Lincoln | 98
Sherman's Army's Jubilation—Its Sudden Stoppage | 99
No Good Portrait of Lincoln | 100
Releas'd Union Prisoners from South | 100
Death of a Pennsylvania Soldier | 103
The Armies Returning | 104
The Grand Review | 105
Western Soldiers | 106
A Soldier on Lincoln | 106
Two Brothers, One South, One North | 107
Some Sad Cases Yet | 108
Calhoun's Real Monument | 109
Hospitals Closing | 109
Typical Soldiers | 111
"Convulsiveness" | 112
Three Years Summ'd Up | 112
The Million Dead, Too, Summ'd Up | 114
The Real War Will Never Get in the Books | 115
An Interregnum Paragraph | 118
New Themes Entered Upon | 119
Entering a Long Farm-Lane | 120
To the Spring and Brook | 121
An Early Summer Reveille | 121

Birds Migrating at Midnight 122
Bumble-Bees 123
Cedar-Apples 126
Summer Sights and Indolencies 127
Sundown Perfume—Quail-Notes—the Hermit Thrush 127
A July Afternoon by the Pond 128
Locusts and Katydids 129
The Lesson of a Tree 130
Autumn Side-Bits 132
The Sky—Days and Nights—Happiness 133
Colors—a Contrast 135
November 8, '76 135
Crows and Crows 136
A Winter Day on the Sea-Beach 137
Sea-Shore Fancies 138
In Memory of Thomas Paine 140
A Two Hours' Ice-Sail 142
Spring Overtures—Recreations 143
One of the Human Kinks 144
An Afternoon Scene 144
The Gates Opening 145
The Common Earth, the Soil 145
Birds and Birds and Birds 146
Full-Starr'd Nights 147
Mulleins and Mulleins 148
Distant Sounds 149
A Sun-Bath—Nakedness 150
The Oaks and I 152
A Quintette 154
The First Frost—Mems 154
Three Young Men's Deaths 155
February Days 158
A Meadow Lark 160
Sundown Lights 161
Thoughts under an Oak—a Dream 161
Clover and Hay Perfume 162
An Unknown 163
Bird-Whistling 163
Horse-Mint 164
Three of Us 164
Death of William Cullen Bryant 165

Jaunt up the Hudson 167
Happiness and Raspberries 167
A Specimen Tramp Family 168
Manhattan from the Bay 169
Human and Heroic New York 171
Hours for the Soul 173
Straw-Color'd and Other Psyches 178
A Night Remembrance 179
Wild Flowers 180
A Civility Too Long Neglected 181
Delaware River—Days and Nights 181
Scenes on Ferry and River—Last Winter's Nights 183
The First Spring Day on Chestnut Street 188
Up the Hudson to Ulster County 190
Days at J. B.'s—Turf-Fires—Spring Songs 191
Meeting a Hermit 193
An Ulster County Waterfall 193
Walter Dumont and His Medal 194
Hudson River Sights 194
Two City Areas, Certain Hours 196
Central Park Walks and Talks 197
A Fine Afternoon, 4 to 6 198
Departing of the Big Steamers 200
Two Hours on the Minnesota 201
Mature Summer Days and Nights 202
Exposition Building—New City Hall—River Trip 203
Swallows on the River 204
Begin a Long Jaunt West 205
In the Sleeper 205
Missouri State 206
Lawrence and Topeka, Kansas 207
The Prairies. *And an Undeliver'd Speech.* 207
On to Denver—a Frontier Incident 209
An Hour on Kenosha Summit 210
An Egotistical "Find" 210
New Senses—New Joys 211
Steam-Power, Telegraphs, &c 211
America's Back-Bone 212
The Parks 213
Art Features 213
Denver Impressions 214

I Turn South—and Then East Again   216
Unfulfill'd Wants—the Arkansas River   217
A Silent Little Follower—the Coreopsis   218
The Prairies and Great Plains in Poetry   219
The Spanish Peaks—Evening on the Plains   220
America's Characteristic Landscape   220
Earth's Most Important Stream   221
Prairie Analogies—the Tree Question   222
Mississippi Valley Literature   222
An Interviewer's Item   224
The Women of the West   225
The Silent General   226
President Hayes's Speeches   227
St. Louis Memoranda   228
Nights on the Mississippi   229
Upon Our Own Land   229
Edgar Poe's Significance   230
Beethoven's Septette   233
A Hint of Wild Nature   233
Loafing in the Woods   234
A Contralto Voice   235
Seeing Niagara to Advantage   236
Jaunting to Canada   237
Sunday with the Insane   237
Reminiscence of Elias Hicks   239
Grand Native Growth   240
A Zollverein Between the U. S. and Canada   240
The St. Lawrence Line   241
The Savage Saguenay   242
Capes Eternity and Trinity   243
Chicoutimi and Ha-Ha Bay   244
The Inhabitants—Good Living   244
Cedar-Plums Like—Names   245
Death of Thomas Carlyle   248
Carlyle from American Points of View   254
A Couple of Old Friends—a Coleridge Bit   263
A Week's Visit to Boston   264
The Boston of To-Day   265
My Tribute to Four Poets   266
Millet's Pictures—Last Items   267
Birds—and a Caution   269

Samples of My Common-Place Book — 270
My Native Sand and Salt Once More — 273
Hot Weather New York — 273
"Custer's Last Rally" — 275
Some Old Acquaintances—Memories — 277
A Discovery of Old Age — 277
A Visit, at the Last, to R. W. Emerson — 278
Other Concord Notations — 280
Boston Common—More of Emerson — 281
An Ossianic Night—Dearest Friends — 282
Only a New Ferry Boat — 283
Death of Longfellow — 284
Starting Newspapers — 286
The Great Unrest of Which We Are Part — 289
By Emerson's Grave — 290
At Present Writing—Personal — 291
After Trying a Certain Book — 292
Final Confessions—Literary Tests — 293
Nature and Democracy—Morality — 294

APPENDICES:

A. Books and Periodicals from Which Passages Were Omitted
   in SDC
   "The Great Army of the Sick." NYT, February 26, 1863 — 296
   "Washington in the Hot Season." NYT, August 16, 1863 — 301
   "Our Wounded and Sick Soldiers." NYT, December 11, 1864 — 302
   " 'Tis But Ten Years Since." Six Papers in NYWG.
       First Paper, January 24, 1874 — 310
       Second Paper, February 7, 1874 — 313
       Third Paper, February 14, 1874 — 314
       Fourth Paper, February 21, 1874 — 316
       Fifth Paper, February 28, 1874 — 318
       Sixth Paper, March 7, 1874 — 319
   Memoranda During the War, 1875–76 — 320
   "A Poet's Recreation." NYTR, July 4, 1878 — 329
   "Winter Sunshine." PT, January 26, 1879 — 330
   "Broadway Revisited." NYTR, May 10, 1879 — 338
   "Real Summer Openings." NYTR, May 17, 1879 — 339
   "These May Afternoons." NYTR, May 24, 1879 — 341
   "Walt Whitman's Impression of Denver and the West." Denver *Daily Tribune*, September 21 [?], 1879 — 343

"Summer Days in Canada." London (Ont.) *Advertiser*, June 22, 1880   345

"Letter from Walt Whitman." London (Ont.) *Advertiser*, August 26, 1880   346

"How I Get Around at Sixty and Take Notes." Six Numbers in *CR*.

    First Number, January 29, 1881   347

    Second Number, April 9, 1881   347

    Third Number, May 7, 1881   347

    Fourth Number, July 16, 1881   348

    Fifth Number, December 3, 1881   348

    Sixth Number, July 15, 1882   351

"Bumble-Bees and Bird-Music." *PA*, May 14, 1881   352

"A Week at West Hills." *NYTR*, August 4, 1881   352

"City Notes in August." *NYTR*, August 15, 1881   354

"Death of Longfellow." *CR*, April 8, 1882   355

"Starting Newspapers." *CC*, June 1, 1882; *NYW*, June 11, 1882   355

"Edgar Poe's Significance." *CR*, June 3, 1882   355

B. Chronology of Walt Whitman's Life and Work   356

Note on the Textual Variants

All textual notes comparing the present text with Whitman's autograph manuscript, or with a printed clipping which he included as manuscript, have reference to the extant printer's copy of *Specimen Days & Collect* unless a different source is specified. The symbol "MS," when used without qualification, always refers to this printer's copy. The symbols used for the titles of books and periodicals are listed under "Abbreviations."

The lines of each section of the text, as identified by Whitman's subtitle, are numbered in a separate sequence. Whitman's footnotes are treated as part of the text which is being edited in the present volume. Variant readings are printed on the lower part of the page which in this edition contains those passages to which they pertain. The initial number in each textual note corresponds with that of the annotated line of the text. Where verbal change is concerned the first entry after this number is the key word or phrase from the line of text annotated; the variant readings follow in reverse chronological order, each reading separated from that preceding by a terminal bracket. When the key phrase is long it is shortened, as indicated by the mark (. . .) of ellipsis. If two or more early versions of a long passage show only minor differences, the later version will be quoted at length and the variants of earlier versions inserted at the appropriate places in brackets. If an earlier text is identical with the key word or phrase, it is not mentioned in the note. Autograph MS variants originating before the initial publication of a passage are noted only when they have special significance for the study of Whitman's life or his literary method.

Whitman's use of the series of periods (leaders, he called them) for punctuation is inconsistent, but because of the importance that has sometimes been attached to this kind of punctuation each use of it has been retained without change. The following variations are not recorded unless they occur in a context annotated for other reasons: the change of initial capitals to lower case letters in common nouns; the use of figures for words to indicate numbers; the shift from "etc." to "&c." or from "ed" to " 'd" in nonsyllabic endings, or the change in the position of the comma before or after quotation marks and marks of parenthesis; and minor changes in punctuation, such as the omission of the comma before "and" in a series and the use of a comma in place of a dash or a colon in place of a semicolon, where they do not affect the meaning of a sentence.

Differences between the corrected printer's copy and the published text of *SDC* represent, with but few exceptions, the revisions made by Whitman in the galley proof, the corrected copy of which has not been available to the present editor and perhaps no longer exists. He has seen the corrected page proofs in the Feinberg Collection. He has also seen Whitman's list of corrections and changes to be made in the plates before the printing of the Glasgow edition of *SDC*. Only a very few changes were made in the plates, which were also used for *CPP* and *CPW*.

Interpolated comments by the present editor in the textual notes, followed where necessary by the identifying abbreviation "ED.," are enclosed in brackets.

Passages from earlier publications omitted in *SDC*, if they are relatively short or closely connected with the context, appear in the textual notes; all others are printed in the Appendix. The contents of the Appendix are listed in chronological order under the titles of the books and periodical articles from which they are drawn. Cross references are provided to assist the reader in locating related passages in the textual notes and in the Appendix.

ABBREVIATIONS

BOOKS

CPW	*Complete Prose Works* (1892)
CPP	*Complete Poems & Prose* (1888)
DV	*Democratic Vistas* (1871)
DVOP	*Democratic Vistas and Other Papers* (London, 1888)
GBF	*Good-Bye My Fancy* (1891)
MDW	*Memoranda During the War* (1875)
NB	*November Boughs* (1888)
SDA	*Specimen Days in America* (London, 1887)
SDC	*Specimen Days & Collect* (1882)
SDC Glasgow	*Specimen Days & Collect* (Glasgow, 1883)
TR	*Two Rivulets* (1876)
UPP	*Uncollected Poetry and Prose of Walt Whitman* (2 vols.), edited by Emory Holloway (1921)

MAGAZINES

CTP	*Cope's Tobacco Plant*
CR	*The Critic*

NEWSPAPERS

CC	The Camden *Courier*
CNR	The Camden *New Republic*
LA	The London (Ontario) *Advertiser*
LE	The London (England) *Examiner*
NYT	The New York *Times*
NYTR	The New York *Tribune*
NYW	The New York *World*
NYDG	The New York *Daily Graphic*
NYWG	The New York *Weekly Graphic*
PA	The Philadelphia *American*
PPRE	The Philadelphia *Press*
PPRO	The Philadelphia *Progress*
PT	The Philadelphia *Times*

Walt Whitman, Prose Works 1892

VOLUME I, SPECIMEN DAYS

Specimen Days

A Happy Hour's Command.

Down in the Woods, July 2d, 1882.—If I do it at all I must delay
no longer. Incongruous and full of skips and jumps as is that huddle of
diary-jottings, war-memoranda of 1862–'65, Nature-notes of 1877–'81,
with Western and Canadian observations afterwards, all bundled up and
tied by a big string, the resolution and indeed mandate comes to me this   5
day, this hour,—(and what a day! what an hour just passing! the luxury
of riant grass and blowing breeze, with all the shows of sun and sky and
perfect temperature, never before so filling me body and soul)—to go
home, untie the bundle, reel out diary-scraps and memoranda, just as they
are, large or small, one after another, into print-pages,* and let the   10
melange's lackings and wants of connection take care of themselves. It will
illustrate one phase of humanity anyhow; how few of life's days and hours
(and they not by relative value or proportion, but by chance) are ever
noted. Probably another point too, how we give long preparations for
some object, planning and delving and fashioning, and then, when the ac-   15
tual hour for doing arrives, find ourselves still quite unprepared, and
tumble the thing together, letting hurry and crudeness tell the story better
than fine work. At any rate I obey my happy hour's command, which
seems curiously imperative. May-be, if I don't do anything else, I shall
send out the most wayward, spontaneous, fragmentary book ever printed.   20

---

* The pages from 8 to 20 are nearly verbatim an off-hand letter of mine
in January, 1882, to an insisting friend. Following, I give some gloomy experi-

A Happy Hour's Command.
This section was printed from four autograph MS pages; two printed clippings attached to the MS were used in the footnote.
   4. afterwards] MS: afterward
  12. anyhow; how] MS: anyhow—how
  20. spontaneous, fragmentary] MS: spontaneous and fragmentary
  21. The pages from 8 to 20] SDA: The earlier pages
  21–24. From the autograph MS through the word "commenced" in line 24.
  21–26. NYWG reads: "During the war, commenced at the close of '62, and all
through '63, '4, and '5, I was much around and with the wounded, both in the Army
Hospitals in Virginia and on the field."

ences. The war of attempted secession has, of course, been the distinguishing event of my time. I commenced at the close of 1862, and continued steadily
25 through '63, '64, and '65, to visit the sick and wounded of the army, both on the field and in the hospitals in and around Washington city. From the first I kept little note-books for impromptu jottings in pencil to refresh my memory of names and circumstances, and what was specially wanted, &c. In these I brief'd cases, persons, sights, occurrences in camp, by the bedside, and not seldom by
30 the corpses of the dead. Some were scratch'd down from narratives I heard and itemized while watching, or waiting, or tending somebody amid those scenes. I have dozens of such little note-books left, forming a special history of those years, for myself alone, full of associations never to be possibly said or sung. I wish I could convey to the reader the associations that attach to these soil'd and
35 creas'd livraisons, each composed of a sheet or two of paper, folded small to carry in the pocket, and fasten'd with a pin. I leave them just as I threw them by after the war, blotch'd here and there with more than one blood-stain, hurriedly written, sometimes at the clinique, not seldom amid the excitement of uncertainty, or defeat, or of action, or getting ready for it, or a march. Most
40 of the pages from 26 to 81 are verbatim copies of those lurid and blood-smutch'd little note-books.

Very different are most of the memoranda that follow. Some time after the war ended I had a paralytic stroke, which prostrated me for several years. In 1876 I began to get over the worst of it. From this date, portions of several

22. The "insisting friend" was probably Dr. R. M. Bucke. An undiscovered letter to Bucke dated January 9, 1882 is mentioned in Whitman's Commonplace Book. The notes pasted together to form printer's copy for SDC pages 8–20 may be the letter.

24–39. After the word "commenced" and continuing through the sentence ending "or a march," from a clipping of the beginning of MDW after the words "During the Union War I commenced". This previously appeared in paragraph 5, under the sub-title "A Step Ten Years Backward, and its Mementoes," of the first of six papers entitled " 'Tis But Ten Years Since" (NYWG, 1874).

26–27. first I kept] NYWG: first I found it necessary to systematize my doings, and, among other things, always kept

28–29. I brief'd cases] NYWG: I noted down cases

29. bedside, and not] NYWG: bedside in hospital, and not

30. corpses of the dead.] MDW continues: "Of the present Volume most of its pages are *verbatim* renderings from such pencillings on the spot."] NYWG reads: "Several of the sketches I propose to give in the papers following are *verbatim* renderings from such pencillings on the spot."

31–32. amid . . . left] MDW: amid those scenes. I have perhaps forty such little note-books left] NYWG: amid these scenes. I have perhaps forty such little books left

33–34. possibly . . . associations] NYWG: possibly written or told. I wish indeed I could convey to the reader a glimpse, or even a few, of the teeming associations

35. creas'd livraisons] MDW and NYWG: creas'd little livraisons

35. of a sheet or two of] NYWG: of two or three sheets of

37. by . . . blotch'd] MDW: by during the War, blotch'd] NYWG: by 10 Years Since, full as they are of scrawls and memoranda, half-illegible to any eyes but mine, blotched

39. or a march.] MDW continues with a passage not reprinted by Whitman after TR. See Appendix XI, 1.

39–41. This sentence from the autograph MS. SDA omits "from 26 to 81" after "pages".

seasons, especially summers, I spent at a secluded haunt down in Camden 45
county, New Jersey—Timber creek, quite a little river (it enters from the great
Delaware, twelve miles away)—with primitive solitudes, winding stream, recluse and woody banks, sweet-feeding springs, and all the charms that birds,
grass, wild-flowers, rabbits and squirrels, old oaks, walnut trees, &c., can bring.
Through these times, and on these spots, the diary from page 83 onward was 50
mostly written.

The COLLECT afterward gathers up the odds and ends of whatever pieces
I can now lay hands on, written at various times past, and swoops all together
like fish in a net. 55

I suppose I publish and leave the whole gathering, first, from that eternal
tendency to perpetuate and preserve which is behind all Nature, authors included; second, to symbolize two or three specimen interiors, personal and other,
out of the myriads of my time, the middle range of the Nineteenth century in
the New World; a strange, unloosen'd, wondrous time. But the book is prob- 60
ably without any definite purpose that can be told in a statement.

Answer to an Insisting Friend.

You ask for items, details of my early life—of genealogy and parentage, particularly of the women of my ancestry, and of its far back

42–49. Through "I" in line 45, printed from the autograph MS; the rest from a
clipping of the *Critic*, April 9, 1881, the second article of a series entitled "How I Get
Around at Sixty and Take Notes."
    45. haunt down] *CR:* haunt of mine down
    47–48. twelve . . . springs,] *CR:* twelve or fourteen miles away)—with its primi-
tive solitudes, its flowing, fresh, winding stream, its recluse banks, its cool, sweet
feeding springs,
    49. wild-flowers, rabbits] *CR:* wild flowers, nooks, rabbits,
    46–49. Lines almost identical with these appeared in paragraph 9 of "Winter
Sunshine," Philadelphia *Times*, January 26, 1879: "Not far off is my own choice
haunt, Timber Creek, with its primitive solitudes, its flowing, fresh, winding stream,
its recluse and woody banks, its cool, sweet feeding-springs, and all the charms that
in genial seasons, the birds, grass, wild flowers, nooks, rabbits and squirrels, old oaks,
walnut trees, etc., can bring."
    50–60. Printed from the autograph MS.
    50. 83] *SDA:* 127
    56–57. included; second] MS: included—second
    59. World; a] MS: World—a

    Answer to an Insisting Friend.
    This section and all others through "Sources of Character—Results—1860"
were printed in *SDC* from MS pages numbered through 20 (*SDC*, 8–21), composed of
autograph sheets of varying sizes and several printed clippings, all pasted together in
sequence. The section titles must have been inserted at the time copy was prepared for
the printer since they are written in the revising red ink and crowded between the
original regular lines in black ink.

Netherlands stock on the maternal side—of the region where I was born
and raised, and my father and mother before me, and theirs before them
—with a word about Brooklyn and New York cities, the times I lived
there as lad and young man. You say you want to get at these details
mainly as the go-befores and embryons of "Leaves of Grass." Very good;
you shall have at least some specimens of them all. I have often thought
of the meaning of such things—that one can only encompass and complete matters of that kind by exploring behind, perhaps very far behind,
themselves directly, and so into their genesis, antecedents, and cumulative stages. Then as luck would have it, I lately whiled away the tedium
of a week's half-sickness and confinement, by collating these very items
for another (yet unfulfill'd, probably abandon'd,) purpose; and if you will
be satisfied with them, authentic in date-occurrence and fact simply, and
told my own way, garrulous-like, here they are. I shall not hesitate to make
extracts, for I catch at any thing to save labor; but those will be the best
versions of what I want to convey.

Genealogy—Van Velsor and Whitman.

The later years of the last century found the Van Velsor family, my
mother's side, living on their own farm at Cold Spring, Long Island, New
York State, near the eastern edge of Queens county, about a mile from the
harbor.* My father's side—probably the fifth generation from the first
English arrivals in New England—were at the same time farmers on their
own land—(and a fine domain it was, 500 acres, all good soil, gently

* Long Island was settled first on the west end by the Dutch, from Holland,
then on the east end by the English—the dividing line of the two nationalities being a little west of Huntington, where my father's folks lived,
and where I was born.

Genealogy—Van Velsor and Whitman.
Lines 1–26 through the words "from one" in line 10, printed from the autograph MS, beginning immediately after the last line of the preceding section, with
the subtitle interlined. Footnote also from the autograph MS. The rest from a clipping
of *NYTR*, August 4, 1881, part of paragraph 7 of "A Week at West Hills." The beginning of the first sentence, cut away from the clipping, is as follows: "The Whitmans on Long Island or in New-England and the Middle States (without going
further back) are generally traceable to".
    10. in Old England] *NYTR:* in England
    12. "True Love"] *NYTR:* True Love
    12–13. and lived . . . became the] *NYTR:* and settled in Weymouth, Mass.,
which place is the

sloping east and south, about one-tenth woods, plenty of grand old trees,) two or three miles off, at West Hills, Suffolk county. The Whitman name in the Eastern States, and so branching West and South, starts undoubtedly from one John Whitman, born 1602, in Old England, where he grew up, married, and his eldest son was born in 1629. He came over in the "True Love" in 1640 to America, and lived in Weymouth, Mass., which place became the mother-hive of the New-Englanders of the name: he died in 1692. His brother, Rev. Zechariah Whitman, also came over in the "True Love," either at that time or soon after, and lived at Milford, Conn. A son of this Zechariah, named Joseph, migrated to Huntington, Long Island, and permanently settled there. Savage's "Genealogical Dictionary" (vol. iv, p. 524) gets the Whitman family establish'd at Huntington, per this Joseph, before 1664. It is quite certain that from that beginning, and from Joseph, the West Hill Whitmans, and all others in Suffolk county, have since radiated, myself among the number. John and Zechariah both went to England and back again divers times; they had large families, and several of their children were born in the old country. We hear of the father of John and Zechariah, Abijah Whitman, who goes over into the 1500's, but we know little about him, except that he also was for some time in America.

These old pedigree-reminiscences come up to me vividly from a visit I made not long since (in my 63d year) to West Hills, and to the burial grounds of my ancestry, both sides. I extract from notes of that visit, written there and then:

The Old Whitman and Van Velsor Cemeteries.

July 29, 1881.—After more than forty years' absence, (except a brief visit, to take my father there once more, two years before he died,) went down Long Island on a week's jaunt to the place where I was born, thirty miles from New York city. Rode around the old familiar spots,

---

14, 16, 21, 24. Zechariah] *NYTR:* Zachariah
15. "True-Love,"] *NYTR:* True Love
15. lived at] *NYTR:* settled at
17–18. "Genealogical Dictionary"] *NYTR:* Genealogical Dictionary
27–30. From the autograph MS.

The Old Whitman and Van Velsor Cemeteries.
Based on clippings from *NYTR*, paragraphs 2, 3, 6, and 9 of "A Week at West Hills," with changes as indicated. For the first paragraph of *NYTR*, omitted from *SDC*, see Appendix XXXIV, *1*.
1–4. For this sentence *NYTR* has: "*July 29*—Down at the native place, after a

5   viewing and pondering and dwelling long upon them, everything coming back to me. Went to the old Whitman homestead on the upland and
took a view eastward, inclining south, over the broad and beautiful farm
lands of my grandfather (1780,) and my father. There was the new
house (1810,) the big oak a hundred and fifty or two hundred years old;
10   there the well, the sloping kitchen-garden, and a little way off even the
well-kept remains of the dwelling of my great-grandfather (1750–'60)
still standing, with its mighty timbers and low ceilings. Near by, a
stately grove of tall, vigorous black-walnuts, beautiful, Apollo-like, the
sons or grandsons, no doubt, of black-walnuts during or before 1776.
15   On the other side of the road spread the famous apple orchard, over
twenty acres, the trees planted by hands long mouldering in the grave
(my uncle Jesse's,) but quite many of them evidently capable of throwing
out their annual blossoms and fruit yet.

I now write these lines seated on an old grave (doubtless of a cen-
20   tury since at least) on the burial hill of the Whitmans of many generations. Fifty and more graves are quite plainly traceable, and as many
more decay'd out of all form—depress'd mounds, crumbled and broken
stones, cover'd with moss—the gray and sterile hill, the clumps of chest-
nuts outside, the silence, just varied by the soughing wind. There is al-
25   ways the deepest eloquence of sermon or poem in any of these ancient
graveyards of which Long Island has so many; so what must this one have
been to me? My whole family history, with its succession of links, from
the first settlement down to date, told here—three centuries concen-
trate on this sterile acre.

30   The next day, July 30, I devoted to the maternal locality, and if possible was still more penetrated and impress'd. I write this paragraph on

long absence. Hadn't been in Huntington Village for over 40 years, and only once
briefly at the Hills during that time."
    4–43. Printed from the clippings.
    4. around the] NYTR: around to all the
    6. me. Went to] NYTR: me from fifty years, with childhood's days and scenes.
Went first to
    6. upland and] NYTR: upland at West Hills, and
    14. After "1776." NYTR begins a new paragraph.
    18. After "fruit yet." NYTR paragraphs 4 and 5, subtitled "The Actual Birth-
Spot," were not reprinted. See Appendix XXXIV, 2.
    19–29. Printed from paragraph 6 of NYTR, subtitled "An Old Long Island Ceme-
tery."
    19. I now write] NYTR: I write
    22. all form—depress'd] NYTR: any form; depressed
    27. My whole] NYTR: A whole
    28. date, told] NYTR: date, is told
    29. sterile acre.] Paragraph 7, which follows in NYTR, was reprinted in "Gene-
alogy—Van Velsor and Whitman," q.v. (above). For paragraph 8 of NYTR, not re-

the burial hill of the Van Velsors, near Cold Spring, the most significant depository of the dead that could be imagin'd, without the slightest help from art, but far ahead of it, soil sterile, a mostly bare plateau-flat of half an acre, the top of a hill, brush and well grown trees and dense woods 35 bordering all around, very primitive, secluded, no visitors, no road (you cannot drive here, you have to bring the dead on foot, and follow on foot.) Two or three-score graves quite plain; as many more almost rubb'd out. My grandfather Cornelius and my grandmother Amy (Naomi) and numerous relatives nearer or remoter, on my mother's side, lie buried 40 here. The scene as I stood or sat, the delicate and wild odor of the woods, a slightly drizzling rain, the emotional atmosphere of the place, and the inferr'd reminiscences, were fitting accompaniments.

The Maternal Homestead.

I went down from this ancient grave place eighty or ninety rods to the site of the Van Velsor homestead, where my mother was born (1795,) and where every spot had been familiar to me as a child and youth (1825-'40.) Then stood there a long rambling, dark-gray, shingle-sided house, with sheds, pens, a great barn, and much open road-space. Now of 5 all those not a vestige left; all had been pull'd down, erased, and the plough and harrow pass'd over foundations, road-spaces and every-thing, for many summers; fenced in at present, and grain and clover grow-ing like any other fine fields. Only a big hole from the cellar, with some little heaps of broken stone, green with grass and weeds, identified the 10 place. Even the copious old brook and spring seem'd to have mostly dwindled away. The whole scene, with what it arous'd, memories of my

printed in SDC, see Appendix XXXIV, 3.
    30–43. Printed from paragraph 9 of "A Week at West Hills," the first under the subtitle "Then On My Mother's Side."
    34. art, but far ahead of it, soil] NYTR: art, soil
    34–35. of half an acre,] NYTR: of an acre
    43. were fitting accompaniments.] NYTR: were such as I never realized before.

The Maternal Homestead.
    Printed from the autograph MS and clippings from NYTR, "A Week at West Hills," paragraph 10, under the subtitle "Then On My Mother's Side," and paragraphs 11 and 12 subtitled " 'Tis Fifty Years Since."
    1–18. From clippings of paragraphs 10 and 11.
    9. from the cellar,] NYTR: from an ancient cellar,
    11. the copious old] NYTR: the great old
    12. dwindled away.] NYTR begins a new paragraph with the subtitle " 'Tis Fifty Years Since."
    12. The whole] NYTR: In some particulars this whole

40 The other, (Hannah Brush,) was an equally noble, perhaps stronger character, lived to be very old, had quite a family of sons, was a natural lady, was in early life a school-mistress, and had great solidity of mind. W. W. himself makes much of the women of his ancestry."—*The same.*

45 Out from these arrieres of persons and scenes, I was born May 31, 1819. And now to dwell awhile on the locality itself—as the successive growth-stages of my infancy, childhood, youth and manhood were all pass'd on Long Island, which I sometimes feel as if I had incorporated. I roam'd, as boy and man, and have lived in nearly all parts, from Brooklyn to Montauk point.

Paumanok, and My Life on It as Child and Young Man.

Worth fully and particularly investigating indeed this Paumanok, (to give the spot its aboriginal name,*) stretching east through Kings, Queens and Suffolk counties, 120 miles altogether—on the north Long Island sound, a beautiful, varied and picturesque series of inlets, "necks"
5 and sea-like expansions, for a hundred miles to Orient point. On the ocean side the great south bay dotted with countless hummocks, mostly small, some quite large, occasionally long bars of sand out two hundred rods to a mile-and-a-half from the shore. While now and then, as at Rockaway and far east along the Hamptons, the beach makes right on the island, the sea
10 dashing up without intervention. Several light-houses on the shores east; a long history of wrecks tragedies, some even of late years. As a youngster, I was in the atmosphere and traditions of many of these wrecks—of one or two almost an observer. Off Hempstead beach for example, was the loss of the ship "Mexico" in 1840, (alluded to in "the Sleepers" in L. of G.)
15 And at Hampton, some years later, the destruction of the brig "Elizabeth," a fearful affair, in one of the worst winter gales, where Margaret Fuller went down, with her husband and child.

Inside the outer bars or beach this south bay is everywhere comparatively shallow; of cold winters all thick ice on the surface. As a boy I
20 often went forth with a chum or two, on those frozen fields, with hand-sled, axe and eel-spear, after messes of eels. We would cut holes in the

39. (Hannah Brush,) was] *Notes:* (Hannah Brush, before marriage,) was
39. noble, perhaps stronger] *Notes:* noble, but stronger
41. mind. W. W. himself] *Notes:* mind. The poet himself
42. Whitman deletes the last sentence of Burroughs' paragraph and also the brackets enclosing the paragraph. The deleted sentence is as follows: "He never speaks of his own mother but as 'dear mother,' his face flush with yearning and pride.]"

ice, sometimes striking quite an eel-bonanza, and filling our baskets with great, fat, sweet, white-meated fellows. The scenes, the ice, drawing the hand-sled, cutting holes, spearing the eels, &c., were of course just such fun as is dearest to boyhood. The shores of this bay, winter and summer, 25 and my doings there in early life, are woven all through L. of G. One sport I was very fond of was to go on a bay-party in summer to gather sea-gull's eggs. (The gulls lay two or three eggs, more than half the size of hen's eggs, right on the sand, and leave the sun's heat to hatch them.)

The eastern end of Long Island, the Peconic bay region, I knew quite 30 well too—sail'd more than once around Shelter island, and down to Montauk—spent many an hour on Turtle hill by the old light-house, on the extreme point, looking out over the ceaseless roll of the Atlantic. I used to like to go down there and fraternize with the blue-fishers, or the annual squads of sea-bass takers. Sometimes, along Montauk peninsula, (it is 35 some 15 miles long, and good grazing,) met the strange, unkempt, half-barbarous herdsmen, at that time living there entirely aloof from society or civilization, in charge, on those rich pasturages, of vast droves of horses, kine or sheep, own'd by farmers of the eastern towns. Sometimes, too, the few remaining Indians, or half-breeds, at that period left on Montauk pen- 40 insula, but now I believe altogether extinct.

More in the middle of the island were the spreading Hempstead plains, then (1830–'40) quite prairie-like, open, uninhabited, rather sterile, cover'd with kill-calf and huckleberry bushes, yet plenty of fair pasture for the cattle, mostly milch-cows, who fed there by hundreds, even thou- 45 sands, and at evening, (the plains too were own'd by the towns, and this was the use of them in common,) might be seen taking their way home, branching off regularly in the right places. I have often been out on the edges of these plains toward sundown, and can yet recall in fancy the interminable cow-processions, and hear the music of the tin or copper bells 50 clanking far or near, and breathe the cool of the sweet and slightly aromatic evening air, and note the sunset.

Through the same region of the island, but further east, extended wide central tracts of pine and scrub-oak, (charcoal was largely made here,) monotonous and sterile. But many a good day or half-day did I 55 have, wandering through those solitary cross-roads, inhaling the peculiar

43–48. Printed from the autograph MS.

Paumanok, and My Life on It as Child and Young Man.
All except Whitman's footnote printed from the autograph MS. The footnote was from what appears to be a newspaper clipping inserted by Whitman as an afterthought. Though Whitman attributes the quotation to John Burroughs, the present editor has not found it in Burroughs' works.

and wild aroma. Here, and all along the island and its shores, I spent intervals many years, all seasons, sometimes riding, sometimes boating, but
generally afoot, (I was always then a good walker,) absorbing fields,
60 shores, marine incidents, characters, the bay-men, farmers, pilots—always
had a plentiful acquaintance with the latter, and with fishermen—went
every summer on sailing trips—always liked the bare sea-beach, south side,
and have some of my happiest hours on it to this day.

As I write, the whole experience comes back to me after the lapse of
65 forty and more years—the soothing rustle of the waves, and the saline
smell—boyhood's times, the clam-digging, barefoot, and with trowsers
roll'd up—hauling down the creek—the perfume of the sedge-meadows—
the hay-boat, and the chowder and fishing excursions;—or, of later years,
little voyages down and out New York bay, in the pilot boats. Those same
70 later years, also, while living in Brooklyn, (1836–'50) I went regularly
every week in the mild seasons down to Coney island, at that time a long,
bare unfrequented shore, which I had all to myself, and where I loved,
after bathing, to race up and down the hard sand, and declaim Homer or
Shakspere to the surf and sea-gulls by the hour. But I am getting ahead
75 too rapidly, and must keep more in my traces.

* "Paumanok, (or Paumanake, or Paumanack, the Indian name of Long
Island,) over a hundred miles long; shaped like a fish—plenty of sea shore,
sandy, stormy, uninviting, the horizon boundless, the air too strong for invalids,
the bays a wonderful resort for aquatic birds, the south-side meadows cover'd
80 with salt hay, the soil of the island generally tough, but good for the locust-tree,
the apple orchard, and the blackberry, and with numberless springs of the
sweetest water in the world. Years ago, among the bay-men—a strong, wild
race, now extinct, or rather entirely changed—a native of Long Island was
called a *Paumanacker*, or *Creole-Paumanacker*."—*John Burroughs*.

76. the Indian name] Clipping: the aboriginal name
77. After "Island,"] and before "over" three or four words were deleted and so
blotted that they are illegible.
78. After "air" and before "too" perhaps two words were deleted and so blotted as
to be illegible.
84. The credit line of the clipping was: "------[word illegible] *of John Burroughs*." All was deleted except "*John Burroughs*."

My First Reading.—Lafayette.
All printed from the autograph MS except the footnote.
In the MS this section is entitled "Brooklyn—My First Reading—Type Set-
ting." In revision "Brooklyn" was deleted. The further revision, presumably in galley

My First Reading.—Lafayette.

From 1824 to '28 our family lived in Brooklyn in Front, Cranberry and Johnson streets. In the latter my father built a nice house for a home, and afterwards another in Tillary street. We occupied them, one after the other, but they were mortgaged, and we lost them. I yet remember Lafayette's visit.* Most of these years I went to the public schools. It 5 must have been about 1829 or '30 that I went with my father and mother to hear Elias Hicks preach in a ball-room on Brooklyn heights. At about the same time employ'd as a boy in an office, lawyers', father and two sons, Clarke's, Fulton street, near Orange. I had a nice desk and window-nook to myself; Edward C. kindly help'd me at my handwriting and 10 composition, and, (the signal event of my life up to that time,) subscribed for me to a big circulating library. For a time I now revel'd in romance-reading of all kinds; first, the "Arabian Nights," all the volumes, an amazing treat. Then, with sorties in very many other directions, took in Walter Scott's novels, one after another, and his poetry, (and continue to 15 enjoy novels and poetry to this day.)

* "On the visit of General Lafayette to this country, in 1824, he came over to Brooklyn in state, and rode through the city. The children of the schools turn'd out to join in the welcome. An edifice for a free public library for youths was just then commencing, and Lafayette consented to stop on his way and 20 lay the corner-stone. Numerous children arriving on the ground, where a huge irregular excavation for the building was already dug, surrounded with heaps of rough stone, several gentlemen assisted in lifting the children to safe or convenient spots to see the ceremony. Among the rest, Lafayette, also helping the children, took up the five-year-old Walt Whitman, and pressing the child a 25 moment to his breast, and giving him a kiss, handed him down to a safe spot in the excavation."—*John Burroughs.*

proof, may have been suggested by the late insertion of the footnote.

17–27. From a clipping of page 80 of *Notes on Walt Whitman as Poet and Person* (1867). Whitman deletes the brackets enclosing the paragraph and also the following words with which the paragraph in *Notes* begins: "Here is one item of his childhood:"

17. in 1824, he] *Notes:* in 1825, he

[Variants of the story of Lafayette's visit to Brooklyn are found in Whitman's *Brooklyniana* (1862), in the 8th and 15th installments (*UPP*, II, 256–257, 284–285), where the date of the laying of the cornerstone of the Apprentices' Library is given as July 4, 1825; and in "Old Brooklyn Days" (*CPW*, 506), where Whitman says he was five years old and refers to "the personal coming of Lafayette in 1824–5 to Brooklyn." See also *Lafayette in Brooklyn*, ed. Burroughs, 1905. The date of the laying of the cornerstone was correctly stated in *Brooklyniana*.—ED.]

Printing Office.—Old Brooklyn.

After about two years went to work in a weekly newspaper and printing office, to learn the trade. The paper was the "Long Island Patriot," owned by S. E. Clements, who was also postmaster. An old printer in the office, William Hartshorne, a revolutionary character, who had seen
5   Washington, was a special friend of mine, and I had many a talk with him about long past times. The apprentices, including myself, boarded with his grand-daughter. I used occasionally to go out riding with the boss, who was very kind to us boys; Sundays he took us all to a great old rough, fortress-looking stone church, on Joralemon street, near where
10   the Brooklyn city hall now is—(at that time broad fields and country roads everywhere around.*) Afterward I work'd on the "Long Island Star," Alden Spooner's paper. My father all these years pursuing his trade as carpenter and builder, with varying fortune. There was a growing family of children—eight of us—my brother Jesse the oldest, myself the second,
15   my dear sisters Mary and Hannah Louisa, my brothers Andrew, George, Thomas Jefferson, and then my youngest brother, Edward, born 1835, and always badly crippled, as I am myself of late years.

* Of the Brooklyn of that time (1830–40) hardly anything remains, except the lines of the old streets. The population was then between ten and twelve
20   thousand. For a mile Fulton street was lined with magnificent elm trees. The character of the place was thoroughly rural. As a sample of comparative values, it may be mention'd that twenty-five acres in what is now the most costly part of the city, bounded by Flatbush and Fulton avenues, were then bought by Mr. Parmentier, a French *emigré*, for $4000. Who remembers the old places

Printing Office.—Old Brooklyn.

All, except part of the footnote, printed from the autograph MS. The MS title, "Printing Office and Country School Teaching," unrevised, was presumably changed in the galley proof.

18–33. From a printed clipping, probably a newspaper, not identified; cut so that "population" (line 19) is the first word; the first sentence and the first word of the second sentence introducing the clipping are in Whitman's autograph. The language of the clipping resembles passages in Whitman's *Brooklyniana* and, still more, the last two paragraphs of an article by Whitman entitled "Old Brooklyn Days," NYMJ, August 3, 1890; this article was reprinted (omitting the two paragraphs above referred to) in GBF under the same title, *q.v.*, *Prose 1892*, II.

20–21. thousand. For . . . character] Clipping: thousand. The character
24. Clipping begins a new paragraph with "Who remembers".
25. of that time? Among] Clipping: of the time with their well known faces? Among

as they were? Who remembers the old citizens of that time? Among the former 25
were Smith & Wood's, Coe Downing's, and other public houses at the ferry,
the old Ferry itself, Love lane, the Heights as then, the Wallabout with the
wooden bridge, and the road out beyond Fulton street to the old toll-gate.
Among the latter were the majestic and genial General Jeremiah Johnson, with
others, Gabriel Furman, Rev. E. M. Johnson, Alden Spooner, Mr. Pierrepont, 30
Mr. Joralemon, Samuel Willoughby, Jonathan Trotter, George Hall, Cyrus P.
Smith, N. B. Morse, John Dikeman, Adrian Hegeman, William Udall, and
old Mr. Duflon, with his military garden.

Growth—Health—Work.

I develop'd (1833–4–5) into a healthy, strong youth (grew too fast,
though, was nearly as big as a man at 15 or 16.) Our family at this period
moved back to the country, my dear mother very ill for a long time, but
recover'd. All these years I was down Long Island more or less every summer, now east, now west, sometimes months at a stretch. At 16, 17, and 5
so on, was fond of debating societies, and had an active membership with
them, off and on, in Brooklyn and one or two country towns on the island.
A most omnivorous novel-reader, these and later years, devour'd everything I could get. Fond of the theatre, also, in New York, went whenever
I could—sometimes witnessing fine performances. 10
1836–7, work'd as compositor in printing offices in New York city.
Then, when little more than eighteen, and for a while afterwards, went to
teaching country schools down in Queens and Suffolk counties, Long Island, and "boarded round." (This latter I consider one of my best experiences and deepest lessons in human nature behind the scenes, and in the 15
masses.) In '39, '40, I started and publish'd a weekly paper in my native

30. others, Gabriel] Clipping: others mentioned at random, mostly passed away
before now, but a few, yet among us, Gabriel

Growth—Health—Work.
All printed from the autograph MS. Some changes in the MS of biographical
interest are noted in the collation.
    1. (1833–4–5)] MS before revision: (1834–5–6)
    3. for a long time, but] MS before revision: for nearly two years, but
    5. at 16, 17, and] MS before revision: at 16, 17, 18 and
    7. Brooklyn and] MS before revision: Brooklyn, New York City, and
    11. 1836–7,] MS before revision: 1834, f,] First Revision: 1835–'6] Second
Revision: 1836–'7
    12. Then, . . . afterwards] MS before revision: Then while still hardly sixteen
years of age, and for two years afterwards] First Revision: Then when little more than
seventeen, and for several months afterwards
    14–15. best experiences] MS before revision: best and deepest experiences

town, Huntington. Then returning to New York city and Brooklyn, work'd on as printer and writer, mostly prose, but an occasional shy at "poetry."

My Passion for Ferries.

Living in Brooklyn or New York city from this time forward, my life, then, and still more the following years, was curiously identified with Fulton ferry, already becoming the greatest of its sort in the world for general importance, volume, variety, rapidity, and picturesqueness. Al-
5 most daily, later, ('50 to '60,) I cross'd on the boats, often up in the pilot-houses where I could get a full sweep, absorbing shows, accompaniments, surroundings. What oceanic currents, eddies, underneath—the great tides of humanity also, with ever-shifting movements. Indeed, I have always had a passion for ferries; to me they afford inimitable, streaming,
10 never-failing, living poems. The river and bay scenery, all about New York island, any time of a fine day—the hurrying, splashing sea-tides—the changing panorama of steamers, all sizes, often a string of big ones outward bound to distant ports—the myriads of white-sail'd schooners, sloops, skiffs, and the marvellously beautiful yachts—the majestic sound
15 boats as they rounded the Battery and came along towards 5, afternoon, eastward bound—the prospect off towards Staten island, or down the Narrows, or the other way up the Hudson—what refreshment of spirit such sights and experiences gave me years ago (and many a time since.) My old pilot friends, the Balsirs, Johnny Cole, Ira Smith, William White, and
20 my young ferry friend, Tom Gere—how well I remember them all.

Broadway Sights.

Besides Fulton ferry, off and on for years, I knew and frequented Broadway—that noted avenue of New York's crowded and mixed hu-

My Passion for Ferries.
From the autograph MS.
18. experiences gave me years] MS before revision: experiences on the waters of Brooklyn and New York always gave me forty to fifty years

Broadway Sights.
Lines 1–18 through the sentence ending "jaded," in line 18, printed from the autograph MS. One MS change is of biographical significance.
15. The visit was about a piece of mine he had publish'd.] MS before revision: The interview was about a piece I had to be published.
18–35. These lines, beginning with "For another" and continuing to the end of the paragraph, were printed from a clipping of the last part of the paragraph subtitled

manity, and of so many notables. Here I saw, during those times, Andrew Jackson, Webster, Clay, Seward, Martin Van Buren, filibuster Walker, Kossuth, Fitz Greene Halleck, Bryant, the Prince of Wales, Charles Dickens, the first Japanese ambassadors, and lots of other celebrities of the time. Always something novel or inspiriting; yet mostly to me the hurrying and vast amplitude of those never-ending human currents. I remember seeing James Fenimore Cooper in a court-room in Chambers street, back of the city hall, where he was carrying on a law case—(I think it was a charge of libel he had brought against some one.) I also remember seeing Edgar A. Poe, and having a short interview with him, (it must have been in 1845 or '6,) in his office, second story of a corner building, (Duane or Pearl street.) He was editor and owner or part owner of "the Broadway Journal." The visit was about a piece of mine he had publish'd. Poe was very cordial, in a quiet way, appear'd well in person, dress, &c. I have a distinct and pleasing remembrance of his looks, voice, manner and matter; very kindly and human, but subdued, perhaps a little jaded. For another of my reminiscences, here on the west side, just below Houston street, I once saw (it must have been about 1832, of a sharp, bright January day) a bent, feeble but stout-built very old man, bearded, swathed in rich furs, with a great ermine cap on his head, led and assisted, almost carried, down the steps of his high front stoop (a dozen friends and servants, emulous, carefully holding, guiding him) and then lifted and tuck'd in a gorgeous sleigh, envelop'd in other furs, for a ride. The sleigh was drawn by as fine a team of horses as I ever saw. (You needn't think all the best animals are brought up nowadays; never was such horseflesh as fifty years ago on Long Island, or south, or in New York city; folks look'd for spirit and mettle in a nag, not tame speed merely.) Well, I, a boy of perhaps thirteen or fourteen, stopp'd and gazed long at the spectacle of that fur-swathed old man, surrounded by friends and servants, and the careful seating of him in the sleigh. I remember the spirited, champing horses, the driver with his whip, and a fellow-driver by his side, for extra pru-

"John Jacob Astor Goes Sleighriding," the ninth of "Broadway Revisited," NYTR, May 10, 1879. For the first two sentences of the paragraph, see Appendix XIX, 2.

18–19. For . . . here on] NYTR: Here, on

19–20. the west . . . once] NYTR: the west side of Broadway, just below Houston, I once

20. been about 1832, of a] NYTR: been between forty-five and fifty years ago, of a

21. stout-built very old] NYTR: stout-built old

26. saw. (You needn't] NYTR: saw. (Folks needn't

28. in New York city;] NYTR: in this city;

30. gazed] NYTR: looked

31. by friends] NYTR: by a cloud of friends

33–34. prudence. The old man,] NYTR: prudence. I had a good look at the old man,

35 dence. The old man, the subject of so much attention, I can almost see now.
It was John Jacob Astor.

The years 1846, '47, and there along, see me still in New York city, working as writer and printer, having my usual good health, and a good time generally.

Omnibus Jaunts and Drivers.

One phase of those days must by no means go unrecorded—namely, the Broadway omnibuses, with their drivers. The vehicles still (I write this paragraph in 1881) give a portion of the character of Broadway—the Fifth avenue, Madison avenue, and Twenty-third street lines yet running.
5 But the flush days of the old Broadway stages, characteristic and copious, are over. The Yellow-birds, the Red-birds, the original Broadway, the Fourth avenue, the Knickerbocker, and a dozen others of twenty or thirty years ago, are all gone. And the men specially identified with them, and giving vitality and meaning to them—the drivers—a strange, natural,
10 quick-eyed and wondrous race—(not only Rabelais and Cervantes would have gloated upon them, but Homer and Shakspere would)—how well I remember them, and must here give a word about them. How many hours, forenoons and afternoons—how many exhilarating night-times I have had —perhaps June or July, in cooler air—riding the whole length of Broad-
15 way, listening to some yarn, (and the most vivid yarns ever spun, and the

34. attention, . . . now.] *NYTR:* attention, and can almost see him now.
The entire clipping about John Jacob Astor is omitted from the text of SDA (London, 1887), p. 29, where the paragraph beginning "The years 1846, '47," (line 36) follows immediately the passage in the preceding paragraph on Poe (line 18).
36–38. Printed from the autograph MS.

Omnibus Jaunts and Drivers.

The original title, "Broadway Omnibusses," was changed in the MS to "Broadway Omnibus Jaunts and Drivers." The word "Broadway" was deleted in the galley proof.
1–3. Through the first syllable of "portion," printed from the autograph MS. The date in line 3 is 1880 in the MS; presumably changed in the proof. The rest of the section is printed from clippings of paragraphs 10–12, subtitled "Old Broadway Drivers," of "Broadway Revisited," *NYTR*, May 10, 1879. In the first clipping the subtitle and the first line ("The stages—the omnibuses—they still give a por-") were cut away.
4. Fifth . . . lines] *NYTR:* Fifth-ave., the Madison-ave. and the Twenty-third-st. lines
5. the old Broadway] *NYTR:* the Broadway
7. twenty or thirty] *NYTR:* twenty and twenty-five
9–10. strange, natural, quick-eyed] *NYTR:* strange, wild, quick-eyed
11. have gloated] *NYTR:* have taken them in and gloated

rarest mimicry)—or perhaps I declaiming some stormy passage from Julius Cæsar or Richard, (you could roar as loudly as you chose in that heavy, dense, uninterrupted street-bass.) Yes, I knew all the drivers then, Broadway Jack, Dressmaker, Balky Bill, George Storms, Old Elephant, his brother Young Elephant (who came afterward,) Tippy, Pop Rice, Big 20 Frank, Yellow Joe, Pete Callahan, Patsy Dee, and dozens more; for there were hundreds. They had immense qualities, largely animal—eating, drinking, women—great personal pride, in their way—perhaps a few slouches here and there, but I should have trusted the general run of them, in their simple good-will and honor, under all circumstances. Not 25 only for comradeship, and sometimes affection—great studies I found them also. (I suppose the critics will laugh heartily, but the influence of those Broadway omnibus jaunts and drivers and declamations and escapades undoubtedly enter'd into the gestation of "Leaves of Grass.")

Plays and Operas Too.

And certain actors and singers, had a good deal to do with the business. All through these years, off and on, I frequented the old Park, the Bowery, Broadway and Chatham-square theatres, and the Italian operas at Chambers-street, Astor-place or the Battery—many seasons was on the free list, writing for papers even as quite a youth. The old Park 5 theatre—what names, reminiscences, the words bring back! Placide,

11. Shakspere would)—how well I] *NYTR:* Shakespeare would.) Well I] [After "would.)" *NYTR* begins a new paragraph.]
12–13. hours, forenoons] *NYTR:* hours—fine forenoons
18. uninterrupted] *NYTR:* unintermitted
18. After "street-bass.)" *NYTR* begins a new paragraph.
18–19. then, Broadway] *NYTR:* then, especially the old ones—Broadway
21. Joe, . . . dozens] *NYTR:* Joe, and dozens
22. were hundreds] *NYTR:* were several hundreds
22. qualities, largely] *NYTR:* qualities. Largely
27–29. of those . . . enter'd] *NYTR:* of these old omnibus drivers, too, has entered

Plays and Operas Too.
Lines 1–5 through "old," from the autograph MS.
In the MS the first sentence originally began: "Plays and operas too (starting from an early date) and certain . . ." In revision the subtitle was indicated by underlining the words "Plays and operas too" with triple lines. The phrase in parentheses was deleted and the first letter of "and" made a capital.
5–23. Beginning with "Park," the text was based on a clipping of part of paragraphs 7 and 8 subtitled "The Old Park Theatre, Too," of "Broadway Revisited," *NYTR*, May 10, 1879.
5. The first part of the first paragraph, cut from the clipping, is as follows: "Then

Clarke, Mrs. Vernon, Fisher, Clara F., Mrs. Wood, Mrs. Seguin, Ellen
Tree, Hackett, the younger Kean, Macready, Mrs. Richardson, Rice—
singers, tragedians, comedians. What perfect acting! Henry Placide in
"Napoleon's Old Guard" or "Grandfather Whitehead,"—or "the Provoked Husband" of Cibber, with Fanny Kemble as Lady Townley—or
Sheridan Knowles in his own "Virginius"—or inimitable Power in "Born
to Good Luck." These, and many more, the years of youth and onward.
Fanny Kemble—name to conjure up great mimic scenes withal—perhaps
the greatest. I remember well her rendering of Bianca in "Fazio," and
Marianna in "the Wife." Nothing finer did ever stage exhibit—the veterans of all nations said so, and my boyish heart and head felt it in every
minute cell. The lady was just matured, strong, better than merely beautiful, born from the footlights, had had three years' practice in London
and through the British towns, and then she came to give America that
young maturity and roseate power in all their noon, or rather forenoon,
flush. It was my good luck to see her nearly every night she play'd at the
old Park—certainly in all her principal characters.

I heard, these years, well render'd, all the Italian and other operas in
vogue, "Sonnambula," "the Puritans," "Der Freischutz," "Huguenots,"
"Fille d'Regiment," "Faust," "Etoile du Nord," "Poliuto," and others.
Verdi's "Ernani," "Rigoletto," and "Trovatore," with Donnizetti's "Lu-
cia" or "Favorita" or "Lucrezia," and Auber's "Massaniello," or Rossini's
"William Tell" and "Gazza Ladra," were among my special enjoyments.
I heard Alboni every time she sang in New York and vicinity—also
Grisi, the tenor Mario, and the baritone Badiali, the finest in the world.

up along the Bowling Green—on by Wall-st.—Trinity Church—the Astor—the Post
Office—the Park. But I must stop a few minutes here to recall (looking across a little
south of the head of Beekman-st.,) a spot of much happiness, my early manhood. The
old"

7. Clara . . . Seguin] *NYTR:* Clara F., Mrs. Seguin
9. What perfect acting!] *NYTR:* What acting!
10–11. or "the Provoked] *NYTR:* or "The Tempest," with Mrs. Knight as Ariel,
and Peter Richings as Caliban—or "The Provoked
13. *NYTR* ends the paragraph with "Born to Good Luck" and begins a new paragraph with "Fanny Kemble!" Whitman inserts the intervening sentence in ink.
14. Fanny Kemble—name] *NYTR:* Fanny Kemble!—Name
17. my boyish heart] *NYTR:* my young heart
23. After "characters." *NYTR* continues with this sentence, lined out in the MS:
"(Strange—but certainly true—that her playing, and the elder Booth's, with Alboni's
and Bettini's singing, gave the first part of the influences that afterwards resulted in
my 'Leaves of Grass.')" This sentence was revised as if Whitman had intended to
use it, then changed his mind. The chief revision was the substitution of "most definite" for "first" before "part of the influences."
24–49. Printed from the autograph MS, although the last sentence, in parentheses,
is almost identical with the first sentence of paragraph 6, *NYTR.*
35. old Booth in] MS before revision: old Booth at his best in

This musical passion follow'd my theatrical one. As boy or young man I had seen, (reading them carefully the day beforehand,) quite all Shakspere's acting dramas, play'd wonderfully well. Even yet I cannot conceive anything finer than old Booth in "Richard Third," or "Lear," (I   35 don't know which was best,) or Iago, (or Pescara, or Sir Giles Overreach, to go outside of Shakspere)—or Tom Hamblin in "Macbeth"—or old Clarke, either as the ghost in "Hamlet," or as Prospero in "the Tempest," with Mrs. Austin as Ariel, and Peter Richings as Caliban. Then other dramas, and fine players in them, Forrest as Metamora or Damon or   40 Brutus—John R. Scott as Tom Cringle or Rolla—or Charlotte Cushman's Lady Gay Spanker in "London Assurance." Then of some years later, at Castle Garden, Battery, I yet recall the splendid seasons of the Havana musical troupe under Maretzek—the fine band, the cool sea-breezes, the unsurpass'd vocalism—Steffanone, Bosio, Truffi, Marini in   45 "Marino Faliero," "Don Pasquale," or "Favorita." No better playing or singing ever in New York. It was here too I afterward heard Jenny Lind. (The Battery—its past associations—what tales those old trees and walks and sea-walls could tell!)

Through Eight Years.

In 1848, '49, I was occupied as editor of the "daily Eagle" newspaper, in Brooklyn. The latter year went off on a leisurely journey and working expedition (my brother Jeff with me) through all the middle States, and down the Ohio and Mississippi rivers. Lived awhile in New

41. or Charlotte] MS before revision: or Henry Placide as Sir Harwood Courtly to Charlotte
43–44. seasons of the Havana] MS before revision: seasons of Italian opera by the Havana
For paragraphs 5 and 6 of "Broadway Revisited," not reprinted, see Appendix XIX, 1.
The first four paragraphs of "Broadway Revisited," not in SDC, were used in GBF, in the section subtitled "New York—the Bay—the Old Name," q.v. in Prose 1892, II.

Through Eight Years.
Lines 1–2 through the word "went," printed from the autograph MS.
1. In 1848, '49, I] MS before revision: In 1847, '48, I
2–16. Beginning with the words "off on a" in line 2, through "at last.)" in line 16, from two clippings of parts of the printed "Personal Note" on the verso of the sheet headed "Remembrance Copy" and inserted in the front of a few copies of MDW intended for presentation to friends.
2–9. The first clipping, through "Hudson;" in line 9, is reprinted in quotation marks, almost word for word, in the "Chronological forecast of Walt Whitman's life" on p. 9 of R. M. Bucke's *Walt Whitman*. Bucke's credit line reads: "*Personal Notes, W. W.*"

5 Orleans, and work'd there on the editorial staff of "daily Crescent" newspaper. After a time plodded back northward, up the Mississippi, and
around to, and by way of the great lakes, Michigan, Huron, and Erie, to
Niagara falls and lower Canada, finally returning through central New
York and down the Hudson; traveling altogether probably 8000 miles this
10 trip, to and fro. '51, '53, occupied in house-building in Brooklyn. (For a
little of the first part of that time in printing a daily and weekly paper,
"the Freeman.") '55, lost my dear father this year by death. Commenced
putting "Leaves of Grass" to press for good, at the job printing office of
my friends, the brothers Rome, in Brooklyn, after many MS. doings and
15 undoings—(I had great trouble in leaving out the stock "poetical"
touches, but succeeded at last.) I am now (1856–'7) passing through my
37th year.

Sources of Character—Results—1860.

To sum up the foregoing from the outset (and, of course, far, far
more unrecorded,) I estimate three leading sources and formative stamps

5–6. work'd . . . newspaper.] First Clipping: worked there.
9–10. down . . . to and fro.] First Clipping: down the Hudson.
9–16. Portions of the Second Clipping, beginning with "traveling" in line 9, are
used by Bucke on pp. 9 and 24 of the biography, but rearranged and without quotation marks.
10. '51, '53, occupied] Second Clipping: 1851–'54,—Occupied
11–12. weekly . . . lost] Second Clipping: weekly newspaper.) 1855,—Lost
13–14. press . . . after] Second Clipping: press, for good after
16–17. The last sentence beginning "I am" was added in the MS.

Sources of Character—Results—1860.
All printed from the autograph MS with very little revision.
[Beginning with the next section, subtitled "Opening of the Secession War"
(SDC, p. 21), and continuing through the last paragraph under the subtitle "The Real
War Will Never Get in the Books" (SDC, p. 81), SDC was printed from pages of
Memoranda During the War, with numerous insertions and deletions in both black
and red ink; inserted subtitles are in red ink. Since the MDW section of *Two Rivulets* (1876) was printed from the same plates as MDW, perhaps even assembled from
previously unused printed sheets of MDW, it is not possible to determine whether
Whitman clipped pages from MDW or TR, or, in some cases at least, used still unbound sheets. The edges suggest that the sheets had not been cut for binding; the
slightly frayed edge on one side could have been made by tearing or roughly cutting
the fold of pages in an unbound signature. For convenience these pages, however
derived, are referred to here as "clippings." Section subtitles in MDW are set in italics
as part of the first line ("side heads," Whitman called them). Parts of this material
had already been printed in the following newspaper articles: "The Great Army of
the Sick" in NYT, Feb. 26, 1863 (reprinted with the title "The Great Army of the
Wounded" in Bucke's *The Wound Dresser*, 1898, pp. 1–10); "Washington in the
Hot Season" in NYT, Aug. 16, 1863; "Our Wounded and Sick Soldiers" in NYT,

to my own character, now solidified for good or bad, and its subsequent
literary and other outgrowth—the maternal nativity-stock brought hither
from far-away Netherlands, for one, (doubtless the best)—the subter-   5
ranean tenacity and central bony structure (obstinacy, wilfulness) which
I get from my paternal English elements, for another—and the combination of my Long Island birth-spot, sea-shores, childhood's scenes, absorp-
tions, with teeming Brooklyn and New York—with, I suppose, my experiences afterward in the secession outbreak, for the third.   10

For, in 1862, startled by news that my brother George, an officer in
the 51st New York volunteers, had been seriously wounded (first Fredericksburg battle, December 13th,) I hurriedly went down to the field of
war in Virginia. But I must go back a little.

Opening of the Secession War.

News of the attack on fort Sumter and *the flag* at Charleston harbor,
S. C., was receiv'd in New York city late at night (13th April, 1861,)

Dec. 11, 1864 (*NYT* subtitle, "Visits Among Army Hospitals, at Washington, on the
Field, and Here in New-York"; reprinted in Bucke's *The Wound Dresser*, pp. 21–46,
with the title "Hospital Visits"); "The Soldiers" in *NYT*, Feb. 28, 1865; and " 'Tis
But Ten Years Since" (hereafter abbreviated "Ten Years"), a series of six articles, or
"Papers," in *NYWG*, Jan. 24, Feb. 7, 14, 21, and 28, and March 7, 1874 (reprinted in
1943, excluding the parts used in *SDC*, by T. O. Mabbott and R. G. Silver in
American Literature, XV, 52–62). All texts printed in Whitman's lifetime are
collated in these notes.]

   Opening of the Secession War.
      Printed from a clipping of *MDW* "Notes," p. 60, beginning about the middle
of the first line of the second paragraph under the subtitle: "Attack on Fort Sumter,
April, 1861." The omitted first paragraph, which was not reprinted in *SDC*, is as follows:
      "What ran through the land, as if by electric nerves, and show'd itself in stupen-
dous and practical action, immediately after the firing on *the Flag* at Fort Sumter—
the Nation ('till then incredulous) flush'd in the face, and all its veins fiercely pulsing
and pounding—the arm'd volunteers instantaneously springing up everywhere—the
tumultuous processions of the regiments—Was it not grand to have lived in such
scenes and days, and be absorb'd by them, and unloosen'd to them?"
      Most of the section was also included in the First Paper of "Ten Years," *NYWG*,
paragraphs 1–3 subtitled "Night of April 13, 1861, in New York—News of the First
Gun Fired Against the Flag, (and the End, Afterwards, of Him Who Fired It.)"
      The clipping is cut so that the first words left are "was receiv'd." The first sentence
in the MS through "S. C.," was written in ink on a separate strip of paper and pasted
at the top of the clipping.
      1–2. News . . . was] *MDW:* The news of the attack on Sumter was] *NYWG:*
The news of the first actual firing on the National Flag—the attack on Fort Sumter—
was
      2. New York city] *NYWG:* New York

and was immediately sent out in extras of the newspapers. I had been to
the opera in Fourteenth street that night, and after the performance was
walking down Broadway toward twelve o'clock, on my way to Brooklyn,
when I heard in the distance the loud cries of the newsboys, who came
presently tearing and yelling up the street, rushing from side to side even
more furiously than usual. I bought an extra and cross'd to the Metropolitan hotel (Niblo's) where the great lamps were still brightly blazing,
and, with a crowd of others, who gather'd impromptu, read the news,
which was evidently authentic. For the benefit of some who had no
papers, one of us read the telegram aloud, while all listen'd silently and
attentively. No remark was made by any of the crowd, which had increas'd
to thirty or forty, but all stood a minute or two, I remember, before they
dispers'd. I can almost see them there now, under the lamps at midnight
again.

National Uprising and Volunteering.

I have said somewhere that the three Presidentiads preceding 1861
show'd how the weakness and wickedness of rulers are just as eligible
here in America under republican, as in Europe under dynastic influences.
But what can I say of that prompt and splendid wrestling with secession
slavery, the arch-enemy personified, the instant he unmistakably show'd
his face? The volcanic upheaval of the nation, after that firing on the flag

---

4. opera . . . that] *NYWG:* opera that
5. Broadway toward twelve] *NYWG:* Broadway, after eleven
8. I bought . . . cross'd] *NYWG:* I felt that subtle magnetic something which
runs through one, on pronounced occasions—bought an extra (10 cents), and crossed
    10. a crowd] *MDW* and *NYWG:* a small crowd
    12–13. and attentively.] *NYWG:* and very attentive.

National Uprising and Volunteering.
Printed from the same clipping, *MDW*, p. 60, with the sidehead: "*The ensuing three Months—The National Uprising and Volunteering.—*" The same material is
found in *NYWG*, paragraphs 1–3, Second Paper of "Ten Years," subtitled "National
Uprising and Enthusiasm, (Yet with a Drawback.)"
    1. I have . . . that] *MDW:* I have said in another place that] *NYWG:* I have
said that
    [Cf. "Ten Years," First Paper, first paragraph of "Our Surging Politics from
1840 to '60"; also cf. "The Eighteenth Presidency!" (ed. Grier, 1956), pp. 22–23,
and a similar passage in "Death of Abraham Lincoln," *q.v., Prose 1892,* II.]
    4–5. wrestling . . . instant] *NYWG:* wrestling with the arch enemy, the instant
    6. face? The] *MDW:* face?......The] *NYWG* begins a new paragraph with
"The volcanic".
    6–8. The volcanic . . . disunion.] *NYWG:* The volcanic upheaval of the bulk of
the Nation, after that unprovoked outrage and taunt, the firing on the flag at
Charleston, so prompt and general, showed something which had been previously in

at Charleston, proved for certain something which had been previously in
great doubt, and at once substantially settled the question of disunion. In
my judgment it will remain as the grandest and most encouraging spectacle yet vouchsafed in any age, old or new, to political progress and   10
democracy. It was not for what came to the surface merely—though that
was important—but what it indicated below, which was of eternal importance. Down in the abysms of New World humanity there had form'd
and harden'd a primal hard-pan of national Union will, determin'd and in
the majority, refusing to be tamper'd with or argued against, confronting   15
all emergencies, and capable at any time of bursting all surface bonds, and
breaking out like an earthquake. It is, indeed, the best lesson of the century, or of America, and it is a mighty privilege to have been part of it.
(Two great spectacles, immortal proofs of democracy, unequall'd in all
the history of the past, are furnish'd by the secession war—one at the be-   20
ginning, the other at its close. Those are, the general, voluntary, arm'd
upheaval, and the peaceful and harmonious disbanding of the armies in
the summer of 1865.)

Contemptuous Feeling.

Even after the bombardment of Sumter, however, the gravity of the
revolt, and the power and will of the slave States for a strong and con-

---

great doubt and at once in my opinion at the time, (and now, after many fluctuations,
permanently confirmed) settled the question of Disunion.

    9. remain as] *NYWG:* remain—and the whole War will, on the National
side—as

    12–13. importance. Down] *MDW:* importance.......Down] *NYWG* begins a
new paragraph with "Down".

    17. like an earthquake.] *NYWG:* like a cosmical earthquake.

    17. It . . . best] *NYWG:* It is the best

    18. to . . . it.] *NYWG:* to have lived in it, and witnessed it, and have been a
part of it.

    18. Paragraph 3 of *NYWG* ends with "part of it." *MDW* inserts a series of seven
periods and continues the paragraph.

    19–23. Sentences in parentheses not in *NYWG.*

    20. by . . . war] *MDW:* by this War

    23. After this paragraph *NYWG* has a paragraph not reprinted. See Appendix
VI, *1.*

    Contemptuous Feeling.

    Printed from the same clipping. *MDW* has the sidehead: *"Contemptuous
National feeling.—" NYWG* has two paragraphs under the subtitle "Supercilious First
Estimate of the Revolt," 5 and 6 of the Second Paper.

    1. Even after . . . the gravity] *NYWG:* At this time, too, through all the North-
ern, Middle and Western States, the gravity

tinued military resistance to national authority, were not at all realized at the North, except by a few. Nine-tenths of the people of the free States
5   look'd upon the rebellion, as started in South Carolina, from a feeling one-half of contempt, and the other half composed of anger and incredulity. It was not thought it would be join'd in by Virginia, North Carolina, or Georgia. A great and cautious national official predicted that it would blow over "in sixty days," and folks generally believ'd the prediction. I remem-
10   ber talking about it on a Fulton ferry-boat with the Brooklyn mayor, who said he only "hoped the Southern fire-eaters would commit some overt act of resistance, as they would then be at once so effectually squelch'd, we would never hear of secession again—but he was afraid they never would have the pluck to really do anything." I remember, too, that a couple of
15   companies of the Thirteenth Brooklyn, who rendezvou'd at the city armory, and started thence as thirty days' men, were all provided with pieces of rope, conspicuously tied to their musket-barrels, with which to bring back each man a prisoner from the audacious South, to be led in a noose, on our men's early and triumphant return!

Battle of Bull Run, July, 1861.

All this sort of feeling was destin'd to be arrested and revers'd by a terrible shock—the battle of first Bull Run—certainly, as we now know it, one of the most singular fights on record. (All battles, and their results, are far more matters of accident than is generally thought; but this was
5   throughout a casualty, a chance. Each side supposed it had won, till the last moment. One had, in point of fact, just the same right to be routed as the other. By a fiction, or series of fictions, the national forces at the last

3–4. realized . . . except] MDW: realized through the North, except] NYWG: realized, except
14. anything." I remember] MDW: anything.'. . . . . . . I remember] NYWG begins a new paragraph with "I".
19. After "return!" MDW ends the paragraph with the following two sentences not in NYWG or other texts: "[This was indeed the general feeling, and came to the surface. Still, there was a very strong Secession party at the North, as I shall mention in a Note further on.]"

Battle of Bull Run, July, 1861.

Printed from three clippings of MDW "Notes," pp. 60–62, with the same subtitle. NYWG has several headings for the material in this section. Paragraphs 7 and 8 of the Second Paper are subtitled "The Flood-Tide Suddenly Ebbs."
3–8. Sentence beginning "All battles" is not enclosed in parentheses in NYWG.
8. Paragraph 8 of NYWG, a single sentence, and paragraph 9, subtitled "The Two Blackest Days," omitted in later texts at this point, were printed, with revisions,

moment exploded in a panic and fled from the field.) The defeated troops commenced pouring into Washington over the Long Bridge at daylight on Monday, 22d—day drizzling all through with rain. The Saturday and Sunday of the battle (20th, 21st,) had been parch'd and hot to an extreme—the dust, the grime and smoke, in layers, sweated in, follow'd by other layers again sweated in, absorb'd by those excited souls—their clothes all saturated with the clay-powder filling the air—stirr'd up everywhere on the dry roads and trodden fields by the regiments, swarming wagons, artillery, &c.—all the men with this coating of murk and sweat and rain, now recoiling back, pouring over the Long Bridge—a horrible march of twenty miles, returning to Washington baffled, humiliated, panic-struck. Where are the vaunts, and the proud boasts with which you went forth? Where are your banners, and your bands of music, and your ropes to bring back your prisoners? Well, there isn't a band playing—and there isn't a flag but clings ashamed and lank to its staff.

The sun rises, but shines not. The men appear, at first sparsely and shame-faced enough, then thicker, in the streets of Washington—appear in Pennsylvania avenue, and on the steps and basement entrances. They come along in disorderly mobs, some in squads, stragglers, companies. Occasionally, a rare regiment, in perfect order, with its officers (some gaps, dead, the true braves,) marching in silence, with lowering faces, stern, weary to sinking, all black and dirty, but every man with his musket, and stepping alive; but these are the exceptions. Sidewalks of Pennsylvania avenue, Fourteenth street, &c., crowded, jamm'd with citizens, darkies, clerks, everybody, lookers-on; women in the windows, curious expressions from faces, as those swarms of dirt-cover'd return'd soldiers there (will they never end?) move by; but nothing said, no comments; half our lookers-on secesh of the most venomous kind—they say nothing; but the

in *MDW* at the end of the section with the sidehead "Battle of Bull Run, July 1861," p. 62, and in *SDC* and *CPW* at the end of the section subtitled "The Stupor Passes—Something Else Begins" (*q.v.*, lines 19–22 and 23–31).

Paragraphs 10–15 of *NYWG* have the subtitle: "Washington City, 22d to 25th July, 1861, After First Bull Run." *MDW* has no new subtitle but makes the first sentence a separate paragraph.

8. The defeated troops] *MDW* and *NYWG:* The troops

14. the air—stirr'd up] *NYWG:* the air, those two days—stirred up

16–17. sweat . . . back,] *MDW:* sweat and Virginia rain—now recoiling back—] *NYWG:* sweat and Virginia rain—now a solid stream recoiling back—

18–19. panic-struck. Where] *MDW:* panic struck!......Where] *NYWG:* panic-struck! Where

20. and your] *NYWG:* and where your

22. *SDC* and *NYWG* end the paragraph with "staff." *MDW* has a series of seven periods and continues the paragraph.

30. *MDW* has a series of nine periods after "the exceptions." and continues the paragraph. *NYWG* ends the paragraph.

devil snickers in their faces.) During the forenoon Washington gets all
over motley with these defeated soldiers—queer-looking objects, strange
eyes and faces, drench'd (the steady rain drizzles on all day) and fearfully worn, hungry, haggard, blister'd in the feet. Good people (but not
40 over-many of them either,) hurry up something for their grub. They put
wash-kettles on the fire, for soup, for coffee. They set tables on the sidewalks—wagon-loads of bread are purchas'd, swiftly cut in stout chunks.
Here are two aged ladies, beautiful, the first in the city for culture and
charm, they stand with store of eating and drink at an improvis'd table of
45 rough plank, and give food, and have the store replenish'd from their
house every half-hour all that day; and there in the rain they stand, active,
silent, white-hair'd, and give food, though the tears stream down their
cheeks, almost without intermission, the whole time. Amid the deep excitement, crowds and motion, and desperate eagerness, it seems strange to
50 see many, very many, of the soldiers sleeping—in the midst of all, sleeping sound. They drop down anywhere, on the steps of houses, up close by
the basements or fences, on the sidewalk, aside on some vacant lot, and
deeply sleep. A poor seventeen or eighteen year old boy lies there, on the
stoop of a grand house; he sleeps so calmly, so profoundly. Some clutch
55 their muskets firmly even in sleep. Some in squads; comrades, brothers,
close together—and on them, as they lay, sulkily drips the rain.

As afternoon pass'd, and evening came, the streets, the bar-rooms,
knots everywhere, listeners, questioners, terrible yarns, bugaboo, mask'd
batteries, our regiment all cut up, &c.—stories and story-tellers, windy,
60 bragging, vain centres of street-crowds. Resolution, manliness, seem to
have abandon'd Washington. The principal hotel, Willard's, is full of
shoulder-straps—thick, crush'd, creeping with shoulder-straps. (I see
them, and must have a word with them. There you are, shoulder-straps!
—but where are your companies? where are your men? Incompetents!

36. Both MDW and NYWG end the paragraph with "their faces.)"
36–37. gets . . . queer-looking] MDW: gets motley with the dirt-cover'd soldiers
—queer-looking] NYWG: gets motley with these dirt-covered soldiers. Queer-looking
41–42. side-walks] NYWG: side walk
48. Both MDW and NYWG end the paragraph with "whole time."
48–49. excitement, crowds] NYWG: excitement (too deep for demonstration) amid
the crowds
57. pass'd and] NYWG: passed on, and
58. terrible yarns,] NYWG: terrible stories,
62–69. Not enclosed in parentheses in NYWG.
68–69. half or one-tenth worthy] NYWG: Half worthy
70–97. Paragraphs 16–18 in NYWG, the first of four subtitled "Is Not Secession
Already Triumphant?—Must Lincoln and His Cabinet Fly?" MDW and SDC continue
under the same subtitle.
75. Union] NYWG: Liberty-Union

never tell me of chances of battle, of getting stray'd, and the like. I think 65
this is your work, this retreat, after all. Sneak, blow, put on airs there in
Willard's sumptuous parlors and bar-rooms, or anywhere—no explanation
shall save you. Bull Run is your work; had you been half or one-tenth
worthy your men, this would never have happen'd.)

Meantime, in Washington, among the great persons and their entou- 70
rage, a mixture of awful consternation, uncertainty, rage, shame, helpless-
ness, and stupefying disappointment. The worst is not only imminent, but
already here. In a few hours—perhaps before the next meal—the secesh
generals, with their victorious hordes, will be upon us. The dream of
humanity, the vaunted Union we thought so strong, so impregnable—lo! 75
it seems already smash'd like a china plate. One bitter, bitter hour—perhaps proud America will never again know such an hour. She must pack
and fly—no time to spare. Those white palaces—the dome-crown'd capitol there on the hill, so stately over the trees—shall they be left—or de-
stroy'd first? For it is certain that the talk among certain of the magnates 80
and officers and clerks and officials everywhere, for twenty-four hours in
and around Washington after Bull Run, was loud and undisguised for
yielding out and out, and substituting the southern rule, and Lincoln
promptly abdicating and departing. If the secesh officers and forces had
immediately follow'd, and by a bold Napoleonic movement had enter'd 85
Washington the first day, (or even the second,) they could have had
things their own way, and a powerful faction north to back them. One of
our returning colonels express'd in public that night, amid a swarm of
officers and gentlemen in a crowded room, the opinion that it was useless
to fight, that the southerners had made their title clear, and that the best 90
course for the national government to pursue was to desist from any further attempt at stopping them, and admit them again to the lead, on the
best terms they were willing to grant. Not a voice was rais'd against this

76. it . . . smash'd] *MDW* and *NYWG:* it is smashed
77. proud America] *NYWG:* proud and dainty personified America
77. such an hour.] *MDW* and *NYWG:* such a bitter hour.
78. Those . . . the] *NYWG:* These white palaces of magnitude and beauty—the
79. trees—shall] *NYWG:* trees—decide quickly—shall
80. *NYWG* ends the paragraph with the sentence ending "destroyed first?" *MDW* has a series of seven periods and continues the paragraph.
80. is . . . magnates] *NYWG:* is not generally known that the talk among the talkers and magnates
83. out and out, and] *NYWG:* out and out to the secession demands, and
86. second,) they] *NYWG:* second) it is certain they
88. returning colonels express'd] *NYWG:* returning Bull Run officers (T. F. Meagher) expressed] *MDW:* returning officers express'd
88–89. a swarm of officers] *NYWG:* a large swarm of other officers
90. clear, and] *MDW* and *NYWG:* clear to their own terms, and

95 judgment, amid that large crowd of officers and gentlemen. (The fact is, the hour was one of the three or four of those crises we had then and afterward, during the fluctuations of four years, when human eyes appear'd at least just as likely to see the last breath of the Union as to see it continue.)

The Stupor Passes—Something Else Begins.

But the hour, the day, the night pass'd, and whatever returns, an hour, a day, a night like that can never again return. The President, recovering himself, begins that very night—sternly, rapidly sets about the task of reorganizing his forces, and placing himself in positions for future 5 and surer work. If there were nothing else of Abraham Lincoln for history to stamp him with, it is enough to send him with his wreath to the memory of all future time, that he endured that hour, that day, bitterer than gall—indeed a crucifixion day—that it did not conquer him—that he unflinchingly stemm'd it, and resolv'd to lift himself and the Union out 10 of it.

Then the great New York papers at once appear'd, (commencing that

94–97. This sentence is the second of two in a separate paragraph in parentheses in *NYWG*. The first of the two, not in *MDW* or *SDC*, is as follows: "(This was Washington 'society,' remember, and it makes the strongest point against Washington I know of."

95–96. had . . . during] *MDW* and *NYWG*: had during

The Stupor Passes—Something Else Begins.

Printed from the same clipping of *MDW*, p. 62. This subtitle does not appear in either *MDW* or *NYWG*.

1–10. This is paragraph 19, the fourth under the subtitle "Is Not Secession," etc.

3. sternly, rapidly] *NYWG*: sternly and rapidly

5. and surer work.] *MDW* and *NYWG*: and greater work.

6. with, it is] *NYWG*: with, it is to be said, (and I say it here,) that it is

8. crucifixion . . . conquer] *NYWG*: crucifixion day—that he endured it, was superior to it, that it did not conquer

10. After "Union out of it." *NYWG* continues with the following sentence, not reprinted, to end the paragraph: "I say that his deed, in this alone, is a first class historic grandeur, fit to stand with all greatest antique and modern samples and personalities, and not afraid of comparison with the best of them."

11–22. This paragraph, 20 in *NYWG*, follows the sentence quoted above, but has the separate subtitle "The New York Press Do Well."

11–12. that evening] *MDW* and *NYWG*: that very evening

13. land with the] *NYWG*: land, with all the

14. ring . . . bugles] *MDW*: ring of clearest, wildest bugles] *NYWG*: ring of bands of clearest, wildest, most stirring bugles

16–18. Names of newspapers are printed in italics in *MDW* and *NYWG*.

20–22. In place of this sentence *NYWG* has the following: "And there is no denying that these loud cheerful clarion tones of the *Herald* and the rest, coming on the

evening, and following it up the next morning, and incessantly through many days afterwards,) with leaders that rang out over the land with the loudest, most reverberating ring of clearest bugles, full of encouragement, hope, inspiration, unfaltering defiance. Those magnificent edi-   15
torials! they never flagg'd for a fortnight. The "Herald" commenced them—I remember the articles well. The "Tribune" was equally cogent and inspiriting—and the "Times," "Evening Post," and other principal papers, were not a whit behind. They came in good time, for they were needed. For in the humiliation of Bull Run, the popular feeling north,   20
from its extreme of superciliousness, recoil'd to the depth of gloom and apprehension.

(Of all the days of the war, there are two especially I can never forget. Those were the day following the news, in New York and Brooklyn, of that first Bull Run defeat, and the day of Abraham Lincoln's death. I   25
was home in Brooklyn on both occasions. The day of the murder we heard the news very early in the morning. Mother prepared breakfast—and other meals afterward—as usual; but not a mouthful was eaten all day by either of us. We each drank half a cup of coffee; that was all. Little was said. We got every newspaper morning and evening, and the frequent   30
extras of that period, and pass'd them silently to each other.)

instant gave the key-note to what followed, on the National side, and soon restored the Union energies with determination five times magnified, and finally plucked the flower safety out of the nettle danger."

20–22. This sentence in SDC and MDW is a revision of paragraph 8 in NYWG, "The Flood-Tide Suddenly Ebbs," to wit: "Then the popular feeling North, from its extreme of superciliousness, recoiled to the depth of gloom and apprehension." [See note to line 8, "Battle of Bull Run, July, 1861."]

23–31. This was paragraph 9 subtitled "The Two Blackest Days." In NYWG the parentheses include only the last five sentences of the paragraph. [See note to line 8, "Battle of Bull Run, July, 1861."]

23. war, there are] NYWG: war, with its fitful long-drawn four years of ups and downs, there are

24. day] NYWG: days

25. that first] NYWG: the first

27–28. and other] NYWG: and the other

28–29. eaten all day by] NYWG: eaten by

31. of . . . to] NYWG: of those days, and passed them to

31. The clipping of MDW, p. 62, ends with this line. The rest of MDW, p. 62, under the subtitle "Sherman's Army's Jubilation, 1865—Its sudden stoppage.—" is used later in SDC under the same subtitle, q.v.

The remainder of "Ten Years," Second Paper, is not used at this point in SDC. Paragraph 21, first under "The Inner Points of the War Can Never Be Written," was not used in SDC. See Appendix VI, 1.

Paragraph 22, same subtitle, was used in part later in SDC, in the section subtitled "The Real War Will Never Get in the Books," lines 37–53, q.v. Paragraph 23, subtitled "What the War Was Really to Decide," was used, with revisions, later in SDC, in "Origins of Attempted Secession," lines 189–197. See Prose 1892, II. The last paragraph, subtitled "Items of My Next," was not used in SDC. See Appendix VI, 1.

Down at the Front.

FALMOUTH, Va., *opposite Fredericksburgh, December 21, 1862.*—
Begin my visits among the camp hospitals in the army of the Potomac.
Spend a good part of the day in a large brick mansion on the banks of the
Rappahannock, used as a hospital since the battle—seems to have receiv'd
only the worst cases. Out doors, at the foot of a tree, within ten yards of
the front of the house, I notice a heap of amputated feet, legs, arms,
hands, &c., a full load for a one-horse cart. Several dead bodies lie near,
each cover'd with its brown woolen blanket. In the door-yard, towards the
river, are fresh graves, mostly of officers, their names on pieces of barrel-
staves or broken boards, stuck in the dirt. (Most of these bodies were subsequently taken up and transported north to their friends.) The large
mansion is quite crowded upstairs and down, everything impromptu, no
system, all bad enough, but I have no doubt the best that can be done;
all the wounds pretty bad, some frightful, the men in their old clothes,
unclean and bloody. Some of the wounded are rebel soldiers and officers,
prisoners. One, a Mississippian, a captain, hit badly in leg, I talk'd with
some time; he ask'd me for papers, which I gave him. (I saw him three
months afterward in Washington, with his leg amputated, doing well.)

Down at the Front.
     Printed from a clipping of a part of page 6, MDW. With this section Whitman
begins to use material from the Third Paper of "Ten Years," NYWG. Much of this
paper had previously been printed in "Our Wounded and Sick Soldiers" in NYT,
Dec. 11, 1864. Subtitle inserted in copy. The material of this section is in the first
three paragraphs of NYWG, subtitled "Battle of First Fredericksburgh—Visits Among
the Wounded." In NYT it is in paragraphs 3–5, subtitled "Camp Hospitals, Fredericksburgh, Near Falmouth, Va." Before this subtitle, NYT has two introductory
paragraphs omitted from later texts. See Appendix III, I.
     1–2. Falmouth . . . among] NYWG: *December 21, 1862.—Began my visits*
among] NYT: Began my visits (Dec. 21, 1862,) among
     2–3. Potomac. Spend] MDW: Potomac. Spent] NYWG: Potomac, about Falmouth,
Va. Spent] NYT: Potomac, under Gen. Burnside. Spent
     4. Rappahannock, used] NYWG and NYT: Rappahannock, immediately oppo-
site Fredericksburgh. It is used
     4. battle—seems] MDW: battle—Seems] NYWG and NYT: battle, and seems
     7. a full load] NYT: about a load
     8. woolen] MDW and NYWG: woollen
     8. towards] NYT: toward
     10. boards] MDW, NYWG, and NYT: board
     11. their friends.) The] MDW: their friends.) . . . . The] [NYWG and
NYT begin a new paragraph with "The".]
     11–12. The large mansion] NYWG: The large brick house] NYT: The house
     12. crowded upstairs and down, everything] NYT: crowded, everything

I went through the rooms, downstairs and up. Some of the men were dying. I had nothing to give at that visit, but wrote a few letters to folks home, mothers, &c. Also talk'd to three or four, who seem'd most suscepti- ble to it, and needing it.

After First Fredericksburg.

December 23 to 31.—The results of the late battle are exhibited everywhere about here in thousands of cases, (hundreds die every day,) in the camp, brigade, and division hospitals. These are merely tents, and sometimes very poor ones, the wounded lying on the ground, lucky if their blankets are spread on layers of pine or hemlock twigs, or small leaves. No cots; seldom even a mattress. It is pretty cold. The ground is frozen hard, and there is occasional snow. I go around from one case to another. I do not see that I do much good to these wounded and dying; but I cannot leave them. Once in a while some youngster holds on to me convulsively, and I do what I can for him; at any rate, stop with him and sit near him for hours, if he wishes it.

Besides the hospitals, I also go occasionally on long tours through the camps, talking with the men, &c. Sometimes at night among the groups around the fires, in their shebang enclosures of bushes. These are curious

---

15. rebel soldiers and officers] *NYT:* rebel officers
18. with his leg] *NYT:* with leg
18–19. doing well.) I] *MDW:* doing well.) . . . . .I] [*NYWG* and *NYT* be- gin a new paragraph with "I".]
22. After "needing it." *MDW* and *NYWG* have a paragraph deleted in copy for *SDC.* See Appendix XI, 2. For paragraphs 5 and 6, *NYWG*, see Appendix VII, 2.

After First Fredericksburg.
Printed from clippings of *MDW*, pp. 6–7. *NYWG* has the same in paragraphs 7–9, Third Paper, subtitled "Hospitals in Camp," and *NYT*, article of Dec. 11, 1864, has the same in paragraphs 6–8, subtitled "Camp Hospitals, Fredericksburgh, Near Falmouth, Va." Subtitle inserted in copy.
1–3. Not in *NYT*, which has the initial sentence: "Am among the regimental, brigade and division hospitals somewhat."
1. battle] *MDW* and *NYWG:* battles
3. These are merely] *NYT:* Few at home realize that these are merely
5. blankets . . . layers] *NYT:* blanket is spread on a layer
5–6. or small leaves.] *NYT:* or some leaves.
6. mattress.] *NYWG* and *NYT:* mattress on the ground.
6–7. The sentence beginning "The ground" is not in *NYT*.
8–9. I do much good . . . dying; but] *MDW:* I do much good, but] *NYWG:* I can do much good, but] *NYT:* I can do any good, but
12. Besides] *NYT:* Beside   14. enclosures] *NYT:* inclosures
14. After "of bushes." *NYWG* inserts the following sentence not found in *NYT:*

15   shows, full of characters and groups. I soon get acquainted anywhere in
camp, with officers or men, and am always well used. Sometimes I go
down on picket with the regiments I know best. As to rations, the army
here at present seems to be tolerably well supplied, and the men have
enough, such as it is, mainly salt pork and hard tack. Most of the regi-
20   ments lodge in the flimsy little shelter-tents. A few have built themselves
huts of logs and mud, with fire-places.

Back to Washington.

January, '63.—Left camp at Falmouth, with some wounded, a few
days since, and came here by Aquia creek railroad, and so on government
steamer up the Potomac. Many wounded were with us on the cars and
boat. The cars were just common platform ones. The railroad journey of
5   ten or twelve miles was made mostly before sunrise. The soldiers guarding the road came out from their tents or shebangs of bushes with rum-
pled hair and half-awake look. Those on duty were walking their posts,
some on banks over us, others down far below the level of the track. I
saw large cavalry camps off the road. At Aquia creek landing were num-
10   bers of wounded going north. While I waited some three hours, I went
around among them. Several wanted word sent home to parents,

"These are curious shows, full of characters and groups, worthy of Zenophon to nar-
rate and Rembrandt to paint." SDC and MDW end this sentence with "groups."
      17. know best. As] MDW: know best.......As] [NYWG and NYT begin new
paragraph with "As".]
      19. as it is, . . . Most] NYWG: as it is. It is mainly salt pork and hard tack.
Most] NYT: as it is. Most
      21. After "with fire-places." NYT has the following sentence (paragraph 9) not
in any other text: "I might give a long list of special cases, interesting items of the
wounded men here, but have not space."
      21. Paragraphs 10–14, NYWG, are not in any other text. See Appendix VII, 3.
      Back to Washington.
      Printed from clippings of parts of pp. 7–8 of MDW. The subtitle is inserted
in SDC. This material, under different subtitles, is found in paragraphs 15–20 of
NYWG, Third Paper of "Ten Years"; it is in paragraph 10–11 and 13–15 of NYT,
Dec. 11, 1864.
      1–14. From paragraph 15, NYWG, subtitled "I Remove to Washington—Sights
on the Road," and paragraph 10, NYT, "Via Aquia Creek, Up the Potomac."
      1. *January, '63.*—Left camp . . . here by] MDW: *Washington, January, '63.*
—Left camp . . . here by] NYWG: *January, '63.*—Left camp . . . here (to
Washington) by] NYT: Left Falmouth, January, 1863, by
      15–28. From paragraphs 16 and 17 in NYWG, subtitled "Wounded Soldiers—
Specimen Cases." In NYT it includes paragraph 11, the first of two subtitled "Com-
mence with Washington Hospitals," and paragraphs 13–15 subtitled "Specimens of

brothers, wives, &c., which I did for them, (by mail the next day from Washington.) On the boat I had my hands full. One poor fellow died going up.

I am now remaining in and around Washington, daily visiting the hospitals. Am much in Patent-office, Eighth street, H street, Armory-square, and others. Am now able to do a little good, having money, (as almoner of others home,) and getting experience. To-day, Sunday afternoon and till nine in the evening, visited Campbell hospital; attended specially to one case in ward 1, very sick with pleurisy and typhoid fever, young man, farmer's son, D. F. Russell, company E, 60th New York, downhearted and feeble; a long time before he would take any interest; wrote a letter home to his mother, in Malone, Franklin county, N. Y., at his request; gave him some fruit and one or two other gifts; envelop'd and directed his letter, &c. Then went thoroughly through ward 6, observ'd every case in the ward, without, I think, missing one; gave perhaps from twenty to thirty persons, each one some little gift, such as oranges, apples, sweet crackers, figs, &c.

Thursday, Jan. 21.—Devoted the main part of the day to Armory-square hospital; went pretty thoroughly through wards F, G, H, and I; some fifty cases in each ward. In ward F supplied the men throughout with writing paper and stamp'd envelope each; distributed in small portions, to proper subjects, a large jar of first-rate preserv'd berries, which

Hospital Visits."
    15. I am now remaining in] *NYT:* Am now (January, February, &c., 1863,) in
    18. experience. To-day] *MDW:* experience . . . . To-day] [*NYWG* begins a new paragraph with "To-day".]
    18. After "experience," *NYT,* paragraph 12, not in other texts, is as follows:
    "I would like to give lists of cases, for there is no end to the interesting ones, but it is impossible without making a large volume, or rather several volumes. I must, therefore, let one or two days' visits, at this time, suffice as specimens of scores and hundreds of subsequent ones, through the ensuing Spring, Summer and Fall, and indeed, down to the present week."
    18–19. To-day, . . . nine in] *NYT:* Sunday, January 25.—Afternoon and till 9 in
    22–23. interest; wrote] *NYT:* interest; soothed and cheered him gently; wrote
    26–27. ward, . . . perhaps] *NYWG:* ward, (without, I think, missing one;) found some cases I thought needed little sums of money; supplied them; (sums of perhaps 30, 20 [*NYT:* 30, 25, 20] or 15 cents;) distributed a pretty bountiful supply of cheerful reading matter, and gave perhaps
    29–52. For these lines *NYWG* has the subtitle "Armory Square Hospital."
    29. *Thursday, Jan. 21.*—] *NYT:* Thursday, Jan. 29.
    29. day to] *NYT:* day, from 11 to 3:30 o'clock, to
    32. each; distributed] *NYWG* and *NYT:* each; also some cheerful reading matter; distributed
    32–33. portions, to proper] *NYT:* portions, about half of it in this ward, to proper
    33–34. berries, . . . cooking. Found] *NYWG:* berries, . . . cooking. In Wards G, H, and I, found] *NYT:* berries; also other small gifts. In Wards G, H and I, found

had been donated to me by a lady—her own cooking. Found several cases
35 I thought good subjects for small sums of money, which I furnish'd. (The
wounded men often come up broke, and it helps their spirits to have even
the small sum I give them.) My paper and envelopes all gone, but distributed a good lot of amusing reading matter; also, as I thought judicious, tobacco, oranges, apples, &c. Interesting cases in ward I; Charles
40 Miller, bed 19, company D, 53d Pennsylvania, is only sixteen years of age,
very bright, courageous boy, left leg amputated below the knee; next bed
to him, another young lad very sick; gave each appropriate gifts. In the
bed above, also, amputation of the left leg; gave him a little jar of raspberries; bed 1, this ward, gave a small sum; also to a soldier on crutches,
45 sitting on his bed near. . . . (I am more and more surprised at the very
great proportion of youngsters from fifteen to twenty-one in the army. I
afterwards found a still greater proportion among the southerners.)

Evening, same day, went to see D. F. R., before alluded to; found
him remarkably changed for the better; up and dress'd—quite a triumph;
50 he afterwards got well, and went back to his regiment. Distributed in the
wards a quantity of note-paper, and forty or fifty stamp'd envelopes, of
which I had recruited my stock, and the men were much in need.

Fifty Hours Left Wounded on the Field.

Here is a case of a soldier I found among the crowded cots in the
Patent-office. He likes to have some one to talk to, and we will listen to him.

35. furnish'd.] *NYT:* furnished in each case.
35–37. *NYWG* and *NYT* omit marks of parenthesis.
35–36. (The wounded men often come up broke, and] *NYT:* The poor wounded
men often come up dead broke, and
39. Interesting] *NYWG:* Very interesting] *NYT:* Some very interesting
42. gave each] *NYT:* gave the two each
43. him a little jar] *NYT:* him part of a jar
45. bed near. . . .] *MDW:* bed near. . . . . . .] *NYWG:* bed near.
45–47. These lines are a separate paragraph in *NYWG;* not in *NYT.*
49–50. quite . . . regiment.] [*NYT* encloses this part of the sentence in parentheses.]
50. regiment. Distributed] *MDW:* regiment. . . . . .Distributed
51–52. forty or fifty . . . in need.] *NYWG:* forty or fifty stamped envelopes, of
which the men were much in need.] *NYT:* 40 or 50 mostly paid envelopes, of which
the men were much in need; also a four-pound bag of ginger-snaps I bought at a
baker's in Seventh-street.

Fifty Hours Left Wounded on the Field.
Printed from clippings of pp. 8 and 9 of *MDW.* Published also, same subtitle,
as paragraphs 21–23, Third Paper of "Ten Years," *NYWG;* and as paragraphs 16–

He got badly hit in his leg and side at Fredericksburgh that eventful
Saturday, 13th of December. He lay the succeeding two days and nights
helpless on the field, between the city and those grim terraces of batteries; 5
his company and regiment had been compell'd to leave him to his fate. To
make matters worse, it happen'd he lay with his head slightly down hill,
and could not help himself. At the end of some fifty hours he was brought
off, with other wounded, under a flag of truce. I ask him how the rebels
treated him as he lay during those two days and nights within reach of 10
them—whether they came to him—whether they abused him? He answers
that several of the rebels, soldiers and others, came to him at one time
and another. A couple of them, who were together, spoke roughly and
sarcastically, but nothing worse. One middle-aged man, however, who
seem'd to be moving around the field, among the dead and wounded, for 15
benevolent purposes, came to him in a way he will never forget; treated
our soldier kindly, bound up his wounds, cheer'd him, gave him a couple
of biscuits and a drink of whiskey and water; asked him if he could eat
some beef. This good secesh, however, did not change our soldier's position, for it might have caused the blood to burst from the wounds, clotted 20
and stagnated. Our soldier is from Pennsylvania; has had a pretty severe
time; the wounds proved to be bad ones. But he retains a good heart, and
is at present on the gain. (It is not uncommon for the men to remain on
the field this way, one, two, or even four or five days.)

2. Patent-office. He likes] *NYWG:* Patent Office—(they have removed most of
the men of late, and are breaking [*NYT:* and broken] up that hospital.) He likes
3. badly hit in his leg] *NYT:* badly wounded in the leg
5–6. batteries; his] *NYWG* and *NYT:* batteries; for his
7. worse, it happen'd he lay] *NYWG* and *NYT:* worse, he lay
9. truce. I] *MDW:* truce. . . . . I] [*NWYG* and *NYT* begin a new paragraph with "I".]
9. I ask] *NYT:* We ask
10. treated . . . during] *NYT:* treated him during
14. but nothing worse.] *NYWG:* but did nothing to him.] *NYT:* but did no act.
16. forget; treated] *NYWG* and *NYT:* forget. This man treated
18. biscuits and a drink] *NYT:* biscuits, gave him a drink
20. wounds, clotted] *NYWG* and *NYT:* wounds, where they were clotted
23–24. In *MDW* this sentence is preceded by a series of nine periods. In *NYWG*
it is a separate paragraph. In *NYT* it is a separate paragraph without parentheses.
For paragraphs 24 and 25, concluding the Third Paper, not printed elsewhere, see Appendix VII, 4.
Immediately following "Fifty Hours Left Wounded On the Field," *NYT* has a
paragraph (19) not afterwards reprinted. See Appendix III, 2.

Hospital Scenes and Persons.

Letter Writing.—When eligible, I encourage the men to write, and myself, when called upon, write all sorts of letters for them, (including love letters, very tender ones.) Almost as I reel off these memoranda, I write for a new patient to his wife. M. de F., of the 17th Connecticut, company H, has just come up (February 17th) from Windmill point, and is received in ward H, Armory-square. He is an intelligent looking man, has a foreign accent, black-eyed and hair'd, a Hebraic appearance. Wants a telegraphic message sent to his wife, New Canaan, Conn. I agree to send the message—but to make things sure I also sit down and write the wife a letter, and despatch it to the post-office immediately, as he fears she will come on, and he does not wish her to, as he will surely get well.

Saturday, January 30th.—Afternoon, visited Campbell hospital. Scene of cleaning up the ward, and giving the men all clean clothes— through the ward (6) the patients dressing or being dress'd—the naked upper half of the bodies—the good-humor and fun—the shirts, drawers, sheets of beds, &c., and the general fixing up for Sunday. Gave J. L. 50 cents.

Wednesday, February 4th.—Visited Armory-square hospital, went pretty thoroughly through wards E and D. Supplied paper and envelopes to all who wish'd—as usual, found plenty of men who needed those articles. Wrote letters. Saw and talk'd with two or three members of the Brooklyn 14th regt. A poor fellow in ward D, with a fearful wound in a fearful condition, was having some loose splinters of bone taken from the neighborhood of the wound. The operation was long, and one of great pain—yet, after it was well commenced, the soldier bore it in silence. He sat up, propp'd—was much wasted—had lain a long time quiet in one

---

Hospital Scenes and Persons.

Printed from clippings of MDW, pp. 9–10.

1–11. This is paragraph 4 of the Fourth Paper of "Ten Years" in NYWG. It may possibly have been influenced by the following paragraph (20) of NYT, under the heading "Writing Letters by the Bedside":

"I do a good deal of this, of course, writing all kinds, including love-letters. Many sick and wounded soldiers have not written home to parents, brothers, sisters, and even wives, for one reason or another, for a long, long time. Some are poor writers, some cannot get paper and envelopes; many have an aversion to writing because they dread to worry the folks at home—the facts about them are so sad to tell. I always encourage the men to write, and promptly write for them."

1. When eligible, I encourage the men] NYWG: Of course when eligible, I generally encourage all the men

position (not for days only but weeks,) a bloodless, brown-skinn'd face, with eyes full of determination—belong'd to a New York regiment. There was an unusual cluster of surgeons, medical cadets, nurses, &c., around his bed—I thought the whole thing was done with tenderness, and done well. In one case, the wife sat by the side of her husband, his sickness typhoid fever, pretty bad. In another, by the side of her son, a mother —she told me she had seven children, and this was the youngest. (A fine, kind, healthy, gentle mother, good-looking, not very old, with a cap on her head, and dress'd like home—what a charm it gave to the whole ward.) I liked the woman nurse in Ward E—I noticed how she sat a long time by a poor fellow who just had, that morning, in addition to his other sickness, bad hemorrhage—she gently assisted him, reliev'd him of the blood, holding a cloth to his mouth, as he coughed it up—he was so weak he could only just turn his head over on the pillow.

One young New York man, with a bright, handsome face, had been lying several months from a most disagreeable wound, receiv'd at Bull Run. A bullet had shot him right through the bladder, hitting him front, low in the belly, and coming out back. He had suffer'd much—the water came out of the wound, by slow but steady quantities, for many weeks— so that he lay almost constantly in a sort of puddle—and there were other disagreeable circumstances. He was of good heart, however. At present comparatively comfortable, had a bad throat, was delighted with a stick of horehound candy I gave him, with one or two other trifles.

Patent-Office Hospital.

February 23.—I must not let the great hospital at the Patent-office pass away without some mention. A few weeks ago the vast area of the second story of that noblest of Washington buildings was crowded close

---

3. These memoranda,] MDW: this memoranda,] NYWG: this sketch,
12–49. All of this, apparently, was printed for the first time in MDW.
22. Brooklyn 14th regt. A] MDW: Brooklyn Fourteenth.........A
31. MDW begins a new paragraph after "and done well."

Patent-Office Hospital.
     Printed from MDW, pp. 10–11, where it has only the sidehead "*Feb.* 23.—"
It was used first in Whitman's article "The Great Army of the Sick," NYT, Feb. 26,
1863, which Bucke reprinted with some changes in *The Wound-Dresser* (pp. 1–9)
as "The Great Army of the Wounded." In NYT the paragraph has the subtitle "The
Patent Office."
     1–2. This sentence not in NYT.
     3. buildings was] NYT: buildings, the Patent Office, was

30
35
40
45

with rows of sick, badly wounded and dying soldiers. They were placed
in three very large apartments. I went there many times. It was a strange,
solemn, and, with all its features of suffering and death, a sort of fascinating sight. I go sometimes at night to soothe and relieve particular cases.
Two of the immense apartments are fill'd with high and ponderous glass
cases, crowded with models in miniature of every kind of utensil, machine or invention, it ever enter'd into the mind of man to conceive; and
with curiosities and foreign presents. Between these cases are lateral openings, perhaps eight feet wide and quite deep, and in these were placed the
sick, besides a great long double row of them up and down through the
middle of the hall. Many of them were very bad cases, wounds and amputations. Then there was a gallery running above the hall in which there
were beds also. It was, indeed, a curious scene, especially at night when lit
up. The glass cases, the beds, the forms lying there, the gallery above, and
the marble pavement under foot—the suffering, and the fortitude to bear
it in various degrees—occasionally, from some, the groan that could not
be repress'd—sometimes a poor fellow dying, with emaciated face and
glassy eye, the nurse by his side, the doctor also there, but no friend, no
relative—such were the sights but lately in the Patent-office. (The
wounded have since been removed from there, and it is now vacant again.)

The White House by Moonlight.

February 24th.—A spell of fine soft weather. I wander about a
good deal, sometimes at night under the moon. To-night took a long look
at the President's house. The white portico—the palace-like, tall, round
columns, spotless as snow—the walls also—the tender and soft moon-

5. many times.] *NYT:* several times.
7. I go sometimes] *NYT:* I went sometimes
7–8. cases. Two] *NYT:* cases; some, I found, needed a little cheering up and
friendly consolation at that time, for they went to sleep better afterward. Two
11. cases are] *NYT:* cases were
12–13. placed the sick, besides] *NYT:* placed many of the sick; besides
16. scene, . . . night] *MDW* and *NYT:* scene at night,
17. the beds, . . . the gallery] *NYT:* the beds, the sick, the gallery
22–23. No marks of parenthesis in *MDW* and *NYT.*
[The paragraph above collated is the only part of the article of Feb. 26, 1863,
which was reprinted in *SDC.* For the rest of the article see Appendix 1, 1.]

The White House by Moonlight.
Printed from a clipping, *MDW,* p. 11. Apparently not previously printed.
2. sometimes at night] *MDW:* especially at night,
3. house. The . . . tall,] *MDW:* House—and here is my splurge about it. The
white portico—the brilliant gas-light shining—the palace-like portico—the tall,
6–7. everywhere a . . . in the air—] *MDW:* everywhere too a soft transparent

light, flooding the pale marble, and making peculiar faint languishing 5
shades, not shadows—everywhere a soft transparent hazy, thin, blue
moon-lace, hanging in the air—the brilliant and extra-plentiful clusters
of gas, on and around the façade, columns, portico, &c.—everything so
white, so marbly pure and dazzling, yet soft—the White House of future
poems, and of dreams and dramas, there in the soft and copious moon— 10
the gorgeous front, in the trees, under the lustrous flooding moon, full of
reality, full of illusion—the forms of the trees, leafless, silent, in trunk and
myriad-angles of branches, under the stars and sky—the White House of
the land, and of beauty and night—sentries at the gates, and by the portico, silent, pacing there in blue overcoats—stopping you not at all, but 15
eyeing you with sharp eyes, whichever way you move.

An Army Hospital Ward.

Let me specialize a visit I made to the collection of barrack-like one-
story edifices, Campbell hospital, out on the flats, at the end of the then
horse railway route, on Seventh street. There is a long building appropri-
ated to each ward. Let us go into ward 6. It contains to-day, I should
judge, eighty or a hundred patients, half sick, half wounded. The edifice 5
is nothing but boards, well whitewash'd inside, and the usual slender-
framed iron bedsteads, narrow and plain. You walk down the central passage, with a row on either side, their feet towards you, and their heads to
the wall. There are fires in large stoves, and the prevailing white of the
walls is reliev'd by some ornaments, stars, circles, &c., made of evergreens. 10
The view of the whole edifice and occupants can be taken at once, for
there is no partition. You may hear groans or other sounds of unendurable

haze, a thin blue moon-lace, hanging in the night in the air—
    10–11. moon—the . . . lustrous] *MDW:* moon—the pure and gorgeous front, in
the trees, under the night-lights, under the lustrous
    13. White House . . . —sentries] *MDW:* White House of the land, the White
House of the night, and of beauty and silence—sentries

An Army Hospital Ward.
    Printed from clippings of *MDW*, pp. 11–12. It first appeared in *NYWG*, "Ten
Years," Fourth Paper, paragraphs 5 and 6.
    1. me specialize a] *NYWG:* me mention a
    2. edifices, Campbell] *MDW:* edifices, call'd Campbell] *NYWG:* edifices, called
the Campbell Hospital,
    2–3. at . . . railway] *NYWG:* at the present end of the horse-railway
    8. towards] *MDW* and *NYWG:* toward
    9. are fires in large] *NYWG:* are two or three large
    10. After "of evergreens." *NYWG* begins a new paragraph.
    12. partition. You may hear] *NYWG:* partition. You see a melancholy spectacle.
You may hear

suffering from two or three of the cots, but in the main there is quiet—
almost a painful absence of demonstration; but the pallid face, the dull'd
15 eye, and the moisture on the lip, are demonstration enough. Most of these
sick or hurt are evidently young fellows from the country, farmers' sons,
and such like. Look at the fine large frames, the bright and broad countenances, and the many yet lingering proofs of strong constitution and physique. Look at the patient and mute manner of our American wounded as
20 they lie in such a sad collection; representatives from all New England,
and from New York, and New Jersey, and Pennsylvania—indeed from all
the States and all the cities—largely from the west. Most of them are entirely without friends or acquaintances here—no familiar face, and
hardly a word of judicious sympathy or cheer, through their sometimes
25 long and tedious sickness, or the pangs of aggravated wounds.

A Connecticut Case.

This young man in bed 25 is H. D. B., of the 27th Connecticut,
company B. His folks live at Northford, near New Haven. Though not
more than twenty-one, or thereabouts, he has knock'd much around the
world, on sea and land, and has seen some fighting on both. When I first
5 saw him he was very sick, with no appetite. He declined offers of money—
said he did not need anything. As I was quite anxious to do something, he
confess'd that he had a hankering for a good home-made rice pudding—
thought he could relish it better than anything. At this time his stomach
was very weak. (The doctor, whom I consulted, said nourishment would
10 do him more good than anything; but things in the hospital, though better
than usual, revolted him.) I soon procured B. his rice-pudding. A Wash-

13. the cots] *MDW* and *NYWG:* the iron cots
18–19. physique. Look . . . wounded as] *NYWG:* physique. I have never seen
a more pathetic sight than the patient and mute manner of our American wounded and
sick soldiers, as

A Connecticut Case.
Printed from a clipping of *MDW,* p. 12. First published, with the same subhead, in *NYWG,* Fourth Paper of "Ten Years," paragraphs 7–9.
3. thereabouts] *NYWG:* thereabout
9–11. No marks of parenthesis in *NYWG.*
11. *NYWG* begins a new paragraph with "I soon".
14. days. This B.] *MDW:* days . . . . This B.] [*NYWG* begins a new paragraph
with "This B."]

Two Brooklyn Boys.
Printed from a clipping of *MDW,* p. 12. In *NYWG,* Fourth Paper, it is
paragraph 10.

ington lady, (Mrs. O'C.), hearing his wish, made the pudding herself, and
I took it up to him the next day. He subsequently told me he lived
upon it for three or four days. This B. is a good sample of the American eastern young man—the typical Yankee. I took a fancy to him, and   15
gave him a nice pipe, for a keepsake. He receiv'd afterwards a box of
things from home, and nothing would do but I must take dinner with
him, which I did, and a very good one it was.

Two Brooklyn Boys.

Here in this same ward are two young men from Brooklyn, members
of the 51st New York. I had known both the two as young lads at
home, so they seem near to me. One of them, J. L., lies there with an
amputated arm, the stump healing pretty well. (I saw him lying on the
ground at Fredericksburgh last December, all bloody, just after the arm   5
was taken off. He was very phlegmatic about it, munching away at a
cracker in the remaining hand—made no fuss.) He will recover, and
thinks and talks yet of meeting the Johnny Rebs.

A Secesh Brave.

The grand soldiers are not comprised in those of one side, any more
than the other. Here is a sample of an unknown southerner, a lad of seventeen. At the War department, a few days ago, I witness'd a presentation
of captured flags to the Secretary. Among others a soldier named Gant,
of the 104th Ohio volunteers, presented a rebel battle-flag, which one of   5

2. of the 51st New York.] *NYWG:* of that war-worn regiment, the Fifty-first New
York.

8. After "Two Brooklyn Boys," Fourth Paper continues with three paragraphs
not reprinted. See Appendix VIII, 3 and 4.

[Paragraphs 14 and 15, completing the section headed "Still More of the Hospitals," are collated with "Hospitals Ensemble," *q.v.* (below). Paragraphs 16–18 subtitled "Long One-Story Wooden Barracks," concluding the Fourth Paper of "Ten
Years," are partly used in "Summer of 1864" and partly in "Gifts—Money—Discrimination," *q.v.* (below).]

A Secesh Brave.

Printed from a clipping of *MDW*, pp. 12–13. It appeared with the same sub-
title in *NYWG* as paragraph 7 of the Fifth Paper of "Ten Years." First printed as "An
Unknown Hero, Though an Enemy," the last paragraph of "The Soldiers" in *NYT*,
March 6, 1865.

1. The grand] *MDW, NYWG*, and *NYT:* The brave, grand

the officers stated to me was borne to the mouth of our cannon and planted there by a boy but seventeen years of age, who actually endeavor'd to stop the muzzle of the gun with fence-rails. He was kill'd in the effort, and the flag-staff was sever'd by a shot from one of our men.

The Wounded from Chancellorsville.

May, '63.—As I write this, the wounded have begun to arrive from Hooker's command from bloody Chancellorsville. I was down among the first arrivals. The men in charge told me the bad cases were yet to come. If that is so I pity them, for these are bad enough. You ought to see the scene of the wounded arriving at the landing here at the foot of Sixth street, at night. Two boat loads came about half-past seven last night. A little after eight it rain'd a long and violent shower. The pale, helpless soldiers had been debark'd, and lay around on the wharf and neighborhood anywhere. The rain was, probably, grateful to them; at any rate they were exposed to it. The few torches light up the spectacle. All around—on the wharf, on the ground, out on side places—the men are lying on blankets, old quilts, &c., with bloody rags bound round heads, arms, and legs. The attendants are few, and at night few outsiders also—only a few hard-work'd transportation men and drivers. (The wounded are getting to be common, and people grow callous.) The men, whatever their condition, lie there, and patiently wait till their turn comes to be taken up. Near by, the ambulances are now arriving in clusters, and one after another is call'd to back up and take its load. Extreme cases are sent

6. stated to me was] *NYT:* stated was

9. After "our men." *MDW* has the following sentence to end the paragraph: "(Perhaps, in that Southern boy of seventeen, untold in history, unsung in poems, altogether named, fell as strong a spirit, and as sweet, as any in all time.)" *NYWG* has the same sentence without the parentheses. *NYT* has the following sentence: "Perhaps, in the boy of seventeen, untold in history, unsung in poems, altogether unnamed, fell as strong a spirit, and as sweet, as any in this war, (and that is as much as to say, any in all time.)"

After Whitman's name at the end of *NYT* appears the following postscript, not reprinted:

"P.S.—As I am now, after an interval, visiting the hospitals again, and among the soldiers, wounded or ill, or in their camps or barracks, as during the past two years, I would like to state that letters by mail, relating to the sick or wounded, directed to me simply to Washington, D. C., will reach me."

The Wounded from Chancellorsville.

Printed from a clipping of *MDW*, p. 13. In *NYWG*, with the same subtitle, it consists of paragraphs 4–6, Fifth Paper of "Ten Years." First printed as paragraphs 21–23, subtitled "After Chancellorsville," in "Our Wounded and Sick Soldiers," *NYT*, Dec. 11, 1864.

off on stretchers. The men generally make little or no ado, whatever their
sufferings. A few groans that cannot be suppress'd, and occasionally a   20
scream of pain as they lift a man into the ambulance. To-day, as I write,
hundreds more are expected, and to-morrow and the next day more, and
so on for many days. Quite often they arrive at the rate of 1000 a day.

A Night Battle, Over a Week Since.

May 12.—There was part of the late battle at Chancellorsville,
(second Fredericksburgh,) a little over a week ago, Saturday, Saturday
night and Sunday, under Gen. Joe Hooker, I would like to give just a
glimpse of—(a moment's look in a terrible storm at sea—of which a few
suggestions are enough, and full details impossible.) The fighting had   5
been very hot during the day, and after an intermission the latter part,
was resumed at night, and kept up with furious energy till 3 o'clock in the
morning. That afternoon (Saturday) an attack sudden and strong by
Stonewall Jackson had gain'd a great advantage to the southern army,
and broken our lines, entering us like a wedge, and leaving things in that   10
position at dark. But Hooker at 11 at night made a desperate push, drove
the secesh forces back, restored his original lines, and resumed his plans.
This night scrimmage was very exciting, and afforded countless strange
and fearful pictures. The fighting had been general both at Chancellorsville and northeast at Fredericksburgh. (We hear of some poor fighting,   15
episodes, skedaddling on our part. I think not of it. I think of the fierce
bravery, the general rule.) One corps, the 6th, Sedgewick's, fights four

1. *May, '63.*—As I write this, the] *NYT:* As I write this, in May, 1863, the
3. charge told] *MDW, NYWG,* and *NYT:* charge of them told
5. here at the foot] *MDW, NYWG,* and *NYT:* here foot
7. The pale,] *MDW, NYWG,* and *NYT:* The poor, pale,
10. After "exposed to it." *NYWG* and *NYT* begin a new paragraph.
11. places—the] *NYT:* places, &c., the
12. with bloody] *MDW* and *NYT:* with the bloody
13. legs. The] *NYT:* legs, &c. The
21. ambulance. To-day] *MDW:* ambulance........To-day] [*NYWG* and *NYT*
make a separate paragraph of the sentence beginning "To-day".]
23. This sentence does not appear in *NYWG* or *NYT.*

A Night Battle, Over a Week Since.
Printed from clippings of *MDW,* all of pp. 14 and 15, and parts of pp. 13 and
16. Apparently this was not previously printed.
1. *MDW* has the following initial sentence, deleted in *SDC:* "We already talk
of Histories of the War, (presently to accumulate)—yes—technical histories of some
things, statistics, official reports, and so on—but shall we ever get histories of the
real things? ...."

dashing and bloody battles in thirty-six hours, retreating in great jeop-
ardy, losing largely but maintaining itself, fighting with the sternest desperation under all circumstances, getting over the Rappahannock only by
the skin of its teeth, yet getting over. It lost many, many brave men, yet
it took vengeance, ample vengeance.

But it was the tug of Saturday evening, and through the night and Sunday morning, I wanted to make a special note of. It was largely in the
woods, and quite a general engagement. The night was very pleasant, at
times the moon shining out full and clear, all Nature so calm in itself,
the early summer grass so rich, and foliage of the trees—yet there the battle raging, and many good fellows lying helpless, with new accessions to
them, and every minute amid the rattle of muskets and crash of cannon,
(for there was an artillery contest too,) the red life-blood oozing out from
heads or trunks or limbs upon that green and dew-cool grass. Patches of
the woods take fire, and several of the wounded, unable to move, are con-
sumed—quite large spaces are swept over, burning the dead also—some
of the men have their hair and beards singed—some, burns on their faces
and hands—others holes burnt in their clothing. The flashes of fire from the
cannon, the quick flaring flames and smoke, and the immense roar—
the musketry so general, the light nearly bright enough for each side to see
the other—the crashing, tramping of men—the yelling—close quarters—
we hear the secesh yells—our men cheer loudly back, especially if Hooker
is in sight—hand to hand conflicts, each side stands up to it, brave, determin'd as demons, they often charge upon us—a thousand deeds are
done worth to write newer greater poems on—and still the woods on fire
—still many are not only scorch'd—too many, unable to move, are burn'd
to death.

Then the camps of the wounded—O heavens, what scene is this?—is
this indeed *humanity*—these butchers' shambles? There are several of
them. There they lie, in the largest, in an open space in the woods, from
200 to 300 poor fellows—the groans and screams—the odor of blood,

19. largely but] *MDW:* largely and
31–32. Patches . . . several of] *MDW:* The woods take fire, and many of
32. move, are] *MDW:* move, (especially some of the divisions in the Sixth Corps,)
are
34. some, burns] *MDW:* some, splatches of burns
35. clothing. The] *MDW:* clothing . . . . The
44. After "burned to death." *MDW* has a series of nine periods and continues the
paragraph with "Then the".
45. camps of] *MDW:* camp of
48. 200 to 300] *MDW:* 500 to 600
51. things. One] *MDW:* things . . . . One
56. boys—many] *MDW:* boys—here is one his face colorless as chalk, lying per-

mixed with the fresh scent of the night, the grass, the trees—that
slaughter-house! O well is it their mothers, their sisters cannot see them
—cannot conceive, and never conceiv'd, these things. One man is shot by
a shell, both in the arm and leg—both are amputated—there lie the rejected members. Some have their legs blown off—some bullets through the
breast—some indescribably horrid wounds in the face or head, all mutilated, sickening, torn, gouged out—some in the abdomen—some mere
boys—many rebels, badly hurt—they take their regular turns with the
rest, just the same as any—the surgeons use them just the same. Such
is the camp of the wounded—such a fragment, a reflection afar off of the
bloody scene—while over all the clear, large moon comes out at times
softly, quietly shining. Amid the woods, that scene of flitting souls—amid
the crack and crash and yelling sounds—the impalpable perfume of the
woods—and yet the pungent, stifling smoke—the radiance of the moon,
looking from heaven at intervals so placid—the sky so heavenly—the
clear-obscure up there, those buoyant upper oceans—a few large placid
stars beyond, coming silently and languidly out, and then disappearing—
the melancholy, draperied night above, around. And there, upon the
roads, the fields, and in those woods, that contest, never one more desperate in any age or land—both parties now in force—masses—no fancy
battle, no semi-play, but fierce and savage demons fighting there—courage and scorn of death the rule, exceptions almost none.

What history, I say, can ever give—for who can know—the mad, determin'd tussle of the armies, in all their separate large and little squads
—as this—each steep'd from crown to toe in desperate, mortal purports?
Who know the conflict, hand-to-hand—the many conflicts in the dark,
those shadowy-tangled, flashing moonbeam'd woods—the writhing
groups and squads—the cries, the din, the cracking guns and pistols—
the distant cannon—the cheers and calls and threats and awful music of
the oaths—the indescribable mix—the officers' orders, persuasions, encouragements—the devils fully rous'd in human hearts—the strong shout,

fectly still, a bullet has perforated the abdomen—life is ebbing fast, there is no help
for him. In the camp of the wounded are many
    57. same. Such] MDW: same . . . . Such
    60. After "quietly shining." MDW begins a new paragraph.
    60. Amid] MDW: Such, amid
    62. smoke—the] MDW: smoke—shed with the
    62–63. moon, looking] MDW: moon, the round, maternal queen, looking
    65. coming . . . out, and] MDW: coming out and
    66. around. And] MDW: around . . . . And
    71. history, I] MDW: history, again I
    76. squads—the cries] MDW: squads—hear through the woods the cries
    79–80. strong shout, Charge] MDW: strong word, Charge

80 *Charge, men, charge*—the flash of the naked sword, and rolling flame
and smoke? And still the broken, clear and clouded heaven—and still
again the moonlight pouring silvery soft its radiant patches over all. Who
paint the scene, the sudden partial panic of the afternoon, at dusk? Who
paint the irrepressible advance of the second division of the Third corps,
85 under Hooker himself, suddenly order'd up—those rapid-filing phantoms
through the woods? Who show what moves there in the shadows, fluid
and firm—to save, (and it did save,) the army's name, perhaps the nation? as there the veterans hold the field. (Brave Berry falls not yet—but
death has mark'd him—soon he falls.)

Unnamed Remains the Bravest Soldier.

Of scenes like these, I say, who writes—who e'er can write the
story? Of many a score—aye, thousands, north and south, of unwrit heroes, unknown heroisms, incredible, impromptu, first-class desperations
—who tells? No history ever—no poem sings, no music sounds, those
5 bravest men of all—those deeds. No formal general's report, nor book in
the library, nor column in the paper, embalms the bravest, north or south,

80–81. and rolling flame and smoke? And] MDW: sword, and many a flame and
smoke—And
82. all. Who] MDW: all? . . . . Who
87–88. nation? as there] MDW: Nation? And there
Two pages (numbered 2 and 3) out of an autograph MS that was apparently
an early draft of all or part of this section survive in the Barrett Collection in the
University of Virginia Library. At the top of the first of these pages the following
passage, which resembles the sentence deleted from MDW (line 1), is crossed out:
"who shall tell the story? We talk I say of histories of this war—have histories of
this war already; and shall have books of full details, hundreds of them. In printed
books, full histories of this war will come. O heavens! what book can give the history
of this war?" Following immediately without a paragraph break, another passage,
not crossed out and quoted here as revised, resembles the last paragraph (lines 81–
102) of the section: "What book—who shall write—for who can know, the mad, the
savage tussle of the armies, in all their separate large & little squads, each steeped
from crown to toe in desperate, mortal purports?—Who know the conflicts hand-to-
hand—who know the scenes there in those dark, those moon-beam'd woods, those
shadowy tangled woods, those groups & squads—hear through the woods the cries,
the din, the wild confusion, the cheers & the oaths, indescribable mix—the officers'
orders, persuasions, encouragements, the devils roused in the men's hearts, the
strong word *Charge, men, charge*, the flash of the unsheathed sword—and still the
clouded heaven & still again the moonlight calm and silvery, pouring soft and
radiant over all.
"Who can tell—who describe that scene of regiments of our forces, not Americans, retreating in the afternoon in wild disorder, rapidly a panic, spreading, rushing, dastardly, growing like magic—when the Commander in chief ordering up his
own old division, the 2d of the 3d Army Corps—when they advance, fluid as surges
but firm as the rocks—who paint what moves slow through the shadows of the falling

east or west. Unnamed, unknown, remain, and still remain, the bravest soldiers. Our manliest—our boys—our hardy darlings; no picture gives them. Likely, the typic one of them (standing, no doubt, for hundreds, thousands,) crawls aside to some bush-clump, or ferny tuft, on receiving   10 his death-shot—there sheltering a little while, soaking roots, grass and soil, with red blood—the battle advances, retreats, flits from the scene, sweeps by—and there, haply with pain and suffering (yet less, far less, than is supposed,) the last lethargy winds like a serpent round him—the eyes glaze in death—none recks—perhaps the burial-squads, in truce, a   15 week afterwards, search not the secluded spot—and there, at last, the Bravest Soldier crumbles in mother earth, unburied and unknown.

Some Specimen Cases.

June 18th.—In one of the hospitals I find Thomas Haley, company M, 4th New York cavalry—a regular Irish boy, a fine specimen of youthful physical manliness—shot through the lungs—inevitably dying—came over to this country from Ireland to enlist—has not a single friend or

night, to save the army's name—who paint the hours that followed—that stern impassive fight, that hurried stemming fight so full of glory & brave Berry falls not yet, but death, invisible death, has marked him & hovers—soon he must fall as soldier loves to fall—thus the corps stood undismayed—thus there amid the night they so far conquered,—amid the dewy night, under the silent-moving moon, the veterans held the field. No panic-soldiers they, but heroes native.

"—Of scenes like these, I say, and such as these—who e'er can write the story? Of many a score yet more & loftier, deeper, aye thousands more than scores of unknown heroisms & unknown heroes and impromptu desperations, who tells? None tells"

Unnamed Remains the Bravest Soldier.

Printed from a clipping of MDW, p. 16; the new subtitle was inserted in the MS. Apparently printed for the first time in MDW. The last paragraph of the MS quoted in the notes to "A Night Battle, Over a Week Since" may have been the beginning of an early draft of this section, since Whitman's notes break off in the middle of a sentence at the end of page 3 of the autograph MS.

  1. who e'er] This is the reading of MDW. SDC and later editions have "whoe'er". The text of MDW is restored, since there is no evidence in the printer's manuscript that a change was intended by Whitman. It must be presumed to be a typographical error that Whitman overlooked in reading proof.

  4. No . . . music] MDW: No history, ever—No poem sings, nor music

  5. nor book] MDW: nor print, nor book

  8. darlings; no] MDW: darlings. Indeed no

  9. them. Likely,] MDW: them. Likely their very names are lost. Likely,

  17. in mother] MDW: in the soil of mother

Some Specimen Cases.

Printed from clippings of MDW, pp. 16–18. This subtitle was inserted in the MS. Apparently printed for the first time in MDW.

acquaintance here—is sleeping soundly at this moment, (but it is the sleep of death)—has a bullet-hole straight through the lung. I saw Tom when first brought here, three days since, and didn't suppose he could live twelve hours—(yet he looks well enough in the face to a casual observer.) He lies there with his frame exposed above the waist, all naked, for coolness, a fine built man, the tan not yet bleach'd from his cheeks and neck. It is useless to talk to him, as with his sad hurt, and the stimulants they give him, and the utter strangeness of every object, face, furniture, &c., the poor fellow, even when awake, is like some frighten'd, shy animal. Much of the time he sleeps, or half sleeps. (Sometimes I thought he knew more than he show'd.) I often come and sit by him in perfect silence; he will breathe for ten minutes as softly and evenly as a young babe asleep. Poor youth, so handsome, athletic, with profuse beautiful shining hair. One time as I sat looking at him while he lay asleep, he suddenly, without the least start, awaken'd, open'd his eyes, gave me a long steady look, turning his face very slightly to gaze easier—one long, clear, silent look—a slight sigh—then turn'd back and went into his doze again. Little he knew, poor death-stricken boy, the heart of the stranger that hover'd near.

W. H. E., Co. F., 2d N. J.—His disease is pneumonia. He lay sick at the wretched hospital below Aquia creek, for seven or eight days before brought here. He was detail'd from his regiment to go there and help as nurse, but was soon taken down himself. Is an elderly, sallow-faced, rather gaunt, gray-hair'd man, a widower, with children. He express'd a great desire for good, strong green tea. An excellent lady, Mrs. W., of Washington, soon sent him a package; also a small sum of money. The doctor said give him the tea at pleasure; it lay on the table by his side, and he used it every day. He slept a great deal; could not talk much, as he grew deaf. Occupied bed 15, ward I, Armory. (The same lady above, Mrs. W., sent the men a large package of tobacco.)

J. G. lies in bed 52, ward I; is of company B, 7th Pennsylvania. I gave him a small sum of money, some tobacco, and envelopes. To a man adjoining also gave twenty-five cents; he flush'd in the face when I offer'd it—refused at first, but as I found he had not a cent, and was very fond of having the daily papers to read, I prest it on him. He was evidently very grateful, but said little.

J. T. L., of company F., 9th New Hampshire, lies in bed 37, ward I. Is very fond of tobacco. I furnish him some; also with a little money. Has gangrene of the feet; a pretty bad case; will surely have to lose three toes.

6. lung. I saw] *MDW:* lung . . . . . . I saw
13. like some frighten'd] *MDW:* like a frighten'd
48. book. Some] *MDW:* book . . . . Some
50. Alexandria—she] *MDW:* Alexandri—she [evidently a misprint in *MDW*]
53. critical case—I] *MDW:* critical, too—I

Is a regular specimen of an old-fashion'd, rude, hearty, New England countryman, impressing me with his likeness to that celebrated singed cat, who was better than she look'd.

Bed 3, ward E, Armory, has a great hankering for pickles, something pungent. After consulting the doctor, I gave him a small bottle of horse-radish; also some apples; also a book. Some of the nurses are excellent. The woman-nurse in this ward I like very much. (Mrs. Wright—a year after-wards I found her in Mansion house hospital, Alexandria—she is a per-fect nurse.)

In one bed a young man, Marcus Small, company K, 7th Maine—sick with dysentery and typhoid fever—pretty critical case—I talk with him often—he thinks he will die—looks like it indeed. I write a letter for him home to East Livermore, Maine—I let him talk to me a little, but not much, advise him to keep very quiet—do most of the talking myself—stay quite a while with him, as he holds on to my hand—talk to him in a cheering, but slow, low and measured manner—talk about his furlough, and going home as soon as he is able to travel.

Thomas Lindly, 1st Pennsylvania cavalry, shot very badly through the foot—poor young man, he suffers horribly, has to be constantly dosed with morphine, his face ashy and glazed, bright young eyes—I give him a large handsome apple, lay it in sight, tell him to have it roasted in the morning, as he generally feels easier then, and can eat a little breakfast. I write two letters for him.

Opposite, an old Quaker lady is sitting by the side of her son, Amer Moore, 2d U. S. artillery—shot in the head two weeks since, very low, quite rational—from hips down paralyzed—he will surely die. I speak a very few words to him every day and evening—he answers pleasantly—wants nothing—(he told me soon after he came about his home affairs, his mother had been an invalid, and he fear'd to let her know his condi-tion.) He died soon after she came.

My Preparations for Visits.

In my visits to the hospitals I found it was in the simple matter of personal presence, and emanating ordinary cheer and magnetism, that I

69–70. pleasantly—wants] MDW: pleasantly—is a handsome fellow—wants

My Preparations for Visits.
Apparently first printed in MDW, p. 18, where it directly follows the last paragraph of "Some Specimen Cases" and is enclosed in parentheses. The subtitle was inserted in the MS.

succeeded and help'd more than by medical nursing, or delicacies, or gifts of money, or anything else. During the war I possess'd the perfection of physical health. My habit, when practicable, was to prepare for starting out on one of those daily or nightly tours of from a couple to four or five hours, by fortifying myself with previous rest, the bath, clean clothes, a good meal, and as cheerful an appearance as possible.

Ambulance Processions.

June 25, Sundown.—As I sit writing this paragraph I see a train of about thirty huge four-horse wagons, used as ambulances, fill'd with wounded, passing up Fourteenth street, on their way, probably, to Columbian, Carver, and mount Pleasant hospitals. This is the way the men come in now, seldom in small numbers, but almost always in these long, sad processions. Through the past winter, while our army lay opposite Fredericksburgh, the like strings of ambulances were of frequent occurrence along Seventh street, passing slowly up from the steamboat wharf, with loads from Aquia creek.

Bad Wounds—the Young.

The soldiers are nearly all young men, and far more American than is generally supposed—I should say nine-tenths are native-born. Among the arrivals from Chancellorsville I find a large proportion of Ohio, Indiana, and Illinois men. As usual, there are all sorts of wounds. Some of the men fearfully burnt from the explosions of artillery caissons. One ward has a long row of officers, some with ugly hurts. Yesterday was perhaps

Ambulance Processions.
     Printed from a clipping of MDW, p. 18, where it was without separate heading. It appeared in NYWG as paragraph 9, subtitled "Ambulances," of the Fifth Paper of "Ten Years." First published in "Our Wounded and Sick Soldiers," NYT, Dec. 11, 1864, as paragraph 27, subtitled "Death of a New-York Soldier."
     1. *June 25, Sundown.*—As I . . . I see] MDW: June 25, (*Thursday, Sundown*).—As I . . . I see] NYWG: June 25 (*Thursday, sundown*).—As I . . . I see] NYT: As I sit writing this paragraph, (sundown, Thursday, June 25,) I see
     8–9. wharf, with loads from] NYWG and NYT: wharf, from

Bad Wounds—the Young.
     Printed from clippings of MDW, pp. 18–19. It appears in NYWG as paragraph 10 of the Fifth Paper of "Ten Years." First published in NYT, Dec. 11, 1864, as

worse than usual. Amputations are going on—the attendants are dressing wounds. As you pass by, you must be on your guard where you look. I saw the other day a gentleman, a visitor apparently from curiosity, in one of the wards, stop and turn a moment to look at an awful wound they   10 were probing. He turn'd pale, and in a moment more he had fainted away and fallen on the floor.

The Most Inspiriting of All War's Shows.

June 29.—Just before sundown this evening a very large cavalry force went by—a fine sight. The men evidently had seen service. First came a mounted band of sixteen bugles, drums and cymbals, playing wild martial tunes—made my heart jump. Then the principal officers, then company after company, with their officers at their heads, making of   5 course the main part of the cavalcade; then a long train of men with led horses, lots of mounted negroes with special horses—and a long string of baggage-wagons, each drawn by four horses—and then a motley rear guard. It was a pronouncedly warlike and gay show; the sabres clank'd, the men look'd young and healthy and strong; the electric tramping of so   10 many horses on the hard road, and the gallant bearing, fine seat, and bright faced appearance of a thousand and more handsome young American men, were so good to see. An hour later another troop went by, smaller in numbers, perhaps three hundred men. They too look'd like serviceable men, campaigners used to field and fight.   15

July 3.—This forenoon, for more than an hour, again long strings of cavalry, several regiments, very fine men and horses, four or five abreast. I saw them in Fourteenth street, coming in town from north. Several hundred extra horses, some of the mares with colts, trotting along. (Appear'd

paragraph 24, the first of three under the subtitle "June, July, Etc.—the Hospitals Full."
 5. men fearfully] *NYWG* and *NYT:* men are fearfully
 5. explosions] *MDW, NYWG,* and *NYT:* explosion
 11. probing. He] *MDW, NYWG,* and *NYT:* probing, &c. He
 12. After this paragraph, *NYT* contains two short paragraphs (25–26) not reprinted. See Appendix III, 3.

The Most Inspiriting of All War's Shows.

 Printed from a clipping of *MDW,* p. 19, where it appears in four paragraphs without subtitle. Not previously published.
 8. baggage-wagons] *MDW:* baggage-waggons
 9. show; the] *MDW:* show. The
 13. to see.] *MDW:* to see—quite set me up for hours.
 13. After the sentence ending "for hours." *MDW* begins a new paragraph.

20 to be a number of prisoners too.) How inspiriting always the cavalry regiments. Our men are generally well mounted, feel good, are young, gay
on the saddle, their blankets in a roll behind them, their sabres clanking at
their sides. This noise and movement and the tramp of many horses' hoofs
has a curious effect upon one. The bugles play—presently you hear them
25 afar off, deaden'd, mix'd with other noises. Then just as they had all
pass'd, a string of ambulances commenc'd from the other way, moving up
Fourteenth street north, slowly wending along, bearing a large lot of
wounded to the hospitals.

Battle of Gettysburg.

July 4th.—The weather to-day, upon the whole, is very fine, warm,
but from a smart rain last night, fresh enough, and no dust, which is a
great relief for this city. I saw the parade about noon, Pennsylvania avenue, from Fifteenth street down toward the capitol. There were three
5 regiments of infantry, (I suppose the ones doing patrol duty here,) two or
three societies of Odd Fellows, a lot of children in barouches, and a squad
of policemen. (A useless imposition upon the soldiers—they have work
enough on their backs without piling the like of this.) As I went down the
Avenue, saw a big flaring placard on the bulletin board of a newspaper
10 office, announcing "Glorious Victory for the Union Army!" Meade had
fought Lee at Gettysburg, Pennsylvania, yesterday and day before, and
repuls'd him most signally, taken 3,000 prisoners, &c. (I afterwards saw
Meade's despatch, very modest, and a sort of order of the day from the
President himself, quite religious, giving thanks to the Supreme, and
15 calling on the people to do the same.) I walk'd on to Armory hospital—
took along with me several bottles of blackberry and cherry syrup, good
and strong, but innocent. Went through several of the wards, announc'd

---

20. too.) How] MDW: too.) . . . . How
21. well . . . gay] MDW: well mounted, they ride well, feel good, are young,
and gay
25. MDW makes a separate paragraph of the sentence beginning "Then just".

Battle of Gettysburg.
Printed from clippings of MDW, pp. 19–20, where it appears as three short
paragraphs with the heading: "*4th July—Battle of Gettysburg.*" Not previously published.
7. policemen. (A] MDW: policemen. (It was a
8. With "As I went" MDW begins a new paragraph.
15. same.)] MDW: same, &c.) [MDW begins a new paragraph after this sentence.]

to the soldiers the news from Meade, and gave them all a good drink of
the syrups with ice water, quite refreshing—prepar'd it all myself, and
serv'd it around. Meanwhile the Washington bells are ringing their sun-   20
down peals for Fourth of July, and the usual fusilades of boys' pistols,
crackers, and guns.

A Cavalry Camp.

I am writing this, nearly sundown, watching a cavalry company
(acting Signal service,) just come in through a shower, making their
night's camp ready on some broad, vacant ground, a sort of hill, in full
view opposite my window. There are the men in their yellow-striped jackets. All are dismounted; the freed horses stand with drooping heads and   5
wet sides; they are to be led off presently in groups, to water. The little
wall-tents and shelter tents spring up quickly. I see the fires already blazing, and pots and kettles over them. Some among the men are driving in
tent-poles, wielding their axes with strong, slow blows. I see great huddles
of horses, bundles of hay, groups of men (some with unbuckled sabres yet   10
on their sides,) a few officers, piles of wood, the flames of the fires, saddles, harness, &c. The smoke streams upward, additional men arrive and
dismount—some drive in stakes, and tie their horses to them; some go with
buckets for water, some are chopping wood, and so on.

July 6th.—A steady rain, dark and thick and warm. A train of   15
six-mule wagons has just pass'd bearing pontoons, great square-end flat-
boats, and the heavy planking for overlaying them. We hear that the Potomac above here is flooded, and are wondering whether Lee will be able
to get back across again, or whether Meade will indeed break him to
pieces. The cavalry camp on the hill is a ceaseless field of observation for   20
me. This forenoon there stand the horses, tether'd together, dripping,

---

19. refreshing—prepar'd . . . around.   Meanwhile]   MDW: refreshing
. . . . .Meanwhile

A Cavalry Camp.

Printed from clippings of MDW, pp. 20–21, where it appears as four paragraphs. Not previously published.

2. shower, making] MDW: shower, and making
6. sides; they] MDW: sides. They
8. them. Some . . . driving] MDW: them. The laggards among the men are
driving
10. hay, groups of men] MDW: hay, men
11–12. fires, saddles] MDW: fires, comrades by two and threes, saddles
20. After "to pieces." MDW begins a new paragraph.
21. horses, tether'd] MDW: horses, huddled, tether'd

steaming, chewing their hay. The men emerge from their tents, dripping also. The fires are half quench'd.

July 10th.—Still the camp opposite—perhaps fifty or sixty tents.
25 Some of the men are cleaning their sabres (pleasant to-day,) some brushing boots, some laying off, reading, writing—some cooking, some sleeping. On long temporary cross-sticks back of the tents are cavalry accoutrements—blankets and overcoats are hung out to air—there are the squads of horses tether'd, feeding, continually stamping and whisking their tails
30 to keep off flies. I sit long in my third story window and look at the scene—a hundred little things going on—peculiar objects connected with the camp that could not be described, any one of them justly, without much minute drawing and coloring in words.

A New York Soldier.

This afternoon, July 22d, I have spent a long time with Oscar F. Wilber, company G, 154th New York, low with chronic diarrhœa, and a bad wound also. He asked me to read him a chapter in the New Testament. I complied, and ask'd him what I should read. He said, "Make your
5 own choice." I open'd at the close of one of the first books of the evangelists, and read the chapters describing the latter hours of Christ, and the scenes at the crucifixion. The poor, wasted young man ask'd me to read the following chapter also, how Christ rose again. I read very slowly, for Oscar was feeble. It pleased him very much, yet the tears were in his eyes.
10 He ask'd me if I enjoy'd religion. I said, "Perhaps not, my dear, in the way you mean, and yet, may-be, it is the same thing." He said, "It is my chief reliance." He talk'd of death, and said he did not fear it. I said, "Why, Oscar, don't you think you will get well?" He said, "I may,

26–27. sleeping. On] *MDW:* sleeping—On
27. are cavalry] *MDW:* are hung saddles and cavalry
30. off flies. I] *MDW:* off flies. I
31. on—peculiar] *MDW:* on—or peculiar

A New York Soldier.
Printed from a clipping of *MDW*, p. 21. It appeared in *NYWG* as paragraph 15, the third from the end, of the Fifth Paper of "Ten Years." First published in *NYT*, Dec. 11, 1864, subtitled "Death of a New-York Soldier."
1. July 22d, I have spent] *NYWG* and *NYT:* July 22, 1863, I spent
3. read him a] *MDW:* read to him a
Paragraphs 29–33 of *NYT* were not reprinted. See Appendix III, 4.

but it is not probable." He spoke calmly of his condition. The wound was
very bad, it discharg'd much. Then the diarrhœa had prostrated him, and   15
I felt that he was even then the same as dying. He behaved very manly
and affectionate. The kiss I gave him as I was about leaving he return'd
fourfold. He gave me his mother's address, Mrs. Sally D. Wilber, Alle-
ghany post-office, Cattaraugus county, N. Y. I had several such interviews
with him. He died a few days after the one just described.   20

Home-Made Music.

August 8th.—To-night, as I was trying to keep cool, sitting by a
wounded soldier in Armory-square, I was attracted by some pleasant
singing in an adjoining ward. As my soldier was asleep, I left him, and
entering the ward where the music was, I walk'd half-way down and took
a seat by the cot of a young Brooklyn friend, S. R., badly wounded in   5
the hand at Chancellorsville, and who has suffer'd much, but at that moment in the evening was wide awake and comparatively easy. He had
turn'd over on his left side to get a better view of the singers, but the
mosquito-curtains of the adjoining cots obstructed the sight. I stept round
and loop'd them all up, so that he had a clear show, and then sat down   10
again by him, and look'd and listen'd. The principal singer was a young
lady-nurse of one of the wards, accompanying on a melodeon, and join'd
by the lady-nurses of other wards. They sat there, making a charming
group, with their handsome, healthy faces, and standing up a little behind
them were some ten or fifteen of the convalescent soldiers, young men,   15
nurses, &c., with books in their hands, singing. Of course it was not such
a performance as the great soloists at the New York opera house take a
hand in, yet I am not sure but I receiv'd as much pleasure under the

Home-Made Music.
Printed from clippings of *MDW*, pp. 21–22, where it is without title. First
published in "Washington in the Hot Season," *NYT*, August 16, 1863, as paragraphs 10–14 subtitled "A Scene in Hospital."
1. *August 8th.*—To-night, as] *MDW: Aug.* 8.—To-night, as] *NYT:* I must give
you a scene from one of the great Government Hospitals here. I go to them every
day to inspirit the drooping cases, and give the men little gifts, sometimes of
articles, sometimes of money. Two or three nights ago, as
2. Armory-square, I] *MDW:* Armory Square, I] *NYT:* Armory-square Hospital, I
8–9. the mosquito-curtains] *MDW* and *NYT:* the plentiful drapery of the mus-
quito curtains
16. hands, singing.] *MDW* and *NYT:* hands, taking part in the singing.
17–18. performance . . . yet I] *NYT:* performance as Medori or Brignoli and
the choruses at your New-York Fourteenth-street take a hand in; but I

circumstances, sitting there, as I have had from the best Italian composi-
tions, express'd by world-famous performers. The men lying up and down
the hospital, in their cots, (some badly wounded—some never to rise
thence,) the cots themselves, with their drapery of white curtains, and the
shadows down the lower and upper parts of the ward; then the silence
of the men, and the attitudes they took—the whole was a sight to look
around upon again and again. And there sweetly rose those voices up to
the high, whitewash'd wooden roof, and pleasantly the roof sent it all
back again. They sang very well, mostly quaint old songs and declamatory hymns, to fitting tunes. Here, for instance:

> My days are swiftly gliding by, and I a pilgrim stranger,
> Would not detain them as they fly, those hours of toil and danger;

20. performers. The men] MDW: performers.......The scene was, indeed, an
impressive one. The men] [NYT: same as MDW except begins new paragraph after
"performers."]
21. wounded—some never] NYT: wounded—and, perhaps, never
24. they took—the whole was] NYT: they took—nothing to interrupt the singing
—and the whole combination was
25. those voices] MDW: those female voices] NYT: those fresh female voices
28. instance:] MDW and NYT: instance, is one of the songs they sang:
28. MDW has in centered capitals above the two stanzas of song the title "Shining
Shores." NYT inserts three stanzas of an entirely different song, entitled "Homeward
Bound" and two short prose paragraphs before the two stanzas of "Shining Shores."
They are as follows:

"HOMEWARD BOUND.
> Out on an ocean all boundless we ride,
>   We're homeward bound—homeward bound;
> Tossed on the waves of a rough, restless tide,
>   Yet homeward bound, homeward bound.
> Far from the safe, quiet harbor we've rode,
> Seeking our Father's celestial abode,
> Promise of which on us each he bestowed,
>   So we're homeward bound.
>
> Wildly the storm sweeps on us where it roars,
>   Yet we're homeward bound;
> Look! yonder lie the bright heavenly shores,
>   Where we're homeward bound.
> Steady, oh! pilot, stand firm at the wheel;
> Steady! we soon shall outweather the gale;
> Oh! how we fly 'neath the loud-cracking sail,
>   As we're homeward bound.
>
> Now toward the harbor of Heaven we glide,
>   We're home at last;
> Softly we drift on its bright silver tide—
>   Yes! we're home at last.
> Glory to God, all our dangers are o'er,
> Stand we secure on the beautiful shore,
> Glory to God we will shout evermore,
>   We're home at last.

For O we stand on Jordan's strand, our friends are passing over,
And just before, the shining shore we may almost discover.

We'll gird our loins my brethren dear, our distant home discerning,
Our absent Lord has left us word, let every lamp be burning,
For O we stand on Jordan's strand, our friends are passing over,   35
And just before, the shining shore we may almost discover.

Abraham Lincoln.

August 12th.—I see the President almost every day, as I happen to live where he passes to or from his lodgings out of town. He never sleeps

"As the strains reverberated through the great edifice of boards, (an excellent place for musical performers,) it was plain to see how it all soothed and was grateful to the men.

"The singers went on; they sang, 'Home, Sweet Home,' and a beautiful hymn called 'Shining Shores.' I saw one of the soldiers near me turn over, and bury his face partially in his pillow; he was probably ashamed to be seen with wet eyes. Since I have mentioned it, let me give a verse or two:"

The two stanzas then follow as in *SDC* except as noted.

29. pilgrim] *MDW* and *NYT:* Pilgrim
32. shore] *MDW* and *NYT:* shores
36. shore] *MDW* and *NYT:* shores

After the two stanzas of "Shining Shores," before the paragraph dated Aug. 12, *MDW* inserts the following paragraph drawn from the two short paragraphs of *NYT* that appeared between the stanzas of "Homeward Bound" and those of "Shining Shores":

"As the strains reverberated through the great edifice of boards, (an excellent place for musical performers,) it was plain to see how it all sooth'd and was grateful to the men. I saw one near me turn over, and bury his face partially in his pillow; he was probably ashamed to be seen with wet eyes."

NYT has the following paragraph, not in *MDW* or *SDC*, immediately following the two stanzas of "Shining Shores":

"Such were the fine and vivifying songs these girls sang there for all our sakes, until quite late in the night. The sounds and scene altogether have made an indelible impression on my memory."

Abraham Lincoln.

Printed from clippings of *MDW*, pp. 22, 23, and 24, where it appears as three separate paragraphs, and a footnote, without subtitle. Substantially the same material was first published in *NYT*, August 16, 1863, the first four paragraphs of the article, subtitled "The President." It was also reprinted as a footnote in Whitman's contribution (pp. 469–475) to the volume *Reminiscences of Abraham Lincoln* (New York, 1886), edited by Allen Thorndike Rice. Whitman precedes the note with the statement: "From my Note-book in 1864, at Washington City, I find this memorandum, under date of August 12." The text is close to that of *MDW* but not identical with it; it is collated here, abbreviated *RAL.* This note was omitted when the Lincoln article was incorporated in *November Boughs.*

1. *August 12th.*—I see] *MDW:* Aug. 12.—I see] *NYT* and *RAL:* I see
2–3. He never sleeps at] *NYT:* Does the reader need to be informed that Mr. Lincoln never reposes at

at the White House during the hot season, but has quarters at a healthy
location some three miles north of the city, the Soldiers' home, a United
5 States military establishment. I saw him this morning about 8½ coming in
to business, riding on Vermont avenue, near L street. He always has a
company of twenty-five or thirty cavalry, with sabres drawn and held upright over their shoulders. They say this guard was against his personal
wish, but he let his counselors have their way. The party makes no great
10 show in uniform or horses. Mr. Lincoln on the saddle generally rides a
good-sized, easy-going gray horse, is dress'd in plain black, somewhat
rusty and dusty, wears a black stiff hat, and looks about as ordinary in
attire, &c., as the commonest man. A lieutenant, with yellow straps, rides
at his left, and following behind, two by two, come the cavalry men, in
15 their yellow-striped jackets. They are generally going at a slow trot, as
that is the pace set them by the one they wait upon. The sabres and accoutrements clank, and the entirely unornamental *cortège* as it trots
towards Lafayette square arouses no sensation, only some curious stranger
stops and gazes. I see very plainly ABRAHAM LINCOLN's dark brown face,
20 with the deep-cut lines, the eyes, always to me with a deep latent sadness
in the expression. We have got so that we exchange bows, and very
cordial ones. Sometimes the President goes and comes in an open barouche. The cavalry always accompany him, with drawn sabres. Often I
notice as he goes out evenings—and sometimes in the morning, when he
25 returns early—he turns off and halts at the large and handsome residence
of the Secretary of War, on K street, and holds conference there. If in

5. military establishment.] NYT: benevolent establishment?
6. L street. He always] MDW: L street. The sight is a significant one, (and
different enough from how and where I first saw him.*) He always] NYT: The sight
is a significant one. He always
[The asterisk refers to a long footnote, MDW, pp. 22–23, describing Whitman's
first sight of Lincoln. This description was transferred, with revisions, to the section
"Death of Abraham Lincoln," SDC, pp. 307–308. See *Prose 1892*, II.]
8–9. shoulders. They . . . way. The party] MDW, NYT, and RAL: shoulders.
The party
10. uniform or . . . generally] MDW and RAL: uniforms or . . . generally]
NYT: uniforms or horses. Mr. Lincoln generally
16. the one they] MDW and RAL: the One they] NYT: the dignitary they
16. After "wait upon." NYT begins a new paragraph.
17–18. *cortège* as it trots towards [MDW and RAL: toward] Lafayette square
arouses] NYT: cortege trots slowly toward Lafayette square. It arouses
19. I see very plainly Abraham Lincoln's dark] NYT: I saw very plainly the
President's dark
20. eyes, always] MDW, NYT, and RAL: eyes, &c., always
21–22. expression. We . . . ones. Sometimes] MDW and RAL: expression. We
have got so that we always exchange bows, and very cordial ones. Sometimes] NYT:
expression. Sometimes
22. MDW, NYT, and RAL begin a new paragraph with "Sometimes".

his barouche, I can see from my window he does not alight, but sits in his vehicle, and Mr. Stanton comes out to attend him. Sometimes one of his sons, a boy of ten or twelve, accompanies him, riding at his right on a pony. Earlier in the summer I occasionally saw the President and his wife, toward the latter part of the afternoon, out in a barouche, on a pleasure ride through the city. Mrs. Lincoln was dress'd in complete black, with a long crape veil. The equipage is of the plainest kind, only two horses, and they nothing extra. They pass'd me once very close, and I saw the President in the face fully, as they were moving slowly, and his look, though abstracted, happen'd to be directed steadily in my eye. He bow'd and smiled, but far beneath his smile I noticed well the expression I have alluded to. None of the artists or pictures has caught the deep, though subtle and indirect expression of this man's face. There is something else there. One of the great portrait painters of two or three centuries ago is needed.

Heated Term.

There has lately been much suffering here from heat; we have had it upon us now eleven days. I go around with an umbrella and a fan. I saw two cases of sun-stroke yesterday, one in Pennsylvania avenue, and another in Seventh street. The City railroad company loses some horses

27–28. in his vehicle] MDW, NYT, and RAL: in the vehicle

30. MDW, NYT, and RAL begin a new paragraph with "Earlier in".

30. summer I . . . President] NYT: Summer you might have seen the President

31. in a barouche] NYT: in barouche

35. moving slowly] MDW, NYT, and RAL: moving slow

36–37. my eye. He . . . smile I] NYT: my eye. I

38. pictures has caught] MDW, NYT, and RAL: pictures have caught

38–39. the deep, though subtle] RAL: the subtle

39–40. There is something else there. [RAL omits this sentence.]

41. After the paragraph ending "centuries ago is needed." NYT has three paragraphs (5–7) not reprinted. See Appendix II, 1.

Heated Term.

Printed from a clipping of MDW, p. 24. Some parts of this paragraph appeared in paragraph 8 of NYT subtitled "Feelings After All"; other parts appeared in paragraph 9 subtitled "Suffering from the Heat."

1–5. These four sentences were drawn from paragraph 9 of NYT.

1. There has] NYT: I have said that there has

1. here from heat; we] MDW: here from heat. We] NYT: here too from heat. We

5   every day. Yet Washington is having a livelier August, and is probably
putting in a more energetic and satisfactory summer, than ever before during its existence. There is probably more human electricity, more population to make it, more business, more light-heartedness, than ever before.
The armies that swiftly circumambiated from Fredericksburgh—
10 march'd, struggled, fought, had out their mighty clinch and hurl at Gettysburg—wheel'd, circumambiated again, return'd to their ways, touching
us not, either at their going or coming. And Washington feels that she
has pass'd the worst; perhaps feels that she is henceforth mistress. So here
she sits with her surrounding hills spotted with guns, and is conscious of a
15 character and identity different from what it was five or six short weeks
ago, and very considerably pleasanter and prouder.

Soldiers and Talks.

Soldiers, soldiers, soldiers, you meet everywhere about the city,
often superb-looking men, though invalids dress'd in worn uniforms, and
carrying canes or crutches. I often have talks with them, occasionally
quite long and interesting. One, for instance, will have been all through
5   the peninsula under McClellan—narrates to me the fights, the marches,
the strange, quick changes of that eventful campaign, and gives glimpses
of many things untold in any official reports or books or journals. These,
indeed, are the things that are genuine and precious. The man was there,
has been out two years, has been through a dozen fights, the superfluous

5–16. These lines, beginning with "Yet Washington," were drawn from paragraph 8 of *NYT*.
10–11. Gettysburg—wheel'd, circumambiated] *SDA:* Gettysburgh—wheel'd,
circumambiated] *MDW* and *NYT:* Gettysburgh, wheeled, have circumambiated
14. hills spotted] *MDW:* hills and shores spotted
15. identity . . . what] *NYT:* identity not only different from of old, but markedly different from what
16. *NYT* has the following paragraph subtitled "Suffering from the Heat" immediately after the paragraph subtitled "Feelings After All," given below, which was
apparently not reprinted.
"I have said that there has lately been much suffering here too from heat. We
have had it upon us now eleven days. I go around with an umbrella and a fan. I saw
two cases of sun-stroke yesterday, one in Pennsylvania-avenue and another in Seventh-
street. The City Railroad Company loses some horses every day. The soda water and
ice-cream trade is tremendous. Confidentially, I am pained to inform you I doubt if
there is any good lager in Washington."

Soldiers and Talks.
Printed (except the footnote) from clippings of *MDW*, pp. 24–25. It first appeared in *NYT* as paragraphs 15–17 subtitled "Soldiers, Talks, Etc.," the last of

flesh of talking is long work'd off him, and he gives me little but the   10
hard meat and sinew. I find it refreshing, these hardy, bright, intuitive,
American young men, (experienc'd soldiers with all their youth.) The vocal play and significance moves one more than books. Then there hangs
something majestic about a man who has borne his part in battles, especially if he is very quiet regarding it when you desire him to unbosom. I   15
am continually lost at the absence of blowing and blowers among these
old-young American militaires. I have found some man or other who has
been in every battle since the war began, and have talk'd with them about
each one in every part of the United States, and many of the engagements
on the rivers and harbors too. I find men here from every State in the   20
Union, without exception. (There are more Southerners, especially border
State men, in the Union army than is generally supposed.*) I now
doubt whether one can get a fair idea of what this war practically is, or
what genuine America is, and her character, without some such experience
as this I am having.   25

* MR. GARFIELD (*In the House of Representatives, April 15, '79.*) "Do
gentlemen know that (leaving out all the border States) there were fifty regiments and seven companies of white men in our army fighting for the Union
from the States that went into rebellion? Do they know that from the single
State of Kentucky more Union soldiers fought under our flag than Napoleon   30
took into the battle of Waterloo? more than Wellington took with all the allied
armies against Napoleon? Do they remember that 186,000 color'd men fought
under our flag against the rebellion and for the Union, and that of that number 90,000 were from the States which went into rebellion?"

the article.
   1. Soldiers, . . . meet] NYT: Soldiers you meet
   2. superb-looking men] MDW: superb looking men] NYT: superb looking young
men
   3. or crutches] NYT: or, perhaps, crutches
  10. and he] MDW and NYT: and now he
  11–12. sinew. I find] MDW: sinew.......I find] [NYT begins a new paragraph with "I find".]
  11. refreshing, these] NYT: refreshing to talk with these
  12–13. The vocal . . . moves] MDW: The vital . . . moves] NYT: The vital
play and significance of their talk moves
  17. After "militaires." NYT begins a new paragraph with the following sentence,
omitted in SDC and MDW: "But in the hospitals I have talked most with the men for
months past."
  17. or other who] MDW and NYT: or another who
  22. The asterisk after "supposed" and the footnote to which it refers are not in
MDW and NYT. The footnote must have been inserted in the galley proof; it appears
in the page proof.
  25. I am having.] NYT: I have had for the past seven or eight months in the
hospitals.
  25. At the end of the NYT article, "Walt Whitman."

Death of a Wisconsin Officer.

Another characteristic scene of that dark and bloody 1863, from notes of my visit to Armory-square hospital, one hot but pleasant summer day. In ward H we approach the cot of a young lieutenant of one of the Wisconsin regiments. Tread the bare board floor lightly here, for the pain
5   and panting of death are in this cot. I saw the lieutenant when he was first brought here from Chancellorsville, and have been with him occasionally from day to day and night to night. He had been getting along pretty well till night before last, when a sudden hemorrhage that could not be stopt came upon him, and to-day it still continues at intervals. Notice
10 that water-pail by the side of the bed, with a quantity of blood and bloody pieces of muslin, nearly full; that tells the story. The poor young man is struggling painfully for breath, his great dark eyes with a glaze already upon them, and the choking faint but audible in his throat. An attendant sits by him, and will not leave him till the last; yet little or nothing can
15 be done. He will die here in an hour or two, without the presence of kith or kin. Meantime the ordinary chat and business of the ward a little way off goes on indifferently. Some of the inmates are laughing and joking, others are playing checkers or cards, others are reading, &c.

I have noticed through most of the hospitals that as long as there is
20 any chance for a man, no matter how bad he may be, the surgeon and nurses work hard, sometimes with curious tenacity, for his life, doing everything, and keeping somebody by him to execute the doctor's orders, and minister to him every minute night and day. See that screen there. As

Death of a Wisconsin Officer.

Printed from clippings of *MDW*, pp. 25–26. This material was originally published in *NYWG*, under the same subtitle, as the first five paragraphs of the Sixth Paper of "Ten Years."

1. Another . . . bloody 1863] *NYWG:* Here is another characteristic scene of the dark and bloody year 1863

3. day. In] *MDW:* day . . . . In] [*NYWG* has a colon after "day" and begins a new paragraph with "In".]

7. He had been] *NYWG:* He has been

11–12. is struggling] *MDW* and *NYWG:* is lying panting, struggling

15. done. He will] *NYWG:* done. The young man will

18. After "reading, &c." *MDW* continues the paragraph.

19–39. These lines in parentheses in *MDW*.

23. and day. See] *MDW:* and day . . . . See] [After "and day." *NYT* begins a new paragraph.

31. After "destroyer." *NYWG* begins a new paragraph.

you advance through the dusk of early candle-light, a nurse will step forth
on tip-toe, and silently but imperiously forbid you to make any noise, or   25
perhaps to come near at all. Some soldier's life is flickering there, sus-
pended between recovery and death. Perhaps at this moment the exhausted frame has just fallen into a light sleep that a step might shake.
You must retire. The neighboring patients must move in their stocking
feet. I have been several times struck with such mark'd efforts—every-   30
thing bent to save a life from the very grip of the destroyer. But when
that grip is once firmly fix'd, leaving no hope or chance at all, the surgeon abandons the patient. If it is a case where stimulus is any relief, the
nurse gives milk-punch or brandy, or whatever is wanted, *ad libitum*.
There is no fuss made. Not a bit of sentimentalism or whining have I seen   35
about a single death-bed in hospital or on the field, but generally impassive
indifference. All is over, as far as any efforts can avail; it is useless to ex-
pend emotions or labors. While there is a prospect they strive hard—at
least most surgeons do; but death certain and evident, they yield the field.

Hospitals Ensemble.

Aug., Sep., and Oct., '63.—I am in the habit of going to all, and to
Fairfax seminary, Alexandria, and over Long bridge to the great Convalescent camp. The journals publish a regular directory of them—a long
list. As a specimen of almost any one of the larger of these hospitals, fancy
to yourself a space of three to twenty acres of ground, on which are   5
group'd ten or twelve very large wooden barracks, with, perhaps, a dozen
or twenty, and sometimes more than that number, small buildings, capa-

---

Hospitals Ensemble.
    Printed from clippings of MDW, pp. 26–27. Lines 1–18 were first published
in NYT, Dec. 11, 1864, as paragraph 34, the first of four subtitled "Specimen of the
Army Hospitals Now in and Around Washington," and the first five lines of 35. For
the remainder of 35 and paragraphs 36–37 see Appendix III, 5. Lines 19–44 appeared for the first time in NYWG, the Fourth Paper (paragraphs 14–15) of "Ten
Years," under the subtitle "Still More of the Hospitals." This section was reprinted
with only minor changes in punctuation as part of a footnote (omitted in NB) to
"Army Hospitals and Cases," *Century Magazine*, October, 1888, Vol. 36, p. 827
(cf. "Last of the War Cases," *Prose 1892*, II).
    1. *Aug., Sep., and Oct.*, '63.—] MDW: *Aug., Sep., and Oct.*, '63—*The Hospitals.*
—] NYT: Not dated, but the two preceding paragraphs are subtitled "March and
April, 1864." The first sentence in NYT—"There are thirty or forty of them."—is
omitted in later texts.
    3–4. This sentence does not appear in NYT.
    4. of the larger of these] NYT: of these
    7. number, small] MDW and NYT: number, of small

ble altogether of accommodating from five hundred to a thousand or fifteen hundred persons. Sometimes these wooden barracks or wards, each of them perhaps from a hundred to a hundred and fifty feet long, are rang'd in a straight row, evenly fronting the street; others are plann'd so as to form an immense V; and others again are ranged around a hollow square. They make altogether a huge cluster, with the additional tents, extra wards for contagious diseases, guard-houses, sutler's stores, chaplain's house; in the middle will probably be an edifice devoted to the offices of the surgeon in charge and the ward surgeons, principal attaches, clerks, &c. The wards are either letter'd alphabetically, ward G, ward K, or else numerically, 1, 2, 3, &c. Each has its ward surgeon and corps of nurses. Of course, there is, in the aggregate, quite a muster of employés, and over all the surgeon in charge. Here in Washington, when these army hospitals are all fill'd, (as they have been already several times,) they contain a population more numerous in itself than the whole of the Washington of ten or fifteen years ago. Within sight of the capitol, as I write, are some thirty or forty such collections, at times holding from fifty to seventy thousand men. Looking from any eminence and studying the topography in my rambles, I use them as landmarks. Through the rich August verdure of the trees, see that white group of buildings off yonder in the outskirts; then another cluster half a mile to the left of the first; then another a mile to the right, and another a mile beyond, and still another between us and the first. Indeed, we can hardly look in any direction but these clusters are dotting the landscape and environs. That little town, as you might suppose it, off there on the brow of a hill, is indeed a town, but of wounds, sickness, and death. It is Finley hospital, northeast of the city, on Kendall green, as it used to be call'd. That other is Campbell hospital. Both are large establishments. I have known these two alone to have from two thou-

15. house; in the] *MDW* and *NYT:* house, &c. In the

17. After "clerks, &c." *MDW* and *NYT* have the following sentence, omitted in *SDC:* "Then around this centre radiate or are gather'd the Wards for the wounded and sick."

17. The wards] *NYT:* "These wards" [beginning a new paragraph].

20. After "in charge." *MDW* begins a new paragraph with the following sentence before continuing with "Here in":

"The newspaper reader off through the agricultural regions, East or West, sees frequent allusions to these Hospitals, but has probably no clear idea of them." This sentence and the remainder of the section are found in *NYWG*, in the Fourth Paper of "Ten Years," under the subtitle "Still More of the Hospitals" beginning with the second paragraph. The first paragraph under that title was omitted from later texts. See Appendix VIII, *4.*

20–21. when . . . are] *MDW* and *NYWG:* when they are

23–24. some . . . holding] *MDW:* some fifty or sixty such collections or camps, at times holding] *NYWG:* some threescore such army collections or camps of the sick and wounded; they have at times held

26. After "as landmarks." *NYWG* begins a new paragraph.

sand to twenty five hundred inmates. Then there is Carver hospital, larger still, a wall'd and military city regularly laid out, and guarded by squads of sentries. Again, off east, Lincoln hospital, a still larger one; and half a mile further Emory hospital. Still sweeping the eye around down the river toward Alexandria, we see, to the right, the locality where the Convalescent camp stands, with its five, eight, or sometimes ten thousand inmates. Even all these are but a portion. The Harewood, Mount Pleasant, Armory-square, Judiciary hospitals, are some of the rest, and all large collections.

A Silent Night Ramble.

October 20th.—To-night, after leaving the hospital at 10 o'clock, (I had been on self-imposed duty some five hours, pretty closely confined,) I wander'd a long time around Washington. The night was sweet, very clear, sufficiently cool, a voluptuous half-moon, slightly golden, the space near it of a transparent blue-gray tinge. I walk'd up Pennsylvania avenue, and then to Seventh street, and a long while around the Patent-office. Somehow it look'd rebukefully strong, majestic, there in the delicate moonlight. The sky, the planets, the constellations all so bright, so calm, so expressively silent, so soothing, after those hospital scenes. I wander'd to and fro till the moist moon set, long after midnight.

Spiritual Characters among the Soldiers.

Every now and then, in hospital or camp, there are beings I meet— specimens of unworldliness, disinterestedness, and animal purity and her-

30. these clusters] *MDW* and *NYWG:* these grim clusters
43. Armory-square, Judiciary] *NYWG:* Armory square, and Judiciary
43. rest, and all large] *MDW* and *NYWG:* rest, already mention'd, and all of them large
44. After "collections." *NYWG* has the following sentence to end the paragraph: "(I have no means of getting at the number of hospitals, camps of sick, &c., holding our sick and wounded soldiers in the whole United States, but at a random guess I should put the number at five hundred.)"

A Silent Night Ramble.
Printed from a clipping of *MDW*, p. 27, where it is without subtitle. Not previously published.
1. *October 20th.*—] *MDW: Oct. 20.*—
5. transparent blue-gray tinge.] *MDW:* transparent tinge.

Spiritual Characters among the Soldiers.
Printed from clippings of *MDW*, pp. 27–28, where it was apparently first published.

oism—perhaps some unconscious Indianian, or from Ohio or Tennessee —on whose birth the calmness of heaven seems to have descended, and whose gradual growing up, whatever the circumstances of work-life or change, or hardship, or small or no education that attended it, the power of a strange spiritual sweetness, fibre and inward health, have also attended. Something veil'd and abstracted is often a part of the manners of these beings. I have met them, I say, not seldom in the army, in camp, and in the hospitals. The Western regiments contain many of them. They are often young men, obeying the events and occasions about them, marching, soldiering, fighting, foraging, cooking, working on farms or at some trade before the war—unaware of their own nature, (as to that, who is aware of his own nature?) their companions only understanding that they are different from the rest, more silent, "something odd about them," and apt to go off and meditate and muse in solitude.

Cattle Droves about Washington.

Among other sights are immense droves of cattle with their drivers, passing through the streets of the city. Some of the men have a way of leading the cattle by a peculiar call, a wild, pensive hoot, quite musical, prolong'd, indescribable, sounding something between the cooing of a pigeon and the hoot of an owl. I like to stand and look at the sight of one of these immense droves—a little way off—(as the dust is great.) There are always men on horseback, cracking their whips and shouting—the cattle low—some obstinate ox or steer attempts to escape—then a lively scene—the mounted men, always excellent riders and on good horses, dash after the recusant, and wheel and turn—a dozen mounted drovers, their great slouch'd, broad-brim'd hats, very picturesque—another dozen on foot—everybody cover'd with dust—long goads in their hands—an immense drove of perhaps 1000 cattle—the shouting, hooting, movement, &c.

10. the hospitals.] MDW: the great Hospitals.

Cattle Droves about Washington.
Printed from a clipping of MDW, p. 28, where it was apparently first published.
3. cattle by] MDW: cattle on by
13. 1000] MDW: 2000

Hospital Perplexity.
Printed from a clipping of MDW, p. 28. The substance of this section was printed in NYWG in the second paragraph of the Fourth Paper of "Ten Years." The

Hospital Perplexity.

To add to other troubles, amid the confusion of this great army of sick, it is almost impossible for a stranger to find any friend or relative, unless he has the patient's specific address to start upon. Besides the directory printed in the newspapers here, there are one or two general directories of the hospitals kept at provost's headquarters, but they are nothing like complete; they are never up to date, and, as things are, with the daily streams of coming and going and changing, cannot be. I have known cases, for instance such as a farmer coming here from northern New York to find a wounded brother, faithfully hunting round for a week, and then compell'd to leave and go home without getting any trace of him. When he got home he found a letter from the brother giving the right address.

Down at the Front.

CULPEPPER, Va., *Feb. '64.*—Here I am pretty well down toward the extreme front. Three or four days ago General S., who is now in chief command, (I believe Meade is absent, sick,) moved a strong force southward from camp as if intending business. They went to the Rapidan; there has since been some manœuvring and a little fighting, but nothing of consequence. The telegraphic accounts given Monday morning last, make entirely too much of it, I should say. What General S. intended we here know not, but we trust in that competent commander. We were somewhat excited, (but not so very much either,) on Sunday, during the day and night, as orders were sent out to pack up and harness, and be ready to evacuate, to fall back towards Washington. But I was very sleepy and went to bed. Some tremendous shouts arousing me during the night, I went forth and found it was from the men above mention'd, who were

first paragraph was not reprinted. See Appendix VIII, *1.*

1. To add to other troubles, amid] *NYWG:* Amid
3–4. Besides . . . there are] *NYWG:* There are
7–10. This sentence is enclosed in parentheses in *MDW.*
11. right address.] *MDW* and *NYWG;* right address in a hospital in Seventh street here.

Down at the Front.

Printed from clippings of *MDW*, pp. 28–29, where it has no subtitle but only the date and place in the first line. Not previously published.
11. towards Washington. But I] *MDW:* toward Washington. I

returning. I talk'd with some of the men; as usual I found them full of
gayety, endurance, and many fine little outshows, the signs of the most excellent good manliness of the world. It was a curious sight to see those
shadowy columns moving through the night. I stood unobserv'd in the
darkness and watch'd them long. The mud was very deep. The men had
their usual burdens, overcoats, knapsacks, guns and blankets. Along and
along they filed by me, with often a laugh, a song, a cheerful word, but
never once a murmur. It may have been odd, but I never before so realized the majesty and reality of the American people *en masse*. It fell upon
me like a great awe. The strong ranks moved neither fast nor slow. They
had march'd seven or eight miles already through the slipping unctuous
mud. The brave First corps stopt here. The equally brave Third corps
moved on to Brandy station. The famous Brooklyn 14th are here, guarding
the town. You see their red legs actively moving everywhere. Then they
have a theatre of their own here. They give musical performances, nearly
everything done capitally. Of course the audience is a jam. It is good sport
to attend one of these entertainments of the 14th. I like to look around at
the soldiers, and the general collection in front of the curtain, more than
the scene on the stage.

Paying the Bounties.

One of the things to note here now is the arrival of the paymaster
with his strong box, and the payment of bounties to veterans re-enlisting.
Major H. is here to-day, with a small mountain of greenbacks, rejoicing
the hearts of the 2d division of the First corps. In the midst of a rickety
shanty, behind a little table, sit the major and clerk Eldridge, with the
rolls before them, and much moneys. A re-enlisted man gets in cash about
$200 down, (and heavy instalments following, as the pay-days arrive,
one after another.) The show of the men crowding around is quite exhilarating; I like to stand and look. They feel elated, their pockets full, and the
ensuing furlough, the visit home. It is a scene of sparkling eyes and

14. men; as] MDW: men. As
16. world. It] MDW: world . . . . It
22. American people *en masse*. It] MDW: American common people proper. It
26. After "Brandy station." MDW begins a new paragraph.
29. is good] MDW: is real good
31. collection in] MDW: collection of eager and handsome young faces in

Paying the Bounties.
Printed from a clipping of MDW, p. 29. Apparently not previously printed.

flush'd cheeks. The soldier has many gloomy and harsh experiences, and this makes up for some of them. Major H. is order'd to pay first all the re-enlisted men of the First corps their bounties and back pay, and then the rest. You hear the peculiar sound of the rustling of the new and crisp greenbacks by the hour, through the nimble fingers of the major and my friend clerk E.

15

Rumors, Changes, &c.

About the excitement of Sunday, and the orders to be ready to start, I have heard since that the said orders came from some cautious minor commander, and that the high principalities knew not and thought not of any such move; which is likely. The rumor and fear here intimated a long circuit by Lee, and flank attack on our right. But I cast my eyes at the mud, which was then at its deepest and palmiest condition, and retired composedly to rest. Still it is about time for Culpepper to have a change. Authorities have chased each other here like clouds in a stormy sky. Before the first Bull Run this was the rendezvous and camp of instruction of the secession troops. I am stopping at the house of a lady who has witness'd all the eventful changes of the war, along this route of contending armies. She is a widow, with a family of young children, and lives here with her sister in a large handsome house. A number of army officers board with them.

5

10

Virginia.

Dilapidated, fenceless, and trodden with war as Virginia is, wherever I move across her surface, I find myself rous'd to surprise and admiration. What capacity for products, improvements, human life, nourishment and expansion. Everywhere that I have been in the Old Dominion, (the subtle mockery of that title now!) such thoughts have fill'd me. The

5

8–9. exhilarating; I like to] MDW: exhilarating. I like well to

Rumors, Changes, &c.
Printed from clippings of MDW, pp. 29–30. Not previously published.
6. its deepest and] MDW: its highest and

Virginia.
Printed from a clipping of MDW, p. 30. Not previously published.

soil is yet far above the average of any of the northern States. And how full of breadth the scenery, everywhere distant mountains, everywhere convenient rivers. Even yet prodigal in forest woods, and surely eligible for all the fruits, orchards, and flowers. The skies and atmosphere most lus-
10   cious, as I feel certain, from more than a year's residence in the State, and movements hither and yon. I should say very healthy, as a general thing. Then a rich and elastic quality, by night and by day. The sun rejoices in his strength, dazzling and burning, and yet, to me, never unpleasantly weakening. It is not the panting tropical heat, but invigorates. The north
15   tempers it. The nights are often unsurpassable. Last evening (Feb. 8,) I saw the first of the new moon, the outlined old moon clear along with it; the sky and air so clear, such transparent hues of color, it seem'd to me I had never really seen the new moon before. It was the thinnest cut crescent possible. It hung delicate just above the sulky shadow of the Blue
20   mountains. Ah, if it might prove an omen and good prophecy for this unhappy State.

Summer of 1864.

I am back again in Washington, on my regular daily and nightly rounds. Of course there are many specialties. Dotting a ward here and

---

7. breadth . . . distant] MDW: breadth is the scenery, everywhere with distant
16. the outlined old] MDW: the old

Summer of 1864.
Printed from clippings of MDW, pp. 30–31, where it consists of two paragraphs with the sideheading "WASHINGTON *Again—Summer of* 1864" and a third paragraph with the sideheading *"Readings."* Parts of this section appear in NYWG, in the Fourth, Fifth, and Sixth Papers of "Ten Years," and parts were originally published in NYT, Dec. 11, 1864. This section was reprinted with only minor changes in punctuation as part of a footnote in "Army Hospitals and Cases" (omitted from that article in NB), *Century Magazine*, October, 1888. Vol. 36, p. 827 (cf. "Last of the War Cases," *Prose 1892*, II).
2–7. The three sentences beginning "Dotting" and ending "(and so do I.)" were first published in NYWG as the first paragraph of the Fifth Paper of "Ten Years."
7. After the sentence ending "(and so do I.)" NYWG, Fifth Paper, has a short paragraph omitted in later texts. See Appendix IX, 1.
7–11. The three sentences beginning "Each" and ending "condition." were first published in NYWG as part of paragraph 17, the second under "Long One-Story Wooden Barracks," in the Fourth Paper of "Ten Years." The first two sentences of this paragraph, not reprinted, are as follows:
"These places unfold a new world to a man. Everywhere I have found most powerful and pathetic, though curiously mute, calls for some form of contribution, or some good office."
For paragraph 16, not reprinted, see Appendix VIII, 5.

there are always cases of poor fellows, long-suffering under obstinate wounds, or weak and dishearten'd from typhoid fever, or the like; mark'd cases, needing special and sympathetic nourishment. These I sit down and either talk to, or silently cheer them up. They always like it hugely, (and so do I.) Each case has its peculiarities, and needs some new adaptation. I have learnt to thus conform—learnt a good deal of hospital wisdom. Some of the poor young chaps, away from home for the first time in their lives, hunger and thirst for affection; this is sometimes the only thing that will reach their condition. The men like to have a pencil, and something to write in. I have given them cheap pocket-diaries, and almanacs for 1864, interleav'd with blank paper. For reading I generally have some old pictorial magazines or story papers—they are always acceptable. Also the morning or evening papers of the day. The best books I do not give, but lend to read through the wards, and then take them to others, and so on; they are very punctual about returning the books. In these wards, or on the field, as I thus continue to go round, I have come to adapt myself to each emergency, after its kind or call, however trivial, however solemn, every one justified and made real under its circumstances—not only visits and cheering talk and little gifts—not only washing and dressing wounds, (I have some cases where the patient is unwilling any one should do this but me)—but passages from the Bible, expounding them, prayer at the bedside, explanations of doctrine, &c. (I think I see my

5

10

15

20

9. young chaps, away] *NYWG:* young men, away

10. for affection; this] *MDW:* for affection. This] *NYWG:* for magnetism, affection. This

11. condition. The men] *MDW:* condition.......The men] [After "condition." *NYWG* adds the following sentence, not reprinted, to end the paragraph: "(Many of the sick are mere boys.)"]

11–17. The five sentences beginning "The men" and ending "the books." were first published in *NYWG*, paragraph 3 of the Fifth Paper of "Ten Years." The first two sentences of that paragraph, not reprinted, are as follows: "Reading matter is always acceptable. I always carry some—the cheerful kind. A good deal of writing is done in every hospital."

13. 1864] *NYWG:* 1863

16. lend . . . and] *MDW: lend . . .* and] *NYWG: lend* to read through, and

17. on; they] *MDW* and *NYWG:* on. They

17. After "the books." *MDW* begins a new paragraph. *NYWG* continues and completes the same paragraph with the following two sentences, not reprinted: "Sometimes I walk slowly through a ward with a couple of quires of note-paper and a package of envelopes, and sing out whoever wants a little paper to signify it. Of course there are plenty of customers."

17–26. The two sentences after "the books." constitute a separate paragraph in *MDW*. They were first published in *NYWG* as paragraph 7, subtitled "Each Emergency Answered—1864-5," of the Sixth Paper of "Ten Years."

17. these wards, or] *NYWG:* these hospitals, or

20–23. circumstances—not . . . but passages] *NYWG:* circumstances. Reading passages

25 friends smiling at this confession, but I was never more in earnest in my life.) In camp and everywhere, I was in the habit of reading or giving recitations to the men. They were very fond of it, and liked declamatory poetical pieces. We would gather in a large group by ourselves, after supper, and spend the time in such readings, or in talking, and occasion-
30 ally by an amusing game called the game of twenty questions.

A New Army Organization Fit for America.

It is plain to me out of the events of the war, north and south, and out of all considerations, that the current military theory, practice, rules and organization, (adopted from Europe from the feudal institutes, with, of course, the "modern improvements," largely from the French,) though
5 tacitly follow'd, and believ'd in by the officers generally, are not at all consonant with the United States, nor our people, nor our days. What it will be I know not—but I know that as entire an abnegation of the present military system, and the naval too, and a building up from radically different root-bases and centres appropriate to us, must eventually result,
10 as that our political system has resulted and become establish'd, different from feudal Europe, and built up on itself from original, perennial, democratic premises. We have undoubtedly in the United States the greatest military power—an exhaustless, intelligent, brave and reliable rank and file—in the world, any land, perhaps all lands. The problem is to organize
15 this in the manner fully appropriate to it, to the principles of the republic, and to get the best service out of it. In the present struggle, as already

---

26–30. These last three sentences of the section are printed in MDW and in NYWG (paragraph 7 of the Sixth Paper) with the separate subtitle "Readings." They constitute a portion of paragraph 51 in NYT, Dec. 11, 1864, subtitled "Reading, Interesting the Men, Etc."

26. In camp and] NYWG: For three years, in these scenes, in Washington, in camp, and] NYT: In Washington, in camp, and

26–27. reading . . . to] MDW, NYWG, and NYT: reading to

28. poetical pieces. We] NYWG: poetical pieces. Scotch or Irish ballads, Macaulay's poetry, one or two of Longfellow's pieces, translations from Schiller, and Miles O'Reilly's pieces were great favorites. I have had many happy evenings with the men. We] NYT: poetical pieces. Miles O'Reilly's pieces were also great favorites. I have had many happy evenings with the men. We

A New Army Organization Fit for America.

Printed from clippings of MDW, pp. 31–32, where it appears as two paragraphs under the subtitle, "A New Army Organization Fit for America Needed." Not previously printed.

seen and review'd, probably three-fourths of the losses, men, lives, &c., have been sheer superfluity, extravagance, waste.

Death of a Hero.

I wonder if I could ever convey to another—to you, for instance, reader dear—the tender and terrible realities of such cases, (many, many happen'd,) as the one I am now going to mention. Stewart C. Glover, company E, 5th Wisconsin—was wounded May 5, in one of those fierce tussles of the Wilderness—died May 21—aged about 20. He was a small and beardless young man—a splendid soldier—in fact almost an ideal American, of his age. He had serv'd nearly three years, and would have been entitled to his discharge in a few days. He was in Hancock's corps. The fighting had about ceas'd for the day, and the general commanding the brigade rode by and call'd for volunteers to bring in the wounded. Glover responded among the first—went out gayly—but while in the act of bearing in a wounded sergeant to our lines, was shot in the knee by a rebel sharpshooter; consequence, amputation and death. He had resided with his father, John Glover, an aged and feeble man, in Batavia, Genesee county, N. Y., but was at school in Wisconsin, after the war broke out, and there enlisted—soon took to soldier-life, liked it, was very manly, was belov'd by officers and comrades. He kept a little diary, like so many of the soldiers. On the day of his death he wrote the following in it, *to-day the doctor says I must die—all is over with me—ah, so young to die.* On another blank leaf he pencill'd to his brother, *dear brother Thomas, I have been brave but wicked—pray for me.*

6. days. What] MDW: days.....What
12. After "democratic premises." MDW begins a new paragraph.
18. After the sentence ending the paragraph, MDW has the following sentence, deleted in SDC: "The body and bulk come out more and more superb—the practical Military system, directing power, crude, illegitimate—worse than deficient, offensive, radically wrong."

Death of a Hero.
Printed from a clipping of MDW, p. 32. Not previously published.
3. mention. Stewart] MDW: mention.......Stewart
5–8. These three sentences were enclosed in parentheses in MDW.
7. American, of his] MDW: American, of common life, of his
8–9. corps. The] MDW: Corps.).......The
13. sharpshooter; consequence,] MDW: sharpshooter. Consequence,
13. death. He] MDW: death.......He
17. comrades. He] MDW: comrades.......He

Hospital Scenes.—Incidents.

It is Sunday afternoon, middle of summer, hot and oppressive, and very silent through the ward. I am taking care of a critical case, now lying in a half lethargy. Near where I sit is a suffering rebel, from the 8th Louisiana; his name is Irving. He has been here a long time, badly wounded, 5 and lately had his leg amputated; it is not doing very well. Right opposite me is a sick soldier-boy, laid down with his clothes on, sleeping, looking much wasted, his pallid face on his arm. I see by the yellow trimming on his jacket that he is a cavalry boy. I step softly over and find by his card that he is named William Cone, of the 1st Maine cavalry, and his folks 10 live in Skowhegan.

Ice Cream Treat.—One hot day toward the middle of June, I gave the inmates of Carver hospital a general ice cream treat, purchasing a large quantity, and, under convoy of the doctor or head nurse, going around personally through the wards to see to its distribution.

15 *An Incident.*—In one of the fights before Atlanta, a rebel soldier, of large size, evidently a young man, was mortally wounded top of the head, so that the brains partially exuded. He lived three days, lying on his back on the spot where he first dropt. He dug with his heel in the ground during that time a hole big enough to put in a couple of ordinary knap-20 sacks. He just lay there in the open air, and with little intermission kept his heel going night and day. Some of our soldiers then moved him to a house, but he died in a few minutes.

Another.—After the battles at Columbia, Tennessee, where we re-puls'd about a score of vehement rebel charges, they left a great many

Hospital Scenes.—Incidents.

Printed from clippings of MDW, pp. 32–33. The subtitle "Hospital Scenes" was inserted in the MS for SDC; the word "Incidents" must have been added in the galley proof.

1–10. This paragraph in MDW has the subtitle "A Slight Glimpse." In NYWG, paragraph 14 of the Sixth Paper of "Ten Years," it has the subtitle "A Glimpse from My Notes"; in NYT, Dec. 11, 1864, where it was first printed (paragraph 44), it has the subtitle "Characteristic Scene in a Ward."

1. afternoon, middle of summer, hot] NYWG and NYT: afternoon (middle of summer, 1864), hot

5. amputated; it is] MDW, NYWG, and NYT: amputated. It is

8. boy. I step] MDW, NYWG, and NYT: boy. He looks so handsome as he sleeps, one must needs go nearer to him. I step

11–14. In NYT this is paragraph 43.

13–14. quantity, . . . around] MDW and NYWG: quantity, . . . nurse of each ward, going around] NYT: quantity, and going around

15–22. First published in MDW.

wounded on the ground, mostly within our range. Whenever any of these   25
wounded attempted to move away by any means, generally by crawling
off, our men without exception brought them down by a bullet. They let
none crawl away, no matter what his condition.

A Yankee Soldier.

As I turn'd off the Avenue one cool October evening into Thirteenth
street, a soldier with knapsack and overcoat stood at the corner inquiring
his way. I found he wanted to go part of the road in my direction, so
we walk'd on together. We soon fell into conversation. He was small and
not very young, and a tough little fellow, as I judged in the evening light,   5
catching glimpses by the lamps we pass'd. His answers were short, but
clear. His name was Charles Carroll; he belong'd to one of the Massachusetts regiments, and was born in or near Lynn. His parents were living,
but were very old. There were four sons, and all had enlisted. Two had
died of starvation and misery in the prison at Andersonville, and one had   10
been kill'd in the west. He only was left. He was now going home, and
by the way he talk'd I inferr'd that his time was nearly out. He made
great calculations on being with his parents to comfort them the rest of
their days.

16. wounded top] *MDW:* wounded in top

A Yankee Soldier.
Printed from a clipping of *MDW*, p. 33. It appeared in *NYWG*, under the
same subtitle, as paragraph 8 of the Fifth Paper of "Ten Years," but was first published in *NYT*, March 6, 1865, as paragraph 3, with the date line "Jan. 28," subtitled "Four Brothers—But One Left." The date "Jan. 28" does not appear in later
texts because the paragraph was transferred from its original place in a sequence
of events occurring in January, 1865, to a sequence of events occurring in *NYWG*
during May and June, 1863, and in *MDW* and later texts in October, 1864. This
change required the insertion indicated in the first line.
    1. Avenue one cool October evening] *NYWG* and *NYT:* avenue one evening
    2. overcoat stood] *MDW, NYWG,* and *NYT:* overcoat on, stood
    10. Andersonville, and] *NYWG:* Andersonville, Ga., and] *NYT:* Andersonville,
Georgia, and
    11. kill'd in the west.] *NYWG* and *NYT:* killed in battle in the west.
    13–14. After "of their days." *NYT* has the following sentence, deleted in later
texts: "Some small offers of hospitality I made he declined."

Union Prisoners South.

Michael Stansbury, 48 years of age, a sea-faring man, a southerner by birth and raising, formerly captain of U. S. light ship Long Shoal, station'd at Long Shoal point, Pamlico sound—though a southerner, a firm Union man—was captur'd Feb. 17, 1863, and has been nearly two years in the Confederate prisons; was at one time order'd releas'd by Governor Vance, but a rebel officer re-arrested him; then sent on to Richmond for exchange—but instead of being exchanged was sent down (as a southern citizen, not a soldier,) to Salisbury, N. C., where he remain'd until lately, when he escap'd among the exchang'd by assuming the name of a dead soldier, and coming up via Wilmington with the rest. Was about sixteen months in Salisbury. Subsequent to October, '64, there were about 11,000 Union prisoners in the stockade; about 100 of them southern unionists, 200 U. S. deserters. During the past winter 1500 of the prisoners, to save their lives, join'd the confederacy, on condition of being assign'd merely to guard duty. Out of the 11,000 not more than 2500 came out; 500 of these were pitiable, helpless wretches—the rest were in a condition to travel. There were often 60 dead bodies to be buried in the morning; the daily average would be about 40. The regular food was a meal of corn, the cob and husk ground together, and sometimes once a week a ration of sorghum molasses. A diminutive ration of meat might possibly come once a month, not oftener. In the stockade, containing the 11,000 men, there was a partial show of tents, not enough for 2000. A large proportion of the men lived in holes in the ground, in the utmost wretchedness. Some froze to death, others had their hands and feet frozen. The rebel guards would occasionally, and on the least pretence, fire into the prison from mere demonism and wantonness. All the horrors that can be named, starvation, lassitude, filth, vermin, despair, swift loss of self-respect, idiocy, insanity,

Union Prisoners South.

Printed from clippings of MDW, pp. 33–34, where it was first published, and where it has the sidehead "Union Prisoners South—Salisbury."
15. duty. Out] MDW: duty, &c. Out
21. oftener. In] MDW: oftener. . . . . . . In
22. not enough for 2000.] MDW: (not enough for 2,000.)
26. named, starvation,] MDW: named, cruelty, starvation,
28. there. Stansbury] MDW: there. . . . . . . Stansbury
31. to the ship] MDW: to light ship
31. boat.) Has] MDW: boat.) . . . . . . Has
33–34. gone. Has] MDW: gone. . . . . . . Has
34. strangely deaden'd] MDW: strangely expressive, deaden'd

and frequent murder, were there. Stansbury has a wife and child living in Newbern—has written to them from here—is in the U. S. light-house employ still—(had been home to Newbern to see his family, and on his re- 30 turn to the ship was captured in his boat.) Has seen men brought there to Salisbury as hearty as you ever see in your life—in a few weeks completely dead gone, much of it from thinking on their condition—hope all gone. Has himself a hard, sad, strangely deaden'd kind of look, as of one chill'd for years in the cold and dark, where his good manly nature had no room 35 to exercise itself.

Deserters.

Oct. 24.—Saw a large squad of our own deserters, (over 300) sur- rounded with a cordon of arm'd guards, marching along Pennsylvania avenue. The most motley collection I ever saw, all sorts of rig, all sorts of hats and caps, many fine-looking young fellows, some of them shame- faced, some sickly, most of them dirty, shirts very dirty and long worn, 5 &c. They tramp'd along without order, a huge huddling mass, not in ranks. I saw some of the spectators laughing, but I felt like anything else but laughing. These deserters are far more numerous than would be thought. Almost every day I see squads of them, sometimes two or three at a time, with a small guard; sometimes ten or twelve, under a larger one. 10 (I hear that desertions from the army now in the field have often averaged 10,000 a month. One of the commonest sights in Washington is a squad of deserters.)

A Glimpse of War's Hell-Scenes.

In one of the late movements of our troops in the valley, (near Up- perville, I think,) a strong force of Moseby's mounted guerillas attack'd a

Deserters.
Printed from a clipping of MDW, p. 34, with the sidehead "Deserters— Saturday, Oct. 21." Not previously printed.
  2. a cordon] MDW: a strong cordon
  8. After "but laughing." MDW begins a new paragraph.
  13. After "of deserters." MDW has the following final sentence: "I often think it curious that the military and civil operations do not clash, but they never do here.)"

A Glimpse of War's Hell-Scenes.
Printed from clippings of MDW, pp. 35–36, where it consists of five para- graphs. Not previously published.

train of wounded, and the guard of cavalry convoying them. The ambulances contain'd about 60 wounded, quite a number of them officers of rank. The rebels were in strength, and the capture of the train and its partial guard after a short snap was effectually accomplish'd. No sooner had our men surrender'd, the rebels instantly commenced robbing the train and murdering their prisoners, even the wounded. Here is the scene or a sample of it, ten minutes after. Among the wounded officers in the ambulances were one, a lieutenant of regulars, and another of higher rank. These two were dragg'd out on the ground on their backs, and were now surrounded by the guerillas, a demoniac crowd, each member of which was stabbing them in different parts of their bodies. One of the officers had his feet pinn'd firmly to the ground by bayonets stuck through them and thrust into the ground. These two officers, as afterwards found on examination, had receiv'd about twenty such thrusts, some of them through the mouth, face, &c. The wounded had all been dragg'd (to give a better chance also for plunder,) out of their wagons; some had been effectually dispatch'd, and their bodies were lying there lifeless and bloody. Others, not yet dead, but horribly mutilated, were moaning or groaning. Of our men who surrender'd, most had been thus maim'd or slaughter'd.

At this instant a force of our cavalry, who had been following the train at some interval, charged suddenly upon the secesh captors, who proceeded at once to make the best escape they could. Most of them got away, but we gobbled two officers and seventeen men, in the very acts just described. The sight was one which admitted of little discussion, as may be imagined. The seventeen captur'd men and two officers were put under guard for the night, but it was decided there and then that they should die. The next morning the two officers were taken in the town, separate places, put in the centre of the street, and shot. The seventeen men were taken to an open ground, a little one side. They were placed in a hollow square, half-encompass'd by two of our cavalry regiments, one of which regiments had three days before found the bloody corpses of three

6. After "accomplish'd." *MDW* begins a new paragraph.
19. bodies were lying] *MDW:* bodies lying
26. men, in] *MDW:* men, as it were in
30. After "should die." *MDW* begins a new paragraph.
33. square, half-encompass'd] *MDW:* square, encompass'd
41. of the seventeen] *MDW:* of their seventeen
42. square, unfasten'd] *MDW:* square, were unfasten'd
45. square. I was] *MDW:* square . . . . . . I was
50–56. This paragraph is enclosed in parentheses in *MDW.*
50. verify] *MDW:* varify
51. places, could] *MDW:* places, &c., could

of their men hamstrung and hung up by the heels to limbs of trees by   35
Moseby's guerillas, and the other had not long before had twelve men,
after surrendering, shot and then hung by the neck to limbs of trees, and
jeering inscriptions pinn'd to the breast of one of the corpses, who had
been a sergeant. Those three, and those twelve, had been found, I say, by
these environing regiments. Now, with revolvers, they form'd the grim   40
cordon of the seventeen prisoners. The latter were placed in the midst of
the hollow square, unfasten'd, and the ironical remark made to them
that they were now to be given "a chance for themselves." A few ran for it.
But what use? From every side the deadly pills came. In a few minutes the
seventeen corpses strew'd the hollow square. I was curious to know   45
whether some of the Union soldiers, some few, (some one or two at least of
the youngsters,) did not abstain from shooting on the helpless men. Not
one. There was no exultation, very little said, almost nothing, yet every
man there contributed his shot.

Multiply the above by scores, aye hundreds—verify it in all the forms   50
that different circumstances, individuals, places, could afford—light it
with every lurid passion, the wolf's, the lion's lapping thirst for blood—
the passionate, boiling volcanoes of human revenge for comrades, brothers
slain—with the light of burning farms, and heaps of smutting, smoulder-
ing black embers—and in the human heart everywhere black, worse   55
embers—and you have an inkling of this war.

Gifts—Money—Discrimination.

As a very large proportion of the wounded came up from the front
without a cent of money in their pockets, I soon discover'd that it was
about the best thing I could do to raise their spirits, and show them that
somebody cared for them, and practically felt a fatherly or brotherly interest in them, to give them small sums in such cases, using tact and   5
discretion about it. I am regularly supplied with funds for this purpose by

Gifts—Money—Discrimination.

Printed from a clipping of MDW, p. 36. All except the sentence beginning
"I provide" (lines 8–10) comes from NYWG, paragraphs 11 and 12 of the Sixth
Paper of "Ten Years," the first two under the subtitle "Gifts—Money—Discrimina-
tion." The sentence beginning "I provide" is from the last paragraph of the Fourth
Paper. The first sentence (lines 1–6) is also found in NYT, Dec. 11, 1864, where
it is paragraph 54, with the subtitle "Little Gifts of Money."
    1. As a . . . wounded came up] MDW: As a . . . wounded still come up]
NYT: A very large proportion of the wounded come up
    2. pockets, I] NYT: pockets. I
    6–8. The sentence beginning "I am regularly" may have originated in para-

good women and men in Boston, Salem, Providence, Brooklyn, and New York. I provide myself with a quantity of bright new ten-cent and five-cent bills, and, when I think it incumbent, I give 25 or 30 cents, or perhaps
10   50 cents, and occasionally a still larger sum to some particular case. As I have started this subject, I take opportunity to ventilate the financial question. My supplies, altogether voluntary, mostly confidential, often seeming quite Providential, were numerous and varied. For instance, there were two distant and wealthy ladies, sisters, who sent regularly, for two
15   years, quite heavy sums, enjoining that their names should be kept secret. The same delicacy was indeed a frequent condition. From several I had *carte blanche.* Many were entire strangers. From these sources, during from two to three years, in the manner described, in the hospitals, I bestowed, as almoner for others, many, many thousands of dollars. I
20   learn'd one thing conclusively—that beneath all the ostensible greed and heartlessness of our times there is no end to the generous benevolence of men and women in the United States, when once sure of their object. Another thing became clear to me—while *cash* is not amiss to bring up the rear, tact and magnetic sympathy and unction are, and ever will be,
25   sovereign still.

Items from My Note Books.

Some of the half-eras'd, and not over-legible when made, memoranda of things wanted by one patient or another, will convey quite a

graph 41, *NYT*, Dec. 11, 1864, the first of two subtitled "Assistance—More About Hospital Visiting as an Art." See Appendix III, 5.

    8–10. The sentence beginning "I provide" was first published in the last paragraph of the Fourth Paper of "Ten Years," where it follows this sentence, the first of the paragraph: "I have already distributed quite a large amount of money, put in my hands for that purpose by benevolent friends." The remaining sentences of the paragraph are as follows: "Then I scatter around a variety of articles, literally too numerous to mention. I regularly carry a haversack with me, and my coat has two of the biggest kind of pockets."

    10. *MDW* and *NYWG* begin a new paragraph with "As I have".

    10–11. As I . . . the] *MDW:* As I have recurr'd to this subject several times, I may take opportunity to ventilate and sum up the] *NYWG:* As I have recurred to this subject several times in the present notes, I may take opportunity to ventilate and sum up the

    18–19. I bestowed, as almoner for others, many, many thousands of dollars.] *NYWG:* I bestowed over $50,000 in money—and considerably more than that amount in other forms.

    25. After "sovereign still." *NYWG* has paragraph 13, Sixth Paper of "Ten Years," which was not afterwards reprinted, though it had been previously published as paragraph 42 of *NYT*, Dec. 11, 1864. See Appendix III, 5.

fair idea. D. S. G., bed 52, wants a good book; has a sore, weak throat; would like some horehound candy; is from New Jersey, 28th regiment. C. H. L., 145th Pennsylvania, lies in bed 6, with jaundice and erysipelas;   5 also wounded; stomach easily nauseated; bring him some oranges, also a little tart jelly; hearty, full-blooded young fellow—(he got better in a few days, and is now home on a furlough.) J. H. G., bed 24, wants an under-shirt, drawers, and socks; has not had a change for quite a while; is evidently a neat, clean boy from New England—(I supplied him; also   10 with a comb, tooth-brush, and some soap and towels; I noticed afterward he was the cleanest of the whole ward.) Mrs. G., lady-nurse, ward F, wants a bottle of brandy—has two patients imperatively requiring stimu-lus—low with wounds and exhaustion. (I supplied her with a bottle of first-rate brandy from the Christian commission rooms.)   15

A Case from Second Bull Run.

Well, poor John Mahay is dead. He died yesterday. His was a pain-ful and long-lingering case, (see p. 30 *ante*.) I have been with him at times for the past fifteen months. He belonged to company A, 101st New York, and was shot through the lower region of the abdomen at second Bull Run, August, '62. One scene at his bedside will suffice for the agonies of nearly   5 two years. The bladder had been perforated by a bullet going entirely through him. Not long since I sat a good part of the morning by his bed-

Items from My Note Books.
Printed from clippings of MDW, p. 37, under the sidehead: "Items Wanted—(From my Note Books.)" Not previously printed.
    4. candy; is] MDW: candy. Is
    4–5. regiment. C.H.L.] MDW: regiment.......C.H.L.
    6. wounded; stomach] MDW: wounded. Stomach
    6. nauseated; bring] MDW: nauseated. Bring
    7. jelly; hearty] MDW: jelly. Hearty
    7. fellow—(he] MDW: fellow. (He
    8. furlough.) J.H.G.] MDW: furlough.).......J.H.G.
    9. socks; has] MDW: socks. Has
    9. while; is] MDW: while. Is
    10. New England—(I] MDW: New England. I
    11. towels; I] MDW: towels. I
    12. ward.) Mrs.] MDW: Ward.......Mrs.

A Case from Second Bull Run.
Printed from a clipping of MDW, p. 37. First published in NYT, Dec. 11, 1864, paragraph 45, with the subtitle: "Death of a Case from Second Bull Run."
    2. and long-lingering case, (see p. 30 *ante*.) I] MDW: and long lingering case, (see p. 10, *ante*.) I] NYT: and lingering case. I] [The reference is to the section "Hospital Scenes and Persons," lines 46–56, *q.v.*]

side, ward E, Armory square. The water ran out of his eyes from the
intense pain, and the muscles of his face were distorted, but he utter'd
nothing except a low groan now and then. Hot moist cloths were applied,
and reliev'd him somewhat. Poor Mahay, a mere boy in age, but old in
misfortune. He never knew the love of parents, was placed in infancy in
one of the New York charitable institutions, and subsequently bound out
to a tyrannical master in Sullivan county, (the scars of whose cowhide
and club remain'd yet on his back.) His wound here was a most disagreeable one, for he was a gentle, cleanly, and affectionate boy. He found
friends in his hospital life, and, indeed, was a universal favorite. He had
quite a funeral ceremony.

Army Surgeons—Aid Deficiencies.

I must bear my most emphatic testimony to the zeal, manliness, and
professional spirit and capacity, generally prevailing among the surgeons,
many of them young men, in the hospitals and the army. I will not say
much about the exceptions, for they are few; (but I have met some of those
few, and very incompetent and airish they were.) I never ceas'd to find
the best men, and the hardest and most disinterested workers, among the
surgeons in the hospitals. They are full of genius, too. I have seen many
hundreds of them and this is my testimony. There are, however, serious
deficiencies, wastes, sad want of system, in the commissions, contributions,
and in all the voluntary, and a great part of the governmental nursing,
edibles, medicines, stores, &c. (I do not say surgical attendance, because
the surgeons cannot do more than human endurance permits.) Whatever
puffing accounts there may be in the papers of the North, this is the actual
fact. No thorough previous preparation, no system, no foresight, no genius.

Army Surgeons—Aid Deficiencies.
  Printed from clippings of MDW, pp. 37–38, where it forms two paragraphs.
This material was originally published in NYT, Dec. 11, 1864, under two discon-
nected subtitles. The first part, lines 1–8, appears as paragraph 56, subtitled "Surgeons, the Young Men." The rest of the paragraph, with some differences, was drawn
from paragraph 40, the second under "Lamentable Deficiencies After Heavy Battles."
  6–7. among the surgeons] MDW and NYT: among these Surgeons
  8. MDW begins a new paragraph with "There are".
  8–11. The sentence beginning "There are" is not in NYT, but in place of it NYT
has several sentences including all of paragraph 39 and the first part of 40. See Appendix III, 5.
  12–13. Whatever puffing accounts] NYT: Whatever pleasant accounts
  15. but never] MDW and NYT: but always miles away; never
  18. noblest men] MDW and NYT: noblest young men
  20. or merely] NYT: or with merely

Always plenty of stores, no doubt, but never where they are needed, and ⏑15 never the proper application. Of all harrowing experiences, none is greater than that of the days following a heavy battle. Scores, hundreds of the noblest men on earth, uncomplaining, lie helpless, mangled, faint, alone, and so bleed to death, or die from exhaustion, either actually untouch'd at all, or merely the laying of them down and leaving them, when there ⏑20 ought to be means provided to save them.

The Blue Everywhere.

This city, its suburbs, the capitol, the front of the White House, the places of amusement, the Avenue, and all the main streets, swarm with soldiers this winter, more than ever before. Some are out from the hospitals, some from the neighboring camps, &c. One source or another, they pour plenteously, and make, I should say, the mark'd feature in the ⏑5 human movement and costume-appearance of our national city. Their blue pants and overcoats are everywhere. The clump of crutches is heard up the stairs of the paymasters' offices, and there are characteristic groups around the doors of the same, often waiting long and wearily in the cold. Toward the latter part of the afternoon, you see the furlough'd men, ⏑10 sometimes singly, sometimes in small squads, making their way to the Baltimore depot. At all times, except early in the morning, the patrol detachments are moving around, especially during the earlier hours of evening, examining passes, and arresting all soldiers without them. They do not question the one-legged, or men badly disabled or maim'd, but all ⏑15 others are stopt. They also go around evenings through the auditoriums of the theatres, and make officers and all show their passes, or other authority, for being there.

The Blue Everywhere.
Printed from a clipping of *MDW*, p. 38. It first appeared as paragraphs 1 and 2, under the subtitle "Soldiers Everywhere—The Patrol.—Feb. '64," in Whitman's article "The Soldiers," *NYT*, March 6, 1865. Reprinted under the same subtitle in *NYWG* as the last two paragraphs of the Fifth Paper of "Ten Years."
4–5. One . . . pour plenteously,] *MDW:* One . . . pour in plenteously,] *NYWG* and *NYT:* Out of one source or another they pour in plenteously,
7–8. heard up] *MDW, NYWG,* and *NYT:* heard, and up
8. paymasters' offices] *NYWG* and *NYT:* Paymaster's offices;
10. cold. Toward] *MDW:* cold . . . . Toward] [*NYWG* and *NYT* begin a new paragraph with "Toward".]
13–14. of evening] *NYWG* and *NYT:* of the evening
14. all soldiers without] *MDW, NYWG,* and *NYT:* all without
16. around evenings through] *MDW, NYWG,* and *NYT:* around through
18. being there.] *NYT:* being here.

A Model Hospital.

Sunday, January 29th, 1865.—Have been in Armory-square this afternoon. The wards are very comfortable, new floors and plaster walls, and models of neatness. I am not sure but this is a model hospital after all, in important respects. I found several sad cases of old lingering wounds. One Delaware soldier, William H. Millis, from Bridgeville, whom I had been with after the battles of the Wilderness, last May, where he receiv'd a very bad wound in the chest, with another in the left arm, and whose case was serious (pneumonia had set in) all last June and July, I now find well enough to do light duty. For three weeks at the time mention'd he just hovered between life and death.

Boys in the Army.

As I walk'd home about sunset, I saw in Fourteenth street a very young soldier, thinly clad, standing near the house I was about to enter. I stopt a moment in front of the door and call'd him to me. I knew that an old Tennessee regiment, and also an Indiana regiment, were temporarily stopping in new barracks, near Fourteenth street. This boy I found belonged to the Tennessee regiment. But I could hardly believe he carried a musket. He was but 15 years old, yet had been twelve months a soldier, and had borne his part in several battles, even historic ones. I ask'd him if

A Model Hospital.

Printed from clippings of MDW, pp. 38–39. The subtitle was inserted in the MS. This paragraph was not used in "Ten Years." It was first published as paragraph 4 in NYT, March 6, 1865, with the subhead "A Sunday Afternoon in Hospital." In NYT, paragraph 3, with subtitle "Four Brothers—But One Left," came between "Soldiers Everywhere—The Patrol.—Feb. '64." and "A Sunday Afternoon in Hospital." It was shifted in later texts to the section "A Yankee Soldier," *q.v.*

   1. *Sunday, January 29th, 1865.*—Have] NYT: Jan. 29.—I have
   2. comfortable, new] MDW and NYT: comfortable, with new
   4. in important] NYT: in most important
   5. William H. Millis] MDW: Wm. H. Millis] NYT: Wm. H. Mills
   10. After "and death." NYT has the following sentence to end the paragraph: "To Dr. Robbins, the ward Surgeon, Dr. Bliss, the Surgeon in charge, and the lady nurse of Ward B, he probably owes his life."

Boys in the Army.

Printed from a clipping of MDW, p. 39, where it is in two paragraphs. It was

he did not suffer from the cold, and if he had no overcoat. No, he did not suffer from cold, and had no overcoat, but could draw one whenever he wish'd. His father was dead, and his mother living in some part of East Tennessee; all the men were from that part of the country. The next forenoon I saw the Tennessee and Indiana regiments marching down the Avenue. My boy was with the former, stepping along with the rest. There were many other boys no older. I stood and watch'd them as they tramp'd along with slow, strong, heavy, regular steps. There did not appear to be a man over 30 years of age, and a large proportion were from 15 to perhaps 22 or 23. They had all the look of veterans, worn, stain'd, impassive, and a certain unbent, lounging gait, carrying in addition to their regular arms and knapsacks, frequently a frying-pan, broom, &c. They were all of pleasant physiognomy; no refinement, nor blanch'd with intellect, but as my eye pick'd them, moving along, rank by rank, there did not seem to be a single repulsive, brutal or markedly stupid face among them.

Burial of a Lady Nurse.

Here is an incident just occurr'd in one of the hospitals. A lady named Miss or Mrs. Billings, who has long been a practical friend of soldiers, and nurse in the army, and had become attached to it in a way that no one can realize but him or her who has had experience, was taken sick, early this winter, linger'd some time, and finally died in the hospital. It was her request that she should be buried among the soldiers, and after

first published in NYT, March 6, 1865, as paragraphs 5–7, under the same subtitle. Not reprinted in "Ten Years."
    4. old Tennessee regiment] MDW: old Tennessee Union regiment] NYT: old campaign Tennessee Union regiment
    8. ones. I] MDW: ones . . . . I] [NYT begins a new paragraph with "I".]
    12. After "country." MDW and NYT begin a new paragraph.
    15. were many other] NYT: were several other
    19. lounging gait] NYT: louping gait
    21. pleasant physiognomy] MDW and NYT: pleasant, even handsome physiognomy

    Burial of a Lady Nurse.
    Printed from a clipping of MDW, p. 39. In the Fifth Paper of "Ten Years," NYWG, it is paragraph 12, the second under the subhead "Women in the War." First printed as paragraph 8 in NYT, March 6, 1865, under the same subhead as in MDW and SDC.
    1. incident just] MDW and NYT: incident that has

the military method. This request was fully carried out. Her coffin was carried to the grave by soldiers, with the usual escort, buried, and a salute fired over the grave. This was at Annapolis a few days since.

Female Nurses for Soldiers.

There are many women in one position or another, among the hospitals, mostly as nurses here in Washington, and among the military stations; quite a number of them young ladies acting as volunteers. They are a help in certain ways, and deserve to be mention'd with respect. Then
5   it remains to be distinctly said that few or no young ladies, under the irresistible conventions of society, answer the practical requirements of nurses for soldiers. Middle-aged or healthy and good condition'd elderly women, mothers of children, are always best. Many of the wounded must be handled. A hundred things which cannot be gainsay'd, must occur and
10   must be done. The presence of a good middle-aged or elderly woman, the magnetic touch of hands, the expressive features of the mother, the silent soothing of her presence, her words, her knowledge and privileges arrived at only through having had children, are precious and final qualifications. It is a natural faculty that is required; it is not merely having a genteel
15   young woman at a table in a ward. One of the finest nurses I met was a red-faced illiterate old Irish woman; I have seen her take the poor wasted naked boys so tenderly up in her arms. There are plenty of excellent clean old black women that would make tip-top nurses.

Female Nurses for Soldiers.
Printed from clippings of *MDW*, pp. 39–40. It is paragraph 11, the first under the subtitle "Women in the War," *NYWG*, Fifth Paper of "Ten Years." First published as paragraph 9 in *NYT*, March 6, 1865, under the subtitle "A Few Words About Female Nurses for Soldiers."
   1–2. another, among the hospitals, mostly] *NYWG:* another, mostly
   2. and among] *NYWG:* and all around among
   3. stations; quite a number of them young] *NYWG:* stations; most of them are young] *NYT:* stations; most of them young
   4. a help] *MDW* and *NYWG:* a great help
   4. with respect] *MDW, NYWG,* and *NYT:* with praise and respect
   6. the practical] *NYWG* and *NYT:* the real practical
   7. for soldiers] *NYWG* and *NYT:* for these collections of soldiers
   9. gainsay'd] *NYWG:* gainsaid
   13–14. qualifications. It is] *MDW:* qualifications. (Mrs. H. J. Wright, of Mansion House Hospital, Alexandria, is one of those good nurses. I have known her for over two years in her labors of love.) It is] [*NYT* same as *MDW* except that *NYT* omits the marks of parenthesis.]

Southern Escapees.

Feb. 23, '65.—I saw a large procession of young men from the
rebel army, (deserters they are call'd, but the usual meaning of the word
does not apply to them,) passing the Avenue to-day. There were nearly
200, come up yesterday by boat from James river. I stood and watch'd
them as they shuffled along, in a slow, tired, worn sort of way; a large   5
proportion of light-hair'd, blonde, light gray-eyed young men among
them. Their costumes had a dirt-stain'd uniformity; most had been
originally gray; some had articles of our uniform, pants on one, vest or
coat on another; I think they were mostly Georgia and North Carolina
boys. They excited little or no attention. As I stood quite close to them,   10
several good looking enough youths, (but O what a tale of misery their
appearance told,) nodded or just spoke to me, without doubt divining pity
and fatherliness out of my face, for my heart was full enough of it. Several
of the couples trudg'd along with their arms about each other, some
probably brothers, as if they were afraid they might somehow get sepa-   15
rated. They nearly all look'd what one might call simple, yet intelligent,
too. Some had pieces of old carpet, some blankets, and others old bags
around their shoulders. Some of them here and there had fine faces, still it
was a procession of misery. The two hundred had with them about half a
dozen arm'd guards. Along this week I saw some such procession, more   20
or less in numbers, every day, as they were brought up by the boat. The
government does what it can for them, and sends them north and west.

15–16. I met . . . illiterate old] *NYWG* and *NYT:* I have met was a red-faced old
[The next paragraph, the last in *NYT*, subtitled "An Unknown Hero, Though an
Enemy," was printed in *SDC* under the subtitle "A Secesh Brave," *q.v.*]

Southern Escapees.
Printed from clippings of *MDW*, pp. 40–42. Apparently not previously published.
    3. passing the] *MDW:* passing along the
    4. 200, come] *MDW:* 200 of them, come
    5. they . . . a large] *MDW:* they pass'd along in a slow, tired, worn sort of
way. There was a curiously large
    8. some had] *MDW:* some among them had
    9. another; I] *MDW:* another. I
    11. enough youths] *MDW:* enough American youths
    15. brothers, as if] *MDW:* brothers; it seem'd as if
    16–17. intelligent, too] *MDW:* intelligent enough, too
    18. shoulders. Some] *MDW:* shoulders, and some
    20. After "arm'd guards." *MDW* begins a new paragraph.

Feb. 27.—Some three or four hundred more escapees from the confederate army came up on the boat. As the day has been very pleasant indeed, (after a long spell of bad weather,) I have been wandering around a good deal, without any other object than to be out-doors and enjoy it; have met these escaped men in all directions. Their apparel is the same ragged, long-worn motley as before described. I talk'd with a number of the men. Some are quite bright and stylish, for all their poor clothes—walking with an air, wearing their old head-coverings on one side, quite saucily. I find the old, unquestionable proofs, as all along the past four years, of the unscrupulous tyranny exercised by the secession government in conscripting the common people by absolute force everywhere, and paying no attention whatever to the men's time being up—keeping them in military service just the same. One gigantic young fellow, a Georgian, at least six feet three inches high, broad-sized in proportion, attired in the dirtiest, drab, well-smear'd rags, tied with strings, his trousers at the knees all strips and streamers, was complacently standing eating some bread and meat. He appear'd contented enough. Then a few minutes after I saw him slowly walking along. It was plain he did not take anything to heart.

Feb. 28.—As I pass'd the military headquarters of the city, not far from the President's house, I stopt to interview some of the crowd of escapees who were lounging there. In appearance they were the same as previously mention'd. Two of them, one about 17, and the other perhaps 25 or '6, I talk'd with some time. They were from North Carolina, born and rais'd there, and had folks there. The elder had been in the rebel service four years. He was first conscripted for two years. He was then kept arbitrarily in the ranks. This is the case with a large proportion of the secession army. There was nothing downcast in these young men's manners; the younger had been soldiering about a year; he was conscripted; there were six brothers (all the boys of the family) in the army, part of them as conscripts, part as volunteers; three had been kill'd; one had escaped about four months ago, and now this one had got away; he was a pleasant and well-talking lad, with the peculiar North Carolina idiom (not at all disagreeable to my ears.) He and the elder one were of the

---

23. *Feb. 27.*—Some] MDW: *Feb. 27, '65.*—Some
24. boat. As] MDW: boat to-day. As
31–35. The sentence beginning "I find" and ending "the same." is enclosed in parentheses in MDW.
35. same. One] MDW: same.) . . . . . . .One
43. to interview some] MDW: to talk with some
50. There was] MDW: There is no shame in leaving such service—was
51, 53, 54. MDW has periods instead of semicolons in these lines, followed in

same company, and escaped together—and wish'd to remain together. They thought of getting transportation away to Missouri, and working there; but were not sure it was judicious. I advised them rather to go to some of the directly northern States, and get farm work for the present. The younger had made six dollars on the boat, with some tobacco he brought; he had three and a half left. The elder had nothing; I gave him a trifle. Soon after, met John Wormley, 9th Alabama, a West Tennessee rais'd boy, parents both dead—had the look of one for a long time on short allowance—said very little—chew'd tobacco at a fearful rate, spitting in proportion—large clear dark-brown eyes, very fine—didn't know what to make of me—told me at last he wanted much to get some clean underclothes, and a pair of decent pants. Didn't care about coat or hat fixings. Wanted a chance to wash himself well, and put on the under-clothes. I had the very great pleasure of helping him to accomplish all those wholesome designs.

March 1st.—Plenty more butternut or clay-color'd escapees every day. About 160 came in to-day, a large portion South Carolinians. They generally take the oath of allegiance, and are sent north, west, or extreme south-west if they wish. Several of them told me that the desertions in their army, of men going home, leave or no leave, are far more numerous than their desertions to our side. I saw a very forlorn looking squad of about a hundred, late this afternoon, on their way to the Baltimore depot.

The Capitol by Gas-Light.

To-night I have been wandering awhile in the capitol, which is all lit up. The illuminated rotunda looks fine. I like to stand aside and look a long, long while, up at the dome; it comforts me somehow. The House and Senate were both in session till very late. I look'd in upon them, but only a few moments; they were hard at work on tax and appropriation bills. I wander'd through the long and rich corridors and apartments under the Senate; an old habit of mine, former winters, and now more satisfaction

each case by a new sentence.

62. nothing; I] MDW: nothing. I

63. trifle. Soon . . . a West] MDW: trifle . . . . Soon after, I met John Wormley, 9th Alabama—is a West

The Capitol by Gas-Light.

Printed without change, except the inserted subtitle, from the same clipping of MDW, p. 42. Not previously published.

than ever. Not many persons down there, occasionally a flitting figure in the distance.

The Inauguration.

March 4.—The President very quietly rode down to the capitol in his own carriage, by himself, on a sharp trot, about noon, either because he wish'd to be on hand to sign bills, or to get rid of marching in line with the absurd procession, the muslin temple of liberty, and pasteboard monitor.
5   I saw him on his return, at three o'clock, after the performance was over. He was in his plain two-horse barouche, and look'd very much worn and tired; the lines, indeed, of vast responsibilities, intricate questions, and demands of life and death, cut deeper than ever upon his dark brown face; yet all the old goodness, tenderness, sadness, and canny shrewdness,
10   underneath the furrows. (I never see that man without feeling that he is one to become personally attach'd to, for his combination of purest, heartiest tenderness, and native western form of manliness.) By his side sat his little boy, of ten years. There were no soldiers, only a lot of civilians on horseback, with huge yellow scarfs over their shoulders, riding around
15   the carriage. (At the inauguration four years ago, he rode down and back again surrounded by a dense mass of arm'd cavalrymen eight deep, with drawn sabres; and there were sharpshooters station'd at every corner on the route.) I ought to make mention of the closing levee of Saturday night last. Never before was such a compact jam in front of the White
20   House—all the grounds fill'd, and away out to the spacious sidewalks. I was there, as I took a notion to go—was in the rush inside with the crowd —surged along the passage-ways, the blue and other rooms, and through the great east room. Crowds of country people, some very funny. Fine music from the Marine band, off in a side place. I saw Mr. Lincoln, drest
25   all in black, with white kid gloves and a claw-hammer coat, receiving, as in duty bound, shaking hands, looking very disconsolate, and as if he would give anything to be somewhere else.

The Inauguration.
    Printed from clippings of MDW, pp. 42–43. Not previously published.
    3. bills, or] MDW: bills, &c., or
    12. western form of] MDW: Western even rudest forms of
    18. After "route.)" MDW begins a new paragraph.
    20. sidewalks. I] MDW: sidewalks I
    23. east room. Crowds] MDW: East room, (upholster'd like a stage parlor.) Crowds
    24. place. I saw] MDW: place . . . . I saw

Attitude of Foreign Governments During the War.

Looking over my scraps, I find I wrote the following during 1864. The happening to our America, abroad as well as at home, these years, is indeed most strange. The democratic republic has paid her to-day the terrible and resplendent compliment of the united wish of all the nations of the world that her union should be broken, her future cut off, and that she should be compell'd to descend to the level of kingdoms and empires ordinarily great. There is certainly not one government in Europe but is now watching the war in this country, with the ardent prayer that the United States may be effectually split, crippled, and dismember'd by it. There is not one but would help toward that dismemberment, if it dared. I say such is the ardent wish to-day of England and of France, as governments, and of all the nations of Europe, as governments. I think indeed it is to-day the real, heartfelt wish of all the nations of the world, with the single exception of Mexico—Mexico, the only one to whom we have ever really done wrong, and now the only one who prays for us and for our triumph, with genuine prayer. Is it not indeed strange? America, made up of all, cheerfully from the beginning opening her arms to all, the result and justifier of all, of Britain, Germany, France and Spain—all here— the accepter, the friend, hope, last resource and general house of all—she who has harm'd none, but been bounteous to so many, to millions, the mother of strangers and exiles, all nations—should now I say be paid this dread compliment of general governmental fear and hatred. Are we indignant? alarm'd? Do we feel jeopardized? No; help'd, braced, concentrated, rather. We are all too prone to wander from ourselves, to affect Europe, and watch her frowns and smiles. We need this hot lesson of general hatred, and henceforth must never forget it. Never again will we trust the moral sense nor abstract friendliness of a single *government* of the old world.

5

10

15

20

25

Attitude of Foreign Governments During the War.

Printed from a clipping of MDW, "Notes," p. 63, where it consists of three paragraphs under the heading, "Attitude of Foreign Governments toward the U. S. during the War of 1861–'65." Not previously published.

    1–2. 1864. The] MDW: 1864, or the latter part of '63: The
    2. MDW begins a new paragraph with "The" after " '63:"
    16. After "prayer." MDW begins a new paragraph.
    22. hatred. Are] MDW: hatred? . . . . Are
    23. feel jeopardized?] MDW: feel wrong'd? jeopardized?

The Weather.—Does It Sympathize with These Times?

Whether the rains, the heat and cold, and what underlies them all, are affected with what affects man in masses, and follow his play of passionate action, strain'd stronger than usual, and on a larger scale than usual—whether this, or no, it is certain that there is now, and has been for twenty months or more, on this American continent north, many a remarkable, many an unprecedented expression of the subtile world of air above us and around us. There, since this war, and the wide and deep national agitation, strange analogies, different combinations, a different sunlight, or absence of it; different products even out of the ground. After every great battle, a great storm. Even civic events the same. On Saturday last, a forenoon like whirling demons, dark, with slanting rain, full of rage; and then the afternoon, so calm, so bathed with flooding splendor from heaven's most excellent sun, with atmosphere of sweetness; so clear, it show'd the stars, long, long before they were due. As the President came out on the capitol portico, a curious little white cloud, the only one in that part of the sky, appear'd like a hovering bird, right over him.

Indeed, the heavens, the elements, all the meteorological influences, have run riot for weeks past. Such caprices, abruptest alternation of frowns and beauty, I never knew. It is a common remark that (as last summer was different in its spells of intense heat from any preceding it,) the winter just completed has been without parallel. It has remain'd so down to the hour I am writing. Much of the daytime of the past month was sulky, with leaden heaviness, fog, interstices of bitter cold, and some insane storms. But there have been samples of another description. Nor earth nor sky ever knew spectacles of superber beauty than some of the nights lately here. The western star, Venus, in the earlier hours of evening, has never been so large, so clear; it seems as if it told something, as if it held rapport indulgent with humanity, with us Americans. Five or six nights since, it hung close by the moon, then a little past its first

The Weather.—Does It Sympathize with These Times?
Printed from clippings of MDW, next after "The Inauguration," pp. 43–44. Not previously published. MDW has "Sympathise" in the title; not corrected on the clipping, but presumably in the galley proof.
    26. nights lately here.] MDW: nights have lately been here.
    32. the miracle] MDW: the unsurpassable miracle

Inauguration Ball.
Printed from a clipping of MDW, p. 44. Not previously published.

quarter. The star was wonderful, the moon like a young mother. The sky, 30
dark blue, the transparent night, the planets, the moderate west wind, the
elastic temperature, the miracle of that great star, and the young and
swelling moon swimming in the west, suffused the soul. Then I heard,
slow and clear, the deliberate notes of a bugle come up out of the silence,
sounding so good through the night's mystery, no hurry, but firm and 35
faithful, floating along, rising, falling leisurely, with here and there a
long-drawn note; the bugle, well play'd, sounding tattoo, in one of the
army hospitals near here, where the wounded (some of them personally so
dear to me,) are lying in their cots, and many a sick boy come down to the
war from Illinois, Michigan, Wisconsin, Iowa, and the rest. 40

Inauguration Ball.

March 6.—I have been up to look at the dance and supper-rooms,
for the inauguration ball at the Patent office; and I could not help thinking, what a different scene they presented to my view a while since, fill'd
with a crowded mass of the worst wounded of the war, brought in from
second Bull Run, Antietam, and Fredericksburgh. To-night, beautiful 5
women, perfumes, the violins' sweetness, the polka and the waltz; then the
amputation, the blue face, the groan, the glassy eye of the dying, the
clotted rag, the odor of wounds and blood, and many a mother's son
amid strangers, passing away untended there, (for the crowd of the
badly hurt was great, and much for nurse to do, and much for surgeon.) 10

Scene at the Capitol.

I must mention a strange scene at the capitol, the hall of Representatives, the morning of Saturday last, (March 4th.) The day just
dawn'd, but in half-darkness, everything dim, leaden, and soaking. In
that dim light, the members nervous from long drawn duty, exhausted,

1. have been] *MDW:* have this moment been
1. the dance] *MDW:* the gorgeous array'd dance
2. Patent office; and I] *MDW:* Patent Office, (which begins in a few hours;)
and I
2–3. thinking, what] *MDW:* thinking of those rooms, where the music will sound
and the dancers' feet presently tread—what
6. waltz; then] *MDW:* waltz; but then,

Scene at the Capitol.
Printed from clippings of *MDW,* pp. 44–45. Not previously published.

5 some asleep, and many half asleep. The gas-light, mix'd with the dingy day-break, produced an unearthly effect. The poor little sleepy, stumbling pages, the smell of the hall, the members with heads leaning on their desks, the sounds of the voices speaking, with unusual intonations—the general moral atmosphere also of the close of this important session—the

10 strong hope that the war is approaching its close—the tantalizing dread lest the hope may be a false one—the grandeur of the hall itself, with its effect of vast shadows up toward the panels and spaces over the galleries —all made a mark'd combination.

In the midst of this, with the suddenness of a thunderbolt, burst one

15 of the most angry and crashing storms of rain and hail ever heard. It beat like a deluge on the heavy glass roof of the hall, and the wind literally howl'd and roar'd. For a moment, (and no wonder,) the nervous and sleeping Representatives were thrown into confusion. The slumberers awaked with fear, some started for the doors, some look'd up with

20 blanch'd cheeks and lips to the roof, and the little pages began to cry; it was a scene. But it was over almost as soon as the drowsied men were actually awake. They recover'd themselves; the storm raged on, beating, dashing, and with loud noises at times. But the House went ahead with its business then, I think, as calmly and with as much deliberation as at

25 any time in its career. Perhaps the shock did it good. (One is not without impression, after all, amid these members of Congress, of both the Houses, that if the flat routine of their duties should ever be broken in upon by some great emergency involving real danger, and calling for first-class personal qualities, those qualities would be found generally

30 forthcoming, and from men not now credited with them.)

A Yankee Antique.

March 27, 1865.—Sergeant Calvin F. Harlowe, company C, 29th Massachusetts, 3d brigade, 1st division, Ninth corps—a mark'd sample of heroism and death, (some may say bravado, but I say *heroism,*

---

8. desks, the] *MDW:* desks asleep, the
15. and hail ever] *MDW:* and wind ever
27. flat routine] *MDW:* flat and selfish routine

   A Yankee Antique.
   Printed from clippings of *MDW*, pp. 45–46. Not previously published.
14–15. The sentence beginning "The rebels" is enclosed in parentheses in *MDW*.
16. Mass.) Harlowe] *MDW:* Mass.) . . . . Harlowe
18. 29th; and] *MDW:* Twenty-Ninth Mass., and
19. four years' campaign] *MDW:* four years campaign
22. officer in the] *MDW:* officer of the

of grandest, oldest order)—in the late attack by the rebel troops, and
temporary capture by them, of fort Steadman, at night. The fort was surprised at dead of night. Suddenly awaken'd from their sleep, and rushing
from their tents, Harlowe, with others, found himself in the hands of the
secesh—they demanded his surrender—he answer'd, *Never while I live.*
(Of course it was useless. The others surrender'd; the odds were too
great.) Again he was ask'd to yield, this time by a rebel captain. Though
surrounded, and quite calm, he again refused, call'd sternly to his comrades to fight on, and himself attempted to do so. The rebel captain then
shot him—but at the same instant he shot the captain. Both fell together
mortally wounded. Harlowe died almost instantly. The rebels were
driven out in a very short time. The body was buried next day, but soon
taken up and sent home, (Plymouth county, Mass.) Harlowe was only
22 years of age—was a tall, slim, dark-hair'd, blue-eyed young man—
had come out originally with the 29th; and that is the way he met his
death, after four years' campaign. He was in the Seven Days fight before
Richmond, in second Bull Run, Antietam, first Fredericksburgh, Vicksburgh, Jackson, Wilderness, and the campaigns following—was as good
a soldier as ever wore the blue, and every old officer in the regiment will
bear that testimony. Though so young, and in a common rank, he had a
spirit as resolute and brave as any hero in the books, ancient or modern
—It was too great to say the words "I surrender"—and so he died.
(When I think of such things, knowing them well, all the vast and
complicated events of the war, on which history dwells and makes its
volumes, fall aside, and for the moment at any rate I see nothing but
young Calvin Harlowe's figure in the night, disdaining to surrender.)

Wounds and Diseases.

The war is over, but the hospitals are fuller than ever, from former
and current cases. A large majority of the wounds are in the arms and

---

23. testimony. Though] *MDW:* testimony . . . . Though
25–26. died. (When] *MDW:* died . . . . . . (When
28. fall aside] *MDW:* fall indeed aside

Wounds and Diseases.
    Printed, except for the footnote, from a clipping of *MDW*, p. 46. Most of the
paragraph clipped from *MDW* is found under the same subtitle in *NYWG*, paragraph
10 of the Sixth Paper of "Ten Years," and was first published under that subtitle as
paragraph 55 in *NYT*, Dec. 11, 1864.
    1–2. The first sentence does not appear in *NYWG* or *NYT*, the paragraph there
beginning "A large majority".

legs. But there is every kind of wound, in every part of the body. I should say of the sick, from my observation, that the prevailing maladies are typhoid fever and the camp fevers generally, diarrhœa, catarrhal affections and bronchitis, rheumatism and pneumonia. These forms of sickness lead; all the rest follow. There are twice as many sick as there are wounded. The deaths range from seven to ten per cent. of those under treatment.*

* In the U. S. Surgeon-General's office since, there is a formal record and treatment of 253,142 cases of wounds by government surgeons. What must have been the number unofficial, indirect—to say nothing of the Southern armies?

Death of President Lincoln.

April 16, '65.—I find in my notes of the time, this passage on the death of Abraham Lincoln: He leaves for America's history and biography, so far, not only its most dramatic reminiscence—he leaves, in my opinion, the greatest, best, most characteristic, artistic, moral personality. Not but that he had faults, and show'd them in the Presidency; but honesty, goodness, shrewdness, conscience, and (a new virtue, unknown to other lands, and hardly yet really known here, but the foundation and tie of all, as the future will grandly develop,) UNIONISM, in its truest and amplest sense, form'd the hard-pan of his character. These he seal'd with his life. The tragic splendor of his death, purging, illuminating all, throws round his form, his head, an aureole that will remain and will grow brighter through time, while history lives, and love of country lasts. By many has this Union been help'd; but if one name, one man, must be pick'd out, he, most of all, is the conservator of it, to the future. He

4. my observation, that] *NYT:* my experience in the hospitals, that
8. from seven to ten per cent.] *NYWG* and *NYT:* from 6 to 10 per cent.
10–13. Printed from an autograph MS.

Death of President Lincoln.
Printed from a clipping of *MDW*, p. 49, the last paragraph of eight in *MDW* under the subtitle "Murder of President Lincoln," pp. 46–49. [The first seven paragraphs are omitted here because they were used in his lecture, "Death of Abraham Lincoln," *q.v.,* in *Prose 1892,* II.]
1–2. The date and the first two lines through "Lincoln:" are from an autograph MS, introducing the clipping. The remainder of the section, the entire paragraph of the clipping, is enclosed in brackets in *MDW*.
4. artistic, moral personality] *MDW:* artistic, Personality

was assassinated—but the Union is not assassinated—*ça ira!* One falls, and   15
another falls. The soldier drops, sinks like a wave—but the ranks of the
ocean eternally press on. Death does its work, obliterates a hundred, a
thousand—President, general, captain, private—but the Nation is immortal.

Sherman's Army's Jubilation—Its Sudden Stoppage.

When Sherman's armies, (long after they left Atlanta,) were marching through South and North Carolina—after leaving Savannah, the news
of Lee's capitulation having been receiv'd—the men never mov'd a mile
without from some part of the line sending up continued, inspiriting
shouts. At intervals all day long sounded out the wild music of those pe-   5
culiar army cries. They would be commenc'd by one regiment or brigade,
immediately taken up by others, and at length whole corps and armies
would join in these wild triumphant choruses. It was one of the characteristic expressions of the western troops, and became a habit, serving as a
relief and outlet to the men—a vent for their feelings of victory, returning   10
peace, &c. Morning, noon, and afternoon, spontaneous, for occasion or
without occasion, these huge, strange cries, differing from any other,
echoing through the open air for many a mile, expressing youth, joy, wildness, irrepressible strength, and the ideas of advance and conquest,
sounded along the swamps and uplands of the South, floating to the skies.   15
('There never were men that kept in better spirits in danger or defeat—
what then could they do in victory?'—said one of the 15th corps to me,
afterwards.) This exuberance continued till the armies arrived at Raleigh.
There the news of the President's murder was receiv'd. Then no more
shouts or yells, for a week. All the marching was comparatively muffled.   20

13. this Union been help'd] MDW: *this Union* been conserv'd and help'd

Sherman's Army's Jubilation—Its Sudden Stoppage.

Printed from clippings of MDW, "Notes," pp. 62–63, subtitled "Sherman's
Army's Jubilation, 1865—Its sudden stoppage." Not previously published. [This section in MDW immediately follows material there arranged under the several subtitles "Attack on Fort Sumter, April, 1861," "The ensuing three Months—The National Uprising and Volunteering," "Contemptuous National feeling," and "Battle of
Bull Run, July, 1861," most of which was used earlier in SDC. See notes to "Opening
of the Secession War" and the four sections next thereafter following.]

5. shouts. At intervals all] MDW: shouts and cries. At intervals every little while,
all

9–10. as a relief] MDW: as relief

18. After "afterwards.)" MDW begins a new paragraph.

It was very significant—hardly a loud word or laugh in many of the regiments. A hush and silence pervaded all.

No Good Portrait of Lincoln.

Probably the reader has seen physiognomies (often old farmers, sea-captains, and such) that, behind their homeliness, or even ugliness, held superior points so subtle, yet so palpable, making the real life of their faces almost as impossible to depict as a wild perfume or fruit-taste, or
5   a passionate tone of the living voice—and such was Lincoln's face, the peculiar color, the lines of it, the eyes, mouth, expression. Of technical beauty it had nothing—but to the eye of a great artist it furnished a rare study, a feast and fascination. The current portraits are all failures—most of them caricatures.

Releas'd Union Prisoners from South.

The releas'd prisoners of war are now coming up from the southern prisons. I have seen a number of them. The sight is worse than any sight of battle-fields, or any collection of wounded, even the bloodiest. There was, (as a sample,) one large boat load, of several hundreds, brought
5   about the 25th, to Annapolis; and out of the whole number only three individuals were able to walk from the boat. The rest were carried ashore and laid down in one place or another. Can those be *men*—those little livid brown, ash-streak'd, monkey-looking dwarfs?—are they really not mummied, dwindled corpses? They lay there, most of them, quite still,
10 but with a horrible look in their eyes and skinny lips (often with not

22. [The three paragraphs following this section in MDW, p. 63, under the subtitle "Attitude of Foreign Governments toward the U. S. during the War of 1861–'65," was used earlier in SDC in the section subtitled "Attitude of Foreign Governments During the War," *q.v.*]

No Good Portrait of Lincoln.
Printed from a clipping of MDW, "Notes," p. 63, subtitled "No Good Portrait of Abraham Lincoln." Not previously published.
  3. palpable, making] MDW: palpable, defying the lines of art, making
  5. voice—and] MDW: voice . . . . . and
  6. expression. Of] MDW: expression, &c. Of
  7. beauty] MDW: *beauty*
  8. fascination. The] MDW: fascination . . . . The
  9. [The following two sections of MDW, pp. 63–66, under the subtitles "The

enough flesh on the lips to cover their teeth.) Probably no more appalling sight was ever seen on this earth. (There are deeds, crimes, that may be forgiven; but this is not among them. It steeps its perpetrators in blackest, escapeless, endless damnation. Over 50,000 have been compell'd to die the death of starvation—reader, did you ever try to realize what *starvation* 15 actually is?—in those prisons—and in a land of plenty.) An indescribable meanness, tyranny, aggravating course of insults, almost incredible—was evidently the rule of treatment through all the southern military prisons. The dead there are not to be pitied as much as some of the living that come from there—if they can be call'd living—many of them are mentally 20 imbecile, and will never recuperate.*

* *From a review of* "ANDERSONVILLE, A STORY OF SOUTHERN MILITARY PRISONS," *published serially in the "Toledo Blade," in 1879, and afterwards in book form.*
"There is a deep fascination in the subject of Andersonville—for that Gol- 25 gotha, in which lie the whitening bones of 13,000 gallant young men, repre- sents the dearest and costliest sacrifice of the war for the preservation of our national unity. It is a type, too, of its class. Its more than hundred hecatombs of dead represent several times that number of their brethren, for whom the prison gates of Belle Isle, Danville, Salisbury, Florence, Columbia, and 30 Cahaba open'd only in eternity. There are few families in the North who have not at least one dear relative or friend among these 60,000 whose sad fortune it was to end their service for the Union by lying down and dying for it in a southern prison pen. The manner of their death, the horrors that cluster'd thickly around every moment of their existence, the loyal, unfaltering stead- 35 fastness with which they endured all that fate had brought them, has never been adequately told. It was not with them as with their comrades in the field, whose every act was perform'd in the presence of those whose duty it was to observe such matters and report them to the world. Hidden from the view of their friends in the north by the impenetrable veil which the military operations 40 of the rebels drew around the so-called confederacy, the people knew next to

War, though with two sides, really One Identity" etc. and "Results South—Now and Hence," are used in "Origins of Attempted Secession." See *Prose 1892*, II.]

Releas'd Union Prisoners from South.
Printed, except for the long footnote, from a clipping of two paragraphs under the same subtitle in MDW, p. 50. Not previously published.
   3. collection] MDW: collections
   10–11. MDW has no marks of parenthesis.
   11. appalling] MDW: appaling
   16. After "plenty.)" MDW begins a new paragraph.
   25–56. Printed from a clipping of an unidentified newspaper, with revisions as indicated.
   26–27. represents the dearest] Clipping: represents to them very much of the dearest
   39. After "to the world." the clipping begins a new paragraph.

nothing of their career or their sufferings. Thousands died there less heeded even than the hundreds who perish'd on the battle-field. Grant did not lose as many men kill'd outright, in the terrible campaign from the Wilderness to the James river—43 days of desperate fighting—as died in July and August at Andersonville. Nearly twice as many died in that prison as fell from the day that Grant cross'd the Rapidan, till he settled down in the trenches before Petersburg. More than four times as many Union dead lie under the solemn soughing pines about that forlorn little village in southern Georgia, than mark the course of Sherman from Chattanooga to Atlanta. The nation stands aghast at the expenditure of life which attended the two bloody campaigns of 1864, which virtually crush'd the confederacy, but no one remembers that more Union soldiers died in the rear of the rebel lines than were kill'd in the front of them. The great military events which stamp'd out the rebellion drew attention away from the sad drama which starvation and disease play'd in those gloomy pens in the far recesses of sombre southern forests."

From a letter of "Johnny Bouquet," in N. Y. Tribune, March 27, '81.

"I visited at Salisbury, N. C., the prison pen or the site of it, from which nearly 12,000 victims of southern politicians were buried, being confined in a pen without shelter, exposed to all the elements could do, to all the disease herding animals together could create, and to all the starvation and cruelty an incompetent and intense caitiff government could accomplish. From the conversation and almost from the recollection of the northern people this place has dropp'd, but not so in the gossip of the Salisbury people, nearly all of whom say that the half was never told; that such was the nature of habitual outrage here that when Federal prisoners escaped the townspeople harbor'd them in their barns, afraid the vengeance of God would fall on them, to deliver even their enemies back to such cruelty. Said one old man at the Boyden House, who join'd in the conversation one evening: 'There were often men buried out of that prison pen still alive. I have the testimony of a surgeon that he has seen them pull'd out of the dead cart with their eyes open and taking notice, but too weak to lift a finger. There was not the least excuse for such treatment, as the confederate government had seized every sawmill in the region, and could just as well have put up shelter for these prisoners as not, wood being plentiful here. It will be hard to make any honest man in Salisbury say that there was the slightest necessity for those prisoners having to live in old tents, caves and holes half-full of water. Representations were made to the Davis government against the officers in charge of it, but no attention was paid to them. Promotion was the punishment for cruelty there. The inmates were skeletons. Hell could have no terrors for any man who died there, except the inhuman keepers.' "

50. After "Atlanta." the clipping begins a new paragraph.
58–81. Printed from a clipping of the *Tribune*.
58–59. of it, from which nearly] MDW: of it, from which Albert D. Richardson escaped and from which nearly
77. After "water." the clipping has the following two sentences, deleted by Whitman: "No respectable and well-advised man here but will say he would rather have

Death of a Pennsylvania Soldier.

*Frank H. Irwin, company E, 93d Pennsylvania—died May 1, '65—
My letter to his mother.*—Dear madam: No doubt you and Frank's
friends have heard the sad fact of his death in hospital here, through his
uncle, or the lady from Baltimore, who took his things. (I have not seen
them, only heard of them visiting Frank.) I will write you a few lines—as   5
a casual friend that sat by his death-bed. Your son, corporal Frank H. Irwin, was wounded near fort Fisher, Virginia, March 25th, 1865—the
wound was in the left knee, pretty bad. He was sent up to Washington,
was receiv'd in ward C, Armory-square hospital, March 28th—the wound
became worse, and on the 4th of April the leg was amputated a little above   10
the knee—the operation was perform'd by Dr. Bliss, one of the best surgeons in the army—he did the whole operation himself—there was a good
deal of bad matter gather'd—the bullet was found in the knee. For a couple of weeks afterwards he was doing pretty well. I visited and sat by him
frequently, as he was fond of having me. The last ten or twelve days of   15
April I saw that his case was critical. He previously had some fever, with
cold spells. The last week in April he was much of the time flighty—but
always mild and gentle. He died first of May. The actual cause of death
was pyæmia, (the absorption of the matter in the system instead of its discharge.) Frank, as far as I saw, had everything requisite in surgical treat-   20
ment, nursing, &c. He had watches much of the time. He was so good
and well-behaved and affectionate, I myself liked him very much. I was in
the habit of coming in afternoons and sitting by him, and soothing him,
and he liked to have me—liked to put his arm out and lay his hand on
my knee—would keep it so a long while. Toward the last he was more   25
restless and flighty at night—often fancied himself with his regiment—
by his talk sometimes seem'd as if his feelings were hurt by being blamed
by his officers for something he was entirely innocent of—said, "I never
in my life was thought capable of such a thing, and never was." At other
times he would fancy himself talking as it seem'd to children or such like,   30
his relatives I suppose, and giving them good advice; would talk to them

gone to his grave than to that pen. Yet it contained some of the flower of the country
in youth and promise."

Death of a Pennsylvania Soldier.

Printed from clippings of MDW, pp. 50–51. Not previously published.
  6. After "death-bed." MDW begins a new paragraph.
19–20. After "discharge.)" MDW begins a new paragraph.

a long while. All the time he was out of his head not one single bad word or idea escaped him. It was remark'd that many a man's conversation in his senses was not half as good as Frank's delirium. He seem'd quite
35 willing to die—he had become very weak and had suffer'd a good deal, and was perfectly resign'd, poor boy. I do not know his past life, but I feel as if it must have been good. At any rate what I saw of him here, under the most trying circumstances, with a painful wound; and among strangers, I can say that he behaved so brave, so composed, and so sweet
40 and affectionate, it could not be surpass'd. And now like many other noble and good men, after serving his country as a soldier, he has yielded up his young life at the very outset in her service. Such things are gloomy— yet there is a text, "God doeth all things well"—the meaning of which, after due time, appears to the soul.
45 I thought perhaps a few words, though from a stranger, about your son, from one who was with him at the last, might be worth while—for I loved the young man, though I but saw him immediately to lose him. I am merely a friend visiting the hospitals occasionally to cheer the wounded and sick. W. W.

The Armies Returning.

May 7.—Sunday.—To-day as I was walking a mile or two south of Alexandria, I fell in with several large squads of the returning Western army, (*Sherman's men* as they call'd themselves) about a thousand in all, the largest portion of them half sick, some convalescents, on their way to a
5 hospital camp. These fragmentary excerpts, with the unmistakable Western physiognomy and idioms, crawling along slowly—after a great campaign, blown this way, as it were, out of their latitude—I mark'd with curiosity, and talk'd with off and on for over an hour. Here and there was one very sick; but all were able to walk, except some of the last, who had
10 given out, and were seated on the ground, faint and despondent. These I

34. After "delirium." MDW begins a new paragraph.
34–35. He seem'd quite willing] MDW: He was perfectly willing

The Armies Returning.

Printed from clippings of MDW, pp. 51–52, where it has no sidehead except the date. Not previously published.
4–5. convalescents, . . . These] MDW: convalescents, &c. These
11. reach was] MDW: reach, (a sort of half-hospital,) was
12. started, accompanying] MDW: started on, accompanying
15–16. to-day; . . . the men] MDW: to-day. It was a strong, attractive, serious sight. We have been having rainy weather. The men

tried to cheer, told them the camp they were to reach was only a little way further over the hill, and so got them up and started, accompanying some of the worst a little way, and helping them, or putting them under the support of stronger comrades.

May 21.—Saw General Sheridan and his cavalry to-day; a strong, attractive sight; the men were mostly young, (a few middle-aged,) superb-looking fellows, brown, spare, keen, with well-worn clothing, many with pieces of water-proof cloth around their shoulders, hanging down. They dash'd along pretty fast, in wide close ranks, all spatter'd with mud; no holiday soldiers; brigade after brigade. I could have watch'd for a week. Sheridan stood on a balcony, under a big tree, coolly smoking a cigar. His looks and manner impress'd me favorably.

May 22.—Have been taking a walk along Pennsylvania avenue and Seventh street north. The city is full of soldiers, running around loose. Officers everywhere, of all grades. All have the weather-beaten look of practical service. It is a sight I never tire of. All the armies are now here (or portions of them,) for to-morrow's review. You see them swarming like bees everywhere.

The Grand Review.

For two days now the broad spaces of Pennsylvania avenue along to Treasury hill, and so by detour around to the President's house, and so up to Georgetown, and across the aqueduct bridge, have been alive with a magnificent sight, the returning armies. In their wide ranks stretching clear across the Avenue, I watch them march or ride along, at a brisk pace, through two whole days—infantry, cavalry, artillery—some 200,-000 men. Some days afterwards one or two other corps; and then, still afterwards, a good part of Sherman's immense army, brought up from Charleston, Savannah, &c.

18. shoulders, hanging] *MDW:* shoulders and hanging
20. soldiers; brigade] *MDW:* soldiers. Quite all Americans. (The Americans are the handsomest race that ever trod the earth.) They came clattering along, brigade

The Grand Review.
    Printed from a clipping of *MDW*, p. 52. Not previously published.
    2–3. The words "and so up to Georgetown, and across the aqueduct bridge," are enclosed in parentheses in *MDW*.
    7. men. Some] *MDW:* men . . . . Some
    7. corps; and] *MDW:* Corps . . . . and

15

20

25

5

Western Soldiers.

May 26–7.—The streets, the public buildings and grounds of Washington, still swarm with soldiers from Illinois, Indiana, Ohio, Missouri, Iowa, and all the Western States. I am continually meeting and talking with them. They often speak to me first, and always show great sociability, and glad to have a good interchange of chat. These Western soldiers are more slow in their movements, and in their intellectual quality also; have no extreme alertness. They are larger in size, have a more serious physiognomy, are continually looking at you as they pass in the street. They are largely animal, and handsomely so. During the war I have been at times with the Fourteenth, Fifteenth, Seventeenth, and Twentieth Corps. I always feel drawn toward the men, and like their personal contact when we are crowded close together, as frequently these days in the street-cars. They all think the world of General Sherman; call him "old Bill," or sometimes "uncle Billy."

A Soldier on Lincoln.

May 28.—As I sat by the bedside of a sick Michigan soldier in hospital to-day, a convalescent from the adjoining bed rose and came to me, and presently we began talking. He was a middle-aged man, belonged to the 2d Virginia regiment, but lived in Racine, Ohio, and had a family there. He spoke of President Lincoln, and said: "The war is over, and many are lost. And now we have lost the best, the fairest, the truest man in America. Take him altogether, he was the best man this country

Western Soldiers.

Printed from clippings of MDW, pp. 52–53. First published in NYWG, Sixth Paper, "Ten Years," under the same subtitle; paragraphs 17 and 18.

 1. *May 26–7.*] NYWG: *May 26–9,* 1865.
 2. Washington, still swarm with] NYWG: Washington swarm all day long with
 3. States. I am] NYWG: States, temporarily camped here in Sherman's returning armies. I am
 5. chat. These] MDW: chat . . . . These] [After "chat." NYWG begins a new paragraph.]
 9–11. The sentence beginning "During" is enclosed in parentheses in MDW.

A Soldier on Lincoln.

Printed from a clipping of MDW, p. 53, where it is without subtitle. Not previously published.

ever produced. It was quite a while I thought very different; but some time before the murder, that's the way I have seen it." There was deep earnestness in the soldier. (I found upon further talk he had known   10
Mr. Lincoln personally, and quite closely, years before.) He was a veteran; was now in the fifth year of his service; was a cavalry man, and had been in a good deal of hard fighting.

Two Brothers, One South, One North.

May 28-9.—I staid to-night a long time by the bedside of a new patient, a young Baltimorean, aged about 19 years, W. S. P., (2d Maryland, southern,) very feeble, right leg amputated, can't sleep hardly at all—has taken a great deal of morphine, which, as usual, is costing more than it comes to. Evidently very intelligent and well bred—very affec-   5
tionate—held on to my hand, and put it by his face, not willing to let me leave. As I was lingering, soothing him in his pain, he says to me suddenly, "I hardly think you know who I am—I don't wish to impose upon you—I am a rebel soldier." I said I did not know that, but it made no difference. Visiting him daily for about two weeks after that, while he   10
lived, (death had mark'd him, and he was quite alone,) I loved him much, always kiss'd him, and he did me. In an adjoining ward I found his brother, an officer of rank, a Union soldier, a brave and religious man, (Col. Clifton K. Prentiss, sixth Maryland infantry, Sixth corps, wounded in one of the engagements at Petersburgh, April 2—linger'd, suffer'd   15
much, died in Brooklyn, Aug. 20, '65.) It was in the same battle both were hit. One was a strong Unionist, the other Secesh; both fought on their respective sides, both badly wounded, and both brought together here after a separation of four years. Each died for his cause.

1-2. in hospital] *MDW:* in a Hospital
9. seen it." There] *MDW:* seen it.". . . . . . .There

Two Brothers, One South, One North.

Printed from a clipping of *MDW*, p. 53. Not previously published. This section was reprinted with only minor changes in punctuation in "Army Hospitals and Cases," *Century Magazine*, October, 1888, Vol. 36, p. 828, but omitted in the article as reprinted in *NB* (cf. "Last of the War Cases," *Prose 1892*, II).
10. difference. Visiting] *MDW:* difference. . . . . . .Visiting
12. After "did me." *MDW* begins a new paragraph.
19. after a separation of] *MDW:* after absence of

Some Sad Cases Yet.

May 31.—James H. Williams, aged 21, 3d Virginia cavalry.— About as mark'd a case of a strong man brought low by a complication of diseases, (laryngitis, fever, debility and diarrhœa,) as I have ever seen— has superb physique, remains swarthy yet, and flushed and red with
5 fever—is altogether flighty—flesh of his great breast and arms tremulous, and pulse pounding away with treble quickness—lies a good deal of the time in a partial sleep, but with low muttering and groans—a sleep in which there is no rest. Powerful as he is, and so young, he will not be able to stand many more days of the strain and sapping heat of yesterday and
10 to-day. His throat is in a bad way, tongue and lips parch'd. When I ask him how he feels, he is able just to articulate, "I feel pretty bad yet, old man," and looks at me with his great bright eyes. Father, John Williams, Millensport, Ohio.

June 9–10.—I have been sitting late to-night by the bedside of a
15 wounded captain, a special friend of mine, lying with a painful fracture of left leg in one of the hospitals, in a large ward partially vacant. The lights were put out, all but a little candle, far from where I sat. The full moon shone in through the windows, making long, slanting silvery patches on the floor. All was still, my friend too was silent, but could not sleep; so I
20 sat there by him, slowly wafting the fan, and occupied with the musings that arose out of the scene, the long shadowy ward, the beautiful ghostly moonlight on the floor, the white beds, here and there an occupant with huddled form, the bed-clothes thrown off. The hospitals have a number of cases of sun-stroke and exhaustion by heat, from the late reviews. There
25 are many such from the Sixth corps, from the hot parade of day before yesterday. (Some of these shows cost the lives of scores of men.)

Sunday, Sep. 10.—Visited Douglas and Stanton hospitals. They are quite full. Many of the cases are bad ones, lingering wounds, and old

Some Sad Cases Yet.

Printed from clippings of MDW, pp. 53–54, where it is without subtitle. Not previously published.

15. a special friend] MDW: a friend
23. After "thrown off." MDW begins a new paragraph.
28–29. old sickness.] MDW: old cases of sickness.
30. them. I] MDW: them.......I

Calhoun's Real Monument.

Printed from clippings of MDW, pp. 54–55. First published in NYWG, the Sixth Paper of "Ten Years," as paragraph 16, the same subtitle, but dated, at the beginning of the first line, "*May 12, 1865.*" In NYWG this section immediately precedes the section subtitled "Western Soldiers." Whitman's reason for removing it from

sickness. There is a more than usual look of despair on the countenances of many of the men; hope has left them. I went through the wards, talking as 30 usual. There are several here from the confederate army whom I had seen in other hospitals, and they recognized me. Two were in a dying condition.

Calhoun's Real Monument.

In one of the hospital tents for special cases, as I sat to-day tending a new amputation, I heard a couple of neighboring soldiers talking to each other from their cots. One down with fever, but improving, had come up belated from Charleston not long before. The other was what we now call an "old veteran," (*i.e.*, he was a Connecticut youth, probably of less than 5 the age of twenty-five years, the four last of which he had spent in active service in the war in all parts of the country.) The two were chatting of one thing and another. The fever soldier spoke of John C. Calhoun's monument, which he had seen, and was describing it. The veteran said: "I have seen Calhoun's monument. That you saw is not the real monu- 10 ment. But I have seen it. It is the desolated, ruined south; nearly the whole generation of young men between seventeen and thirty destroyed or maim'd; all the old families used up—the rich impoverish'd, the plantations cover'd with weeds, the slaves unloos'd and become the masters, and the name of southerner blacken'd with every shame—all that is Calhoun's 15 real monument."

Hospitals Closing.

October 3.—There are two army hospitals now remaining. I went to the largest of these (Douglas) and spent the afternoon and evening. There

---

this sequence is not apparent, but one consequence of the shift probably was the insertion of the word "belated" in line 4.
  3–4. up belated from] *NYWG:* up from
  10. "I have] *MDW* and *NYWG:* "*I* have
  10. That] *MDW* and *NYWG:* *That*
  12. thirty] *MDW* and *NYWG:* fifty
  15–16. that is Calhoun's real] *MDW* and *NYWG:* *that* is Calhoun's *real*

  Hospitals Closing.
  Printed, except the last paragraph, from a clipping of *MDW*, p. 55, where it is without the subtitle. Not previously published.
    1. are two] *MDW:* are only two

are many sad cases, old wounds, incurable sickness, and some of the wounded from the March and April battles before Richmond. Few realize how sharp and bloody those closing battles were. Our men exposed themselves more than usual; press'd ahead without urging. Then the southerners fought with extra desperation. Both sides knew that with the successful chasing of the rebel cabal from Richmond, and the occupation of that city by the national troops, the game was up. The dead and wounded were unusually many. Of the wounded the last lingering driblets have been brought to hospital here. I find many rebel wounded here, and have been extra busy to-day 'tending to the worst cases of them with the rest.

Oct., Nov. and Dec., '65—Sundays.—Every Sunday of these months visited Harewood hospital out in the woods, pleasant and recluse, some two and a half or three miles north of the capitol. The situation is healthy, with broken ground, grassy slopes and patches of oak woods, the trees large and fine. It was one of the most extensive of the hospitals, now reduced to four or five partially occupied wards, the numerous others being vacant. In November, this became the last military hospital kept up by the government, all the others being closed. Cases of the worst and most incurable wounds, obstinate illness, and of poor fellows who have no homes to go to, are found here.

Dec. 10—Sunday.—Again spending a good part of the day at Harewood. I write this about an hour before sundown. I have walk'd out for a few minutes to the edge of the woods to soothe myself with the hour and scene. It is a glorious, warm, golden-sunny, still afternoon. The only noise is from a crowd of cawing crows, on some trees three hundred yards distant. Clusters of gnats swimming and dancing in the air in all directions. The oak leaves are thick under the bare trees, and give a strong and delicious perfume. Inside the wards everything is gloomy. Death is there. As I enter'd, I was confronted by it the first thing; a corpse of a poor soldier, just dead, of typhoid fever. The attendants had just straighten'd the limbs, put coppers on the eyes, and were laying it out.

3. cases, old wounds, incurable] *MDW:* cases, some old wounds, some of incurable
4. Richmond. Few] *MDW:* Richmond . . . . (Few
4–12. Beginning with "Few realize" *MDW* encloses the rest of this paragraph in parentheses.
10. many. Of the wounded the last] *MDW:* many . . . . Of the wounded, both our own and the rebel, the last
17. hospitals, now] *MDW:* Hospitals—but now
19. being vacant. In] *MDW:* being entirely vacant. The patients are the leavings of the other Hospitals; many of them very sad cases indeed. In
21. wounds, obstinate] *MDW:* wounds, and obstinate
24. Harewood. I write this about] *MDW:* Harewood. As I write this, it is about
30. perfume. Inside] *MDW:* perfume . . . . Inside
31. thing; a corpse] *MDW:* thing. A corpse

The roads.—A great recreation, the past three years, has been in
taking long walks out from Washington, five, seven, perhaps ten miles   35
and back; generally with my friend Peter Doyle, who is as fond of it as I
am. Fine moonlight nights, over the perfect military roads, hard and
smooth—or Sundays—we had these delightful walks, never to be forgotten. The roads connecting Washington and the numerous forts around
the city, made one useful result, at any rate, out of the war.   40

Typical Soldiers.

Even the typical soldiers I have been personally intimate with,—it
seems to me if I were to make a list of them it would be like a city
directory. Some few only have I mention'd in the foregoing pages—most
are dead—a few yet living. There is Reuben Farwell, of Michigan,
(little 'Mitch;') Benton H. Wilson, color-bearer, 185th New York; Wm.   5
Stansberry; Manvill Winterstein, Ohio; Bethuel Smith; Capt. Simms, of
51st New York, (kill'd at Petersburgh mine explosion,) Capt. Sam.
Pooley and Lieut. Fred. McReady, same reg't. Also, same reg't., my
brother, George W. Whitman—in active service all through, four years,
re-enlisting twice—was promoted, step by step, (several times im-   10
mediately after battles,) lieutenant, captain, major and lieut. colonel—was
in the actions at Roanoke, Newbern, 2d Bull Run, Chantilly, South
Mountain, Antietam, Fredericksburgh, Vicksburgh, Jackson, the bloody
conflicts of the Wilderness, and at Spottsylvania, Cold Harbor, and afterwards around Petersburgh; at one of these latter was taken prisoner, and   15
pass'd four or five months in secesh military prisons, narrowly escaping
with life, from a severe fever, from starvation and half-nakedness in the
winter. (What a history that 51st New York had! Went out early—
march'd, fought everywhere—was in storms at sea, nearly wreck'd—
storm'd forts—tramp'd hither and yon in Virginia, night and day, sum-   20

34–40. Not previously published; from an autograph MS.

Typical Soldiers.

Printed from a clipping of MDW, "Notes," p. 59. Not previously published.
   1–2. I have . . . it] MDW: I was personally intimate with, and knew well
—it
   7. Petersburgh] MDW: Petersburg
   9. Whitman—in active] MDW: Whitman—in '61 a young man working in
Brooklyn as a carpenter—was not supposed to have any taste for soldiering—but
volunteer'd in the ranks at once on the breaking out of the War—continued in active
   15. Petersburgh; at] MDW: Petersburg. At
   15. latter was] MDW: latter he was
   18–22. In MDW the lines in parentheses are a separate paragraph enclosed in
brackets; the sentence beginning "I strengthen" is a separate paragraph.

mer of '62—afterwards Kentucky and Mississippi—re-enlisted—was in all the engagements and campaigns, as above.) I strengthen and comfort myself much with the certainty that the capacity for just such regiments, (hundreds, thousands of them) is inexhaustible in the United States, and
25 that there isn't a county nor a township in the republic—nor a street in any city—but could turn out, and, on occasion, would turn out, lots of just such typical soldiers, whenever wanted.

"Convulsiveness."

As I have look'd over the proof-sheets of the preceding pages, I have once or twice fear'd that my diary would prove, at best, but a batch of convulsively written reminiscences. Well, be it so. They are but parts of the actual distraction, heat, smoke and excitement of those times. The war
5 itself, with the temper of society preceding it, can indeed be best described by that very word *convulsiveness*.

Three Years Summ'd Up.

During those three years in hospital, camp or field, I made over six hundred visits or tours, and went, as I estimate, counting all, among from

26. would] MDW: *would*
27. typical soldiers] MDW: *Typical Soldiers*
27. After "whenever wanted." MDW ("Notes," pp. 59–60) has two short paragraphs not reprinted in SDC. See Appendix XI, 4.

"Convulsiveness."
Printed from a clipping of MDW, "Notes," p. 59, where it is the first paragraph, immediately preceding the paragraphs subtitled "Typical Soldiers."
1. preceding pages, I] MDW: preceding Memoranda, I
2. my diary would] MDW: my little tract would
3. but parts] MDW: but items, parts
4. times. The war] MDW: times—of the qualities that then and there took shape. The War

Three Years Summ'd Up.
Printed from clippings of MDW, pp. 55–56. Originally published in two paragraphs, subtitled "The Three Years," as the conclusion of the Sixth Paper of "Ten Years," in NYWG.
The first sentence of NYWG, not reprinted, is as follows: "With these lines—though I have only broached or suggested the exhaustless stores of romance, daring, pathos, &c., of the war—I must conclude my sketches."
1. During those three . . . I] MDW: During my past three . . . I] NYWG: During my three years in the army hospitals, and in the field, ending in 1865, I

eighty thousand to a hundred thousand of the wounded and sick, as sustainer of spirit and body in some degree, in time of need. These visits varied from an hour or two, to all day or night; for with dear or critical   5
cases I generally watch'd all night. Sometimes I took up my quarters in the hospital, and slept or watch'd there several nights in succession. Those three years I consider the greatest privilege and satisfaction, (with all their feverish excitements and physical deprivations and lamentable sights,) and, of course, the most profound lesson of my life. I can say that   10
in my ministerings I comprehended all, whoever came in my way, northern or southern, and slighted none. It arous'd and brought out and decided undream'd-of depths of emotion. It has given me my most fervent views of the true *ensemble* and extent of the States. While I was with wounded and sick in thousands of cases from the New England States, and from   15
New York, New Jersey, and Pennsylvania, and from Michigan, Wisconsin, Ohio, Indiana, Illinois, and all the Western States, I was with more or less from all the States, North and South, without exception. I was with many from the border States, especially from Maryland and Virginia, and found, during those lurid years 1862–63, far more Union southerners,   20
especially Tennesseans, than is supposed. I was with many rebel officers and men among our wounded, and gave them always what I had, and tried to cheer them the same as any. I was among the army teamsters considerably, and, indeed, always found myself drawn to them. Among the black soldiers, wounded or sick, and in the contraband camps, I also   25

   2. visits or tours, and] *NYWG:* visits, and
   2. estimate, counting all, among] *MDW* and *NYWG:* estimate, among
   6. I generally watch'd] *MDW:* I always watch'd] *NYWG:* I watched
   7. After "succession." *NYWG* begins a new paragraph.
   10. lesson of] *MDW* and *NYWG:* lesson and reminiscence, of
   11–12. all, . . . none. It arous'd] *MDW:* all, . . . none. It afforded me, too,
the perusal of those subtlest, rarest, divinest volumes of Humanity, laid bare in its
inmost recesses, and of actual life and death, better than the finest, most labor'd narratives, histories, poems in the libraries. It arous'd] *NYWG: all* and slighted none.
(Perhaps I am a little vain about it.) It afforded me, too, the perusal of those infinite,
subtlest, rarest volumes of Humanity, laid bare in its inmost recesses, and of actual
life and death, better than the finest, most labored shams in the libraries. It aroused
   13. my most] *MDW* and *NYWG:* my plainest and most
   14. I was with] *NYWG:* I have been with
   17. and all the] *NYWG:* and the
   17. I was with] *NYWG:* I have been with
   18. I was with] *NYWG:* I have been with
   20. years 1862–63] *MDW* and *NYWG:* years 1862–65
   [This change is not indicated on Whitman's copy prepared for the printers of
SDC. Presumably it was made on the galley proof.]
   21. I was with] *NYWG:* I have been with
   22. gave] *NYWG:* given
   23. I was among] *NYWG:* I have been among
   24. found] *NYWG:* find

took my way whenever in their neighborhood, and did what I could for them.

The Million Dead, Too, Summ'd Up.

The dead in this war—there they lie, strewing the fields and woods and valleys and battle-fields of the south—Virginia, the Peninsula—Malvern hill and Fair Oaks—the banks of the Chickahominy—the ter-races of Fredericksburgh—Antietam bridge—the grisly ravines of
5   Manassas—the bloody promenade of the Wilderness—the varieties of the *strayed* dead, (the estimate of the War department is 25,000 national soldiers kill'd in battle and never buried at all, 5,000 drown'd—15,000 inhumed by strangers, or on the march in haste, in hitherto unfound localities—2,000 graves cover'd by sand and mud by Mississippi freshets,
10   3,000 carried away by caving-in of banks, &c.,)—Gettysburgh, the West, Southwest—Vicksburgh—Chattanooga—the trenches of Peters-burgh—the numberless battles, camps, hospitals everywhere—the crop reap'd by the mighty reapers, typhoid, dysentery, inflammations—and blackest and loathesomest of all, the dead and living burial-pits, the
15   prison-pens of Andersonville, Salisbury, Belle-Isle, &c., (not Dante's pictured hell and all its woes, its degradations, filthy torments, excell'd those prisons)—the dead, the dead, the dead—*our* dead—or South or North, ours all, (all, all, all, finally dear to me)—or East or West—Atlantic coast or Mississippi valley—somewhere they crawl'd to die,
20   alone, in bushes, low gullies, or on the sides of hills—(there, in secluded spots, their skeletons, bleach'd bones, tufts of hair, buttons, fragments of clothing, are occasionally found yet)—our young men once so handsome and so joyous, taken from us—the son from the mother, the husband from the wife, the dear friend from the dear friend—the clusters of camp
25   graves, in Georgia, the Carolinas, and in Tennessee—the single graves

The Million Dead, Too, Summ'd Up.
    Printed from clippings of MDW, pp. 56–57, where the sidehead is "The Million Dead, too, summ'd up—The Unknown." Not previously published.
    11. Vicksburgh] MDW: Vicksburg
    19. valley—somewhere] MDW: Valley—Some where
    25–26. graves left in] MDW: graves in
    31. entire saturated] MDW: entire is saturated
    33. forever, in every future grain] MDW: forever, and every grain
    38. are now, I believe, over] MDW: are over
    42. we see, and ages] MDW: we see, and see, and ages
    44. In MDW the word "Unknown." is printed in heavy black type, all capitals, in the center of the next line space.

left in the woods or by the road-side, (hundreds, thousands, obliterated) —the corpses floated down the rivers, and caught and lodged, (dozens, scores, floated down the upper Potomac, after the cavalry engagements, the pursuit of Lee, following Gettysburgh)—some lie at the bottom of the sea—the general million, and the special cemeteries in almost all the   30 States—the infinite dead—(the land entire saturated, perfumed with their impalpable ashes' exhalation in Nature's chemistry distill'd, and shall be so forever, in every future grain of wheat and ear of corn, and every flower that grows, and every breath we draw)—not only Northern dead leavening Southern soil—thousands, aye tens of thousands, of   35 Southerners, crumble to-day in Northern earth.

And everywhere among these countless graves—everywhere in the many soldier Cemeteries of the Nation, (there are now, I believe, over seventy of them)—as at the time in the vast trenches, the depositories of slain, Northern and Southern, after the great battles—not only where the   40 scathing trail passed those years, but radiating since in all the peaceful quarters of the land—we see, and ages yet may see, on monuments and gravestones, singly or in masses, to thousands or tens of thousands, the significant word **Unknown.**

(In some of the cemeteries nearly *all* the dead are unknown. At   45 Salisbury, N. C., for instance, the known are only 85, while the unknown are 12,027, and 11,700 of these are buried in trenches. A national monument has been put up here, by order of Congress, to mark the spot —but what visible, material monument can ever fittingly commemorate that spot?)   50

The Real War Will Never Get in the Books.

And so good-bye to the war. I know not how it may have been, or may be, to others—to me the main interest I found, (and still, on recollec-

---

45. In MDW this line is printed without paragraph indention.
50. After this line, ending this section, MDW continues with two paragraphs, pp. 57–58, without subtitle, not afterwards reprinted. See Appendix XI, 3.

The Real War Will Never Get in the Books.
Printed from clippings of MDW, pp. 4–6, where it is without subtitle. Only the last paragraph of this section was previously published: in NYWG, part of paragraph 20, the second under the subtitle "The Inner Points of the War Can Never Be Written," Second Paper of "Ten Years."
1. The first sentence, not in MDW, is inserted in MS.
2. interest I] MDW: interest of the War, I

tion, find,) in the rank and file of the armies, both sides, and in those specimens amid the hospitals, and even the dead on the field. To me the
5   points illustrating the latent personal character and eligibilities of these States, in the two or three millions of American young and middle-aged men, North and South, embodied in those armies—and especially the one-third or one-fourth of their number, stricken by wounds or disease at some time in the course of the contest—were of more significance even
10   than the political interests involved. (As so much of a race depends on how it faces death, and how it stands personal anguish and sickness. As, in the glints of emotions under emergencies, and the indirect traits and asides in Plutarch, we get far profounder clues to the antique world than all its more formal history.)
15   Future years will never know the seething hell and the black infernal background of countless minor scenes and interiors, (not the official surface-courteousness of the Generals, not the few great battles) of the Secession war; and it is best they should not—the real war will never get in the books. In the mushy influences of current times, too, the fervid
20   atmosphere and typical events of those years are in danger of being totally forgotten. I have at night watch'd by the side of a sick man in the hospital, one who could not live many hours. I have seen his eyes flash and burn as he raised himself and recurr'd to the cruelties on his surrender'd brother, and mutilations of the corpse afterward. (See, in the
25   preceding pages, the incident at Upperville—the seventeen kill'd as in the description, were left there on the ground. After they dropt dead, no

---

    3–4. find,) in . . . hospitals,] *MDW:* find,) in those specimens, and in the ambulance, the Hospital,
      7. those armies] *MDW:* the armies
    10–11. on how it faces death] *MDW:* on what it thinks of death
    13. Plutarch, we] *MDW:* Plutarch, &c., we
    16–17. interiors, (not . . . battles) of] *MDW:* interiors, (not the few great battles) of
    18–19. not—the . . . In] *MDW:* not. In
    19. times, too, the] *MDW:* times the
    23. he raised himself and recurr'd] *MDW:* he recurr'd
    24–25. the preceding pages] *MDW:* the following pages
    30. minutiae] *MDW:* minutia
    33. language, . . . his appetite] *MDW:* language, his appetite
    37–53. Most of this was published in *NYWG*, in paragraph 22, the second under the subtitle "The Inner Points of the War Can Never Be Written," in the Second Paper of "Ten Years." Paragraph 21, the first under that subtitle, was not reprinted. See Appendix VI, 1.
    37–39. The first two sentences of this paragraph appear in *MDW* but not in *NYWG*.
    37. The preceding notes may] *MDW:* The present Memoranda may

one touch'd them—all were made sure of, however. The carcasses were left for the citzens to bury or not, as they chose.)

Such was the war. It was not a quadrille in a ball-room. Its interior history will not only never be written—its practicality, minutiæ of deeds and passions, will never be even suggested. The actual soldier of 1862–'65, North and South, with all his ways, his incredible dauntlessness, habits, practices, tastes, language, his fierce friendship, his appetite, rankness, his superb strength and animality, lawless gait, and a hundred unnamed lights and shades of camp, I say, will never be written—perhaps must not and should not be.

The preceding notes may furnish a few stray glimpses into that life, and into those lurid interiors, never to be fully convey'd to the future. The hospital part of the drama from '61 to '65, deserves indeed to be recorded. Of that many-threaded drama, with its sudden and strange surprises, its confounding of prophecies, its moments of despair, the dread of foreign interference, the interminable campaigns, the bloody battles, the mighty and cumbrous and green armies, the drafts and bounties—the immense money expenditure, like a heavy-pouring constant rain—with, over the whole land, the last three years of the struggle, an unending, universal mourning-wail of women, parents, orphans—the marrow of the tragedy concentrated in those Army Hospitals—(it seem'd sometimes as if the whole interest of the land, North and South, was one vast central hospital, and all the rest of the affair but flanges)—those forming the untold and unwritten history of the war—infinitely greater (like life's) than the few

30

35

40

45

50

38. interiors, never] MDW: interiors of the period, never

38–39. future. The hospital] MDW: future. For that purpose, and for what goes along with it, the Hospital

39–40. recorded. Of] MDW: recorded—(I but suggest it.) Of

40. Of that many-threaded drama, with] NYWG: Through this time—indeed through the whole of the vast and many-threaded drama of conflict that followed, with

43–44. cumbrous . . . rain—with] NYWG: cumbrous and fresh armies, the volunteering and drafts and bounties—with

45. land, . . . an] NYWG: land, North and South, an

46–49. orphans—the . . . the untold] MDW: [the same except it omits "Army" before "Hospitals" in line 47.] NYWG: orphans—while of the military movements of all those, and the ups and downs from 1861 to 1865, the ostensible statistics, numbers, dates, &c., have been put on record, (though much is yet behind to be gradually unearthed, disentangled, clarified, and to furnish points in History, Literature, Art, and even Philosophy, for ages and ages to come,) there was ever going on, in by-scenes or behind the scenes, South and North, a mass of complicated weft and warp of subordinate occurrences, not at the time registered, and perhaps never will be—though in some respects it identifies the most important part of the whole. This formed, and will ever form, the vast Untold

50. of the war] NYWG: of our Civil War

scraps and distortions that are ever told or written. Think how much, and of importance, will be—how much, civic and military, has already been —buried in the grave, in eternal darkness.

An Interregnum Paragraph.

Several years now elapse before I resume my diary. I continued at Washington working in the Attorney-General's department through '66 and '67, and some time afterward. In February '73 I was stricken down by paralysis, gave up my desk, and migrated to Camden, New Jersey, where I lived during '74 and '75, quite unwell—but after that began to grow better; commenc'd going for weeks at a time, even for months, down in the country, to a charmingly recluse and rural spot along Timber creek, twelve or thirteen miles from where it enters the Delaware river. Domicil'd at the farm-house of my friends, the Staffords, near by, I lived half the time along this creek and its adjacent fields and lanes. And it is to my life here that I, perhaps, owe partial recovery (a sort of second wind, or semi-renewal of the lease of life) from the prostration of 1874–'75. If the notes of that outdoor life could only prove as glowing to you, reader

51. scraps and distortions] *NYWG*: scraps and ends and distortions
53. darkness.] *MDW*: darkness!. . . . . . .But to my Memoranda.] *NYWG*: darkness!
53. In *MDW* this paragraph is followed by the section subtitled "Falmouth, Va., opposite Fredericksburgh, December 21, 1862." (In *SDC* "After First Fredericksburg," *q.v.*) In *NYWG* it is followed by a paragraph subtitled "What the War Was Really to Decide." Part of this paragraph is used as the last sentence of paragraph 6 of "Origins of Attempted Secession," *Prose 1892*, II, *q.v.*

An Interregnum Paragraph.
Printed from an autograph MS and two short clippings from the second installment, April 9, 1881, of Whitman's series in the *Critic* entitled "How I Get Around at Sixty and Take Notes."
1–8. Through the sentence ending "river." printed from an autograph MS.
9–12. Beginning with "Domicil'd" and ending with "1874–'75," printed from a clipping of the last six lines of paragraph 2 of the *Critic* article. Lines much like them were previously printed as paragraph 10 of the article "Winter Sunshine" in the Philadelphia *Times*, Jan. 26, 1879. The *PT* lines are included in the collation.
9. farm-house of my friends] *CR:* farm of my friends] *PT:* farm of my dear and valued friends
9–10. I lived . . . along] *CR:* I lived along] *PT:* I have passed good parts of the last two or three summers along
10–11. And . . . that] *CR:* And it is to my experiences and my outdoor life here that] *PT:* And indeed it is to my experiences and my outdoor life here—conquering, catching the health and physical virtue of Nature, by close and persistent contact with it at first hand—that
11. owe partial] *PT:* owe recovery, or partial
11–12. from the prostration of 1874–'75.] *CR:* from my prostration of 1873–

dear, as the experience itself was to me. Doubtless in the course of the
following, the fact of invalidism will crop out, (I call myself *a half-*   15
Paralytic these days, and reverently bless the Lord it is no worse,) between some of the lines—but I get my share of fun and healthy hours, and
shall try to indicate them. (The trick is, I find, to tone your wants and
tastes low down enough, and make much of negatives, and of mere daylight and the skies.)   20

New Themes Entered Upon.

1876, '77.—I find the woods in mid-May and early June my best
places for composition.* Seated on logs or stumps there, or resting on rails,
nearly all the following memoranda have been jotted down. Wherever I
go, indeed, winter or summer, city or country, alone at home or traveling,
I must take notes—(the ruling passion strong in age and disablement, and   5
even the approach of—but I must not say it yet.) Then underneath the
following excerpta—crossing the *t's* and dotting the *i's* of certain moderate movements of late years—I am fain to fancy the foundations of quite a
lesson learn'd. After you have exhausted what there is in business, politics,

'76.] *PT:* from my paralysis of 1873, '74, '75 and '76.
    12–20. These lines, beginning "If the notes," printed from a clipping of the last
nine lines of the first paragraph of *CR.*
    12–13. If . . . could] *CR:* If they could
    14–15. Doubtless . . . the fact] *CR:* Doubtless the fact
    17–18. hours, and . . . them. (The] *CR:* hours—and try to indicate them here.
(The
    20. The first six lines of *CR,* paragraph 1, not reprinted, are as follows:
    "*April 4, '81.*—Some might think the following notes out of keeping with the
weather this season. On the contrary, (I suggest), just as you want red and orange
in your present room-trimmings, and reserve pale-blue and green till August, my summer reminiscences may well come in for latter winter reading." [For the first nine
lines of *CR,* paragraph 2 (except the first eleven words, to wit: "Frequent portions of
the last four years, especially summers, I have") see "A Happy Hour's Command"
(above, lines 45–49). For *CR,* paragraph 3, see "An Early Summer Reveille" (below,
lines 15–18).]
    New Themes Entered Upon.
    Printed from an autograph MS and a clipping of the first two paragraphs of
the first number of "How I Get Around," *Critic,* Jan. 29, 1881.
    1–3. The first two sentences were printed from an autograph MS.
    3–17. Printed from the clipping.
    3–4. Wherever . . . alone] *CR: Jan.* 26, 1881.—Wherever I go yet, winter or
summer, city or down in the country, or alone
    7. excerpta] *CR:* excerpts
    8. foundations] *CR:* foundation
    9–10. business, . . . on—have] *CR:* business, literature, politics, conviviality,
love, and even religion—have

10 conviviality, love, and so on—have found that none of these finally satisfy, or permanently wear—what remains? Nature remains; to bring out from their torpid recesses, the affinities of a man or woman with the open air, the trees, fields, the changes of seasons—the sun by day and the stars of heaven by night. We will begin from these convictions. Literature flies so
15 high and is so hotly spiced, that our notes may seem hardly more than breaths of common air, or draughts of water to drink. But that is part of our lesson.

Dear, soothing, healthy, restoration-hours—after three confining years of paralysis—after the long strain of the war, and its wounds and death.

20 * Without apology for the abrupt change of field and atmosphere—after what I have put in the preceding fifty or sixty pages—temporary episodes, thank heaven!—I restore my book to the bracing and buoyant equilibrium of concrete outdoor Nature, the only permanent reliance for sanity of book or human life.
25 Who knows, (I have it in my fancy, my ambition,) but the pages now ensuing may carry ray of sun, or smell of grass or corn, or call of bird, or gleam of stars by night, or snow-flakes falling fresh and mystic, to denizen of heated city house, or tired workman or workwoman?—or may-be in sick-room or prison—to serve as cooling breeze, or Nature's aroma, to some fever'd
30 mouth or latent pulse.

Entering a Long Farm-Lane.

As every man has his hobby-liking, mine is for a real farm-lane fenced by old chestnut-rails gray-green with dabs of moss and lichen, copious weeds and briers growing in spots athwart the heaps of stray-pick'd stones at the fence bases—irregular paths worn between, and
5 horse and cow tracks—all characteristic accompaniments marking and scenting the neighborhood in their seasons—apple-tree blossoms in forward April—pigs, poultry, a field of August buckwheat, and in another

11–12. remains; . . . the affinities] CR: remains. To bring out from their torpid recess, (where in nineteen cases out of twenty they sleep the sleep of death,) the affinities
13. trees, fields, the] CR: trees, birds, the
14. night. We . . . convictions.] CR: night. So cheap, so close at hand—little things, perhaps, yet unending, unpalling medicine to the soul, when all else has failed. That dumb Nature—but not cold or bloodless—full of eloquence, emotion, nourishment.
Even though crudely, we will begin and carry out our notes from these convictions.
15. that our notes may] CR: that they may
18–19. Printed from an autograph MS.
20–30. This footnote was also printed from an autograph MS; the first paragraph

the long flapping tassels of maize—and so to the pond, the expansion of
the creek, the secluded-beautiful, with young and old trees, and such
recesses and vistas.   10

To the Spring and Brook.

So, still sauntering on, to the spring under the willows—musical as
soft clinking glasses—pouring a sizeable stream, thick as my neck, pure
and clear, out from its vent where the bank arches over like a great brown
shaggy eyebrow or mouth-roof—gurgling, gurgling ceaselessly—meaning, saying something, of course (if one could only translate it)—always   5
gurgling there, the whole year through—never giving out—oceans of
mint, blackberries in summer—choice of light and shade—just the place
for my July sun-baths and water-baths too—but mainly the inimitable soft
sound-gurgles of it, as I sit there hot afternoons. How they and all grow
into me, day after day—everything in keeping—the wild, just-palpable   10
perfume, and the dapple of leaf-shadows, and all the natural-medicinal,
elemental-moral influences of the spot.

Babble on, O brook, with that utterance of thine! I too will express
what I have gather'd in my days and progress, native, subterranean, past
—and now thee. Spin and wind thy way—I with thee, a little while, at any   15
rate. As I haunt thee so often, season by season, thou knowest reckest not
me, (yet why be so certain? who can tell?)—but I will learn from thee,
and dwell on thee—receive, copy, print from thee.

An Early Summer Reveille.

Away then to loosen, to unstring the divine bow, so tense, so long.
Away, from curtain, carpet, sofa, book—from "society"—from city house,

in pencil on white paper, the second in black ink on gray paper.

Entering a Long Farm-Lane.
Printed from an autograph MS.

To the Spring and Brook.
Printed from an autograph MS, mostly in pencil.

An Early Summer Reveille.
Printed from an autograph MS in several pieces and from a brief clipping of
the *Critic*, paragraph 3, second number of "How I Get Around."
1–14. Printed from an autograph MS.

street, and modern improvements and luxuries—away to the primitive winding, aforementioned wooded creek, with its untrimm'd bushes and turfy banks—away from ligatures, tight boots, buttons, and the whole cast-iron civilizee life—from entourage of artificial store, machine, studio, office, parlor—from tailordom and fashion's clothes—from any clothes, perhaps, for the nonce, the summer heats advancing, there in those watery, shaded solitudes. Away, thou soul, (let me pick thee out singly, reader dear, and talk in perfect freedom, negligently, confidentially,) for one day and night at least, returning to the naked source-life of us all— to the breast of the great silent savage all-acceptive Mother. Alas! how many of us are so sodden—how many have wander'd so far away, that return is almost impossible.

But to my jottings, taking them as they come, from the heap, without particular selection. There is little consecutiveness in dates. They run any time within nearly five or six years. Each was carelessly pencilled in the open air, at the time and place. The printers will learn this to some vexation perhaps, as much of their copy is from those hastily-written first notes.

Birds Migrating at Midnight.

Did you ever chance to hear the midnight flight of birds passing through the air and darkness overhead, in countless armies, changing their early or late summer habitat? It is something not to be forgotten. A friend called me up just after 12 last night to mark the peculiar noise of unusually immense flocks migrating north (rather late this year.) In the silence, shadow and delicious odor of the hour, (the natural perfume belonging to the night alone,) I thought it rare music. You could *hear* the characteristic motion—once or twice "the rush of mighty wings," but

15–19. Printed from *CR*.
15. But to my jottings] *CR:* But let me proceed to the jottings
16. little consecutiveness] *CR:* no consecutiveness
17. within nearly five or six years] *CR:* within the last three or four years
17–18. was . . . at] *CR:* was pencilled in the open air, and at
19–20. This last sentence was printed from an autograph MS.

Birds Migrating at Midnight.

Printed from an autograph MS, much revised. The first sentence originally began "May 18, '82—" but the date is marked out in red ink.

Bumble-Bees.

Printed from four clippings of an article entitled "Bumble-Bees and Bird-Music" in the Philadelphia *American*, May 14, 1881, consisting of ten of the eighteen

oftener a velvety rustle, long drawn out—sometimes quite near—with continual calls and chirps, and some song-notes. It all lasted from 12 till after 3. Once in a while the species was plainly distinguishable; I could make out the bobolink, tanager, Wilson's thrush, white-crown'd sparrow, and occasionally from high in the air came the notes of the plover.

Bumble-Bees.

May-month—month of swarming, singing, mating birds—the bumble-bee month—month of the flowering lilac—(and then my own birth-month.) As I jot this paragraph, I am out just after sunrise, and down towards the creek. The lights, perfumes, melodies—the blue birds, grass birds and robins, in every direction—the noisy, vocal, natural concert. For undertones, a neighboring wood-pecker tapping his tree, and the distant clarion of chanticleer. Then the fresh earth smells—the colors, the delicate drabs and thin blues of the perspective. The bright green of the grass has receiv'd an added tinge from the last two days' mildness and moisture. How the sun silently mounts in the broad clear sky, on his day's journey! How the warm beams bathe all, and come streaming kissingly and almost hot on my face.

A while since the croaking of the pond frogs and the first white of the dog-wood blossoms. Now the golden dandelions in endless profusion, spotting the ground everywhere. The white cherry and pear-blows—the wild violets, with their blue eyes looking up and saluting my feet, as I saunter the wood-edge—the rosy blush of budding apple-trees—the light-clear emerald hue of the wheat-fields—the darker green of the rye—a warm elasticity pervading the air—the cedar-bushes profusely deck'd with their little brown apples—the summer fully awakening—the con-

paragraphs of the article. Most of the rest of the article was included in later pages of *SDC*.

1. May-month—month of] *PA:* May is here—the month for
3. After "birth-month.)" *PA* has the following sentence not reprinted: "This summer is at least three weeks behind-hand; but from appearances will yet make it up." *PA* begins a new paragraph with "As I".
4. down . . . creek. The] *PA:* down an old farm lane towards a creek running in from the Delaware river 12 miles off. The
9–10. two days' . . . How] *PA:* two days. How
13. A while since the] *PA:* A few days since, the
15. everywhere. The] *PA:* everywhere. So May comes with her shows, lugging and whirling April apace! The
18. emerald hue of] *PA:* emerald green of
19. a warm] *PA:* a moist and warm

vocation of black birds, garrulous flocks of them, gathering on some tree, and making the hour and place noisy as I sit near.

Later.—Nature marches in procession, in sections, like the corps of an army. All have done much for me, and still do. But for the last two days it has been the great wild bee, the humble-bee, or "bumble," as the children call him. As I walk, or hobble, from the farm-house down to the creek, I traverse the before-mention'd lane, fenced by old rails, with many splits, splinters, breaks, holes, &c., the choice habitat of those crooning, hairy insects. Up and down and by and between these rails, they swarm and dart and fly in countless myriads. As I wend slowly along, I am often accompanied with a moving cloud of them. They play a leading part in my morning, midday or sunset rambles, and often dominate the landscape in a way I never before thought of—fill the long lane, not by scores or hundreds only, but by thousands. Large and vivacious and swift, with wonderful momentum and a loud swelling perpetual hum, varied now and then by something almost like a shriek, they dart to and fro, in rapid flashes, chasing each other, and (little things as they are,) conveying to me a new and pronounc'd sense of strength, beauty, vitality and movement. Are they in their mating season? or what is the meaning of this plenitude, swiftness, eagerness, display? As I walk'd, I thought I was follow'd by a particular swarm, but upon observation I saw that it was a rapid succession of changing swarms, one after another.

As I write, I am seated under a big wild-cherry tree—the warm day temper'd by partial clouds and a fresh breeze, neither too heavy nor light —and here I sit long and long, envelop'd in the deep musical drone of these bees, flitting, balancing, darting to and fro about me by hundreds— big fellows with light yellow jackets, great glistening swelling bodies, stumpy heads and gauzy wings—humming their perpetual rich mellow boom. (Is there not a hint in it for a musical composition, of which it

---

22. [The following seven paragraphs of *PA*, omitted at this point, were later used: the first in "Birds and Birds and Birds" (*q.v.*); the next two in "A Couple of Old Friends—A Coleridge Bit" (*q.v.*); and the next four in "An Unknown" and "Bird-Whistling." (*q.v.*).

23–96. These lines, subtitled "Bumble-Bees," follow "Bird-Whistling" in *PA*.

23. *Later.*—Nature] *PA: Middle of May.*—Nature

24. army. All] *PA:* army. The black birds, bluebirds, frogs, dandelions and lilacs advented and had their season, and engrossed my interest. All

26. After "call him." *PA* begins a new paragraph.

27. traverse . . . with] *PA:* traverse a lane of some 80 rods, fenced by old chestnut rails, of drab and straw color—rails with

29. down and by] *PA:* down this lane, and by

43. write, I am seated under] *PA:* write this I am seated on a stout flat old rail, down the lane under

50–51. some bumble-bee symphony?) How it all nourishes] *PA:* some "Bumble-

should be the back-ground? some bumble-bee symphony?) How it all
nourishes, lulls me, in the way most needed; the open air, the rye-fields,
the apple orchards. The last two days have been faultless in sun, breeze,
temperature and everything; never two more perfect days, and I have
enjoy'd them wonderfully. My health is somewhat better, and my spirit at
peace. (Yet the anniversary of the saddest loss and sorrow of my life is
close at hand.)

Another jotting, another perfect day: forenoon, from 7 to 9, two hours
envelop'd in sound of bumble-bees and bird-music. Down in the apple-
trees and in a neighboring cedar were three or four russet-back'd
thrushes, each singing his best, and roulading in ways I never heard
surpass'd. Two hours I abandon myself to hearing them, and indolently
absorbing the scene. Almost every bird I notice has a special time in the
year—sometimes limited to a few days—when it sings its best; and now is
the period of these russet-backs. Meanwhile, up and down the lane, the
darting, droning, musical bumble-bees. A great swarm again for my
entourage as I return home, moving along with me as before.

As I write this, two or three weeks later, I am sitting near the brook
under a tulip tree, 70 feet high, thick with the fresh verdure of its young
maturity—a beautiful object—every branch, every leaf perfect. From top
to bottom, seeking the sweet juice in the blossoms, it swarms with myriads
of these wild bees, whose loud and steady humming makes an undertone
to the whole, and to my mood and the hour. All of which I will bring to a
close by extracting the following verses from Henry A. Beers's little
volume:

> "As I lay yonder in tall grass
> A drunken bumble-bee went past
> Delirious with honey toddy.
> The golden sash about his body

Bee Symphony?") How it all soothes, nourishes
50. *PA* begins a new paragraph with "How it all".
51. needed; the] *PA:* needed! The
57. day: forenoon] *PA:* day. Forenoon
61. to hearing] *PA:* to merely hearing
62. After "the scene." *PA* begins a new paragraph.
66. entourage] *PA: entourage*
67–96. In *PA* this paragraph has the separate subtitle "A Sonata to End With."
67. this, . . . am] *PA:* this I am
70. bottom, . . . it] *PA:* bottom, it
72. will bring] *PA:* will just bring
75–96. These lines constitute all but the last ten lines of the poem "Bumblebee"
in Beers's volume *Odds and Ends: Verses Humorous, Occasional, and Miscellaneous,*
Boston, 1878. They are quoted accurately in *PA* and *SDC* except for very minor
changes in punctuation.

Scarce kept it in his swollen belly
80   Distent with honeysuckle jelly.
Rose liquor and the sweet-pea wine
Had fill'd his soul with song divine;
Deep had he drunk the warm night through,
His hairy thighs were wet with dew.
85   Full many an antic he had play'd
While the world went round through sleep and shade.
Oft had he lit with thirsty lip
Some flower-cup's nectar'd sweets to sip,
When on smooth petals he would slip,
90   Or over tangled stamens trip,
And headlong in the pollen roll'd,
Crawl out quite dusted o'er with gold;
Or else his heavy feet would stumble
Against some bud, and down he'd tumble
95   Amongst the grass; there lie and grumble
In low, soft bass—poor maudlin bumble!"

Cedar-Apples.

As I journey'd to-day in a light wagon ten or twelve miles through
the country, nothing pleas'd me more, in their homely beauty and novelty
(I had either never seen the little things to such advantage, or had never
noticed them before) than that peculiar fruit, with its profuse clear-
5   yellow dangles of inch-long silk or yarn, in boundless profusion spotting
the dark-green cedar bushes—contrasting well with their bronze tufts—
the flossy shreds covering the knobs all over, like a shock of wild hair on
elfin pates. On my ramble afterward down by the creek I pluck'd one from
its bush, and shall keep it. These cedar-apples last only a little while
10   however, and soon crumble and fade.

96. After the poem PA has the following paragraph, not reprinted:
"My notes are written off-hand in the latitude of middle New Jersey. Though
they describe what I see—what appears to me—I dare say the expert ornithologist
or entomologist will detect more than one slip in them. W. W."

Cedar-Apples.
Printed from an autograph MS. The date, April 25, is deleted in the MS,
probably because in the SDC arrangement it was chronologically out of order. Other
revisions in the MS were made apparently for the same reason.

Summer Sights and Indolencies.

June 10th.—As I write, 5½ P.M., here by the creek, nothing can exceed the quiet splendor and freshness around me. We had a heavy shower, with brief thunder and lightning, in the middle of the day; and since, overhead, one of those not uncommon yet indescribable skies (in quality, not details or forms) of limpid blue, with rolling silver-fringed clouds, and a pure-dazzling sun. For underlay, trees in fulness of tender foliage—liquid, reedy, long-drawn notes of birds—based by the fretful mewing of a querulous cat-bird, and the pleasant chippering-shriek of two kingfishers. I have been watching the latter the last half hour, on their regular evening frolic over and in the stream; evidently a spree of the liveliest kind. They pursue each other, whirling and wheeling around, with many a jocund downward dip, splashing the spray in jets of diamonds—and then off they swoop, with slanting wings and graceful flight, sometimes so near me I can plainly see their dark-gray feather-bodies and milk-white necks.

Sundown Perfume—Quail-Notes—the Hermit-Thrush.

June 19th, 4 to 6½, P.M.—Sitting alone by the creek—solitude here, but the scene bright and vivid enough—the sun shining, and quite a fresh wind blowing (some heavy showers last night,) the grass and trees looking their best—the clare-obscure of different greens, shadows, half-shadows, and the dappling glimpses of the water, through recesses— the wild flageolet-note of a quail near by—the just-heard fretting of some hylas down there in the pond—crows cawing in the distance—a drove of young hogs rooting in soft ground near the oak under which I sit—some come sniffing near me, and then scamper away, with grunts. And still the

Summer Sights and Indolencies.
Printed from an autograph MS in pencil with ink revisions. The date in pencil "June—'76 or 7" is crossed out and "June 10" in ink written in; changed to "June 10th," evidently in proof.

Sundown Perfume—Quail-Notes—the Hermit-Thrush.
Printed from an autograph MS, in black ink. The title, inserted, originally began "Cedar-Perfume," later changed to its present form. Near the top of the page " '76" has been written in pencil and crossed out.
4. clare-obscure] MS: clare-oscuro

10   clear notes of the quail—the quiver of leaf-shadows over the paper as I
write—the sky aloft, with white clouds, and the sun well declining to the
west—the swift darting of many sand-swallows coming and going, their
holes in a neighboring marl-bank—the odor of the cedar and oak, so
palpable, as evening approaches—perfume, color, the bronze-and-gold
15   of nearly ripen'd wheat—clover-fields, with honey-scent—the well-up
maize, with long and rustling leaves—the great patches of thriving potatoes, dusky green, fleck'd all over with white blossoms—the old, warty,
venerable oak above me—and ever, mix'd with the dual notes of the quail,
the soughing of the wind through some near-by pines.

20   As I rise for return, I linger long to a delicious song-epilogue (is it the
hermit-thrush?) from some bushy recess off there in the swamp, repeated
leisurely and pensively over and over again. This, to the circle-gambols of
the swallows flying by dozens in concentric rings in the last rays of sunset, like flashes of some airy wheel.

A July Afternoon by the Pond.

The fervent heat, but so much more endurable in this pure air—the
white and pink pond-blossoms, with great heart-shaped leaves; the glassy
waters of the creek, the banks, with dense bushery, and the picturesque
beeches and shade and turf; the tremulous, reedy call of some bird from
5   recesses, breaking the warm, indolent, half-voluptuous silence; an occasional wasp, hornet, honey-bee or bumble (they hover near my hands or
face, yet annoy me not, nor I them, as they appear to examine, find nothing, and away they go)—the vast space of the sky overhead so clear, and
the buzzard up there sailing his slow whirl in majestic spirals and discs;
10   just over the surface of the pond, two large slate-color'd dragon-flies,
with wings of lace, circling and darting and occasionally balancing themselves quite still, their wings quivering all the time, (are they not showing
off for my amusement?)—the pond itself, with the sword-shaped calamus; the water snakes—occasionally a flitting blackbird, with red dabs

A July Afternoon by the Pond.
Printed from a clipping of the Philadelphia *Times*, January 26, 1879, being
paragraph 31 of "Winter Sunshine" and the twentieth under the subtitle "Thumb-
Nail Jottings at Timber Creek."
5. indolent, half-voluptuous] *PT:* indolent, perfumed, half-voluptuous
10. pond, two] *PT:* pond, the two
10. slate-color'd dragon-flies] *PT:* slate-colored beetles, dragon-flies
14–15. snakes . . . on] *PT:* snakes, and occasionally the flitting blackbird,
with the red dabs I see on

on his shoulders, as he darts slantingly by—the sounds that bring out the   15
solitude, warmth, light and shade—the quawk of some pond duck—
(the crickets and grasshoppers are mute in the noon heat, but I hear the
song of the first cicadas;)—then at some distance the rattle and whirr of
a reaping machine as the horses draw it on a rapid walk through a rye
field on the opposite side of the creek—(what was the yellow or light-   20
brown bird, large as a young hen, with short neck and long-stretch'd legs
I just saw, in flapping and awkward flight over there through the trees?)
—the prevailing delicate, yet palpable, spicy, grassy, clovery perfume to
my nostrils; and over all, encircling all, to my sight and soul, the free
space of the sky, transparent and blue—and hovering there in the west, a   25
mass of white-gray fleecy clouds the sailors call "shoals of mackerel"—
the sky, with silver swirls like locks of toss'd hair, spreading, expanding—
a vast voiceless, formless simulacrum—yet may-be the most real reality
and formulator of everything—who knows?

Locusts and Katydids.

Aug. 22.—Reedy monotones of locust, or sounds of katydid—I
hear the latter at night, and the other both day and night. I thought the
morning and evening warble of birds delightful; but I find I can listen to
these strange insects with just as much pleasure. A single locust is now
heard near noon from a tree two hundred feet off, as I write—a long   5
whirring, continued, quite loud noise graded in distinct whirls, or swinging circles, increasing in strength and rapidity up to a certain point, and
then a fluttering, quietly tapering fall. Each strain is continued from one
to two minutes. The locust-song is very appropriate to the scene—gushes,
has meaning, is masculine, is like some fine old wine, not sweet, but far   10
better than sweet.

But the katydid—how shall I describe its piquant utterances? One
sings from a willow-tree just outside my open bedroom window, twenty
yards distant; every clear night for a fortnight past has sooth'd me to

23. palpable, spicy] *PT:* palpable enough, spicy
26–27. mackerel"—the sky] *PT:* mackerel." The Sky
29. After this paragraph, which concludes the "jottings" printed in *PT,* the
next ten paragraphs (32–41) were not reprinted. See Appendix XVI, 5.

   Locusts and Katydids.
   Printed from an autograph MS. The year "77" after "Aug. 22" is crossed out.
   4–17. Written on two small pieces of white paper. The rest of the MS is in purple
ink, revised in pencil and black ink, on gray paper.

15 sleep. I rode through a piece of woods for a hundred rods the other
evening, and heard the katydids by myriads—very curious for once; but I
like better my single neighbor on the tree.

Let me say more about the song of the locust, even to repetition; a
long, chromatic, tremulous crescendo, like a brass disk whirling round
20 and round, emitting wave after wave of notes, beginning with a certain
moderate beat or measure, rapidly increasing in speed and emphasis,
reaching a point of great energy and significance, and then quickly and
gracefully dropping down and out. Not the melody of the singing-bird—
far from it; the common musician might think without melody, but surely
25 having to the finer ear a harmony of its own; monotonous—but what a
swing there is in that brassy drone, round and round, cymballine—or like
the whirling of brass quoits.

The Lesson of a Tree.

Sept. 1.—I should not take either the biggest or the most picturesque tree to illustrate it. Here is one of my favorites now before me, a
fine yellow poplar, quite straight, perhaps 90 feet high, and four thick at
the butt. How strong, vital, enduring! how dumbly eloquent! What sug-
5 gestions of imperturbability and *being*, as against the human trait of
mere *seeming*. Then the qualities, almost emotional, palpably artistic,
heroic, of a tree; so innocent and harmless, yet so savage. It *is*, yet says
nothing. How it rebukes by its tough and equable serenity all weathers,
this gusty-temper'd little whiffet, man, that runs indoors at a mite of rain
10 or snow. Science (or rather half-way science) scoffs at reminiscence of
dryad and hamadryad, and of trees speaking. But, if they don't, they do
as well as most speaking, writing, poetry, sermons—or rather they do a
great deal better. I should say indeed that those old dryad-reminiscences
are quite as true as any, and profounder than most reminiscences we get.
15 ("Cut this out," as the quack mediciners say, and keep by you.) Go and
sit in a grove or woods, with one or more of those voiceless companions,
and read the foregoing, and think.

One lesson from affiliating a tree—perhaps the greatest moral lesson
anyhow from earth, rocks, animals, is that same lesson of inherency, of
20 *what is*, without the least regard to what the looker on (the critic) sup-
poses or says, or whether he likes or dislikes. What worse—what more

The Lesson of a Tree.
Printed, except the footnote, from several pages of autograph MS. At the

general malady pervades each and all of us, our literature, education, attitude toward each other, (even toward ourselves,) than a morbid trouble about *seems*, (generally temporarily seems too,) and no trouble at all, or hardly any, about the sane, slow-growing, perennial, real parts of character, books, friendship, marriage—humanity's invisible foundations and hold-together? (As the all-basis, the nerve, the great-sympathetic, the plenum within humanity, giving stamp to everything, is necessarily invisible.)

Aug. 4, 6 p.m.—Lights and shades and rare effects on tree-foliage and grass—transparent greens, grays, &c., all in sunset pomp and dazzle. The clear beams are now thrown in many new places, on the quilted, seam'd, bronze-drab, lower tree-trunks, shadow'd except at this hour—now flooding their young and old columnar ruggedness with strong light, unfolding to my sense new amazing features of silent, shaggy charm, the solid bark, the expression of harmless impassiveness, with many a bulge and gnarl unreck'd before. In the revealings of such light, such exceptional hour, such mood, one does not wonder at the old story fables, (indeed, why fables?) of people falling into love-sickness with trees, seiz'd extatic with the mystic realism of the resistless silent strength in them—*strength*, which after all is perhaps the last, completest, highest beauty.

Trees I am familiar with here.

Oaks, (many kinds—one sturdy old fellow, vital, green, bushy, five feet thick at the butt, I sit under every day.)
Cedars, plenty.
Tulip trees, (*Liriodendron*, is of the magnolia family—I have seen it in Michigan and southern Illinois, 140 feet high and 8 feet thick at the butt*; does not transplant well; best rais'd from seeds—the lumbermen call it yellow poplar.)
Sycamores.
Gum-trees, both sweet and sour.
Beeches.
Black-walnuts.
Sassafras.

Willows.
Catalpas.
Persimmons.
Mountain-ash.
Hickories.
Maples, many kinds.
Locusts.
Birches.
Dogwood.
Pine.
the Elm.
Chestnut.
Linden.
Aspen.
Spruce.
Hornbeam.
Laurel.
Holly.

top of the first MS page appears the date " '76," and after that the months "June Sept. Aug." All are crossed out. The footnote is from a newspaper clipping. SDA omits the note from the Woodstown *Register*.

* There is a tulip poplar within sight of Woodstown, which is twenty feet around, three feet from the ground, four feet across about eighteen feet up the trunk, which is broken off about three or four feet higher up. On the south side an arm has shot out from which rise two stems, each to about ninety-one or ninety-two feet from the ground. Twenty-five (or more) years since the cavity in the butt was large enough for, and nine men at one time, ate dinner therein. It is supposed twelve to fifteen men could now, at one time, stand within its trunk. The severe winds of 1877 and 1878 did not seem to damage it, and the two stems send out yearly many blossoms, scenting the air immediately about it with their sweet perfume. It is entirely unprotected by other trees, on a hill.—*Woodstown, N. J., "Register," April 15, '79.*

Autumn Side-Bits.

Sept. 20.—Under an old black oak, glossy and green, exhaling aroma—amid a grove the Albic druids might have chosen—envelop'd in the warmth and light of the noonday sun, and swarms of flitting insects—with the harsh cawing of many crows a hundred rods away—here I sit in solitude, absorbing, enjoying all. The corn, stack'd in its cone-shaped stacks, russet-color'd and sere—a large field spotted thick with scarlet-gold pumpkins—an adjoining one of cabbages, showing well in their green and pearl, mottled by much light and shade—melon patches, with their bulging ovals, and great silver-streak'd, ruffled, broad-edged leaves —and many an autumn sight and sound beside—the distant scream of a flock of guinea-hens—and pour'd over all the September breeze, with pensive cadence through the tree tops.

Another Day.—The ground in all directions strew'd with *debris* from a storm. Timber creek, as I slowly pace its banks, has ebb'd low, and shows reaction from the turbulent swell of the late equinoctial. As I look around, I take account of stock—weeds and shrubs, knolls, paths, occasional stumps, some with smooth'd tops, (several I use as seats of rest, from place to place, and from one I am now jotting these lines,)—frequent wild-flowers, little white, star-shaped things, or the cardinal red of the lobelia, or the cherry-ball seeds of the perennial rose, or the many-threaded vines winding up and around trunks of trees.

Autumn Side-Bits.
Printed from clippings of the first number, dated January 29, 1881, of the *Critic* series "How I Get Around," paragraphs 8–10, subtitled "Autumn Scenes and Sights" and dated "Sept. 20, '76."
    2. aroma—amid] CR: aroma, and four to five feet thick at the butt—amid
16–17. paths, occasional] CR: paths, butterflies—occasional

Oct. 1, 2 and 3.—Down every day in the solitude of the creek. A serene autumn sun and westerly breeze to-day (3d) as I sit here, the water surface prettily moving in wind-ripples before me. On a stout old beech at the edge, decayed and slanting, almost fallen to the stream, yet with life and leaves in its mossy limbs, a gray squirrel, exploring, runs up and down, flirts his tail, leaps to the ground, sits on his haunches upright as he sees me, (a Darwinian hint?) and then races up the tree again.

Oct. 4.—Cloudy and coolish; signs of incipient winter. Yet pleasant here, the leaves thick-falling, the ground brown with them already; rich coloring, yellows of all hues, pale and dark-green, shades from lightest to richest red—all set in and toned down by the prevailing brown of the earth and gray of the sky. So, winter is coming; and I yet in my sickness. I sit here amid all these fair sights and vital influences, and abandon myself to that thought, with its wandering trains of speculation.

The Sky—Days and Nights—Happiness.

Oct. 20.—A clear, crispy day—dry and breezy air, full of oxygen. Out of the sane, silent, beauteous miracles that envelope and fuse me—trees, water, grass, sunlight, and early frost—the one I am looking at most to-day is the sky. It has that delicate, transparent blue, peculiar to autumn, and the only clouds are little or larger white ones, giving their still and spiritual motion to the great concave. All through the earlier day (say from 7 to 11) it keeps a pure, yet vivid blue. But as noon approaches the color gets lighter, quite gray for two or three hours—then still paler for a spell, till sun-down—which last I watch dazzling through the interstices of a knoll of big trees—darts of fire and a gorgeous show of light-yellow, liver-color and red, with a vast silver glaze askant on the water—the transparent shadows, shafts, sparkle, and vivid colors beyond all the paintings ever made.

I don't know what or how, but it seems to me mostly owing to these skies, (every now and then I think, while I have of course seen them every day of my life, I never really saw the skies before,) I have had this

20–21. wild-flowers, little] CR: wild-flowers, some of rare beauty—little
33. After "of the sky." CR begins a new paragraph.

The Sky—Days and Nights—Happiness.

Printed from several pages of autograph MS. The year, " '76," is crossed out in the date.
1–13. Written in pencil on white paper.

autumn some wondrously contented hours—may I not say perfectly happy ones? As I've read, Byron just before his death told a friend that he had known but three happy hours during his whole existence. Then

20 there is the old German legend of the king's bell, to the same point. While I was out there by the wood, that beautiful sunset through the trees, I thought of Byron's and the bell story, and the notion started in me that I was having a happy hour. (Though perhaps my best moments I never jot down; when they come I cannot afford to break the charm by inditing

25 memoranda. I just abandon myself to the mood, and let it float on, carrying me in its placid extasy.)

What is happiness, anyhow? Is this one of its hours, or the like of it? —so impalpable—a mere breath, an evanescent tinge? I am not sure—so let me give myself the benefit of the doubt. Hast Thou, pellucid, in Thy

30 azure depths, medicine for case like mine? (Ah, the physical shatter and troubled spirit of me the last three years.) And dost Thou subtly mystically now drip it through the air invisibly upon me?

Night of Oct. 28.—The heavens unusually transparent—the stars out by myriads—the great path of the Milky Way, with its branch, only

35 seen of very clear nights—Jupiter, setting in the west, looks like a huge hap-hazard splash, and has a little star for companion.

> Clothed in his white garments,
> Into the round and clear arena slowly entered the brahmin,
> Holding a little child by the hand,
40 > Like the moon with the planet Jupiter in a cloudless night-sky.
> > *Old Hindu Poem.*

Early in November.—At its farther end the land already described opens into a broad grassy upland field of over twenty acres, slightly sloping to the south. Here I am accustom'd to walk for sky views and

45 effects, either morning or sundown. To-day from this field my soul is calm'd and expanded beyond description, the whole forenoon by the clear blue arching over all, cloudless, nothing particular, only sky and daylight. Their soothing accompaniments, autumn leaves, the cool dry air, the faint

33. In the MS this date is *"Night of Oct. 11."*

37–40. The verses are written in pencil on a separate piece of white paper and pasted on.

38. The words "round and clear" are inserted above the line in pencil. The word "walk" is written in the line, crossed out, and the word "entered" written after it. The word "brahmin" is inserted above the line in ink.

40. "Mars" was originally written in the line, crossed out, and the word "Jupiter" written above it.

[The source of these verses has not been identified. The circumstances under which they appear in the MS suggest the possibility that Whitman wrote them himself.—ED.]

aroma—crows cawing in the distance—two great buzzards wheeling gracefully and slowly far up there—the occasional murmur of the wind, sometimes quite gently, then threatening through the trees—a gang of farm-laborers loading corn-stalks in a field in sight, and the patient horses waiting.

50

Colors—a Contrast.

Such a play of colors and lights, different seasons, different hours of the day—the lines of the far horizon where the faint-tinged edge of the landscape loses itself in the sky. As I slowly hobble up the lane toward day-close, an incomparable sunset shooting in molten sapphire and gold, shaft after shaft, through the ranks of the long-leaved corn, between me and the west.

5

Another day.—The rich dark green of the tulip-trees and the oaks, the gray of the swamp-willows, the dull hues of the sycamores and black-walnuts, the emerald of the cedars (after rain,) and the light yellow of the beeches.

10

November 8, '76.

The forenoon leaden and cloudy, not cold or wet, but indicating both. As I hobble down here and sit by the silent pond, how different from the excitement amid which, in the cities, millions of people are now waiting news of yesterday's Presidential election, or receiving and discussing the result—in this secluded place uncared-for, unknown.

5

Colors—a Contrast.
Printed from an autograph MS. The words "—A Contrast" are added in red ink.
7. *Another day.* [The MS originally read "Late in September," but this was crossed out and "October" inserted in red ink. This is not deleted in the MS but was presumably changed to "*Another day.*" in galley proof.]

November 8, '76.
Printed from an autograph MS.
5. After the sentence ending "unknown." the following sentence is deleted in the MS: "Important as are the issues of the election I yield myself to try it all by this place, under the clear sky, in the final balance and test of Nature in the open air."

Crows and Crows.

Nov. 14.—As I sit here by the creek, resting after my walk, a warm languor bathes me from the sun. No sound but a cawing of crows, and no motion but their black flying figures from overhead, reflected in the mirror of the pond below. Indeed a principal feature of the scene to-day is
5 these crows, their incessant cawing, far or near, and their countless flocks and processions moving from place to place, and at times almost darkening the air with their myriads. As I sit a moment writing this by the bank, I see the black, clear-cut reflection of them far below, flying through the watery looking-glass, by ones, twos, or long strings. All last night I heard
10 the noises from their great roost in a neighboring wood.

Crows and Crows.
Printed from an autograph MS page made up of two sheets, a white one, partly cut away at the top, written in pencil, evidently the original, at the top of which a new beginning is written in black ink. The original title, in black ink, was "Crows—Indian Summer." Then "—Indian Summer" is crossed out and the words "and Crows" added in red ink.

A Winter Day on the Sea-Beach.
Printed chiefly from CR clippings of paragraphs 3–5 of the first number, January 29, 1881, of "How I Get Around," the first three under the subtitle "A Fine Winter Day on the Beach." Parts of the CR article seem to be revisions of the two paragraphs (42–43) subtitled "The Vast Salt Flat Meadows" and the first, second, and fourth paragraphs (44, 45, and 47) under the subtitle "Atlantic City" in the article "Winter Sunshine," PT, January 26, 1879. The clippings are revised in black and red ink.
1–7. Printed from an autograph MS in black ink. Whitman's subtitle, in red ink, is inserted above these lines.
1–3. This sentence, though cut away from the clipping, is almost identical with the first sentence of CR under the subtitle "A Fine Winter Day on the Beach." It also somewhat resembles the first lines of PT.
1. bright December mid-day] CR: bright half-winter mid-day
2. by a little] CR: by little
3–7. This sentence is not in CR. Parts of it resemble paragraph 2 of PT. The first two paragraphs of "Winter Sunshine" (dated January 24) are as follows:
"As I went to bed a few Saturday nights ago, it entered my head all of a sudden, decidedly yet quietly, that if the coming morn was fine, I would take a trip across Jersey by the Camden and Atlantic Railroad through to the sea.
"Luck for me! A bright clear sunrise—after a good night's rest—crisp, champagne-like winter atmosphere—brief toilet and partial bath—a trill of song to welcome the day and clinch my own contented mood—and then a good breakfast, cooked by the hands I love. (How much better it makes the victuals taste!)"
7–32. Printed from CR clippings.
7–11. These lines may be compared with the following two paragraphs (42–43) of PT, subtitled "The Vast Salt Flat Meadows":
"After this a broad region of interminable salt-bay meadows, intersected with

ILLUSTRATIONS

BIBLIOGRAPHICAL NOTE

The first nine pages of this section are reproductions of Whitman's autograph manuscript for "Hours for the Soul." For an explanation for and an analysis of the differences between this manuscript and the final version printed in *Specimen Days & Collect*, see notes, pages 172–78.

July . . . in the country again.
. . . wonderful con-
junction of . . . that goes to make
those occasional miracle-hours after
sunset — near and yet . . .
Perfect, or nearly perfect, days, I
notice, are not . . . very uncommon;
but the combinations needed for perfect
nights are exceptionally few *and rare* even in a
life-time.) (run on

To-day's Sunset left things pretty
clear. The larger stars were visible
soon as the shades allow'd. A while
after 8 three or four great black clouds
suddenly rose, seemingly from different
points, and sweeping with broad swirls
of wind, but no thunder, underspread
the orbs from view everywhere, and
indicated a violent heat-storm. But
without storm the clouds blackness and
swept ? . . . potent and instantaneous pause,
all, vanish'd as suddenly as they had
risen, and from a little after 9 till
12 the atmosphere and the whole show
above were in that state of exceptional
clearness and glory just alluded to.

In the north-west turn'd the Great Dipper with its pointers round the Cynosure. A little south of east the Scorpion was fully up, with red Antares glowing in its neck; while dominating Jupiter swam, an hour and a half risen, in the east — (no moon till after 11.)

A large part of the sky seem'd just laid in great splashes of phosphorus. You could look deeper in, farther through, than usual. The orbs — thick as heads of wheat in a field. Not that there was any special brilliancy either — nothing near as sharp as some keen winter nights, but a curious general luminousness throughout to sight, senses, and soul. The latter had most to do with it. (I am convinced that there are hours of Nature, especially of the atmosphere, address'd to the soul. Night transcends for that purpose what the proudest day can do.) Now indeed, to me, if never before, the heavens declared the glory of God. It was to the full the sky of the Bible, of Arabia and Egypt, of the prophets and shepherds, and of the oldest poems. There in abstraction and stillness, (I had gone off by myself to absorb the scene, to have the spell unbroken,) the copiousness, removedness, vitality, loose-clear-crowdedness, of that stellar concave spreading overhead, softly absorbed into me, rising so free, interminably high, stretching east, west, north, south — and I, though but a point in the centre below, embodying all, (run in

As if for the first time indeed Creation noiselessly sank into and through my soul, its placid and untellable lesson, beyond — O so infinitely beyond — any thing by rote of art, books, sermons, or from science old or new. (run in

The spirit's hour — religion's hour — the visible suggestion of God in Space and Time — now definitely indicated for once, if never again. The untold pointed at — the heavens all paved with it. The Milky Way as if some superhuman Symphony, some universal ode, disdaining syllable and sound — a flash and glance of Deity to the soul. All silently — the indescribable night and stars — far off and silently.

The Dawn — July 23 — This morning an hour before sunrise a spectacle wrought on the same background yet of different beauty and meaning.

The moon is well up in the heavens, and past her half, shining brightly. The air and sky of that cynical-clear Minerva-like quality, virgin cool — not the weight of senti-ment mystery, or passious ecstasy in definable — not the religious sense, the varied All distill'd and sublima-ted into one emotion, of the night just described. Every star now clean-cut, showing for just what it is, there in the colorless ether. The character of the heralded morning ineffably sweet and fresh and limpid, but for the es-thetic sense alone and for purity with-out sentiment. I have itemized the night — but dare I attempt the cloud-less dawn? (What subtle tie is this between one's soul and the break of day? Alike, and yet no two nights or morning shows ever exactly alike.) Preceded by an immense star, almost unearthly in its effusion of white splendor, with two or three long unequal spoke-rays of diamond radiance, shedding down

shedding down through the fresh morning
air - almost an ½ hour of this - and then
the sunrise.

The East. / What a subject for a
poem ! indeed where else a more pregnant
one ? Where one more idealistic-real,
more subtle-expanding, more sensuous.
delicate ! The East - answering all lands,
all peoples ages, peoples, touching all
senses here, immediate, every day - and
yet so indescribably distant - such retrospect. The East - long stretching - so
losing itself - the Orient - the gardens of -
Asia - the womb of history and song
and mythology - forth-issuing all those
strange biblic cavalcades,
Florid with blood, pensive, rapt with musings, hot
with passion
Sultry with perfume, with ample and flowing garments,
With sunburnt vision, intense soul and glittering eyes.

Always the East - old, how incalculably
old ! And yet here the same - ours yet -
fresh as a rose to every morning, every
life, to-day - and always will be.

Sept. 17. 78. — Another presentative
same theme, just befor sunrise again,
(a favorite hour with me.) The clear gray
sky, a faint glow in the dull liver-color
of the east, and the cool fresh odor and
moisture — the cattle and horses off there
~~quietly~~ grazing in the fields — the planet ~~star~~
Venus again, two hours high. For
sounds, the chirping of crickets in the
grass, the ~~crowing~~ clarion of Chanticleer,
and the distant cawing of an early crow.
Quietly over the low dense fringe of
cedars and pines soon rises that dazzling red
transparent disk of quiet ✗ flame, and the low
sheets of white vapor roll and roll
into dissolution.
~~Moon and stars~~
~~The Moon~~ — May 18 '78 — I went to
bed early last night, but found myself
waked shortly after 12, and turning
awhile sleepless and mentally feverish,
rose, ~~so~~ dress'd myself, sallied forth and
down the lane. The full moon, some
three or four hours up — a sprinkle of
light and less light clouds just lazily
moving — Jupiter an hour high — and here

in the heavens, amid the languid clouds,
a star after star disappearing and appearing again. So beautifully veil'd and
varied — the air with that early-summer
perfume, not at all damp or raw — at
times Luna emerging in richest brightness for minutes, and then partially
envelopt. It was that silent time
between 1 and 3 oclock. Far-off a
whip-poor-will plied his notes incessantly. ¶ The rare nocturnal scene —
how completely it pacified and sooth'd
me. Is there not something about the
moon, some relation or reminder, which
no poem or literature has ever caught?
In very old and primitive ballads I have
come across lines or asides that suggest
it.) After a while the clouds mostly
clear'd, and as the moon swam
on she carried, shimmering and shifting,
delicate color-effects of pellucid green
and tawny vapor. I conclude with
an extract (some writer in the Tribune
May 16, '78;) — "No one ever gets tired of
the moon. Goddess that she is by dower

of her ~~eternal~~ beauty. She is a true
woman by her tact — knows the charm
of being seldom seen, of coming by surprise and staying but a little while;
never wears the same dress two nights
running, nor all night the same way;
commends herself to the matter-of-fact
people by her usefulness, and makes her
uselessness adored by poets, artists, and all
lovers in all lands; lends herself to
every symbolism and to every emblem
— is Diana's bow and Venus's mirror,
and Mary's throne; is a sickle, a
scarf, an eye-brow, his face or her
face, as looked at, by her or by him;
is the madman's hell, the poets' heaven,
the baby's toy, the philosopher's study —
and while her admirers follow her
footsteps and hang on her lovely looks,
she knows how to keep her woman's
secret — her other side — unguess'd and
unguessable."

Feb. 9. '80 – Just before 10 p.m., cold and entirely clear again, the show overhead, bearing south-west of wonderful and crowded magnificence. The moon in her third quarter – the clusters of the Hyades and Pleiades, with the planet Mars between – in full crossing-sprawl in the sky the great Egyptian X. (Sirius, Procyon, and the main stars in the constellations of the Ship, the Dove, and of Orion) – just north of east Bootes and in his knee Arcturus, an hour high, mounting the heaven, ambitiously large and sparkling, as if he meant to challenge with Sirius the stellar supremacy.

With the sentiment of the stars such nights I get all the free margins and indefiniteness of music and poetry, fused in geometry's utmost exactness.

Sent to N Y Critic
pub April 8 '82

Death of Longfellow

Camden April 3 '82 —

I have just returned from a ~~week~~
couple of weeks down in the some
~~old piney~~ ~~and~~ ~~primitive~~ + woods, where I love to
go occasionally, away from parlors,
pavements and ~~men~~ the newspapers and
magazines, — ~~It~~ ~~and~~ ~~there~~ — and where, in the shade
~~sides &~~
of + cedars and a tangle of old laurel
~~in the silence, the mottled light, and the spring earth smell,~~
trees and vines, the news of Longfellow's
first
death reach'd me! For want of any thing
better, ~~I give some of the reflections~~
~~in response as any~~ let me twine lightly
twine
~~some of the reflections~~ that ~~floated~~
~~through~~ ~~on~~ the ₰ in
~~as with the reflections~~

~~as with the~~ a spring of this the
sweet   in the ~~dark~~ dead leaves
ground-ivy ~~braid~~ ~~so plentiful~~ ~~here~~ at my
feet ~~with~~ ~~or~~ with ~~some~~ reflections from
~~on that~~ half hour   there in the ~~woods~~ silence of
~~that there~~ alone, ~~and lay it~~
Jersey
the ~~woods~~ in the mottled light, ~~and the~~ ~~Spring~~
the Jersey woods;
smells & ~~spring~~ and lay it
as my ~~humble~~ contribution to on
bard's grave.
the dead ~~poet~~ ~~from~~

(brev
caps) A Lincoln reminiscence.

As is well known,
Story-telling was often with Abra
President Lincoln a weapon which
he employed with great skill. Very
often he could not give a point
blank reply or comment – and these
indirections, (sometimes funny,
but not always so,) were probably
                   possible.
the best responses we recorded or
unrecorded. In the gloomiest period
of the war, he had a call from
a large delegation of bank presidents. In the talk after business
was settled one of the big Dons
asked Mr. Lincoln if his confidence in
the future, and in the permanence of
the Union was not beginning to
be shaken – whereupon the homely
President told a little story. "When
I was a young man in Illinois," said
he. "I boarded for a time with a
Deacon of the Presbyterian church.
One night I was roused from my sleep
by a rap at the door & I heard the deacon's voice exclaiming 'Arise Abraham
the day of judgment has come'. I sprang
from my bed & rushed to the window.
and saw the stars fall, in great showers.
But looking back of them in the heavens
I saw all the grand old constellations
with which I was so well acquainted,
fixed and immovable and true in
their places. Gentlemen, the
world did not come to an end then,
nor will the Union now."

For the inauguration of the Thos: Paine bust
written out in the woods

Kirkwood (White Horse)
N J
Oct 2 '76.
W W

Some 35 years ago, in New York
City, at Tammany Hall, of which place
I was then a frequenter.)

Some 35 years ago in
New York city, I ~happen'd to become~ quite well
acquainted with Thomas Paine's
~perhaps~ most intimate chum, and ~certainly~ later
years ~very frequent~ companion — a remarkably
fine old man, Col. Fellows; who
may yet be remembered by some
stray relicts of that ~place and~
period and spot. ~you will allow me I will~
~first give~ description of the Colonel himself.
~The Colonel at Tammany Hall,~
~of which I was then a frequenter.~
He was tall, ~of military bearing~ aged about 75 I should
think, ~thick &~ hair white as snow, clean
shaved on the face, dress'd very
neatly, a tail coat of blue cloth
with metal buttons, buff vest,
pantaloons of drab color, and his
neck breast and wrists showing ~fair~
~the whitest of~ linen. ~Under all circumstances~
~Always~ fine
manners; a good but not profuse

A Winter Day on the Sea-Beach.

One bright December mid-day lately I spent down on the New Jersey sea-shore, reaching it by a little more than an hour's railroad trip over the old Camden and Atlantic. I had started betimes, fortified by nice strong coffee and a good breakfast (cook'd by the hands I love, my dear sister Lou's—how much better it makes the victuals taste, and then   5 assimilate, strengthen you, perhaps make the whole day comfortable afterwards.) Five or six miles at the last, our track enter'd a broad region of salt grass meadows, intersected by lagoons, and cut up everywhere by watery runs. The sedgy perfume, delightful to my nostrils, reminded me of "the mash" and south bay of my native island. I could have journey'd   10 contentedly till night through these flat and odorous sea-prairies. From

lagoons and cut into everywhere by watery runs—the strong sedgy perfume, delightful to my nostrils, all reminding me again of "the mash" and the continuous South Bay of old Long Island. The Atlantic City *Review* says: 'We believe the day when some effort will be put forth to reclaim the meadows between this place and Absecon, or which span almost the entire Jersey coast, is not far distant. It can be utilized by a system of dyking and drainage, for where the experiment has been tried the soil has been discovered to be remarkably rich and productive. The salt water drained away, the meadows are no longer miry, but form a solid bottom, the soil resembling that of Illinois.'

"Passing right through five or six miles (I could have journeyed with delight for a hundred) of these odorous sea prairies we come to the end—the Camden and Atlantic depot, within good gunshot of the beach. I no sooner land from the cars than I meet impromptu with young Mr. English (of the just mentioned *Review* newspaper), who treats me with all brotherly and gentlemanly kindness, posts me up about things, puts me on the best roads and starts me right."

10. native island] *CR:* native Long Island

11. After "sea-prairies." *CR* begins a new paragraph.

11–25. These lines repeat parts of the second, third, and fourth paragraphs under the subtitle "Atlantic City" in *PT*. The first (44), from which little or nothing is taken, is as follows:

"A flat, still sandy, still meadowy region (some of the old hummocks with their hard sedge, in tufts, still remaining)—an island, but good hard roads and plenty of them, really pleasant streets, very little show of trees, shrubbery, etc., but in lieu of them a superb range of ocean beach—miles and miles of it, for driving, walking, bathing—a real Sea Beach City indeed, with salt waves and sandy shores ad libitum."

11–15. Corresponding to these two sentences *PT* has the following paragraph (45), the second under "Atlantic City":

"I had a fine and bracing drive along the smooth sand (the carriage wheels hardly made a dent in it). The bright sun, the sparkling waves, the foam, the view— Brigantine beach, a sail here and there in the distance—the ragged wreck-timbers of the stranded Rockaway—the vital, vast, monotonous sea—all the fascination of simple, uninterrupted space, shore, salt atmosphere, sky (people who go there often and get used to it get infatuated and won't go anywhere else), were the items of my drive."

Paragraph 46, the third under "Atlantic City," was not reprinted. See Appendix XVI, *6.*

half-past 11 till 2 I was nearly all the time along the beach, or in sight of
the ocean, listening to its hoarse murmur, and inhaling the bracing and
welcome breezes. First, a rapid five-mile drive over the hard sand—our
carriage wheels hardly made dents in it. Then after dinner (as there
were nearly two hours to spare) I walk'd off in another direction, (hardly
met or saw a person,) and taking possession of what appear'd to have been
the reception-room of an old bath-house range, had a broad expanse of
view all to myself—quaint, refreshing, unimpeded—a dry area of sedge
and Indian grass immediately before and around me—space, simple, unornamented space. Distant vessels, and the far-off, just visible trailing
smoke of an inward bound steamer; more plainly, ships, brigs, schooners,
in sight, most of them with every sail set to the firm and steady wind.

The attractions, fascinations there are in sea and shore! How one
dwells on their simplicity, even vacuity! What is it in us, arous'd by
those indirections and directions? That spread of waves and gray-
white beach, salt, monotonous, senseless—such an entire absence of art,
books, talk, elegance—so indescribably comforting, even this winter day
—grim, yet so delicate-looking, so spiritual—striking emotional, impalpable depths, subtler than all the poems, paintings, music, I have ever read,
seen, heard. (Yet let me be fair, perhaps it is because I have read those
poems and heard that music.)

Sea-Shore Fancies.

Even as a boy, I had the fancy, the wish, to write a piece, perhaps a
poem, about the sea-shore—that suggesting, dividing line, contact, junction, the solid marrying the liquid—that curious, lurking something, (as

14. sand—our] CR: sand; our
15–25. These lines are identical with paragraph 47 of PT, the fourth under the
subtitle "Atlantic City," except as noted.
19. a dry] PT: the dry
20. me—space, simple] PT: me—space, with a sort of grimness about it—
simple
21. space. Distant] PT: space. In front, as far as I could see, and right and left,
plenty of beach, only broken by a few unpainted wooden houses, on piles, here and
there—distant
22. steamer; more] PT: steamer. More
23. sight, most] PT: sight in the distance. How silently, spiritually, like phantoms
(even in the midst of the bright sunshine and the objective world around me), they
glide away off there—most
24–25. Corresponding to these lines PT has the following, to end paragraph 47:
"How the main attraction and fascination are in sea and shore! How the soul dwells
on their simplicity, eternity, grimness, absence of art!"
Paragraphs 48–60, the remainder of the PT article, were not reprinted. See
Appendix XVI, 7.

doubtless every objective form finally becomes to the subjective spirit,) which means far more than its mere first sight, grand as that is—blending the real and ideal, and each made portion of the other. Hours, days, in my Long Island youth and early manhood, I haunted the shores of Rockaway or Coney island, or away east to the Hamptons or Montauk. Once, at the latter place, (by the old lighthouse, nothing but sea-tossings in sight in every direction as far as the eye could reach,) I remember well, I felt that I must one day write a book expressing this liquid, mystic theme. Afterward, I recollect, how it came to me that instead of any special lyrical or epical or literary attempt, the sea-shore should be an invisible *influence*, a pervading gauge and tally for me, in my composition. (Let me give a hint here to young writers. I am not sure but I have unwittingly follow'd out the same rule with other powers besides sea and shores—avoiding them, in the way of any dead set at poetizing them, as too big for formal handling—quite satisfied if I could indirectly show that we have met and fused, even if only once, but enough—that we have really absorb'd each other and understand each other.)

There is a dream, a picture, that for years at intervals, (sometimes quite long ones, but surely again, in time,) has come noiselessly up before me, and I really believe, fiction as it is, has enter'd largely into my practical life—certainly into my writings, and shaped and color'd them. It is nothing more or less than a stretch of interminable white-brown sand, hard and smooth and broad, with the ocean perpetually, grandly, rolling in upon it, with slow-measured sweep, with rustle and hiss and foam, and many a thump as of low bass drums. This scene, this picture, I say, has risen before me at times for years. Sometimes I wake at night and can hear and see it plainly.

25. simplicity, even] *CR:* simplicity, eternity, even
29. striking emotional] *CR:* striking, emotional

Sea-Shore Fancies.

Printed from clippings, paragraphs 6 and 7, of the first *Critic* article, the fourth and fifth paragraphs under the subtitle "A Fine Winter Day on the Beach." Whitman's subtitle is inserted in red ink; revisions are in both black and red ink.

5–6. that . . . the] *CR:* that is—the blending of the
6–7. in . . . youth] *CR:* in youth
12. recollect, how] *CR:* recollect how
13. attempt, the sea-shore should] *CR:* attempt, it should
18. could indirectly] *CR:* could suggest them—could indirectly
21. There is a dream, a picture] *CR: A Sea Vision.*—There is a dream, a simple yet strange picture
30. The last sentence in *CR* under this subtitle, crossed out on the clipping, is as follows: "What country, or what else anyhow, I do not define; but the vast and lonesome beach is there—an unknown, unsailed, untrod sea and shore."

In Memory of Thomas Paine.

Spoken at Lincoln Hall, Philadelphia, Sunday, Jan. 28, '77, for 140th anniversary of T. P.'s birth-day.

Some thirty-five years ago, in New York city, at Tammany hall, of which place I was then a frequenter, I happen'd to become quite well acquainted with Thomas Paine's perhaps most intimate chum, and certainly his later years' very frequent companion, a remarkably fine old man, Col. Fellows, who may yet be remember'd by some stray relics of that period and spot. If you will allow me, I will first give a description of the Colonel himself. He was tall, of military bearing, aged about 78 I should think, hair white as snow, clean-shaved on the face, dress'd very neatly, a tail-coat of blue cloth with metal buttons, buff vest, pantaloons of drab color, and his neck, breast and wrists showing the whitest of linen. Under all circumstances, fine manners; a good but not profuse talker, his wits still fully about him, balanced and live and undimm'd as ever. He kept pretty fair health, though so old. For employment—for he was poor —he had a post as constable of some of the upper courts. I used to think him very picturesque on the fringe of a crowd holding a tall staff, with his erect form, and his superb, bare, thick-hair'd, closely-cropt white head. The judges and young lawyers, with whom he was ever a favorite, and the subject of respect, used to call him Aristides. It was the general opinion among them that if manly rectitude and the instincts of absolute justice remain'd vital anywhere about New York City Hall, or Tammany, they were to be found in Col. Fellows. He liked young men, and enjoy'd to leisurely talk with them over a social glass of toddy, after his day's work, (he on these occasions never drank but one glass,) and it was at reiterated meetings of this kind in old Tammany's back parlor of those days, that he told me much about Thomas Paine. At one of our interviews he gave me a minute account of Paine's sickness and death. In short, from those talks, I was and am satisfied that my old friend, with his mark'd advantages,

In Memory of Thomas Paine.

Printed from proof sheets, the same presumably from which Whitman read and from which the article in *NYTR* (January 29, 1877) titled "Walt Whitman on Thomas Paine" was printed. Since in Whitman's MS these pages are numbered 105¼ and 105½ their inclusion in *SDC* was probably an afterthought. In place of the italicized lines below the title in *SDC*, *NYTR* has the following: "Philadelphia, Jan. 28.—At a public meeting here to-night in memory of Thomas Paine's 140th birthday, Walt Whitman made these remarks:". The text is collated with both the proof and *NYTR*. An autograph MS, now in the Feinberg Collection, has the following endorsement: "For the inauguration of the Thos. Paine bust. Written out

had mentally, morally and emotionally gauged the author of "Common Sense," and besides giving me a good portrait of his appearance and manners, had taken the true measure of his interior character.   30

Paine's practical demeanor, and much of his theoretical belief, was a mixture of the French and English schools of a century ago, and the best of both. Like most old-fashion'd people, he drank a glass or two every day, but was no tippler, nor intemperate, let alone being a drunkard. He lived simply and economically, but quite well—was always cheery and cour-   35 teous, perhaps occasionally a little blunt, having very positive opinions upon politics, religion, and so forth. That he labor'd well and wisely for the States in the trying period of their parturition, and in the seeds of their character, there seems to me no question. I dare not say how much of what our Union is owning and enjoying to-day—its independence—its   40 ardent belief in, and substantial practice of, radical human rights—and the severance of its government from all ecclesiastical and superstitious dominion—I dare not say how much of all this is owing to Thomas Paine, but I am inclined to think a good portion of it decidedly is.

But I was not going either into an analysis or eulogium of the man. I   45 wanted to carry you back a generation or two, and give you by indirection a moment's glance—and also to ventilate a very earnest and I believe authentic opinion, nay conviction, of that time, the fruit of the interviews I have mention'd, and of questioning and cross-questioning, clench'd by my best information since, that Thomas Paine had a noble personality, as ex-   50 hibited in presence, face, voice, dress, manner, and what may be call'd his atmosphere and magnetism, especially the later years of his life. I am sure of it. Of the foul and foolish fictions yet told about the circumstances of his decease, the absolute fact is that as he lived a good life, after its kind, he died calmly and philosophically, as became him. He served the   55 embryo Union with most precious service—a service that every man, woman and child in our thirty-eight States is to some extent receiving the benefit of to-day—and I for one here cheerfully, reverently throw my

in the woods, Kirkwood (White Horse) Oct. 2, '76 WW" The proof was probably set from a MS of later date than this one.

3–4. certainly his later years'] *NYTR* and Proof: certainly later years

5. stray relics of] *NYTR* and Proof: stray relicts of

6–25. These lines, after "and spot." through "Thomas Paine.", are omitted from *NYTR*, the omission indicated by three asterisks.

7. 78] Proof: 75

8. hair white] Proof: hair thick and white

30. measure of his interior] *NYTR* and Proof: measure not only of his exterior but interior

30. *NYTR* continues the paragraph after "interior character."

58. cheerfully, reverently] *NYTR* and Proof: cheerfully and reverently

60 pebble on the cairn of his memory. As we all know, the season demands—
or rather, will it ever be out of season?—that America learn to better
dwell on her choicest possession, the legacy of her good and faithful men
—that she well preserve their fame, if unquestion'd—or, if need be, that
she fail not to dissipate what clouds have intruded on that fame, and
burnish it newer, truer and brighter, continually.

A Two Hours' Ice-Sail.

Feb. 3, '77.—From 4 to 6 P.M. crossing the Delaware, (back
again at my Camden home,) unable to make our landing, through the ice;
our boat stanch and strong and skilfully piloted, but old and sulky, and
poorly minding her helm. (*Power*, so important in poetry and war, is also
5 first point of all in a winter steamboat, with long stretches of ice-packs to
tackle.) For over two hours we bump'd and beat about, the invisible ebb,
sluggish but irresistible, often carrying us long distances against our will.
In the first tinge of dusk, as I look'd around, I thought there could not be
presented a more chilling, arctic, grim-extended, depressing scene. Every-
10 thing was yet plainly visible; for miles north and south, ice, ice, ice,
mostly broken, but some big cakes, and no clear water in sight. The
shores, piers, surfaces, roofs, shipping, mantled with snow. A faint winter
vapor hung a fitting accompaniment around and over the endless whitish
spread, and gave it just a tinge of steel and brown.

15 *Feb.* 6.—As I cross home in the 6 P.M. boat again, the transparent
shadows are filled everywhere with leisurely falling, slightly slanting,
curiously sparse but very large, flakes of snow. On the shores, near and
far, the glow of just-lit gas-clusters at intervals. The ice, sometimes in
hummocks, sometimes floating fields, through which our boat goes crunch-

A Two Hours' Ice-Sail.
Printed from a clipping of paragraphs 6–8 of the *Critic*, fourth number of
"How I Get Around," July 16, 1881, same subtitle as in SDC. (In the *Critic*,
through an error, both the issue of May 7, 1881, and the issue of July 16, 1881, are
designated "No. 3.")
    1. *Feb.* 3, '77.—From] CR: *Feb.* 16, '79.—From
    1–2. Delaware, . . . unable] CR: Delaware, unable
    3. boat stanch] CR: boat, (the Philadelphia, Capt. Hand,) staunch
    7. After "our will." CR begins a new paragraph.
    15. *Feb.* 6.—As] CR: *Feb:* 22.—As
    19. boat goes] CR: boat (the Pennsylvania, Capt. Walton) goes

ing. The light permeated by that peculiar evening haze, right after sunset,   20
which sometimes renders quite distant objects so distinctly.

Spring Overtures—Recreations.

Feb. 10.—The first chirping, almost singing, of a bird to-day.
Then I noticed a couple of honey-bees spirting and humming about the
open window in the sun.

Feb. 11.—In the soft rose and pale gold of the declining light, this
beautiful evening, I heard the first hum and preparation of awakening   5
spring—very faint—whether in the earth or roots, or starting of insects, I
know not—but it was audible, as I lean'd on a rail (I am down in my
country quarters awhile,) and look'd long at the western horizon. Turning
to the east, Sirius, as the shadows deepen'd, came forth in dazzling splendor. And great Orion; and a little to the north-east the big Dipper, stand-   10
ing on end.

Feb. 20.—A solitary and pleasant sundown hour at the pond, exercising arms, chest, my whole body, by a tough oak sapling thick as my
wrist, twelve feet high—pulling and pushing, inspiring the good air.
After I wrestle with the tree awhile, I can feel its young sap and virtue   15
welling up out of the ground and tingling through me from crown to toe,
like health's wine. Then for addition and variety I launch forth in my
vocalism; shout declamatory pieces, sentiments, sorrow, anger, &c., from
the stock poets or plays—or inflate my lungs and sing the wild tunes and
refrains I heard of the blacks down south, or patriotic songs I learn'd in   20
the army. I make the echoes ring, I tell you! As the twilight fell, in a
pause of these ebullitions, an owl somewhere the other side of the creek
sounded *too-oo-oo-oo-oo*, soft and pensive (and I fancied a little sarcastic)
repeated four or five times. Either to applaud the negro songs—or perhaps an ironical comment on the sorrow, anger, or style of the stock poets.   25

Spring Overtures—Recreations.
    Printed from an autograph MS and a clipping of the *Critic*, paragraphs
13–15 of the first number of "How I Get Around," Jan. 29, 1881, subtitled "Spring
Overtures."
    1–11. These lines are from the clipping.
    1. *Feb. 10.*—The] CR: *Feb. 10. '77.*—The
    4. *Feb. 11.*—In] CR: *Feb. 11.—Dusk.*—In
    7–8. rail . . . and] CR: rail and
    8. After "horizon." CR begins a new paragraph.
    11. After this line, the name "Walt Whitman." in CR.
    12–25. Printed from an autograph MS, where its subtitle "Twilight Recreation"
has been crossed out. Since the page is numbered 106½ in the MS, its inclusion was
probably an afterthought.

One of the Human Kinks.

How is it that in all the serenity and lonesomeness of solitude, away off here amid the hush of the forest, alone, or as I have found in prairie wilds, or mountain stillness, one is never entirely without the instinct of looking around, (I never am, and others tell me the same of themselves,
5 confidentially,) for somebody to appear, or start up out of the earth, or from behind some tree or rock? Is it a lingering, inherited remains of man's primitive wariness, from the wild animals? or from his savage ancestry far back? It is not at all nervousness or fear. Seems as if something unknown were possibly lurking in those bushes, or solitary places.
10 Nay, it is quite certain there is—some vital unseen presence.

An Afternoon Scene.

Feb. 22.—Last night and to-day rainy and thick, till mid-afternoon, when the wind chopp'd round, the clouds swiftly drew off like curtains, the clear appear'd, and with it the fairest, grandest, most wondrous rainbow I ever saw, all complete, very vivid at its earth-ends, spreading
5 vast effusions of illuminated haze, violet, yellow, drab-green, in all directions overhead, through which the sun beam'd—an indescribable utterance of color and light, so gorgeous yet so soft, such as I had never witness'd before. Then its continuance: a full hour pass'd before the last of those earth-ends disappear'd. The sky behind was all spread in trans-
10 lucent blue, with many little white clouds and edges. To these a sunset, filling, dominating the esthetic and soul senses, sumptuously, tenderly, full. I end this note by the pond, just light enough to see, through the evening shadows, the western reflections in its water-mirror surface, with inverted figures of trees. I hear now and then the *flup* of a pike leaping
15 out, and rippling the water.

One of the Human Kinks.
Printed from a clipping of the *Critic*, the first paragraph of the fourth number of "How I Get Around," July 16, 1881, where it has the same subtitle.
2. forest, . . . in] CR: forest woods where I am jotting this note, alone, or in

An Afternoon Scene.
Printed from a clipping of the *Critic*, paragraphs 2 and 3, fourth number; same subtitle as in SDC.
1. Feb. 22.—Last] CR: Feb: 22, '78.—Last

The Gates Opening.

April 6.—Palpable spring indeed, or the indications of it. I am sitting in bright sunshine, at the edge of the creek, the surface just rippled by the wind. All is solitude, morning freshness, negligence. For companions my two kingfishers sailing, winding, darting, dipping, sometimes capriciously separate, then flying together. I hear their guttural twittering again and again; for awhile nothing but that peculiar sound. As noon approaches other birds warm up. The reedy notes of the robin, and a musical passage of two parts, one a clear delicious gurgle, with several other birds I cannot place. To which is join'd, (yes, I just hear it,) one low purr at intervals from some impatient hylas at the pond-edge. The sibilant murmur of a pretty stiff breeze now and then through the trees. Then a poor little dead leaf, long frost-bound, whirls from somewhere up aloft in one wild escaped freedom-spree in space and sunlight, and then dashes down to the waters, which hold it closely and soon drown it out of sight. The bushes and trees are yet bare, but the beeches have their wrinkled yellow leaves of last season's foliage largely left, frequent cedars and pines yet green, and the grass not without proofs of coming fulness. And over all a wonderfully fine dome of clear blue, the play of light coming and going, and great fleeces of white clouds swimming so silently.

The Common Earth, the Soil.

The soil, too—let others pen-and-ink the sea, the air, (as I sometimes try)—but now I feel to choose the common soil for theme—naught else. The brown soil here, (just between winter-close and opening spring and vegetation)—the rain-shower at night, and the fresh smell next morning—the red worms wriggling out of the ground—the dead leaves, the incipient grass, and the latent life underneath—the effort to start

12. After "full." *CR* begins a new paragraph.

The Gates Opening.
Printed from an autograph MS; subtitle added in red ink.

The Common Earth, the Soil.
Printed from an autograph MS, where it follows the preceding section and was originally a part of it. The separate subtitle was inserted in red ink between lines regularly spaced.

something—already in shelter'd spots some little flowers—the distant emerald show of winter wheat and the rye-fields—the yet naked trees, with clear interstices, giving prospects hidden in summer—the tough fal-
10 low and the plow-team, and the stout boy whistling to his horses for en-couragement—and there the dark fat earth in long slanting stripes up-turn'd.

Birds and Birds and Birds.

A little later—bright weather.—An unusual melodiousness, these days, (last of April and first of May) from the blackbirds; indeed all sorts of birds, darting, whistling, hopping or perch'd on trees. Never be-fore have I seen, heard, or been in the midst of, and got so flooded and
5 saturated with them and their performances, as this current month. Such oceans, such successions of them. Let me make a list of those I find here:

Black birds (plenty,)	Meadow-larks (plenty,)
Ring doves,	Cat-birds (plenty,)
Owls,	Cuckoos,
Woodpeckers,	Pond snipes (plenty,)
King-birds,	Cheewinks,
Crows (plenty,)	Quawks,
Wrens,	Ground robins,
Kingfishers,	Ravens,
Quails,	Gray snipes,
Turkey-buzzards,	Eagles,
Hen-hawks,	High-holes,
Yellow birds,	Herons,
Thrushes,	Tits,
Reed birds,	Woodpigeons.

Early came the

Blue birds,	Meadow lark,
Killdeer,	White-bellied swallow,

Birds and Birds and Birds.
Printed mostly from a clipping of the Philadelphia *American*, paragraph 4 of "Bumble-Bees and Bird Music," May 14, 1881, where it is without the subtitle, inserted in red ink.
1–3. These lines, through the word "birds," are written in; the first words of the paragraph in *PA*, "Birds and birds and birds,—" were deleted so that the first word left on the clipping is "darting."
7–20. The following are deleted from the list of birds in *PA*: "Blue birds (plenty,)" after "Black birds (plenty,)"; "Robins (plenty,)," after "Ring-doves";

Plover,	Sandpiper,	
Robin,	Wilson's thrush,	25
Woodcock,	Flicker.	

Full-Starr'd Nights.

May 21.—Back in Camden. Again commencing one of those unusually transparent, full-starr'd, blue-black nights, as if to show that
however lush and pompous the day may be, there is something left in the
not-day that can outvie it. The rarest, finest sample of long-drawn-out
clear-obscure, from sundown to 9 o'clock. I went down to the Delaware, 5
and cross'd and cross'd. Venus like blazing silver well up in the west. The
large pale thin crescent of the new moon, half an hour high, sinking
languidly under a bar-sinister of cloud, and then emerging. Arcturus right
overhead. A faint fragrant sea-odor wafted up from the south. The gloam-
ing, the temper'd coolness, with every feature of the scene, indescribably 10
soothing and tonic—one of those hours that give hints to the soul, impossible to put in a statement. (Ah, where would be any food for spirituality
without night and the stars?) The vacant spaciousness of the air, and the
veil'd blue of the heavens, seem'd miracles enough.

As the night advanc'd it changed its spirit and garments to ampler 15
stateliness. I was almost conscious of a definite presence, Nature silently
near. The great constellation of the Water-Serpent stretch'd its coils over
more than half the heavens. The Swan with outspread wings was flying
down the Milky Way. The northern Crown, the Eagle, Lyra, all up
there in their places. From the whole dome shot down points of light, rap- 20
port with me, through the clear blue-black. All the usual sense of motion,
all animal life, seem'd discarded, seem'd a fiction; a curious power, like
the placid rest of Egyptian gods, took possession, none the less potent for
being impalpable. Earlier I had seen many bats, balancing in the luminous
twilight, darting their black forms hither and yon over the river; but now 25
they altogether disappear'd. The evening star and the moon had gone.

"Flickers," after "Turkey-buzzards"; "Killdeer," after "Meadow-larks (plenty,)";
"Plover," after "Eagles".
  21–26. This list is added in MS.

Full-Starr'd Nights.

Printed from three pages of autograph MS in black ink. Whitman's first title
for this section was "Nights for the Soul," written in black ink, but that is crossed
out and the present title written above it in red ink. The MS has almost no corrections,
apparently a fair copy of earlier drafts. On the third page the date " '77" at the top
is crossed out.

Alertness and peace lay calmly couching together through the fluid universal shadows.

Aug. 26.—Bright has the day been, and my spirits an equal *forzando*. Then comes the night, different, inexpressibly pensive, with its own tender and temper'd splendor. Venus lingers in the west with a voluptuous dazzle unshown hitherto this summer. Mars rises early, and the red sulky moon, two days past her full; Jupiter at night's meridian, and the long curling-slanted Scorpion stretching full view in the south, Aretusneck'd. Mars walks the heavens lord-paramount now; all through this month I go out after supper and watch for him; sometimes getting up at midnight to take another look at his unparallel'd lustre. (I see lately an astronomer has made out through the new Washington telescope that Mars has certainly one moon, perhaps two.) Pale and distant, but near in the heavens, Saturn precedes him.

Mulleins and Mulleins.

Large, placid mulleins, as summer advances, velvety in texture, of a light greenish-drab color, growing everywhere in the fields—at first earth's big rosettes in their broad-leav'd low cluster-plants, eight, ten, twenty leaves to a plant—plentiful on the fallow twenty-acre lot, at the end of the lane, and especially by the ridge-sides of the fences—then close to the ground, but soon springing up—leaves as broad as my hand, and the lower ones twice as long—so fresh and dewy in the morning—stalks now four or five, even seven or eight feet high. The farmers, I find, think the mullein a mean unworthy weed, but I have grown to a fondness for it.

Mulleins and Mulleins.

Printed from an autograph MS much like that of the preceding section except that it has more revisions. The original title was "Mulleins," in black ink. The words "and Mulleins" were added in red ink. At the top of the first of the two pages is penciled "tr this to 78," suggesting that it was first written at an earlier date. The date, in black ink, in the first line was first written "May, '78"; then "May" was crossed out and "June" written in; then both "June" and " '78" were crossed out. The words "as summer advances," in the first line, do not appear in the MS.

16. Originally Whitman had a period after "musing" and after that the following lines: "And who can say they may not, after their sort, realize me brooding near them? Henceforth, to me, what goes with them too—musical chatter of black-bird, and the deep drone of wild bees—the sunrise and the pomp of clouds—the deepening verdure of tulip trees, and the thin strata of gray vapor in the distance—these,". These lines were crossed out in red ink; the period was also deleted and the dash inserted after "musing" in red ink.

A passage in "Winter Sunshine," PT, January 26, 1879, resembles this section but is not its source. See Appendix XVI, 4.

Every object has its lesson, enclosing the suggestion of everything else— 10
and lately I sometimes think all is concentrated for me in these hardy,
yellow-flower'd weeds. As I come down the lane early in the morning, I
pause before their soft wool-like fleece and stem and broad leaves, glittering with countless diamonds. Annually for three summers now, they and I
have silently return'd together; at such long intervals I stand or sit 15
among them, musing—and woven with the rest, of so many hours and
moods of partial rehabilitation—of my sane or sick spirit, here as near
at peace as it can be.

Distant Sounds.

The axe of the wood-cutter, the measured thud of a single thresh-
ing-flail, the crowing of chanticleer in the barn-yard, (with invariable
responses from other barn-yards,) and the lowing of cattle—but most of
all, or far or near, the wind—through the high tree-tops, or through low
bushes, laving one's face and hands so gently, this balmy-bright noon, the 5
coolest for a long time, (Sept. 2)—I will not call it *sighing*, for to me it is
always a firm, sane, cheery expression, though a monotone, giving many
varieties, or swift or slow, or dense or delicate. The wind in the patch of
pine woods off there—how sibilant. Or at sea, I can imagine it this moment, tossing the waves, with spirts of foam flying far, and the free 10
whistle, and the scent of the salt—and that vast paradox somehow with
all its action and restlessness conveying a sense of eternal rest.

Other adjuncts.—But the sun and moon here and these times. As
never more wonderful by day, the gorgeous orb imperial, so vast, so

Distant Sounds.
  Printed from clippings of the *Critic*, the second number of "How I Get
Around," April 9, 1881, paragraphs 6–9, the last four under the subtitle "By the
Pond." The first two paragraphs under this subtitle in the *Critic* appear later in SDC
with the title "Horse-Mint," *q.v.*
  1. The axe] CR: *Distant sounds.*—The axe
  3. cattle—but most] CR: cattle, contribute the sounds. And now that swinging
whirr most seasonable—two locusts, one quite near, with proud, brassy, cymbaline,
continued, undulating song—the other just audible, far off, as if answering him.
(The katy-did and locust now o'nights instead of as three months ago the Hylas,
the bull-frog of the marsh, and the early tree-toad.) *The wind.*—But most
  4. CR begins a new paragraph with "*The wind.*"
  6. The date, Sept. 2, is out of sequence.
  9. there—how sibilant] CR: there—how curious, how sibilant
  12. After "eternal rest." CR, paragraph 8, not reprinted, is as follows:
  "*Brook-babbling.*—Out of the bank rapidly emerges a little volume of water as
thick as my ankle—cool and clear, and no sweeter-tasting have I ever met. I love to

15 ardently, lovingly hot—so never a more glorious moon of nights, especially the last three or four. The great planets too—Mars never before so
flaming bright, so flashing-large, with slight yellow tinge, (the astronomers say—is it true?—nearer to us than any time the past century)—and
well up, lord Jupiter, (a little while since close by the moon)—and in the
20 west, after the sun sinks, voluptuous Venus, now languid and shorn of
her beams, as if from some divine excess.

A Sun-Bath—Nakedness.

Sunday, Aug. 27.—Another day quite free from mark'd prostration
and pain. It seems indeed as if peace and nutriment from heaven subtly
filter into me as I slowly hobble down these country lanes and across
fields, in the good air—as I sit here in solitude with Nature—open, voice-
5 less, mystic, far removed, yet palpable, eloquent Nature. I merge myself
in the scene, in the perfect day. Hovering over the clear brook-water, I am
sooth'd by its soft gurgle in one place, and the hoarser murmurs of its
three-foot fall in another. Come, ye disconsolate, in whom any latent eligibility is left—come get the sure virtues of creek-shore, and wood and
10 field. Two months (July and August, '77,) have I absorb'd them, and
they begin to make a new man of me. Every day, seclusion—every day at
least two or three hours of freedom, bathing, no talk, no bonds, no dress,
no books, no *manners.*

Shall I tell you, reader, to what I attribute my already much-restored
15 health? That I have been almost two years, off and on, without drugs
and medicines, and daily in the open air. Last summer I found a particu-

rest in the shade of the willows close by this glossy rattler, as it runs along its bed
over pebbles, with a couple of little falls, on its way to the big creek. By the soft-
turbulent fount I stay long, abandoning myself dreamily to the liquid music, many a
happy, negative half-hour."

A Sun-Bath—Nakedness.
Printed from an autograph MS and a clipping.
1–13. From a clipping of the *Critic*, paragraph 10, the first under the subtitle
"Convalescent Hours," in the second number of "How I Get Around."
1. *Sunday, Aug. 27.*—Another] CR: *Sunday, Aug: 27, '77.*—Another
6. brook-water, I] CR: brook-water, how I
10. (July and August, '77,)] CR: (July and August)
11. they begin to make] CR: they already make
14–69. The autograph pages from which these lines were printed have been
revised for the printer chiefly to adjust the dates named to an altered chronology.
At the top of the first of the four pages Whitman wrote in pencil " '77 under Nakedness." This is crossed out, and under it is written "under '78 Aug." This too is crossed

larly secluded little dell off one side by my creek, originally a large dug-
out marl-pit, now abandon'd, fill'd with bushes, trees, grass, a group of
willows, a straggling bank, and a spring of delicious water running right
through the middle of it, with two or three little cascades. Here I retreated   20
every hot day, and follow it up this summer. Here I realize the meaning of
that old fellow who said he was seldom less alone than when alone. Never
before did I get so close to Nature; never before did she come so close to
me. By old habit, I pencill'd down from time to time, almost automatically,
moods, sights, hours, tints and outlines, on the spot. Let me specially   25
record the satisfaction of this current forenoon, so serene and primitive,
so conventionally exceptional, natural.

An hour or so after breakfast I wended my way down to the recesses
of the aforesaid dell, which I and certain thrushes, cat-birds, &c., had all to
ourselves. A light south-west wind was blowing through the tree-tops. It   30
was just the place and time for my Adamic air-bath and flesh-brushing
from head to foot. So hanging clothes on a rail near by, keeping old
broadbrim straw on head and easy shoes on feet, havn't I had a good time
the last two hours! First with the stiff-elastic bristles rasping arms, breast,
sides, till they turn'd scarlet—then partially bathing in the clear waters   35
of the running brook—taking everything very leisurely, with many rests
and pauses—stepping about barefooted every few minutes now and then
in some neighboring black ooze, for unctuous mud-bath to my feet—a brief
second and third rinsing in the crystal running waters—rubbing with
the fragrant towel—slow negligent promenades on the turf up and down   40
in the sun, varied with occasional rests, and further frictions of the bristle-
brush—sometimes carrying my portable chair with me from place to place,
as my range is quite extensive here, nearly a hundred rods, feeling quite

out, but the date in heavy ink, " '77" in the upper left-hand corner, is not crossed out.
These and similar dates at the tops of MS pages were apparently Whitman's directions to himself for the organization of his materials at different times. Some at least
of the notes seem to have been first written in the late summer of 1876 or early in
the summer of 1877, though it is not possible to determine precisely.

14. my already much-restored] MS: my somewhat restored
15. been almost two years,] MS: been a year,
16. Last summer I found] MS: I found
20–21. Here . . . summer.] MS: Here I retreated every hot day, during June,
July, and August.

In pencil at top of the third page: "?76" At left of this in heavy ink "1878".

24. from time] SDC: from to time [an obvious error; here corrected.]
25. The first paragraph on this MS page begins as follows: "July 18—A SUN-
BATH—NAKEDNESS. Yesterday and to-day fine in temperature, the heavens film'd
with slight clouds just veiling the sun—welcome enough after the midsummer glare
almost uninterrupted the last three weeks." All of this is crossed out, leaving the paragraph beginning with the next sentence, "Let me specially," etc., which the printer
is directed to run in with the preceding paragraph.

secure from intrusion, (and that indeed I am not at all nervous about, if
45   it accidentally happens.)

As I walk'd slowly over the grass, the sun shone out enough to show
the shadow moving with me. Somehow I seem'd to get identity with each
and every thing around me, in its condition. Nature was naked, and I
was also. It was too lazy, soothing, and joyous-equable to speculate about.
50   Yet I might have thought somehow in this vein: Perhaps the inner never
lost rapport we hold with earth, light, air, trees, &c., is not to be realized
through eyes and mind only, but through the whole corporeal body, which
I will not have blinded or bandaged any more than the eyes. Sweet, sane,
still Nakedness in Nature!—ah if poor, sick, prurient humanity in cities
55   might really know you once more! Is not nakedness then indecent? No,
not inherently. It is your thought, your sophistication, your fear, your re-
spectability, that is indecent. There come moods when these clothes of ours
are not only too irksome to wear, but are themselves indecent. Perhaps indeed he or she to whom the free exhilarating extasy of nakedness in Na-
60   ture has never been eligible (and how many thousands there are!) has not
really known what purity is—nor what faith or art or health really is.
(Probably the whole curriculum of first-class philosophy, beauty, heroism,
form, illustrated by the old Hellenic race—the highest height and deepest
depth known to civilization in those departments—came from their natu-
65   ral and religious idea of Nakedness.)

Many such hours, from time to time, the last two summers—I attribute my partial rehabilitation largely to them. Some good people may
think it a feeble or half-crack'd way of spending one's time and thinking.
May-be it is.

The Oaks and I.

Sept. 5, '77.—I write this, 11 A.M., shelter'd under a dense oak by
the bank, where I have taken refuge from a sudden rain. I came down
here, (we had sulky drizzles all the morning, but an hour ago a lull,) for
the before-mention'd daily and simple exercise I am fond of—to pull on

66. last two summers] MS before revision: last three summers

The Oaks and I.

Printed from clippings of the *Critic*, second number of "How I Get Around,"
April 9, 1881, paragraphs 11 and 12, the second and third under the subtitle
"Convalescent Hours."

3–4. for . . . daily] CR: for a daily

that young hickory sapling out there—to sway and yield to its tough-limber upright stem—haply to get into my old sinews some of its elastic fibre and clear sap. I stand on the turf and take these health-pulls moderately and at intervals for nearly an hour, inhaling great draughts of fresh air. Wandering by the creek, I have three or four naturally favorable spots where I rest—besides a chair I lug with me and use for more deliberate occasions. At other spots convenient I have selected, besides the hickory just named, strong and limber boughs of beech or holly, in easy-reaching distance, for my natural gymnasia, for arms, chest, trunk-muscles. I can soon feel the sap and sinew rising through me, like mercury to heat. I hold on boughs or slender trees caressingly there in the sun and shade, wrestle with their innocent stalwartness—and *know* the virtue thereof passes from them into me. (Or may-be we interchange—may-be the trees are more aware of it all than I ever thought.)

But now pleasantly imprison'd here under the big oak—the rain dripping, and the sky cover'd with leaden clouds—nothing but the pond on one side, and the other a spread of grass, spotted with the milky blossoms of the wild carrot—the sound of an axe wielded at some distant wood-pile—yet in this dull scene, (as most folks would call it,) why am I so (almost) happy here and alone? Why would any intrusion, even from people I like, spoil the charm? But am I alone? Doubtless there comes a time—perhaps it has come to me—when one feels through his whole being, and pronouncedly the emotional part, that identity between himself subjectively and Nature objectively which Schelling and Fichte are so fond of pressing. How it is I know not, but I often realize a presence here—in clear moods I am certain of it, and neither chemistry nor reasoning nor esthetics will give the least explanation. All the past two summers it has been strengthening and nourishing my sick body and soul, as never before. Thanks, invisible physician, for thy silent delicious medicine, thy day and night, thy waters and thy airs, the banks, the grass, the trees, and e'en the weeds!

11. convenient I have] *CR:* convenient (since I am on the details of my convalescence) I have
14. can soon feel] *CR:* can almost feel
15. on boughs] *CR:* on to boughs
25. Doubtless there] *CR:* Perhaps there
29. here—in] *CR:* here—though nor humanity nor its voice, hardly its sign at all —is here. In

A Quintette.

While I have been kept by the rain under the shelter of my great oak, (perfectly dry and comfortable, to the rattle of the drops all around,) I have pencill'd off the mood of the hour in a little quintette, which I will give you:

5
                At vacancy with Nature,
                Acceptive and at ease,
                Distilling the present hour,
                Whatever, wherever it is,
                And over the past, oblivion.

10
Can you get hold of it, reader dear? and how do you like it anyhow?

The First Frost—Mems.

Where I was stopping I saw the first palpable frost, on my sunrise walk, October 6; all over the yet-green spread a light blue-gray veil, giving a new show to the entire landscape. I had but little time to notice it, for the sun rose cloudless and mellow-warm, and as I returned along the
5 lane it had turn'd to glittering patches of wet. As I walk I notice the bursting pods of wild-cotton, (Indian hemp they call it here,) with flossy-silky contents, and dark red-brown seeds—a startled rabbit—I pull a handful of the balsamic life-everlasting and stuff it down in my trowsers-pocket for scent.

A Quintette.

Printed from clippings of the *Critic*, second number of "How I Get Around," consisting of paragraphs 13 and 14, the last under the subtitle "Convalescent Hours." In the *Critic* "A Quintette" is in italics at the beginning of the first line.
    8. Whatever, wherever] CR: Whate'er, where'er
    9. And over] CR: As over
  10. After this line CR has the name "Walt Whitman."

The First Frost—Mems.

Printed from an autograph MS, where the word "Mems" does not appear. It was presumably inserted in the galley proof.

Three Young Men's Deaths.

Printed from clippings of *Cope's Tobacco Plant*, April, 1879, pp. 818–819, where it has the same title. The title was cut from the clipping, but inserted in red

Three Young Men's Deaths.

December 20.—Somehow I got thinking to-day of young men's deaths—not at all sadly or sentimentally, but gravely, realistically, perhaps a little artistically. Let me give the following three cases from budgets of personal memoranda, which I have been turning over, alone in my room, and resuming and dwelling on, this rainy afternoon. Who is there to whom the theme does not come home? Then I don't know how it may be to others, but to me not only is there nothing gloomy or depressing in such cases—on the contrary, as reminiscences, I find them soothing, bracing, tonic.

Erastus Haskell.—[I just transcribe verbatim from a letter written by myself in one of the army hospitals, 16 years ago, during the secession war.] *Washington, July 28, 1863.*—Dear M.,—I am writing this in the hospital, sitting by the side of a soldier, I do not expect to last many hours. His fate has been a hard one—he seems to be only about 19 or 20— Erastus Haskell, company K, 141st N. Y.—has been out about a year, and sick or half-sick more than half that time—has been down on the peninsula—was detail'd to go in the band as fifer-boy. While sick, the surgeon told him to keep up with the rest—(probably work'd and march'd too long.) He is a shy, and seems to me a very sensible boy—has fine manners—never complains—was sick down on the peninsula in an old storehouse—typhoid fever. The first week this July was brought up here— journey very bad, no accommodations, no nourishment, nothing but hard jolting, and exposure enough to make a well man sick; (these fearful journeys do the job for many)—arrived here July 11th—a silent dark-

ink. The date "Dec. 20, 1877" is written in ink at the beginning of the first line, but "1877" must have been deleted in proof.

    1–9. This paragraph is enclosed in brackets in *CTP*, with "W.W." after the last sentence inside the final bracket.

    1. *December 20.*—Somehow] *CTP:* [Camden, New Jersey, U. S. America; Dec., 1878.—Somehow

      5. room, . . . this] *CTP:* room, this

      9. tonic.] *CTP:* tonic. W. W.]

    10. In *CTP* this name is centered on the page above the paragraph.

    11–12. during . . . war] *CTP:* during our American Secession War

    12. "*Washington, July 28, 1863.*" [Sixteen years after this date would be 1879. Evidently Whitman overlooked this discrepancy when he changed the date of this section to 1877. The original of this letter is not published in Miller's volume and is not named in his checklist as a lost letter, but in a note to Letter 65 (p. 131: Vol. I) he says the letter is apparently lost.—ED.]

    21. fever. The] *CTP:* fever; the

25 skinn'd Spanish-looking youth, with large very dark blue eyes, peculiar
looking. Doctor F. here made light of his sickness—said he would recover
soon, &c.; but I thought very different, and told F. so repeatedly; (I came
near quarreling with him about it from the first)—but he laugh'd, and
would not listen to me. About four days ago, I told Doctor he would in my
30 opinion lose the boy without doubt—but F. again laugh'd at me. The next
day he changed his opinion—I brought the head surgeon of the post—he
said the boy would probably die, but they would make a hard fight for
him.

The last two days he has been lying panting for breath—a pitiful
35 sight. I have been with him some every day or night since he arrived. He
suffers a great deal with the heat—says little or nothing—is flighty the last
three days, at times—knows me always, however—calls me "Walter"—
(sometimes calls the name over and over and over again, musingly, ab-
stractedly, to himself.) His father lives at Breesport, Chemung county,
40 N. Y., is a mechanic with large family—is a steady, religious man; his
mother too is living. I have written to them, and shall write again to-day
—Erastus has not receiv'd a word from home for months.

As I sit here writing to you, M., I wish you could see the whole scene.
This young man lies within reach of me, flat on his back, his hands clasp'd
45 across his breast, his thick black hair cut close; he is dozing, breathing
hard, every breath a spasm—it looks so cruel. He is a noble youngster,—
I consider him past all hope. Often there is no one with him for a long
while. I am here as much as possible.

WILLIAM ALCOTT, fireman. *Camden, Nov., 1874.*—Last Monday
50 afternoon his widow, mother, relatives, mates of the fire department, and
his other friends, (I was one, only lately it is true, but our love grew
fast and close, the days and nights of those eight weeks by the chair of
rapid decline, and the bed of death,) gather'd to the funeral of this young
man, who had grown up, and was well-known here. With nothing special,
55 perhaps, to record, I would give a word or two to his memory. He seem'd
to me not an inappropriate specimen in character and elements, of that
bulk of the average good American race that ebbs and flows perennially

27. I came] *CTP:* I come
49–78. These two paragraphs had previously been published as "Death of a
Fireman" in the *New Republic*, Camden, N. J., Nov. 14, 1874.
49. In *CTP* "William Alcott, fireman" is removed from the first line and placed
in capital letters in the center of the page, above the paragraph.
49. William . . . Last] *CTP:* Camden, Nov., 1874.—Last] *CNR:* William Alcott,
aged 26 years.—Last
54. here. With] *CNR:* in Camden. With
58. this scum of] *CNR:* this skim of

beneath this scum of eructations on the surface. Always very quiet in manner, neat in person and dress, good temper'd—punctual and industrious
at his work, till he could work no longer—he just lived his steady, square,   60
unobtrusive life, in its own humble sphere, doubtless unconscious of itself. (Though I think there were currents of emotion and intellect un-
develop'd beneath, far deeper than his acquaintances ever suspected—or
than he himself ever did.) He was no talker. His troubles, when he had
any, he kept to himself. As there was nothing querulous about him in life,   65
he made no complaints during his last sickness. He was one of those persons that while his associates never thought of attributing any particular
talent or grace to him, yet all insensibly, really, liked Billy Alcott.

I, too, loved him. At last, after being with him quite a good deal—
after hours and days of panting for breath, much of the time unconscious,   70
(for though the consumption that had been lurking in his system, once
thoroughly started, made rapid progress, there was still great vitality in
him, and indeed for four or five days he lay dying, before the close,) late
on Wednesday night, Nov. 4th, where we surrounded his bed in silence,
there came a lull—a longer drawn breath, a pause, a faint sigh—another—   75
a weaker breath, another sigh—a pause again and just a tremble—and
the face of the poor wasted young man (he was just 26,) fell gently over,
in death, on my hand, on the pillow.

CHARLES CASWELL.—[I extract the following, verbatim, from a letter
to me dated September 29, from my friend John Burroughs, at Esopus-on-   80
Hudson, New York State.] S. was away when your picture came, attending his sick brother, Charles—who has since died—an event that has sad-
den'd me much. Charlie was younger than S., and a most attractive young
fellow. He work'd at my father's, and had done so for two years. He was
about the best specimen of a young country farm-hand I ever knew. You   85
would have loved him. He was like one of your poems. With his great
strength, his blond hair, his cheerfulness and contentment, his universal
good will, and his silent manly ways, he was a youth hard to match. He
was murder'd by an old doctor. He had typhoid fever, and the old fool
bled him twice. He lived to wear out the fever, but had not strength to   90

60. work, till] *CNR:* work, at the house cor. Fifth and Arch sts., till
77. man (he was just 26,) fell] *CNR:* man fell
78. The *CNR* article has "Walt Whitman." at the end.
79. In *CTP* the name "Charles Caswell" is placed in the center of the page,
above the paragraph.
80. September 29, from] *CTP:* Sept. 29, 1878, from
81. After the sentence in brackets, *CTP* begins a new paragraph.
[This letter has not otherwise been published. Some of the details, together with
some not in Whitman's account, can be seen in *The Heart of Burroughs's Journals,*
ed. Clara Barrus, under date of Sept. 22, 1878, pp. 77–78.—ED.]

rally. He was out of his head nearly all the time. In the morning, as he died in the afternoon, S. was standing over him, when Charlie put up his arms around S.'s neck, and pull'd his face down and kiss'd him. S. said he knew then the end was near. (S. stuck to him day and night to the last.)

95 When I was home in August, Charlie was cradling on the hill, and it was a picture to see him walk through the grain. All work seem'd play to him. He had no vices, any more than Nature has, and was belov'd by all who knew him.

I have written thus to you about him, for such young men belong to
100 you; he was of your kind. I wish you could have known him. He had the sweetness of a child, and the strength and courage and readiness of a young Viking. His mother and father are poor; they have a rough, hard farm. His mother works in the field with her husband when the work presses. She has had twelve children.

February Days.

February 7, 1878.—Glistening sun to-day, with slight haze, warm enough, and yet tart, as I sit here in the open air, down in my country retreat, under an old cedar. For two hours I have been idly wandering around the woods and pond, lugging my chair, picking out choice spots
5 to sit awhile—then up and slowly on again. All is peace here. Of course, none of the summer noises or vitality; to-day hardly even the winter ones. I amuse myself by exercising my voice in recitations, and in ringing the changes on all the vocal and alphabetical sounds. Not even an echo; only the cawing of a solitary crow, flying at some distance. The pond is one

February Days.

Printed from clippings from the Philadelphia *Times*, paragraphs 12–22 of the article titled "Winter Sunshine," Jan. 26, 1879. These are the first eleven paragraphs of "Jottings" from his earlier notes. For the introductory paragraph to these "Jottings" see Appendix XVI, 2.

  1. Glistening] *PT:* A glistening
  1. haze, warm] *PT:* haze, delicious, warm
  2–3. air, . . . For] *PT:* air, under an old cedar, writing this. For
  4. my chair] *PT:* my old chair
  5. After "on again." *PT* begins a new paragraph.
  6. vitality; to-day] *PT:* vitality; and to-day
  9. After "some distance." *PT* begins a new paragraph.
  9–10. is one bright] *PT:* is wonderful, still, glassy—a bright
  11. and an occasional] *PT:* and the occasional
  13. After "snow left." *PT* has the following sentence completing the paragraph and two additional short paragraphs, omitted in *SDC:*
  "The distant whistle of the locomotive, the just-heard chanticleers of neighboring farms, give a soothing vitality-echo to the scene.
  "How the warm, bright, blessed sun falls upon me, as I sit here—bathing

bright, flat spread, without a ripple—a vast Claude Lorraine glass, in 10
which I study the sky, the light, the leafless trees, and an occasional
crow, with flapping wings, flying overhead. The brown fields have a few
white patches of snow left.

Feb. 9.—After an hour's ramble, now retreating, resting, sitting
close by the pond, in a warm nook, writing this, shelter'd from the breeze, 15
just before noon. The *emotional* aspects and influences of Nature! I, too,
like the rest, feel these modern tendencies (from all the prevailing intellec-
tions, literature and poems,) to turn everything to pathos, ennui, morbidity, dissatisfaction, death. Yet how clear it is to me that those are not
the born results, influences of Nature at all, but of one's own distorted, 20
sick or silly soul. Here, amid this wild, free scene, how healthy, how joyous, how clean and vigorous and sweet!

Mid-afternoon.—One of my nooks is south of the barn, and here I
am sitting now, on a log, still basking in the sun, shielded from the wind.
Near me are the cattle, feeding on corn-stalks. Occasionally a cow or the 25
young bull (how handsome and bold he is!) scratches and munches the far
end of the log on which I sit. The fresh milky odor is quite perceptible,
also the perfume of hay from the barn. The perpetual rustle of dry corn-
stalks, the low sough of the wind round the barn gables, the grunting of
pigs, the distant whistle of a locomotive, and occasional crowing of chanti- 30
cleers, are the sounds.

Feb. 19.—Cold and sharp last night—clear and not much wind
—the full moon shining, and a fine spread of constellations and little and
big stars—Sirius very bright, rising early, preceded by many-orb'd
Orion, glittering, vast, sworded, and chasing with his dog. The earth 35

me all over! The Sunshine, with its thin transparent haze—why have I not written a
poem on it? So vast, so spiritual—the source of all—priceless, yet costing nothing—
vouchsafed to every one, to every thing—without which—ah, without which, indeed!
   "Yes—to write the poem of the Sunshine—it were a work for the flush of youth—
or, better still, for full maturity—not for an old, banged-up man like me."
   16. before noon. The *emotional*] *PT:* before noon, the sun shining bright. The
eloquent, vital stillness of Nature, here! The *emotional*
   18. everything to pathos] *PT:* everything even in rude Nature to pathos
   23. barn] *PT:* barn-yard
   27–28. perceptible, also] *PT:* perceptible, and also
   28. of hay] *PT:* of the hay
   29–30. of pigs, . . . occasional] *PT:* of the pigs, and the occasional
   31. After "the sounds." *PT* has the following brief paragraph, omitted in *SDC:*
   "Over all else, so vast, so clear, the marvels of the sky and light! Every day they
come, silent and spiritual—and so we reck not of them—but really what greater, what
more beautiful marvels are there—or can there ever be?"
   32. *Feb. 19.*—Cold] *PT:* FEBRUARY 19—Noon.—Cold
   35–36. his dog. . . . over the] *PT:* his dogs. The earth hard frozen on the
surface and a stiff glare of ice on the

hard frozen, and a stiff glare of ice over the pond. Attracted by the calm splendor of the night, I attempted a short walk, but was driven back by the cold. Too severe for me also at 9 o'clock, when I came out this morning, so I turn'd back again. But now, near noon, I have walk'd down the lane, basking all the way in the sun (this farm has a pleasant southerly exposure,) and here I am, seated under the lee of a bank, close by the water. There are blue-birds already flying about, and I hear much chirping and twittering and two or three real songs, sustain'd quite awhile, in the mid-day brilliance and warmth. (There! that is a true carol, coming out boldly and repeatedly, as if the singer meant it.) Then as the noon strengthens, the reedy trill of the robin—to my ear the most cheering of bird-notes. At intervals, like bars and breaks (out of the low murmur that in any scene, however quiet, is never entirely absent to a delicate ear,) the occasional crunch and cracking of the ice-glare congeal'd over the creek, as it gives way to the sunbeams—sometimes with low sigh—sometimes with indignant, obstinate tug and snort.

(Robert Burns says in one of his letters: "There is scarcely any earthly object gives me more—I do not know if I should call it pleasure—but something which exalts me—something which enraptures me—than to walk in the shelter'd side of a wood in a cloudy winter day, and hear the stormy wind howling among the trees, and raving over the plain. It is my best season of devotion." Some of his most characteristic poems were composed in such scenes and seasons.)

A Meadow Lark.

March 16.—Fine, clear, dazzling morning, the sun an hour high, the air just tart enough. What a stamp in advance my whole day receives

---

37–38. by the cold. Too] *PT:* by the cold. Cold too

38. *PT* begins a new paragraph with "Cold too".

41–42. the water. . . . already] *PT:* the water, writing these. There are blue birds, robins, etc., already

46–47. of bird-notes.] *PT:* of all bird-notes.

47. After "bird-notes." *PT* begins a new paragraph.

49–50. ice-glare . . . as] *PT:* ice-glare, as

51. After "and snort." *PT* has two paragraphs that were omitted from *SDC.* See Appendix XVI, *3.*

52–58. These lines were printed from an autograph MS pasted below the clippings.

A Meadow Lark.
Printed from an autograph MS.

from the song of that meadow lark perch'd on a fence-stake twenty rods distant! Two or three liquid-simple notes, repeated at intervals, full of careless happiness and hope. With its peculiar shimmering-slow progress and rapid-noiseless action of the wings, it flies on a ways, lights on another stake, and so on to another, shimmering and singing many minutes.

Sundown Lights.

May 6, 5 P.M.—This is the hour for strange effects in light and shade—enough to make a colorist go delirious—long spokes of molten silver sent horizontally through the trees (now in their brightest tenderest green,) each leaf and branch of endless foliage a lit-up miracle, then lying all prone on the youthful-ripe, interminable grass, and giving the blades not only aggregate but individual splendor, in ways unknown to any other hour. I have particular spots where I get these effects in their perfection. One broad splash lies on the water, with many a rippling twinkle, offset by the rapidly deepening black-green murky-transparent shadows behind, and at intervals all along the banks. These, with great shafts of horizontal fire thrown among the trees and along the grass as the sun lowers, give effects more and more peculiar, more and more superb, unearthly, rich and dazzling.

Thoughts under an Oak—a Dream.

June 2.—This is the fourth day of a dark northeast storm, wind and rain. Day before yesterday was my birthday. I have now enter'd on my 6oth year. Every day of the storm, protected by overshoes and a water-

Sundown Lights.
Printed with title inserted in red ink, from a clipping of the Philadelphia *Times*, Jan. 26, 1879, where it has only the sidehead and consists of the single paragraph next following the omitted paragraphs under "February Days" beginning "*Authors, Etc.*"

 1. *May 6, 5 P.M.*—This] *PT:* MAY 6, SUNDOWN LIGHTS—5 P.M.—This
 2. long spokes of] *PT:* long counter shafts of
 10. These, with great] *PT:* These, with the late afternoon songs of the birds—great

Thoughts under an Oak—a Dream.
Printed with subtitle inserted in red ink, from a clipping of the Philadelphia *Times*, Jan. 26, 1879, where it consists of the three paragraphs following "Sundown Lights" without a separate heading except the date "June 2, 1878" in the first line.

proof blanket, I regularly come down to the pond, and ensconce myself
under the lee of the great oak; I am here now writing these lines. The
dark smoke-color'd clouds roll in furious silence athwart the sky; the soft
green leaves dangle all round me; the wind steadily keeps up its hoarse,
soothing music over my head—Nature's mighty whisper. Seated here in
solitude I have been musing over my life—connecting events, dates, as
links of a chain, neither sadly nor cheerily, but somehow, to-day here under the oak, in the rain, in an unusually matter-of-fact spirit.

But my great oak—sturdy, vital, green—five feet thick at the butt. I
sit a great deal near or under him. Then the tulip tree near by—the
Apollo of the woods—tall and graceful, yet robust and sinewy, inimitable
in hang of foliage and throwing-out of limb; as if the beauteous, vital,
leafy creature could walk, if it only would. (I had a sort of dream-trance
the other day, in which I saw my favorite trees step out and promenade up,
down and around, very curiously—with a whisper from one, leaning
down as he pass'd me, *We do all this on the present occasion, exception-*
ally, just for you.)

Clover and Hay Perfume.

July 3d, 4th, 5th.—Clear, hot, favorable weather—has been a good
summer—the growth of clover and grass now generally mow'd. The familiar delicious perfume fills the barns and lanes. As you go along you see
the fields of grayish white slightly tinged with yellow, the loosely stack'd
grain, the slow-moving wagons passing, and farmers in the fields with
stout boys pitching and loading the sheaves. The corn is about beginning
to tassel. All over the middle and southern states the spear-shaped bat-
talia, multitudinous, curving, flaunting—long, glossy, dark-green plumes
for the great horseman, earth. I hear the cheery notes of my old acquaintance Tommy quail; but too late for the whip-poor-will, (though I heard

5. of the great oak; I] *PT:* of a great oak. I
8. After "whisper." *PT* begins a new paragraph.
11. After "Spirit." *PT* begins a new paragraph.
20. The two short paragraphs in *PT* next following the three paragraphs under
date of June 2, are dated June 10, and are not reprinted though they resemble the
section "Mulleins and Mulleins," *q.v.* For these two paragraphs (23–24) see Appendix XVI, 4.

Clover and Hay Perfume.
Printed from an autograph MS; subtitle inserted in red ink.

one solitary lingerer night before last.) I watch the broad majestic flight of a turkey-buzzard, sometimes high up, sometimes low enough to see the lines of his form, even his spread quills, in relief against the sky. Once or twice lately I have seen an eagle here at early candle-light flying low.

An Unknown.

June 15.—To-day I noticed a new large bird, size of a nearly grown hen—a haughty, white-bodied dark-wing'd hawk—I suppose a hawk from his bill and general look—only he had a clear, loud, quite musical, sort of bell-like call, which he repeated again and again, at intervals, from a lofty dead tree-top, overhanging the water. Sat there a long time, and I on the opposite bank watching him. Then he darted down, skimming pretty close to the stream—rose slowly, a magnificent sight, and sail'd with steady wide-spread wings, no flapping at all, up and down the pond two or three times, near me, in circles in clear sight, as if for my delectation. Once he came quite close over my head; I saw plainly his hook'd bill and hard restless eyes.

Bird-Whistling.

How much music (wild, simple, savage, doubtless, but so tart-sweet,) there is in mere whistling. It is four-fifths of the utterance of birds. There are all sorts and styles. For the last half-hour, now, while I have been sitting here, some feather'd fellow away off in the bushes has been re-peating over and over again what I may call a kind of throbbing whistle. And now a bird about the robin size has just appear'd, all mulberry red, flitting among the bushes—head, wings, body, deep red, not very bright —no song, as I have heard. *4 o'clock:* There is a real concert going on

An Unknown.
Printed from a clipping of the Philadelphia *American*, May 14, 1881, para-graph 7 of the article "Bumble-Bees and Bird-Music." The date in the first line was inserted in ink.

Bird-Whistling.
Printed from a clipping of *PA*, May 14, 1881, including paragraphs 8–10 of the article "Bumble-Bees and Bird-Music."
2. in mere whistling] *PA:* in whistling
5. After "whistle." *PA* begins a new paragraph.
8–9. concert going on around] *PA:* concert around

around me—a dozen different birds pitching in with a will. There have
10 been occasional rains, and the growths all show its vivifying influences.
As I finish this, seated on a log close by the pond-edge, much chirping and
trilling in the distance, and a feather'd recluse in the woods near by is
singing deliciously—not many notes, but full of music of almost human
sympathy—continuing for a long, long while.

Horse-Mint.

Aug. 22.—Not a human being, and hardly the evidence of one, in
sight. After my brief semi-daily bath, I sit here for a bit, the brook
musically brawling, to the chromatic tones of a fretful cat-bird somewhere
off in the bushes. On my walk hither two hours since, through fields and
5 the old lane, I stopt to view, now the sky, now the mile-off woods on the
hill, and now the apple orchards. What a contrast from New York's or
Philadelphia's streets! Everywhere great patches of dingy-blossom'd
horse-mint wafting a spicy odor through the air, (especially evenings.)
Everywhere the flowering boneset, and the rose-bloom of the wild bean.

Three of Us.

July 14.—My two kingfishers still haunt the pond. In the bright
sun and breeze and perfect temperature of to-day, noon, I am sitting here
by one of the gurgling brooks, dipping a French water-pen in the limpid
crystal, and using it to write these lines, again watching the feather'd
5 twain, as they fly and sport athwart the water, so close, almost touching
into its surface. Indeed there seem to be three of us. For nearly an hour I

---

9. will. There] *PA:* will. I wish I could even measurably describe it, and how I
enjoy it, all to myself—for the spot here is a perfect rural solitude otherwise. *Sunset.*
—There
    9. After "otherwise" *PA* begins a new paragraph.
    10. rains, . . . all] *PA:* rains—and the grass, clover, young wheat and rye, po-
tatoes, early onions, peas, and other growths, all
    14. After "long while." *PA* has the sentence, omitted in *SDC:* "Can it be the her-
mit thrush?"

Horse-Mint.
    Printed from a clipping of *CR,* second number of "How I Get Around," para-
graphs 4 and 5, the first two under the subtitle "By the Pond." This item is out of
sequence in *SDC.* (See notes on "Distant Sounds.") Subtitle inserted in red ink.
    1. *Aug. 22.*—Not a] *CR: Aug: 22, '77.*—As I leisurely write this, (with a
French water pen, dipping every two or three minutes in the brook,) and pause and
look around from time to time, nothing could be more secluded or naturally free, cool,
luxuriant, than the scene I am in the midst of. Not a

indolently look and join them while they dart and turn and take their airy gambols, sometimes far up the creek disappearing for a few moments, and then surely returning again, and performing most of their flight within sight of me, as if they knew I appreciated and absorb'd their vitality, spirituality, faithfulness, and the rapid, vanishing, delicate lines of moving yet quiet electricity they draw for me across the spread of the grass, the trees, and the blue sky. While the brook babbles, babbles, and the shadows of the boughs dapple in the sunshine around me, and the cool west by-nor'-west wind faintly soughs in the thick bushes and tree tops.

Among the objects of beauty and interest now beginning to appear quite plentifully in this secluded spot, I notice the humming-bird, the dragon-fly with its wings of slate-color'd gauze, and many varieties of beautiful and plain butterflies, idly flapping among the plants and wild posies. The mullein has shot up out of its nest of broad leaves, to a tall stalk towering sometimes five or six feet high, now studded with knobs of golden blossoms. The milk-weed, (I see a great gorgeous creature of gamboge and black lighting on one as I write,) is in flower, with its delicate red fringe; and there are profuse clusters of a feathery blossom waving in the wind on taper stems. I see lots of these and much else in every direction, as I saunter or sit. For the last half hour a bird has persistently kept up a simple, sweet, melodious song, from the bushes. (I have a positive conviction that some of these birds sing, and others fly and flirt about here, for my especial benefit.)

Death of William Cullen Bryant.

New York City.—Came on from West Philadelphia, June 13, in the 2 P.M. train to Jersey city, and so across and to my friends, Mr. and Mrs.

2. my brief semi-daily] *CR:* my semi-daily
4. After "bushes." *PA* begins a new paragraph.

Three of Us.
Printed from an autograph MS, purple ink on white paper, revised in red and black ink and in pencil.
1. MS has "July 14, '77," but "'77" is crossed out.
3–4. The phrase "dipping . . . lines" is inserted in the MS in black ink.

Death of William Cullen Bryant.
Printed from clippings of *NYTR*, July 4, 1878; paragraphs 2–4 of "A Poet's Recreation," 2–3 subtitled "Impromptu Start—Death of Mr. Bryant," and 4 subtitled "The Funeral." Whitman's title, written at the top of the clipping, was originally "Funeral of William Cullen Bryant." Revised on the clipping. For paragraph 1, not reprinted, see Appendix xv, 1.
1. *New York City.*—Came on] *NYTR:* Came on

J. H. J., and their large house, large family (and large hearts,) amid which I feel at home, at peace—away up on Fifth avenue, near Eighty-sixth street, quiet, breezy, overlooking the dense woody fringe of the park —plenty of space and sky, birds chirping, and air comparatively fresh and odorless. Two hours before starting, saw the announcement of William Cullen Bryant's funeral, and felt a strong desire to attend. I had known Mr. Bryant over thirty years ago, and he had been markedly kind to me. Off and on, along that time for years as they pass'd, we met and chatted together. I thought him very sociable in his way, and a man to become attach'd to. We were both walkers, and when I work'd in Brooklyn he several times came over, middle of afternoons, and we took rambles miles long, till dark, out towards Bedford or Flatbush, in company. On these occasions he gave me clear accounts of scenes in Europe—the cities, looks, architecture, art, especially Italy—where he had travel'd a good deal.

June 14.—The Funeral.—And so the good, stainless, noble old citizen and poet lies in the closed coffin there—and this is his funeral. A solemn, impressive, simple scene, to spirit and senses. The remarkable gathering of gray heads, celebrities—the finely render'd anthem, and other music—the church, dim even now at approaching noon, in its light from the mellow-stain'd windows—the pronounc'd eulogy on the bard who loved Nature so fondly, and sung so well her shows and seasons— ending with these appropriate well-known lines:

> I gazed upon the glorious sky,
>   And the green mountains round,
> And thought that when I came to lie
>   At rest within the ground,
> 'Twere pleasant that in flowery June,
> When brooks send up a joyous tune,
>   And groves a cheerful sound,

7. After "odorless." *NYTR* begins a new paragraph.
7. starting, saw] *NYTR:* starting from Philadelphia, saw
10. and on, along that time for years as they pass'd, we met] *NYTR:* and on, then, as time passed, we met
12–13. work'd in Brooklyn] *NYTR:* worked on *The Eagle* newspaper, in Brooklyn
14. dark, out towards Bedford or Flatbush, in] *NYTR:* dark, in
26–34. The verses are the second stanza, slightly misquoted, of Bryant's "June."
31. joyous tune] *NYTR* and Bryant: cheerful tune
32. cheerful sound] Bryant: joyous sound
Paragraphs 5, 6, and 7 of the *NYTR* article were not reprinted. See Appendix xv, 2.

Jaunt up the Hudson.
Printed from a clipping of paragraph 8, same article, with the subtitle "The

The sexton's hand, my grave to make,
The rich green mountain turf should break.

Jaunt up the Hudson.

June 20th.—On the "Mary Powell," enjoy'd everything beyond precedent. The delicious tender summer day, just warm enough—the constantly changing but ever beautiful panorama on both sides of the river —(went up near a hundred miles)—the high straight walls of the stony Palisades—beautiful Yonkers, and beautiful Irvington—the never-ending hills, mostly in rounded lines, swathed with verdure,—the distant turns, like great shoulders in blue veils—the frequent gray and brown of the tall-rising rocks—the river itself, now narrowing, now expanding—the white sails of the many sloops, yachts, &c., some near, some in the distance—the rapid succession of handsome villages and cities, (our boat is a swift traveler, and makes few stops)—the Race—picturesque West Point, and indeed all along—the costly and often turreted mansions forever showing in some cheery light color, through the woods—make up the scene.

Happiness and Raspberries.

June 21.—Here I am, on the west bank of the Hudson, 80 miles north of New York, near Esopus, at the handsome, roomy, honeysuckle-and-rose-embower'd cottage of John Burroughs. The place, the perfect June days and nights, (leaning toward crisp and cool,) the hospitality of J. and Mrs. B., the air, the fruit, (especially my favorite dish, currants and raspberries, mixed, sugar'd, fresh and ripe from the bushes—I pick 'em myself)—the room I occupy at night, the perfect bed, the window giving an ample view of the Hudson and the opposite shores, so wonderful toward sunset, and the rolling music of the RR. trains, far over there—the

River in June." Whitman indicates his new subtitle by underlining four words of the first sentence and deleting unused words.

    1. *June 20th.*—On the "Mary Powell," enjoy'd] *NYTR: June 20th.*—Another jaunt up the Hudson, this time in the afternoon, on the Mary Powell. Enjoyed

    2. day, just warm] *NYTR:* day, just cool enough, just warm

    8. rocks, the river] *NYTR:* rocks, the glistening river

    13. the scene.] *NYTR:* the scene, and my trip.

Happiness and Raspberries.

    Printed from a clipping of paragraph 9, same article, with the subtitle "Peace, Happiness and Raspberries."

    3. Burroughs. The] *NYTR:* Burroughs and Mrs. B.—finding myself, (to use a slang phrase of the young fellows years ago) "as happy as the law allows." The

10   peaceful rest—the early Venus-heralded dawn—the noiseless splash of
sunrise, the light and warmth indescribably glorious, in which, (soon as
the sun is well up,) I have a capital rubbing and rasping with the flesh-
brush—with an extra scour on the back by Al. J., who is here with us—
all inspiriting my invalid frame with new life, for the day. Then, after
15   some whiffs of morning air, the delicious coffee of Mrs. B., with the cream,
strawberries, and many substantials, for breakfast.

A Specimen Tramp Family.

June 22.—This afternoon we went out (J. B., Al. and I) on quite a
drive around the country. The scenery, the perpetual stone fences, (some
venerable old fellows, dark-spotted with lichens)—the many fine locust-
trees—the runs of brawling water, often over descents of rock—these,
5   and lots else. It is lucky the roads are first-rate here, (as they are,) for
it is up or down hill everywhere, and sometimes steep enough. B. has a
tip-top horse, strong, young, and both gentle and fast. There is a great
deal of waste land and hills on the river edge of Ulster county, with a
wonderful luxuriance of wild flowers and bushes—and it seems to me I
10   never saw more vitality of trees—eloquent hemlocks, plenty of locusts and
fine maples, and the balm of Gilead, giving out aroma. In the fields and
along the road-sides unusual crops of the tall-stemm'd wild daisy, white as
milk and yellow as gold.
    We pass'd quite a number of tramps, singly or in couples—one squad,
15   a family in a rickety one-horse wagon, with some baskets evidently their
work and trade—the man seated on a low board, in front, driving—the
gauntish woman by his side, with a baby well bundled in her arms, its
little red feet and lower legs sticking out right towards us as we pass'd—
and in the wagon behind, we saw two (or three) crouching little children.

10. the noiseless splash] *NYTR:* the limitless splash
16. strawberries, . . . for] *NYTR:* strawberries and other things, for

A Specimen Tramp Family.
Printed from clippings of paragraphs 10 and 11, same article, under the subtitle "A Specimen Tramp Family Out of Thousands."
    5. else. It] *NYTR:* else with them, do me so much good! It
10. saw more vitality of] *NYTR:* saw such a vital growth of
14. pass'd . . . tramps] *NYTR:* passed many tramps
18–19. pass'd—and in] *NYTR:* passed—and in the huddle of baskets and meagre
"plunder" in
21. held confab] *NYTR:* held long confab
23–24. camp for] *NYTR:* camp there for
27. but somehow her] *NYTR:* but her

It was a queer, taking, rather sad picture. If I had been alone and on foot, I should have stopp'd and held confab. But on our return nearly two hours afterward, we found them a ways further along the same road, in a lonesome open spot, haul'd aside, unhitch'd, and evidently going to camp for the night. The freed horse was not far off, quietly cropping the grass. The man was busy at the wagon, the boy had gather'd some dry wood, and was making a fire—and as we went a little further we met the woman afoot. I could not see her face, in its great sun-bonnet, but somehow her figure and gait told misery, terror, destitution. She had the rag-bundled, half-starv'd infant still in her arms, and in her hands held two or three baskets, which she had evidently taken to the next house for sale. A little barefoot five-year old girl-child, with fine eyes, trotted behind her, clutching her gown. We stopp'd, asking about the baskets, which we bought. As we paid the money, she kept her face hidden in the recesses of her bonnet. Then as we started, and stopp'd again, Al., (whose sympathies were evidently arous'd,) went back to the camping group to get another basket. He caught a look of her face, and talk'd with her a little. Eyes, voice and manner were those of a corpse, animated by electricity. She was quite young—the man she was traveling with, middle-aged. Poor woman— what story was it, out of her fortunes, to account for that inexpressibly scared way, those glassy eyes, and that hollow voice?

Manhattan from the Bay.

June 25.—Returned to New York last night. Out to-day on the waters for a sail in the wide bay, southeast of Staten island—a rough, tossing ride, and a free sight—the long stretch of Sandy Hook, the highlands of Navesink, and the many vessels outward and inward bound. We came

29. hands held two] *NYTR:* hands carried two
32. baskets, which] *NYTR:* baskets, one of which
33. we paid] *NYTR:* we bargained and paid

Manhattan from the Bay.

Printed from a clipping of paragraphs 12–14, same article, revised in black and red ink and in pencil. The subtitle "The Bay—Sandy Hook" of paragraph 12 is crossed out. Whitman's subtitle is in pencil.
1. Out to-day] *NYTR:* Again out to-day
2. sail in] *NYTR:* sail—this time with bevies of handsome, intellectual, jovial, well-drest Sorosis ladies—circumnavigating Staten Island, by way of Kill von Kull. Spent much of the day very comfortably up in the pilot-house with Mr. Judd, one of the owners of the boat, Mr. Croly, and the captain. Lunch on board. In due time, out in

5   up through the midst of all, in the full sun. I especially enjoy'd the last
hour or two. A moderate sea-breeze had set in; yet over the city, and the
waters adjacent, was a thin haze, concealing nothing, only adding to the
beauty. From my point of view, as I write amid the soft breeze, with a
sea-temperature, surely nothing on earth of its kind can go beyond this
10   show. To the left the North river with its far vista—nearer, three or four
war-ships, anchor'd peacefully—the Jersey side, the banks of Wee-
hawken, the Palisades, and the gradually receding blue, lost in the distance—to the right the East river—the mast-hemm'd shores—the grand
obelisk-like towers of the bridge, one on either side, in haze, yet plainly
15   defin'd, giant brothers twain, throwing free graceful interlinking loops
high across the tumbled tumultuous current below—(the tide is just
changing to its ebb)—the broad water-spread everywhere crowded—no,
not crowded, but thick as stars in the sky—with all sorts and sizes of sail
and steam vessels, plying ferry-boats, arriving and departing coasters,
20   great ocean Dons, iron-black, modern, magnificent in size and power, fill'd
with their incalculable value of human life and precious merchandise—
with here and there, above all, those daring, careening things of grace and
wonder, those white and shaded swift-darting fish-birds, (I wonder if
shore or sea elsewhere can outvie them,) ever with their slanting spars,
25   and fierce, pure, hawk-like beauty and motion—first-class New York sloop
or schooner yachts, sailing, this fine day, the free sea in a good wind. And
rising out of the midst, tall-topt, ship-hemm'd, modern, American, yet
strangely oriental, V-shaped Manhattan, with its compact mass, its spires,

5. up through the] *NYTR:* up in the
6. or two. A] *NYTR:* or two, approaching New-York. A
8. After "the beauty." *NYTR:* begins a new paragraph with the separate subtitle
(deleted), "The City from the Bay."
8. write . . . breeze] *NYTR:* write (for this is jotted on the spot) amid the
soft June breeze
9. earth of its kind can] *NYTR:* earth can
12. the gradually receding blue] *NYTR:* the blue
16. tumultuous current below] *NYTR:* tumultuous river below
19–20. coasters, great] *NYTR:* coasters, long strings or fastened groups of canal
barges in tow—great
25–26. motion . . . the free] *NYTR:* motion—those first-class New-York sloop
or schooner yachts, sailing of a fine day, in a free
26. After "good wind." *NYTR* begins a new paragraph.
27. midst, tall-topt] *NYTR:* midst of all this, our own superb, tall-topt
28. Manhattan] *NYTR:* New-York
29. edifices group'd at] *NYTR:* edifices artistically group'd or disposed at
32. After "surface below." *NYTR* continues the paragraph with the following lines,
deleted on the clipping: "(Other skies and bays—other cities, scenes of the sort, I
know not—but fairer, more vivid, characteristic scene than this, I know can not
be met, around the world.)" For paragraph 15, not reprinted, see Appendix xv, 3.

its cloud-touching edifices group'd at the centre—the green of the trees,
and all the white, brown and gray of the architecture well blended, as I   30
see it, under a miracle of limpid sky, delicious light of heaven above, and
June haze on the surface below.

Human and Heroic New York.

The general subjective view of New York and Brooklyn—(will not
the time hasten when the two shall be municipally united in one, and
named Manhattan?)—what I may call the human interior and exterior of
these great seething oceanic populations, as I get it in this visit, is to
me best of all. After an absence of many years, (I went away at the out-   5
break of the secession war, and have never been back to stay since,) again
I resume with curiosity the crowds, the streets I knew so well, Broadway,
the ferries, the west side of the city, democratic Bowery—human appearances and manners as seen in all these, and along the wharves, and in the
perpetual travel of the horse-cars, or the crowded excursion steamers, or in   10
Wall and Nassau streets by day—in the places of amusement at night—
bubbling and whirling and moving like its own environment of waters—
endless humanity in all phases—Brooklyn also—taken in for the last three
weeks. No need to specify minutely—enough to say that (making all al-
lowances for the shadows and side-streaks of a million-headed-city) the   15
brief total of the impressions, the human qualities, of these vast cities, is

Human and Heroic New York.
Printed from a clipping of paragraphs 16 and 17 of the same article, subtitled "Human and Heroic New-York. (The Main Point After All.)" The first two
sentences of paragraph 16, omitted from *SDC*, are as follows:
"And now I wind up with what these off-hand descriptive sketches are for. In
cities or in men, shall not the emotions and the soul tally the outward material investment?"
2. united in] *NYTR:* united, as they are now socially and naturally united, in
5. away at] *NYTR:* away from New-York at
7. well, Broadway] *NYTR:* well, and was brought up amid—Broadway
8. city, democratic Bowery] *NYTR:* city, and then Democratic Bowery
11. day—in the] *NYTR:* day, and the
13. endless humanity in all phases—Brooklyn] *NYTR:* endless New-York humanity in all its phases—and Brooklyn
14. After "three weeks." *NYTR* begins a new paragraph.
14. No need] *NYTR:* And now, no need
15–17. the brief . . . Alertness] *NYTR:* the general and brief total of the impressions, of the humanity-qualities, so to speak, of these vast cities, is to me, inspiring, promising, comforting, even heroic, beyond any present hasty means of statement at my command. Alertness

to me comforting, even heroic, beyond statement. Alertness, generally fine physique, clear eyes that look straight at you, a singular combination of reticence and self-possession, with good nature and friendliness—a pre-
20 vailing range of according manners, taste and intellect, surely beyond any elsewhere upon earth—and a palpable outcropping of that personal com- radeship I look forward to as the subtlest, strongest future hold of this many-item'd Union—are not only constantly visible here in these mighty channels of men, but they form the rule and average. To-day, I should
25 say—defiant of cynics and pessimists, and with a full knowledge of all their exceptions—an appreciative and perceptive study of the current hu- manity of New York gives the directest proof yet of successful Democ- racy, and of the solution of that paradox, the eligibility of the free and fully developed individual with the paramount aggregate. In old age,
30 lame and sick, pondering for years on many a doubt and danger for this republic of ours—fully aware of all that can be said on the other side—I find in this visit to New York, and the daily contact and rapport with its myriad people, on the scale of the oceans and tides, the best, most effective medicine my soul has yet partaken—the grandest physical habitat and sur-
35 roundings of land and water the globe affords—namely, Manhattan is- land and Brooklyn, which the future shall join in one city—city of superb democracy, amid superb surroundings.

20. of according manners] *NYTR:* of manners
22–23. this many-item'd Union] *NYTR:* this Union
27–28. of successful Democracy] *NYTR:* of modern civilization, Democracy
33. people, on] *NYTR:* people, all phases, all degrees, and on
34. partaken—the grandest] *NYTR:* partaken. For spiritual America, in heroic, individual, practical human results in physical and moral perfection, and on a large and averaged scale, has been my dream (my friends say)—and is so yet, more pas- sionately than ever. And here the materialization and fruit are surely not only begin- ning but already established, in the grandest
37. After this paragraph, the last of the article, *NYTR* has Whitman's name as author.

Hours for the Soul.

Printed from clippings of the sixth number of "How I Get Around," *Critic,* July 15, 1882. The fifth and sixth numbers have the altered title "How I Still Get Around and Take Notes." The autograph MS (abbreviated FMS) here collated with the printed texts, which is from the collection of Mr. Charles E. Feinberg, shows no typesetter's smudges. It is probably a fair copy originally intended for SDC, since the pages are numbered in the sequence of the printer's copy of SDC. The copy sent to the *Critic* was perhaps made from it. After the *Critic* issue of July 15 became available, Whitman substituted clippings from it for FMS, "Hours for the Soul." FMS has the numbers 1 through 9 in the upper right-hand corner and the numbers 137 through 145 in the top center of the pages. The substituted pages from clippings of CR are numbered 137 through 139. The next page of the SDC printer's copy would then

Hours for the Soul.

July 22d, 1878.—Living down in the country again. A wonderful conjunction of all that goes to make those sometime miracle-hours after sunset—so near and yet so far. Perfect, or nearly perfect days, I notice, are not so very uncommon; but the combinations that make perfect nights are few, even in a life time. We have one of those perfections to-night. 5 Sunset left things pretty clear; the larger stars were visible soon as the shades allow'd. A while after 8, three or four great black clouds suddenly rose, seemingly from different points, and sweeping with broad swirls of wind but no thunder, underspread the orbs from view everywhere, and indicated a violent heat-storm. But without storm, clouds, blackness and 10 all, sped and vanish'd as suddenly as they had risen; and from a little after 9 till 11 the atmosphere and the whole show above were in that state of exceptional clearness and glory just alluded to. In the northwest turned the Great Dipper with its pointers round the Cynosure. A little south of east the constellation of the Scorpion was fully up, with red Antares 15 glowing in its neck; while dominating, majestic Jupiter swam, an hour

properly be 140, but it bears the notation "140–146," showing that Whitman did not renumber his pages after the substitution. Since the *Commonplace Book* notes that the printer's copy for *Specimen Days* had all been "done" by Sept. 26, and that it came out Oct. 1, Whitman must have made the substitution at the last minute, directing the printer, top of page 137: "Duplicated print from 'Critic' ". The revisions in FMS were not incorporated in SDC.

The title "Hours for the Soul" is in FMS but not in CR. The first paragraph of CR, not in SDC nor FMS, is as follows:

"*Camden, N. J., July* 10, 1882.—Plunging in the budget of notes and memoranda written on the spot, the accumulations of idle hours, and fishing up thence from the past, we pay our respects this time quite altogether to the nights, and the moon and stars."

1–42. CR has five paragraphs under the subtitle "An Exceptional Night." This title does not appear in FMS and is deleted in SDC.

1. The first sentence is not in CR. In FMS it is inserted above the original first line.

2. those sometime miracle-hours] FMS: those occasional miracle-hours

4–5. combinations . . . even] FMS: combinations needed for perfect nights are exceptionally few and rare even

5. FMS originally began a new paragraph after "life time," but it is marked in the same ink "run in". CR begins a new paragraph after "to-night."

5–6. We have . . . clear; the] FMS: To-day's sunset left things pretty clear. The

10–11. storm, clouds, . . . vanish'd] FMS: storm, the clouds, blackness and all, swept by [words blotted] and instantaneous hand, vanish'd

12. 9 till 11] FMS: 9 till 12

15. the . . . Scorpion] FMS: the Scorpion

16. dominating, majestic Jupiter] FMS: dominating Jupiter

and a half risen, in the east—(no moon till after 11.) A large part of
the sky seem'd just laid in great splashes of phosphorus. You could look
deeper in, farther through, than usual; the orbs thick as heads of wheat in
20 a field. Not that there was any special brilliancy either—nothing near as
sharp as I have seen of keen winter nights, but a curious general luminousness throughout to sight, sense, and soul. The latter had much to do with
it. (I am convinced there are hours of Nature, especially of the atmosphere, mornings and evenings, address'd to the soul. Night transcends,
25 for that purpose, what the proudest day can do.) Now, indeed, if never
before, the heavens declared the glory of God. It was to the full the sky
of the Bible, of Arabia, of the prophets, and of the oldest poems. There,
in abstraction and stillness, (I had gone off by myself to absorb the scene,
to have the spell unbroken,) the copiousness, the removedness, vitality,
30 loose-clear-crowdedness, of that stellar concave spreading overhead,
softly absorb'd into me, rising so free, interminably high, stretching east,
west, north, south—and I, though but a point in the centre below, embodying all.

As if for the first time, indeed, creation noiselessly sank into and
35 through me its placid and untellable lesson, beyond—O, so infinitely beyond!—anything from art, books, sermons, or from science, old or new.
The spirit's hour—religion's hour—the visible suggestion of God in space
and time—now once definitely indicated, if never again. The untold
pointed at—the heavens all paved with it. The Milky Way, as if some su-

17. After "after 11.)" CR begins a new paragraph and FMS originally began a
new paragraph, marked "run in".

19. usual; the] CR and FMS: usual. The

21. sharp . . . keen] FMS: sharp as some keen

22. had much to] FMS: had most to

23. convinced there] FMS: convinced that there

23–24. atmosphere, . . . address'd] FMS: atmosphere, address'd

25. After "can do.)" CR begins a new paragraph.

25. indeed, if] FMS: indeed to me, if

27. Arabia, . . . and of] FMS: Arabia and Egypt, of the prophets and shepherds, and of

33. After "embodying all." FMS originally began a new paragraph, marked "run
in". CR begins a new paragraph.

35. through me its] FMS: through my soul its] FMS originally: through me its

36. anything from art] FMS: any thing by rote of art] FMS originally: any thing
from art

36. After "old or new." FMS originally began a new paragraph, marked "run in".

38. now . . . if] FMS: now definitely indicated for once, if] FMS originally:
now once definitely indicated, if

40. some . . . disdaining] FMS: some universal ode disdaining] FMS originally:
some ode of universal space, disdaining

perhuman symphony, some ode of universal vagueness, disdaining sylla- 40
ble and sound—a flashing glance of Deity, address'd to the soul. All silently—the indescribable night and stars—far off and silently.

THE DAWN.—*July 23.*—This morning, between one and two hours
before sunrise, a spectacle wrought on the same background, yet of quite
different beauty and meaning. The moon well up in the heavens, and past 45
her half, is shining brightly—the air and sky of that cynical-clear, Minerva-like quality, virgin cool—not the weight of sentiment or mystery, or
passion's ecstasy indefinable—not the religious sense, the varied All, distill'd and sublimated into one, of the night just described. Every star now
clear-cut, showing for just what it is, there in the colorless ether. The char- 50
acter of the heralded morning, ineffably sweet and fresh and limpid, but
for the esthetic sense alone, and for purity without sentiment. I have
itemized the night—but dare I attempt the cloudless dawn? (What subtle
tie is this between one's soul and the break of day? Alike, and yet no
two nights or morning shows ever exactly alike.) Preceded by an immense 55
star, almost unearthly in its effusion of white splendor, with two or three
long unequal spoke-rays of diamond radiance, shedding down through the
fresh morning air below—an hour of this, and then the sunrise.

THE EAST.—What a subject for a poem! Indeed, where else a more
pregnant, more splendid one? Where one more idealistic-real, more sub- 60
tle, more sensuous-delicate? The East, answering all lands, all ages, peoples; touching all senses, here, immediate, now—and yet so indescribably
far off—such retrospect! The East—long-stretching—so losing itself—

41. a flashing . . . to] FMS: a flash and glance of Deity to
43. The subtitle "The Dawn" is centered above the paragraph in CR. In FMS it
is at the beginning of the line, directed to be moved. After the date, FMS had " '78"
which is crossed out.
43–44. morning, . . . before] FMS: morning an hour before
44–45. of quite different] FMS: of different
45. moon well] FMS: moon is well
46. half, is shining] FMS: half, shining
46. brightly—the air] CR and FMS: brightly. The air
49. one, of] FMS : one emotion, of
52. After "sentiment." CR begins a new paragraph. FMS originally had a new
paragraph, marked "run in".
55. After "alike.)" FMS, in revision, indicates a paragraph where originally there
was none.
58. air below—an] CR: air below—almost an] FMS: air—almost an
59. The subtitle "The East" is centered above the paragraph in CR. In FMS it
was originally in the first line, directed to be moved.
60. pregnant, more splendid one? Where] FMS: pregnant one? Where
60–61. subtle, more] FMS: subtle-expanding, more
62–63. immediate, . . . such] FMS: immediate, every day—and yet so indescribably distant—such

65 the orient, the gardens of Asia, the womb of history and song—forth-issuing all those strange, dim cavalcades—

> Florid with blood, pensive, rapt with musings, hot with passion,
> Sultry with perfume, with ample and flowing garments,
> With sunburnt visage, intense soul and glittering eyes.

70 Always the East—old, how incalculably old! And yet here the same—ours yet, fresh as a rose, to every morning, every life, to-day—and always will be.

Sept. 17.—Another presentation—same theme—just before sunrise again, (a favorite hour with me.) The clear gray sky, a faint glow in the dull liver-color of the east, the cool fresh odor and the moisture—the cattle 75 and horses off there grazing in the fields—the star Venus again, two hours high. For sounds, the chirping of crickets in the grass, the clarion of chanticleer, and the distant cawing of an early crow. Quietly over the dense fringe of cedars and pines rises that dazzling, red, transparent disk of flame, and the low sheets of white vapor roll and roll into dissolution.

80 The Moon.—*May 18.*—I went to bed early last night, but found myself waked shortly after 12, and, turning awhile sleepless and mentally feverish, I rose, dress'd myself, sallied forth and walk'd down the lane. The full moon, some three or four hours up—a sprinkle of light and less-light clouds just lazily moving—Jupiter an hour high in the east, and here 85 and there throughout the heavens a random star appearing and disappearing. So, beautifully veil'd and varied—the air, with that early-summer perfume, not at all damp or raw—at times Luna languidly emerging in richest brightness for minutes, and then partially envelop'd again. Far off a whip-poor-will plied his notes incessantly. It was that silent time between 90 1 and 3.

64–65. song—forth-issuing] FMS: song and mythology—forth-issuing

65. those . . . cavalcades—] FMS: those biblic cavalcades,

66–68. These are lines 28–32 of "A Broadway Pageant" except that both the 1881 and the 1892 editions of *Leaves of Grass* have "with" before "intense" in the third line. CR is identical with SDC, but FMS has "sunburnt vision" for "sunburnt visage."

72. After the date, FMS originally had " '78" but it is crossed out.

74. east, the] FMS: east, and the

74. and the moisture] FMS: and moisture

75. the star Venus] FMS: the planet Venus] FMS originally: the star Venus

77–78. the dense] CR: the low, dense] FMS: the low dense

78. pines rises] CR: pines, rises] FMS: pines soon rises] FMS originally: pines rises

79. of flame] FMS: of quiet flame

80. The subtitle "The Moon" is centered above the paragraph in CR. In FMS the original subtitle was "The Moon" at the beginning of the first line, but this is crossed out and "Moon and Stars" written above it. After the date, " '78" is crossed out, but

The rare nocturnal scene, how soon it sooth'd and pacified me! Is there not something about the moon, some relation or reminder, which no poem or literature has yet caught? (In very old and primitive ballads I have come across lines or asides that suggest it.) After a while the clouds mostly clear'd, and as the moon swam on, she carried, shimmering and shifting, delicate color-effects of pellucid green and tawny vapor. Let me conclude this part with an extract, (some writer in the "Tribune," May 16, 1878:)

No one ever gets tired of the moon. Goddess that she is by dower of her eternal beauty, she is a true woman by her tact—knows the charm of being seldom seen, of coming by surprise and staying but a little while; never wears the same dress two nights running, nor all night the same way; commends herself to the matter-of-fact people by her usefulness, and makes her uselessness adored by poets, artists, and all lovers in all lands; lends herself to every symbolism and to every emblem; is Diana's bow and Venus's mirror and Mary's throne; is a sickle, a scarf, an eyebrow, his face or her face, as look'd at by her or by him; is the madman's hell, the poet's heaven, the baby's toy, the philosopher's study; and while her admirers follow her footsteps, and hang on her lovely looks, she knows how to keep her woman's secret—her other side—unguess'd and unguessable.

Furthermore.—February 19, 1880.—Just before 10 P.M. cold and entirely clear again, the show overhead, bearing southwest, of wonderful and crowded magnificence. The moon in her third quarter—the clusters of the Hyades and Pleiades, with the planet Mars between—in full crossing sprawl in the sky the great Egyptian X, (Sirius, Procyon, and the main stars in the constellations of the Ship, the Dove, and of Orion;) just north of east Bootes, and in his knee Arcturus, an hour high, mount-

left in CR.
82. and walk'd down] FMS: and down
84–86. high . . . So,] FMS: high—and here in the heavens, amid the languid clouds, star after star disappearing and appearing again. So,
87. Luna languidly emerging] FMS: Luna emerging
88. envelop'd again.] FMS: envelopt.
88–90. In FMS the sentence beginning "Far off" follows the one beginning "It was".
91. scene, . . . me!] FMS: scene—how completely it pacified and sooth'd me.
92–93. no poem or] FMS: no poet or] FMS originally: no poem or
94. After "suggest it.)" CR begins a new paragraph.
96–97. Let me conclude this part with] FMS: I conclude with
99–110. This extract, not indented, is copied out in Whitman's handwriting in FMS.
111–122. These two paragraphs are on a separate page in FMS and were apparently not originally a part of the section "Hours for the Soul."
111. The subtitle "*Furthermore*" is centered above the page in CR, in small capitals. It does not appear at all in FMS. The date in FMS is "Feb. 9, '80."

ing the heaven, ambitiously large and sparkling, as if he meant to challenge with Sirius the stellar supremacy.

120   With the sentiment of the stars and moon such nights I get all the
free margins and indefiniteness of music or poetry, fused in geometry's utmost exactness.

Straw-Color'd and Other Psyches.

Aug. 4.—A pretty sight! Where I sit in the shade—a warm day, the
sun shining from cloudless skies, the forenoon well advanc'd—I look over
a ten-acre field of luxuriant clover-hay, (the second crop)—the livid-ripe
red blossoms and dabs of August brown thickly spotting the prevailing
5   dark-green. Over all flutter myriads of light-yellow butterflies, mostly
skimming along the surface, dipping and oscillating, giving a curious animation to the scene. The beautiful, spiritual insects! straw-color'd
Psyches! Occasionally one of them leaves his mates, and mounts, perhaps
spirally, perhaps in a straight line in the air, fluttering up, up, till literally
10 out of sight. In the lane as I came along just now I noticed one spot,
ten feet square or so, where more than a hundred had collected, holding a
revel, a gyration-dance, or butterfly good-time, winding and circling,
down and across, but always keeping within the limits. The little creatures have come out all of a sudden the last few days, and are now
15 very plentiful. As I sit outdoors, or walk, I hardly look around without
somewhere seeing two (always two) fluttering through the air in amorous
dalliance. Then their inimitable color, their fragility, peculiar motion—
and that strange, frequent way of one leaving the crowd and mounting up,
up in the free ether, and apparently never returning. As I look over the
20 field, these yellow-wings everywhere mildly sparkling, many snowy blossoms of the wild carrot gracefully bending on their tall and taper stems—
while for sounds, the distant guttural screech of a flock of guinea-hens
comes shrilly yet somehow musically to my ears. And now a faint growl
of heat-thunder in the north—and ever the low rising and falling wind-
25 purr from the tops of the maples and willows.

    Aug. 20.—Butterflies and butterflies, (taking the place of the bum-
ble-bees of three months since, who have quite disappear'd), continue to
flit to and fro, all sorts, white, yellow, brown, purple—now and then some

---

120. stars and moon such] CR and FMS: stars such
121. music or poetry] FMS: music and poetry
122. After this last line of the article, CR has the name "Walt
Whitman."

gorgeous fellow flashing lazily by on wings like artists' palettes dabb'd with every color. Over the breast of the pond I notice many white ones, crossing, pursuing their idle capricious flight. Near where I sit grows a tall-stemm'd weed topt with a profusion of rich scarlet blossoms, on which the snowy insects alight and dally, sometimes four or five of them at a time. By-and-by a humming-bird visits the same, and I watch him coming and going, daintily balancing and shimmering about. These white butterflies give new beautiful contrasts to the pure greens of the August foliage, (we have had some copious rains lately,) and over the glistening bronze of the pond-surface. You can tame even such insects; I have one big and handsome moth down here, knows and comes to me, likes me to hold him up on my extended hand.

Another Day, later.—A grand twelve-acre field of ripe cabbages with their prevailing hue of malachite green, and floating-flying over and among them in all directions myriads of these same white butterflies. As I came up the lane to-day I saw a living globe of the same, two to three feet in diameter, many scores cluster'd together and rolling along in the air, adhering to their ball-shape, six or eight feet above the ground.

A Night Remembrance.

Aug. 25, 9–10 A.M.—I sit by the edge of the pond, everything quiet, the broad polish'd surface spread before me—the blue of the heavens and the white clouds reflected from it—and flitting across, now and then, the reflection of some flying bird. Last night I was down here with a friend till after midnight; everything a miracle of splendor—the glory of the stars, and the completely rounded moon—the passing clouds, silver and luminous-tawny—now and then masses of vapory illuminated scud—and silently by my side my dear friend. The shades of the trees, and patches of moonlight on the grass—the softly blowing breeze, and just-palpable odor of the neighboring ripening corn—the indolent and spiritual night, inexpressibly rich, tender, suggestive—something altogether to filter through one's soul, and nourish and feed and soothe the memory long afterwards.

Straw-Color'd and Other Psyches.
Printed from four pieces of white paper, in pencil, pasted on gray sheets filled out in black ink. In the first line is the date: "*Aug: 4, '78.*" The year is crossed out.

A Night Remembrance.
Printed from an autograph MS page; subtitle in red ink.

Wild Flowers.

This has been and is yet a great season for wild flowers; oceans of them line the roads through the woods, border the edges of the water-runlets, grow all along the old fences, and are scatter'd in profusion over the fields. An eight-petal'd blossom of gold-yellow, clear and bright, with a brown tuft in the middle, nearly as large as a silver half-dollar, is very common; yesterday on a long drive I noticed it thickly lining the borders of the brooks everywhere. Then there is a beautiful weed cover'd with blue flowers, (the blue of the old Chinese teacups treasur'd by our grand-aunts,) I am continually stopping to admire—a little larger than a dime, and very plentiful. White, however, is the prevailing color. The wild carrot I have spoken of; also the fragrant life-everlasting. But there are all hues and beauties, especially on the frequent tracts of half-open scrub-oak and dwarf-cedar hereabout—wild asters of all colors. Notwithstanding the frost-touch the hardy little chaps maintain themselves in all their bloom. The tree-leaves, too, some of them are beginning to turn yellow or drab or dull green. The deep wine-color of the sumachs and gum-trees is already visible, and the straw-color of the dog-wood and beech. Let me give the names of some of these perennial blossoms and friendly weeds I have made acquaintance with hereabout one season or another in my walks:

wild azalea,	dandelions,
wild honeysuckle,	yarrow,
wild roses,	coreopsis,
golden rod,	wild pea,
larkspur,	woodbine,
early crocus,	elderberry,
sweet flag, (great patches of it,)	poke-weed,
creeper, trumpet-flower,	sun-flower,
scented marjoram,	chamomile,
snakeroot,	violets,

Wild Flowers.
Printed from three pages of autograph MS, written in black ink on gray paper; subtitle inserted in pencil.
17. After "dog-wood and beech." MS has the following passage, deleted perhaps because it is out of place in this context:
"How it is I know not, but the wild-flowers do me more good, and always attract me more, along the creek-banks and over the half-sterile fields, than the choicest hot-house products. (Is it the same in my mind with people? Are not the working farmers, mechanics, boatmen, drivers, railroad-men more emotional and racy? more possessing the natural flavors of fruits, grains, and the aroma of woods?)"

A Civility Too Long Neglected.
Printed from a page of autograph MS.

Solomon's seal,	clematis,
sweet balm,	bloodroot,
mint, (great plenty,)	swamp magnolia,
wild geranium,	milk-weed,
wild heliotrope,	wild daisy, (plenty,) 35
burdock,	wild chrysanthemum.

A Civility Too Long Neglected.

The foregoing reminds me of something. As the individualities I would mainly portray have certainly been slighted by folks who make pictures, volumes, poems, out of them—as a faint testimonial of my own gratitude for many hours of peace and comfort in half-sickness, (and not by any means sure but they will somehow get wind of the compliment,) I   5
hereby dedicate the last half of these Specimen Days to the

bees,	crows,
black-birds,	millers,
dragon-flies,	mosquitoes,
pond-turtles,	butterflies, 10
mulleins, tansy, peppermint,	wasps and hornets,
moths (great and little, some splendid fellows,)	cat birds (and all other birds,) cedars,
glow-worms, (swarming millions of them indescribably strange and beautiful at night over the pond and creek,)	tulip-trees, (and all other trees,) 15 and to the spots and memories of those days, and of the creek.
water-snakes,	

Delaware River—Days and Nights.

April 5, 1879.—With the return of spring to the skies, airs, waters of the Delaware, return the sea-gulls. I never tire of watching their broad

Delaware River—Days and Nights.
Printed from clippings of an article entitled "Only Crossing the Delaware," the Philadelphia *Progress,* April 5, 1879. This was a weekly published and edited by Whitman's friend John W. Forney, established November 16, 1878. Whitman cut away from the clipping the title, the subtitle ("A Mirror for Men and Women"), inserting the new subtitle in red ink, and the first paragraph, which is as follows:
"The Delaware river—opening Spring, on it—the preceding Winter, and the ice —some starry nights—the Camden and Philadelphia Ferry—only these and nothing more, are the threads of my off hand yarn, (I may as well notify you, reader dear, in advance.)"
2. Delaware, return . . . tire of] *SDA:* Delaware, depart the sea-gulls. I never tired of] *CPP:* Delaware, depart the sea-gulls. I never tire of

and easy flight, in spirals, or as they oscillate with slow unflapping wings, or look down with curved beak, or dipping to the water after food. The crows, plenty enough all through the winter, have vanish'd with the ice. Not one of them now to be seen. The steamboats have again come forth —bustling up, handsome, freshly painted, for summer work—the Columbia, the Edwin Forrest, (the Republic not yet out,) the Reybold, the Nelly White, the Twilight, the Ariel, the Warner, the Perry, the Taggart, the Jersey Blue—even the hulky old Trenton—not forgetting those saucy little bull-pups of the current, the steamtugs.

But let me bunch and catalogue the affair—the river itself, all the way from the sea—cape Island on one side and Henlopen light on the other—up the broad bay north, and so to Philadelphia, and on further to Trenton;—the sights I am most familiar with, (as I live a good part of the time in Camden, I view matters from that outlook)—the great arrogant, black, full-freighted ocean steamers, inward or outward bound—the ample width here between the two cities, intersected by Windmill island—an occasional man-of-war, sometimes a foreigner, at anchor, with her guns and port-holes, and the boats, and the brown-faced sailors, and the regular oar-strokes, and the gay crowds of "visiting day"—the frequent large and handsome three-masted schooners, (a favorite style of marine build, hereabout of late years,) some of them new and very jaunty, with their white-gray sails and yellow pine spars—the sloops dashing along in a fair wind —(I see one now, coming up, under broad canvas, her gaff-topsail shining in the sun, high and picturesque—what a thing of beauty amid the sky and waters!)—the crowded wharf-slips along the city—the flags of different nationalities, the sturdy English cross on its ground of blood, the French tricolor, the banner of the great North German empire, and the Italian and the Spanish colors—sometimes, of an afternoon, the whole

3. they oscillate with] *SDA:* they oscillated with
5. winter, have vanish'd] *SDA:* winter, have also vanish'd] *CPP:* winter, also vanish'd
6. After "now to be seen." *PPRO* begins a new paragraph with the following three sentences (deleted in the clipping): "Spring is indeed preparing for, all sorts of ways, this river. A week ago I noticed the faintest yellow-green tinge on the neighboring maples and willow trees. Also plain signs of travel, trade, freight."
6–7. steamboats . . . bustling] *PPRO:* steamboats of last Summer have again come forth—some are in their slips, some going or coming, some just bustling
12. the affair—the] *PPRO:* the whole affair: The
14. and on further to] *PPRO:* and further on to
15–16. live . . . in] *PPRO:* live in
17. bound—the ample] *PPRO:* bound—the never ending variety of shores—the many white sails or black smoke pipes in motion on the open stream—the ample
18. by Windmill] *PPRO:* by old Windmill
21–22. frequent . . . three-masted] *PPRO:* frequent three-masted
33–34. aft—and, . . . the] *PPRO:* aft—the

scene enliven'd by a fleet of yachts, in a half calm, lazily returning from a race down at Gloucester;—the neat, rakish, revenue steamer "Hamilton" in mid-stream, with her perpendicular stripes flaunting aft—and, turning the eyes north, the long ribands of fleecy-white steam, or dingy-black smoke, stretching far, fan-shaped, slanting diagonally across from the Kensington or Richmond shores, in the west-by-south-west wind. 35

Scenes on Ferry and River—Last Winter's Nights.

Then the Camden ferry. What exhilaration, change, people, business, by day. What soothing, silent, wondrous hours, at night, crossing on the boat, most all to myself—pacing the deck, alone, forward or aft. What communion with the waters, the air, the exquisite *chiaroscuro*—the sky and stars, that speak no word, nothing to the intellect, yet so eloquent, 5 so communicative to the soul. And the ferry men—little they know how much they have been to me, day and night—how many spells of listlessness, ennui, debility, they and their hardy ways have dispell'd. And the pilots—captains Hand, Walton, and Giberson by day, and captain Olive at night; Eugene Crosby, with his strong young arm so often supporting, 10 circling, convoying me over the gaps of the bridge, through impediments, safely aboard. Indeed all my ferry friends—captain Frazee the superintendent, Lindell, Hiskey, Fred Rauch, Price, Watson, and a dozen more. And the ferry itself, with its queer scenes—sometimes children suddenly born in the waiting-houses (an actual fact—and more than once)—some- 15 times a masquerade party, going over at night, with a band of music, dancing and whirling like mad on the broad deck, in their fantastic

Scenes on Ferry and River—Last Winter's Nights.
Printed from clippings of the same article as the preceding section. Subtitle, not in *PPRO*, inserted in red ink.
2. hours, at] *PPRO:* hours I have had, at
2–3. night, . . . pacing] *PPRO:* night, certain trips—pacing
3. alone, forward] *PPRO:* alone—forward
8. debility, they] *PPRO:* debility, (in my half paralysis), they
8–9. the pilots— . . . by] *PPRO:* the pilots—Captain Hand and Captain Walton by
10. night; Eugene] *PPRO:* night; and my special friend Eugene
12–14. superintendent, . . . more. And] *PPRO:* Superintendent (gentlemanly and Democratic, with his clear eye to business, but his full-blooded human heart the centre of all)—Lindell, Moore, Thompson, Tilghman, Hiskey, Fred Rauch, Frazee, Will Clark, Charley Baker, the Middletons, Tom Logan, Billy Button, and a dozen more, all my friends, and the engine-men, R. R. conductors, and news-agents. And
15–16. waiting-houses . . . sometimes] *PPRO:* waiting-houses—sometimes

dresses; sometimes the astronomer, Mr. Whitall, (who posts me up in
points about the stars by a living lesson there and then, and answering
20   every question)—sometimes a prolific family group, eight, nine, ten, even
twelve! (Yesterday, as I cross'd, a mother, father, and eight children, waiting in the ferry-house, bound westward somewhere.)

I have mention'd the crows. I always watch them from the boats. They
play quite a part in the winter scenes on the river, by day. Their black
25   splatches are seen in relief against the snow and ice everywhere at that
season—sometimes flying and flapping—sometimes on little or larger
cakes, sailing up or down the stream. One day the river was mostly clear
—only a single long ridge of broken ice making a narrow stripe by itself,
running along down the current for over a mile, quite rapidly. On this
30   white stripe the crows were congregated, hundreds of them—a funny procession—("half mourning" was the comment of some one.)

Then the reception room, for passengers waiting—life illustrated
thoroughly. Take a March picture I jotted there two or three weeks since.
Afternoon, about 3½ o'clock, it begins to snow. There has been a mati-
35   nee performance at the theater—from 4¼ to 5 comes a stream of homeward bound ladies. I never knew the spacious room to present a gayer,
more lively scene—handsome, well-drest Jersey women and girls, scores
of them, streaming in for nearly an hour—the bright eyes and glowing
faces, coming in from the air—a sprinkling of snow on bonnets or dresses
40   as they enter—the five or ten minutes' waiting—the chatting and laughing—(women can have capital times among themselves, with plenty of
wit, lunches, jovial abandon)—Lizzie, the pleasant-manner'd waiting-
room woman—for sound, the bell-taps and steam-signals of the departing
boats with their rhythmic break and undertone—the domestic pictures,

---

18–20. No marks of parenthesis in *PPRO*.
20. eight] *PPRO: eight*
28. a narrow stripe] *PPRO:* a stripe
29. for over a mile, quite] *PPRO:* for two miles, quite
31. some one.)] *PPRO:* some one—indeed it was a sort of Chintz pattern.)
32. waiting—life] *PPRO:* waiting. Here is life
33. a March picture] *PPRO:* a picture
35. performance . . . from] *PPRO:* performance of Pinafore; and from
36. spacious room to] *PPRO:* spacious fine new room (about 50 feet square,
high, dome-lit ceiling) to
38. them, streaming] *PPRO:* them, couples or groups by themselves—streaming
44. rhythmic break] *PPRO:* rhythmic, frequent break
45–46. countrymen—the] *PPRO:* countrymen—good-looking fellows, some young,
some old—the
47. of . . . represented] *PPRO:* of the Comedy Human, represented
47–48. Then outside some] *PPRO:* Then the moving panorama outside—some
48–49. boat. Towards] *PPRO:* boat—towards
49. stream gradually thickening] *PPRO:* stream rapidly thickening

mothers with bevies of daughters, (a charming sight)—children, country- 45
men—the railroad men in their blue clothes and caps—all the various
characters of city and country represented or suggested. Then outside
some belated passenger frantically running, jumping after the boat. Towards six o'clock the human stream gradually thickening—now a pressure of vehicles, drays, piled railroad crates—now a drove of cattle, mak- 50
ing quite an excitement, the drovers with heavy sticks, belaboring the
steaming sides of the frighten'd brutes. Inside the reception room, business bargains, flirting, love-making, *eclaircissements*, proposals—pleasant, sober-faced Phil coming in with his burden of afternoon papers—or
Jo, or Charley (who jump'd in the dock last week, and saved a stout lady 55
from drowning,) to replenish the stove, after clearing it with long crow-
bar poker.

Besides all this "comedy human," the river affords nutriment of a
higher order. Here are some of my memoranda of the past winter, just as
pencill'd down on the spot. 60

A January Night.—Fine trips across the wide Delaware to-night.
Tide pretty high, and a strong ebb. River, a little after 8, full of ice,
mostly broken, but some large cakes making our strong-timber'd steamboat hum and quiver as she strikes them. In the clear moonlight they
spread, strange, unearthly, silvery, faintly glistening, as far as I can see. 65
Bumping, trembling, sometimes hissing like a thousand snakes, the tide-
procession, as we wend with or through it, affording a grand undertone,
in keeping with the scene. Overhead, the splendor indescribable; yet something haughty, almost supercilious, in the night. Never did I realize more
latent sentiment, almost *passion*, in those silent interminable stars up 70
there. One can understand, such a night, why, from the days of the Phar-

52. brutes. Inside] *PPRO:* brutes—inside

53. *eclaircissements*, proposals] *PPRO: eclaircissements*, even proposals

56–57. long crow-bar poker.] *PPRO:* long poker.

58–60. The first sentence is written in ink on a slip of paper, in the copy, pasted
above a clipping beginning with the second sentence; in *PPRO* this second sentence
is partly clipped away. The entire paragraph in *PPRO* between the one ending
"poker." and the one beginning "*A January Night*" is as follows:

"The reader has discovered by this time that my piece indeed gives nothing more
than a few simple, idle experiences, night and day, crossing from Federal street,
Camden, to the foot of Market street, Philadelphia. Let me print some of my memoranda of the past winter, just as pencill'd down on the spot."

61. the wide Delaware] *PPRO:* the Delaware

63–64. our . . . hum] *PPRO:* our boat hum

64–65. moonlight they spread] *PPRO:* moonlight the ice spreads

66. trembling, sometimes hissing] *PPRO:* trembling, hissing

67. it, affording a] *PPRO:* it, affords a

68–69. splendor . . . something] *PPRO:* splendor is indescribable. Yet there
seems something

70. in those silent] *PPRO:* in the silent

aohs or Job, the dome of heaven, sprinkled with planets, has supplied the
subtlest, deepest criticism on human pride, glory, ambition.

Another Winter Night.—I don't know anything more *filling* than to
75 be on the wide firm deck of a powerful boat, a clear, cool, extra-moonlight
night, crushing proudly and resistlessly through this thick, marbly, glistening ice. The whole river is now spread with it—some immense cakes.
There is such weirdness about the scene—partly the quality of the light,
with its tinge of blue, the lunar twilight—only the large stars holding their
80 own in the radiance of the moon. Temperature sharp, comfortable for motion, dry, full of oxygen. But the sense of power—the steady, scornful,
imperious urge of our strong new engine, as she ploughs her way through
the big and little cakes.

Another.—For two hours I cross'd and recross'd, merely for pleasure
85 —for a still excitement. Both sky and river went through several changes.
The first for awhile held two vast fan-shaped echelons of light clouds,
through which the moon waded, now radiating, carrying with her an aureole of tawny transparent brown, and now flooding the whole vast with
clear vapory light-green, through which, as through an illuminated veil,
90 she moved with measur'd womanly motion. Then, another trip, the heavens would be absolutely clear, and Luna in all her effulgence. The big
Dipper in the north, with the double star in the handle much plainer than
common. Then the sheeny track of light in the water, dancing and rippling. Such transformations; such pictures and poems, inimitable.

95 *Another.*—I am studying the stars, under advantages, as I cross to-
night. (It is late in February, and again extra clear.) High toward the
west, the Pleiades, tremulous with delicate sparkle, in the soft heavens.

72. has supplied] *PPRO:* has been the choicest theme of bibles, poems—has supplied
75. on the . . . boat, a] *PPRO:* on a powerful boat of a
76. through this thick] *PPRO:* through the thick
78. is such weirdness] *PPRO:* is a weirdness
82. engine, as] *PPRO:* engine and boat, as
84–85. pleasure— . . . Both] *PPRO:* pleasure. Both
86. awhile held two] *PPRO:* awhile had two
94. transformations; such] *PPRO:* transformations! Such
94. inimitable.] *PPRO:* inimitable, unsuspected, unrecorded!
100. stage, with] *PPRO:* stage, the sky, with
101. shoulder, . . . Kings] *PPRO:* shoulders, and the Three Kings
102. star. Going] *PPRO:* star. Northward, the Great Dipper, with handle down.
Elsewhere, the Sickle—the great W, or double triangle in Cassiopea—and a myriad
of others. Going
102. *PPRO* begins a new paragraph after "myriad of others."
102. ashore, (I] *PPRO:* ashore, yet, for a long time, (I
104. the echoing calls] *PPRO:* the calls
105. &c.; amid] *PPRO:* &c. Amid

Aldebaran, leading the V-shaped Hyades—and overhead Capella and her kids. Most majestic of all, in full display in the high south, Orion, vast-spread, roomy, chief histrion of the stage, with his shiny yellow rosette on his shoulder, and his three Kings—and a little to the east, Sirius, calmly arrogant, most wondrous single star. Going late ashore, (I couldn't give up the beauty and soothingness of the night,) as I staid around, or slowly wander'd, I heard the echoing calls of the railroad men in the West Jersey depot yard, shifting and switching trains, engines, &c.; amid the general silence otherways, and something in the acoustic quality of the air, musical, emotional effects, never thought of before. I linger'd long and long, listening to them.

Night of March 18, '79.—One of the calm, pleasantly cool, exqui-sitely clear and cloudless, early spring nights—the atmosphere again that rare vitreous blue-black, welcom'd by astronomers. Just at 8, evening, the scene overhead of certainly solemnest beauty, never surpass'd. Venus nearly down in the west, of a size and lustre as if trying to outshow herself, before departing. Teeming, maternal orb—I take you again to myself. I am reminded of that spring preceding Abraham Lincoln's mur-der, when I, restlessly haunting the Potomac banks, around Washington city, watch'd you, off there, aloof, moody as myself:

> As we walk'd up and down in the dark blue so mystic,
> As we walk'd in silence the transparent shadowy night,
> As I saw you had something to tell, as you bent to me night after night,
> As you droop'd from the sky low down, as if to my side, (while the
>   other stars all look'd on,)
> As we wander'd together the solemn night.

106–107. air, musical] *PPRO:* air, (what a great difference, different times, in the same sounds!) these calls had musical

110. atmosphere again that] *PPRO:* atmosphere that

111. astronomers. Just] *PPRO:* astronomers. The stars all out, in full splendor, nothing to intercept the heavenly show to its best advantage, (no moon till almost morning). Just

115. of that spring] *PPRO:* of the Spring

115–116. murder, when] *PPRO:* murder, fourteen years ago, just this time of year (last of March and first part of April) when

118–123. These lines are quoted from Section 8 of the 1876 text of "When Lilacs Last in the Door-yard Bloom'd." The first line quoted here is not retained in later texts of the poem, and the "we" of the second line quoted is changed to "I" in later texts.

121. droop'd] [*SDC, CP,* and all other texts except *SDA* have "droop." Since this is obviously a typographical error, and since the clipping of *PPRO* has "droop'd," the misprint, which went through several editions supervised by Whitman without being noticed, is here corrected.]

123. This truncated line is printed as in *PPRO.* In all book texts of *Leaves of Grass* (with variations in punctuation) the full line reads: "As we wander'd together the solemn night, (for something, I know not what, kept me from sleep;)"

With departing Venus, large to the last, and shining even to the edge
125 of the horizon, the vast dome presents at this moment, such a spectacle!
Mercury was visible just after sunset—a rare sight. Arcturus is now risen,
just north of east. In calm glory all the stars of Orion hold the place of
honor, in meridian, to the south—with the Dog-star a little to the left.
And now, just rising, Spica, late, low, and slightly veil'd. Castor, Regulus
130 and the rest, all shining unusually clear, (no Mars or Jupiter or moon till
morning.) On the edges of the river, many lamps twinkling—with two or
three huge chimneys, a couple of miles up, belching forth molten, steady
flames, volcano-like, illuminating all around—and sometimes an electric
or calcium, its Dante-Inferno gleams, in far shafts, terrible, ghastly-power-
135 ful. Of later May nights, crossing, I like to watch the fishermen's little
buoy-lights—so pretty, so dreamy—like corpse candles—undulating
delicate and lonesome on the surface of the shadowy waters, floating with
the current.

The First Spring Day on Chestnut Street.

Winter relaxing its hold, has already allow'd us a foretaste of
spring. As I write, yesterday afternoon's softness and brightness, (after the
morning fog, which gave it a better setting, by contrast,) show'd Chestnut street—say between Broad and Fourth—to more advantage in its
5   various asides, and all its stores, and gay-dress'd crowds generally, than
for three months past. I took a walk there between one and two. Doubtless, there were plenty of hard-up folks along the pavements, but nine-

---

126. Mercury was visible] *PPRO:* Mercury has been visible
127. stars of] *PPRO:* stars and clusters of
130. Jupiter or moon till] *PPRO:* Jupiter till
131. After "morning.)" *PPRO* begins a new paragraph.
134–135. After "powerful." *PPRO* begins a new paragraph.
135. Of later May] *PPRO:* Of May
135. fishermen's] *PPRO:* fisherman's
138. In *PPRO* the author's name, "Walt Whitman," follows the last sentence.

The First Spring Day on Chestnut Street.
Printed from a clipping of the Philadelphia *Progress*, an article by the same
title, March 8, 1879. In the upper left-hand corner the words in black ink "Progress,
March '79" are lined out.
4. street—say] *SDA:* street, Philadelphia—say
5. its stores] *PPRO:* its handsome women, stores
6–7. two. Doubtless] *PPRO:* two. I will not dwell on the balminess of the day.
(Six times was I accosted with the amiable remark: 'Fine weather overhead, but there

tenths of the myriad-moving human panorama to all appearance seem'd
flush, well-fed, and fully-provided. At all events it was good to be on
Chestnut street yesterday. The peddlers on the sidewalk—("sleeve-but-   10
tons, three for five cents")—the handsome little fellow with canary-bird
whistles—the cane men, toy men, toothpick men—the old woman squatted
in a heap on the cold stone flags, with her basket of matches, pins and
tape—the young negro mother, sitting, begging, with her two little coffee-
color'd twins on her lap—the beauty of the cramm'd conservatory of rare   15
flowers, flaunting reds, yellows, snowy lilies, incredible orchids, at the
Baldwin mansion near Twelfth street—the show of fine poultry, beef, fish,
at the restaurants—the china stores, with glass and statuettes—the lus-
cious tropical fruits—the street cars plodding along, with their tintinnabu-
lating bells—the fat, cab-looking, rapidly driven one-horse vehicles of the   20
post-office, squeez'd full of coming or going letter-carriers, so healthy and
handsome and manly-looking, in their gray uniforms—the costly books,
pictures, curiosities, in the windows—the gigantic policemen at most of
the corners—will all be readily remember'd and recognized as features of
this principal avenue of Philadelphia. Chestnut street, I have discover'd, is   25
not without individuality, and its own points, even when compared with
the great promenade-streets of other cities. I have never been in Europe,
but acquired years' familiar experience with New York's, (perhaps the
world's,) great thoroughfare, Broadway, and possess to some extent a
personal and saunterer's knowledge of St. Charles street in New Orleans,   30
Tremont street in Boston, and the broad trottoirs of Pennsylvania avenue in Washington. Of course it is a pity that Chestnut were not two or
three times wider; but the street, any fine day, shows vividness, motion,
variety, not easily to be surpass'd. (Sparkling eyes, human faces, magnet-

ain't many going that way.') Doubtless
    6–7. *PPRO* begins a new paragraph with "Doubtless".
    7. folks . . . pavements,] *PPRO:* folks even along these pavements;
    10. yesterday. The peddlers] *PPRO:* yesterday. ("Give me health and a day,"
says Emerson, "and I will make the pomp of emperors ridiculous.") The peddlers
    10. *PPRO* begins a new paragraph with "The peddlers."
    10–11. *PPRO* does not have the marks of parenthesis.
    12. men, toothpick] *PPRO:* men, and toothpick
    13. matches, pins] *PPRO:* matches, or pins
    15. the beauty] *PPRO:* the wondrous, indescribable beauty
    18–19. the luscious tropical] *SDA:* luscious tropical] *PPRO:* the gorgeous
tropical
    21. letter-carriers, so healthy] *PPRO:* letter-carriers, every one of them healthy
    25. After "Philadelphia." *PPRO* begins a new paragraph.
    26. own points] *PPRO:* own racy points
    31. Tremont street] *PPRO:* Washington street
    32. that Chestnut] *PPRO:* that our Chestnut
    33. but the] *PPRO:* but as it is, the

35 ism, well-dress'd women, ambulating to and fro—with lots of fine things
in the windows—are they not about the same, the civilized world over?)

> How fast the flitting figures come!
> The mild, the fierce, the stony face;
> Some bright with thoughtless smiles—and some
40 > Where secret tears have left their trace.

A few days ago one of the six-story clothing stores along here had the
space inside its plate-glass show-window partition'd into a little corral,
and litter'd deeply with rich clover and hay, (I could smell the odor outside,) on which reposed two magnificent fat sheep, full-sized but young—
45 the handsomest creatures of the kind I ever saw. I stopp'd long and long,
with the crowd, to view them—one lying down chewing the cud, and one
standing up, looking out, with dense-fringed patient eyes. Their wool,
of a clear tawny color, with streaks of glistening black—altogether a queer
sight amidst that crowded promenade of dandies, dollars and drygoods.

Up the Hudson to Ulster County.

April 23.—Off to New York on a little tour and visit. Leaving the
hospitable, home-like quarters of my valued friends, Mr. and Mrs. J. H.
Johnston—took the 4 P.M. boat, bound up the Hudson, 100 miles or so.
Sunset and evening fine. Especially enjoy'd the hour after we passed Coz-
5 zens's landing—the night lit by the crescent moon and Venus, now

35. women] *PPRO:* femmes
37–40. This is the second stanza of W. C. Bryant's "The Crowded Street."
41. the six-story] *PPRO:* the great six-story
43. the odor] *PPRO:* its odor
49. After this line the following sentence, concluding the article in *PPRO*, together with the name "Walt Whitman" is deleted: "The little corral, strewed with
fragrant hay, and those stately sheep, as I looked at them through the plate glass—
were they not, at two or three removes, a sort of test and criticism on the whole
show?"

Up the Hudson to Ulster County.
Printed from a clipping of the *NYTR* article entitled "Real Summer Openings,"
May 17, 1879, including all or parts of paragraphs 2–4 of that article. Whitman's
new subtitle was written in red ink above the clipping. For the first paragraph,
omitted in *SDC*, see Appendix XX, *1.*
1–9. These lines include part of paragraph 2 and all of 3, under the subhead
"Countless Villas and Mansions."
1. The first sentence, not in *NYTR*, is inserted in black ink above the clipping.
3. Johnston] *SDA:* Johnson
3. took] *NYTR:* taking

swimming in tender glory, and now hid by the high rocks and hills of the western shore, which we hugg'd close. (Where I spend the next ten days is in Ulster county and its neighborhood, with frequent morning and evening drives, observations of the river, and short rambles.)

April 24—Noon.—A little more and the sun would be oppressive. The bees are out gathering their bread from willows and other trees. I watch them returning, darting through the air or lighting on the hives, their thighs covered with the yellow forage. A solitary robin sings near. I sit in my shirt sleeves and gaze from an open bay-window on the indolent scene—the thin haze, the Fishkill hills in the distance—off on the river, a sloop with slanting mainsail, and two or three little shad-boats. Over on the railroad opposite, long freight trains, sometimes weighted by cylinder-tanks of petroleum, thirty, forty, fifty cars in a string, panting and rumbling along in full view, but the sound soften'd by distance.

Days at J. B.'s—Turf-Fires—Spring Songs.

April 26.—At sunrise, the pure clear sound of the meadow lark. An hour later, some notes, few and simple, yet delicious and perfect, from the bush-sparrow—towards noon the reedy trill of the robin. To-day is the fairest, sweetest yet—penetrating warmth—a lovely veil in the air, partly heat-vapor and partly from the turf-fires everywhere in patches on the farms. A group of soft maples near by silently bursts out in crimson tips, buzzing all day with busy bees. The white sails of sloops and schooners

10

15

5

3. After the sentence ending "miles or so." *NYTR* has the following, which was deleted on the clipping: "As always, the river, its panorama as I wend along, seems inimitable, increases in interest and variety. This time the absence of foliage gives me better views of the countless handsome country houses: I find I never realized how thickly scattered they are, and how continuous, all the way by the banks, and as far back as you can see."

4. *NYTR* begins a new paragraph with "Sunset".

10–19. This paragraph is drawn from the first part of paragraph 4.

19. After "by distance." *NYTR* has the following, deleted on the clipping: "High up the shore, plainly, as I look, in relief against the background of the dark woods, is the white Grecian-temple-showing house of Mr. L., a millionaire, of the Astor connection—the site, on a lofty bank, with graceful slope, its crest line straight and even for over a mile—I suppose with farm-lands back—certainly to appearance, everything grand and attractive—with the L. family off to Europe, a year past, and, as I hear, hard work to spend half their income, they have so much."

Days at J. B.'s—Turf-Fires—Spring Songs.

Printed from clippings of *NYTR*, the same article as the preceding section. This section includes paragraph 5, the fourth under the subtitle "Countless Villas and Mansions" and paragraphs 6–9 under other subheads.

7. bees. The] *NYTR:* bees, filling their baskets with pollen. The

glide up or down the river; and long trains of cars, with ponderous roll, or faint bell notes, almost constantly on the opposite shore. The earliest wild
10 flowers in the woods and fields, spicy arbutus, blue liverwort, frail anemone, and the pretty white blossoms of the bloodroot. I launch out in slow rambles, discovering them. As I go along the roads I like to see the farmers' fires in patches, burning the dry brush, turf, debris. How the smoke crawls along, flat to the ground, slanting, slowly rising, reaching away,
15 and at last dissipating. I like its acrid smell—whiffs just reaching me— welcomer than French perfume.

The birds are plenty; of any sort, or of two or three sorts, curiously, not a sign, till suddenly some warm, gushing, sunny April (or even March) day—lo! there they are, from twig to twig, or fence to fence, flirt-
20 ing, singing, some mating, preparing to build. But most of them *en passant*—a fortnight, a month in these parts, and then away. As in all phases, Nature keeps up her vital, copious, eternal procession. Still, plenty of the birds hang around all or most of the season—now their love-time, and era of nest-building. I find flying over the river, crows, gulls and hawks. I
25 hear the afternoon shriek of the latter, darting about, preparing to nest. The oriole will soon be heard here, and the twanging *meoeow* of the catbird; also the king-bird, cuckoo and the warblers. All along, there are three peculiarly characteristic spring songs—the meadow-lark's, so sweet, so alert and remonstrating (as if he said, "don't you see?" or, "can't you
30 understand?")—the cheery, mellow, human tones of the robin—(I have been trying for years to get a brief term, or phrase, that would identify and describe that robin-call)—and the amorous whistle of the high-hole. Insects are out plentifully at midday.

April 29.—As we drove lingering along the road we heard, just
35 after sundown, the song of the wood-thrush. We stopp'd without a word,

---

12. After "discovering them." NYTR begins a new paragraph, the first of two subtitled "Turf Fires—Spring Sights—the Birds."
16. perfume.] NYTR: perfumes.] [After "perfumes." NYTR begins a new paragraph.]
17. plenty; of] NYTR: plenty, busy migrating. Of
24. find flying] NYTR: find blue-birds, robins, turtle-doves, black-birds, sparrows and larks, and, flying
26. *meoeow*] NYTR: meoeow
27. After "the warblers." NYTR begins a new paragraph, the first of two subtitled "Characteristic Spring Songs."
27–28. along, . . . three] NYTR: along there have been three
28. songs—the] NYTR: songs; the
29. NYTR has "Don't" and "Can't" for "don't" and "can't".
31–32. identify . . . robin-call)—and] NYTR: identify it)—and
36. a sweet] NYTR: a wild, sweet

and listen'd long. The delicious notes—a sweet, artless, voluntary, simple anthem, as from the flute-stops of some organ, wafted through the twilight—echoing well to us from the perpendicular high rock, where, in some thick young trees' recesses at the base, sat the bird—fill'd our senses, our souls.   40

Meeting a Hermit.

I found in one of my rambles up the hills a real hermit, living in a lonesome spot, hard to get at, rocky, the view fine, with a little patch of land two rods square. A man of youngish middle age, city born and raised, had been to school, had travel'd in Europe and California. I first met him once or twice on the road, and pass'd the time of day, with   5 some small talk; then, the third time, he ask'd me to go along a bit and rest in his hut (an almost unprecedented compliment, as I heard from others afterwards.) He was of Quaker stock, I think; talk'd with ease and moderate freedom, but did not unbosom his life, or story, or tragedy, or whatever it was.   10

An Ulster County Waterfall.

I jot this mem. in a wild scene of woods and hills, where we have come to visit a waterfall. I never saw finer or more copious hemlocks, many of them large, some old and hoary. Such a sentiment to them, secretive, shaggy—what I call weather-beaten and let-alone—a rich underlay of ferns, yew sprouts and mosses, beginning to be spotted with the early   5 summer wild-flowers. Enveloping all, the monotone and liquid gurgle

40. After "our senses, our souls." NYTR has four paragraphs, deleted in SDC (the first three crossed out on the clipping, the fourth cut away). See Appendix xx, 2.

Meeting a Hermit.

Printed from a clipping of NYTR, paragraph 18, same subtitle, of "Real Summer Openings."

5. road, and pass'd] NYTR: road, had passed
7. as I heard] SDA: as I have heard
For paragraphs 19 and 20, omitted in SDC, see Appendix xx, 3.

An Ulster County Waterfall.

Printed from a clipping of NYTR, same article, paragraph 21, same subhead.
3. them, secretive] NYTR: them, and all, secretive
5-6. early . . . Enveloping] NYTR: early wild flowers before-mentioned. Enveloping
6. monotone and] NYTR: monotone of blended base and

from the hoarse impetuous copious fall—the greenish-tawny, darkly transparent waters, plunging with velocity down the rocks, with patches of milk-white foam—a stream of hurrying amber, thirty feet wide, risen far 10 back in the hills and woods, now rushing with volume—every hundred rods a fall, and sometimes three or four in that distance. A primitive forest, druidical, solitary and savage—not ten visitors a year—broken rocks everywhere—shade overhead, thick underfoot with leaves—a just palpable wild and delicate aroma.

Walter Dumont and His Medal.

As I saunter'd along the high road yesterday, I stopp'd to watch a man near by, ploughing a rough stony field with a yoke of oxen. Usually there is much geeing and hawing, excitement, and continual noise and expletives, about a job of this kind. But I noticed how different, how easy 5 and wordless, yet firm and sufficient, the work of this young ploughman. His name was Walter Dumont, a farmer, and son of a farmer, working for their living. Three years ago, when the steamer "Sunnyside" was wreck'd of a bitter icy night on the west bank here, Walter went out in his boat—was the first man on hand with assistance—made a way through the 10 ice to shore, connected a line, perform'd work of first-class readiness, daring, danger, and saved numerous lives. Some weeks after, one evening when he was up at Esopus, among the usual loafing crowd at the country store and post-office, there arrived the gift of an unexpected official gold medal for the quiet hero. The impromptu presentation was made to him on 15 the spot, but he blush'd, hesitated as he took it, and had nothing to say.

Hudson River Sights.

It was a happy thought to build the Hudson river railroad right along the shore. The grade is already made by nature; you are sure of

11–12. forest, druidical] *NYTR:* forest of hemlocks and cedars, druidical
13. leaves—a] *NYTR:* leaves—and a

Walter Dumont and His Medal.
Printed from clippings of *NYTR*, same article, paragraph 22.
7. "Sunnyside"] *NYTR:* Sunnyside
13–14. unexpected . . . for] *NYTR:* unexpected handsome gold medal (either from the Government or the New-York Life Saving Society), for
For paragraph 23, "Conclusion," omitted in *SDC*, see Appendix xx, 4.

Hudson River Sights.
Printed from clippings of *NYTR*, "Real Summer Openings," paragraphs 14–17, under several headings. Subtitle inserted in red ink.

ventilation one side—and you are in nobody's way. I see, hear, the locomotives and cars, rumbling, roaring, flaming, smoking, constantly, away off there, night and day—less than a mile distant, and in full view by day. I like both sight and sound. Express trains thunder and lighten along; of freight trains, most of them very long, there cannot be less than a hundred a day. At night far down you see the headlight approaching, coming steadily on like a meteor. The river at night has its special character-beauties. The shad fishermen go forth in their boats and pay out their nets—one sitting forward, rowing, and one standing up aft dropping it properly—marking the line with little floats bearing candles, conveying, as they glide over the water, an indescribable sentiment and doubled brightness. I like to watch the tows at night, too, with their twinkling lamps, and hear the husky panting of the steamers; or catch the sloops' and schooners' shadowy forms, like phantoms, white, silent, indefinite, out there. Then the Hudson of a clear moonlight night.

But there is one sight the very grandest. Sometimes in the fiercest driving storm of wind, rain, hail or snow, a great eagle will appear over the river, now soaring with steady and now overhended wings—always confronting the gale, or perhaps cleaving into, or at times literally *sitting* upon it. It is like reading some first-class natural tragedy or epic, or hearing martial trumpets. The splendid bird enjoys the hubbub—is adjusted and equal to it—finishes it so artistically. His pinions just oscillating—the position of his head and neck—his resistless, occasionally varied flight—now a swirl, now an upward movement—the black clouds driving—the angry wash below—the hiss of rain, the wind's piping (perhaps the ice colliding, grunting)—he tacking or jibing—now, as it were, for a change, abandoning himself to the gale, moving with it with such velocity—and now, resuming control, he comes up against it, lord of the situation and the storm—lord, amid it, of power and savage joy.

Sometimes (as at present writing,) middle of sunny afternoon, the old "Vanderbilt" steamer stalking ahead—I plainly hear her rhythmic, slush-

1–20. From paragraphs 14 and 15, subtitled "The River a Hundred Miles Up."
7. long, there] NYTR: long, seems to me there
9. After "meteor." NYTR begins a new paragraph.
15. husky panting] NYTR: husky, rhythmic, alternate panting
17. Then the] NYTR: Then, too, the
17. night.] NYTR: night!
18–31. From paragraph 16, subtitled "A Sight for an Artist."
18. grandest.] NYTR: grandest!
21. times literally] NYTR: times poised, literally
24. His . . . oscillating] NYTR: His vast pinions proudly oscillating
29. velocity—and] NYTR: velocity!—and
30. against it, lord] NYTR: against the wind, lord
32–43. From paragraph 17, subtitled "A Specimen 'Tow' on the River."

35 ing paddles—drawing by long hawsers an immense and varied following string, ("an old sow and pigs," the river folks call it.) First comes a big barge, with a house built on it, and spars towering over the roof; then canal boats, a lengthen'd, clustering train, fasten'd and link'd together— the one in the middle, with high staff, flaunting a broad and gaudy flag— others with the almost invariable lines of new-wash'd clothes, drying; two 40 sloops and a schooner aside the tow—little wind, and that adverse—with three long, dark, empty barges bringing up the rear. People are on the boats: men lounging, women in sun-bonnets, children, stovepipes with streaming smoke.

Two City Areas, Certain Hours.

NEW YORK, *May 24, '79.*—Perhaps no quarters of this city (I have return'd again for awhile,) make more brilliant, animated, crowded, spectacular human presentations these fine May afternoons than the two I am now going to describe from personal observation. First: that area compris-
5 ing Fourteenth street (especially the short range between Broadway and Fifth avenue) with Union square, its adjacencies, and so retrostretching down Broadway for half a mile. All the walks here are wide, and the spaces ample and free—now flooded with liquid gold from the last two hours of powerful sunshine. The whole area at 5 o'clock, the days of my
10 observations, must have contain'd from thirty to forty thousand finely-dress'd people, all in motion, plenty of them good-looking, many beautiful women, often youths and children, the latter in groups with their nurses— the trottoirs everywhere close-spread, thick-tangled, (yet no collision, no trouble,) with masses of bright color, action, and tasty toilets; (surely

33. "Vanderbilt"] *NYTR:* Vanderbilt
34. paddles—drawing] *NYTR:* paddles—attached, drawing
34. hawsers an immense] *NYTR:* hawsers, her immense
42. children, stovepipes] *NYTR:* children—and stovepipes

Two City Areas, Certain Hours.
Printed from a clipping of *NYTR,* paragraphs 1–2 of "These May Afternoons," May 24, 1879. This section has no subtitle in *NYTR,* but corresponds to the first item of the general series of subheads at the beginning of the article. Subtitle for *SDC* inserted in red ink.
    1. The date is omitted here in *NYTR;* inserted in black ink above the clipping.
    1. this city] *NYTR:* the city
    1–2. The parenthetical statement, not in *NYTR,* is inserted in black ink.
    11. motion, . . . good-looking] *NYTR:* motion, some of them young and good-looking

the women dress better than ever before, and the men do too.) As if New 15
York would show these afternoons what it can do in its humanity, its
choicest physique and physiognomy, and its countless prodigality of loco-
motion, dry goods, glitter, magnetism, and happiness.

Second: also from 5 to 7 P.M. the stretch of Fifth avenue, all the way
from the Central Park exits at Fifty-ninth street, down to Fourteenth, es- 20
pecially along the high grade by Fortieth street, and down the hill. A Mississippi of horses and rich vehicles, not by dozens and scores, but hundreds
and thousands—the broad avenue filled and cramm'd with them—a
moving, sparkling, hurrying crush, for more than two miles. (I wonder
they don't get block'd, but I believe they never do.) Altogether it is to me 25
the marvel sight of New York. I like to get in one of the Fifth avenue
stages and ride up, stemming the swift-moving procession. I doubt if London or Paris or any city in the world can show such a carriage carnival
as I have seen here five or six times these beautiful May afternoons.

Central Park Walks and Talks.

May 16 to 22.—I visit Central Park now almost every day, sitting,
or slowly rambling, or riding around. The whole place presents its very
best appearance this current month—the full flush of the trees, the plentiful white and pink of the flowering shrubs, the emerald green of the grass
spreading everywhere, yellow dotted still with dandelions—the specialty 5
of the plentiful gray rocks, peculiar to these grounds, cropping out, miles
and miles—and over all the beauty and purity, three days out of four, of
our summer skies. As I sit, placidly, early afternoon, off against Ninetieth
street, the policeman, C. C., a well-form'd sandy-complexion'd young fel-

---

14. of bright color] *NYTR:* of sunny color
20. Central Park] *NYTR:* Park
21–22. Mississippi of] *NYTR:* Mississippi chaos of
23–24. a moving] *NYTR:* one moving
26–27. Fifth . . . procession.] *NYTR:* Fifth Avenue Stages of the later afternoon, and ride up, stemming the swift-moving panorama.

   Central Park Walks and Talks.
   Printed from a clipping of paragraphs 3–5 of the same article; subtitle as
in SDC.
   1–2. day, sitting] *NYTR:* day—off and on, indeed, for the last three or four weeks
—sitting
   3. month—the full] *NYTR:* month, especially these latter days of it. The full
   6. of . . . gray] *NYTR:* of gray
   8. After "summer skies." *NYTR* begins a new paragraph.
   9–10. fellow, comes] *NYTR:* fellow, dressed in citizen's clothes, comes

10   low, comes over and stands near me. We grow quite friendly and chatty
forthwith. He is a New Yorker born and raised, and in answer to my
questions tells me about the life of a New York Park policeman, (while he
talks keeping his eyes and ears vigilantly open, occasionally pausing and
moving where he can get full views of the vistas of the road, up and
15   down, and the spaces around.) The pay is $2.40 a day (seven days to a
week)—the men come on and work eight hours straight ahead, which is
all that is required of them out of the twenty-four. The position has more
risks than one might suppose—for instance if a team or horse runs away
(which happens daily) each man is expected not only to be prompt, but to
20   waive safety and stop wildest nag or nags—(*do it*, and don't be thinking
of your bones or face)—give the alarm-whistle too, so that other guards
may repeat, and the vehicles up and down the tracks be warn'd. Injuries to
the men are continually happening. There is much alertness and quiet
strength. (Few appreciate, I have often thought, the Ulyssean capacity,
25   derring do, quick readiness in emergencies, practicality, unwitting devotion and heroism, among our American young men and working-people
—the firemen, the railroad employés, the steamer and ferry men, the police, the conductors and drivers—the whole splendid average of native
stock, city and country.) It is good work, though; and upon the whole,
30   the Park force members like it. They see life, and the excitement keeps
them up. There is not so much difficulty as might be supposed from
tramps, roughs, or in keeping people "off the grass." The worst trouble of
the regular Park employé is from malarial fever, chills, and the like.

A Fine Afternoon, 4 to 6.

Ten thousand vehicles careering through the Park this perfect afternoon. Such a show! and I have seen all—watch'd it narrowly, and at my

12. of . . . (while] *NYTR:* of the Park Police (while
15. After "around.)" *NYTR* begins a new paragraph. The first sentence of this
paragraph, deleted on the clipping, is as follows: "The Force are all to have—or already have—new suits this Summer; the Department supplies the rig."
18. suppose—for] *NYTR:* suppose; for
20. nags—(*do it*] *NYTR:* nags (*do it*
23. happening. There] *NYTR:* happening—there
24. (Few appreciate] *NYTR:* (Few know
27. steamer and ferry men] *NYTR:* steamer men
28. of native] *NYTR:* of Mechanics, of native
32. grass." The] *NYTR:* grass," etc. The

A Fine Afternoon, 4 to 6.

Printed from a clipping of the same article, paragraph 6, subtitled "The Car-
riage-Riding Classes," and paragraphs 7-8, subtitled "The Horseback Road."

leisure. Private barouches, cabs and coupés, some fine horseflesh—lap-dogs, footmen, fashions, foreigners, cockades on hats, crests on panels—the full oceanic tide of New York's wealth and "gentility." It was an impressive, rich, interminable circus on a grand scale, full of action and color in the beauty of the day, under the clear sun and moderate breeze. Family groups, couples, single drivers—of course dresses generally elegant—much "style," (yet perhaps little or nothing, even in that direction, that fully justified itself.) Through the windows of two or three of the richest carriages I saw faces almost corpse-like, so ashy and listless. Indeed the whole affair exhibited less of sterling America, either in spirit or countenance, than I had counted on from such a select mass-spectacle. I suppose, as a proof of limitless wealth, leisure, and the aforesaid "gentility," it was tremendous. Yet what I saw those hours (I took two other occasions, two other afternoons to watch the same scene,) confirms a thought that haunts me every additional glimpse I get of our top-loftical general or rather exceptional phases of wealth and fashion in this country—namely, that they are ill at ease, much too conscious, cased in too many cerements, and far from happy—that there is nothing in them which we who are poor and plain need at all envy, and that instead of the perennial smell of the grass and woods and shores, their typical redolence is of soaps and essences, very rare may be, but suggesting the barber shop—something that turns stale and musty in a few hours anyhow.

Perhaps the show on the horseback road was prettiest. Many groups (threes a favorite number,) some couples, some singly—many ladies—frequently horses or parties dashing along on a full run—fine riding the rule—a few really first-class animals. As the afternoon waned, the wheel'd carriages grew less, but the saddle-riders seemed to increase. They linger'd long—and I saw some charming forms and faces.

---

1. *NYTR* has the following, which *SDC* shifts to a center subtitle: "*A fine after-noon, 4 to 6.—*"

1–2. afternoon.] *NYTR:* afternoon!

9. (yet . . . nothing] *NYTR:* (yet nothing

12. affair exhibited] *NYTR:* affair, I must say, exhibited

12. in spirit] *NYTR:* in promise, spirit

16. scene,) confirms a] *NYTR:* scene), adds strength to a

19–20. ease, . . . and] *NYTR:* ease, and

22. is of] *NYTR:* is but of

24. After "anyhow." *NYTR* has the subtitle "The Horseback Road."

26. (threes a] *NYTR:* (threes were a

27–28. rule—a] *NYTR:* rule—not a

28. After "animals." *NYTR* begins a new paragraph.

30. and faces.] *NYTR:* and faces—the handsomest girls and the finest looking young men.

Departing of the Big Steamers.

May 15.—A three hours' bay-trip from 12 to 3 this afternoon, accompanying "the City of Brussels" down as far as the Narrows, in behoof of some Europe-bound friends, to give them a good send off. Our spirited little tug, the "Seth Low," kept close to the great black "Brussels," sometimes one side, sometimes the other, always up to her, or even pressing ahead, (like the blooded pony accompanying the royal elephant.) The whole affair, from the first, was an animated, quick-passing, characteristic New York scene; the large, good-looking, well-dress'd crowd on the wharf-end—men and women come to see their friends depart, and bid them God-speed—the ship's sides swarming with passengers—groups of bronze-faced sailors, with uniform'd officers at their posts—the quiet directions, as she quickly unfastens and moves out, prompt to a minute—the emotional faces, adieus and fluttering handkerchiefs, and many smiles and some tears on the wharf—the answering faces, smiles, tears and fluttering handkerchiefs, from the ship—(what can be subtler and finer than this play of faces on such occasions in these responding crowds?—what go more to one's heart?)—the proud, steady, noiseless cleaving of the grand oceaner down the bay—we speeding by her side a few miles, and then turning, wheeling, amid a babel of wild hurrahs, shouted partings, ear-splitting steam whistles, kissing of hands and waving of handkerchiefs.

This departing of the big steamers, noons or afternoons—there is no better medicine when one is listless or vapory. I am fond of going down Wednesdays and Saturdays—their more special days—to watch them

Departing of the Big Steamers.
Printed from clippings of the same article, paragraphs 9–10; subtitle as in *SDC.*
    2. No quotation marks in *NYTR.*
    3. After "send off." *NYTR* has the following sentence, deleted on the clipping: "Never did sun, winds, waters, shipping, bay-spaces, and their sights, more absorb into me—more exhilarate me."
    4. No quotation marks in *NYTR.*
    7. was an animated] *NYTR:* was another animated
    9. women come] *NYTR:* women indiscriminately, come
    18. side . . . and] *NYTR:* side a-ways, and
    22. steamers, noons or afternoons—there] *NYTR:* steamers, too, noons or afternoons, is one of the New-York sights that I love. There
    28. crowd has] *NYTR:* crowd such occasions has
    31–32. No quotation marks in *NYTR.*

and the crowds on the wharves, the arriving passengers, the general bustle   25
and activity, the eager looks from the faces, the clear-toned voices, (a
travel'd foreigner, a musician, told me the other day she thinks an American crowd has the finest voices in the world,) the whole look of the great,
shapely black ships themselves, and their groups and lined sides—in
the setting of our bay with the blue sky overhead. Two days after the   30
above I saw the "Britannic," the "Donau," the "Helvetia" and the "Schie-
dam" steam out, all off for Europe—a magnificent sight.

Two Hours on the Minnesota.

From 7 to 9, aboard the United States school-ship Minnesota, lying
up the North river. Captain Luce sent his gig for us about sundown, to the
foot of Twenty-third street, and receiv'd us aboard with officer-like hospitality and sailor heartiness. There are several hundred youths on the
Minnesota to be train'd for efficiently manning the government navy. I   5
like the idea much; and, so far as I have seen to-night, I like the way it
is carried out on this huge vessel. Below, on the gun-deck, were gather'd
nearly a hundred of the boys, to give us some of their singing exercises,
with a melodeon accompaniment, play'd by one of their number. They
sang with a will. The best part, however, was the sight of the young fel-   10
lows themselves. I went over among them before the singing began, and
talk'd a few minutes informally. They are from all the States; I asked for
the Southerners, but could only find one, a lad from Baltimore. In age,
apparently, they range from about fourteen years to nineteen or twenty.
They are all of American birth, and have to pass a rigid medical examina-   15
tion; well-grown youths, good flesh, bright eyes, looking straight at you,

---

32. out, all off] *NYTR:* out, off
Paragraph 11, the third of this section, omitted in *SDC*, is as follows:
"(It did not add to my good spirits this ride up and down the bay, to see most of
the passing first-class ships, or those at anchor, flying the British, German, French
or other foreign flags—seldom the Stars and Stripes. We met the State of Indiana
coming in, the Red Cross aft. The Brussels we went down with, the same.)"

Two Hours on the Minnesota.
    Printed from a clipping of the same article, paragraph 12; subtitle as in *SDC*.
   1. From 7 to 9,] *NYTR:* Then the same evening, from 7 to 9,
   4–5. are . . . to be] *NYTR:* are 200 youths on the Minnesota, (by a just passed
bill of Congress the number will soon be increased to 600), to be
   6. and, so far] *NYTR:* and, as far
   12. a few . . . They] *NYTR:* a moment. They
   14. fourteen years to] *NYTR:* fourteen to
   15–16. examination; well-grown] *NYTR:* examination. Well-grown

30   As I cross the Delaware, one of the deck-hands, F. R., tells me how a
woman jump'd overboard and was drown'd a couple of hours since. It
happen'd in mid-channel—she leap'd from the forward part of the boat,
which went over her. He saw her rise on the other side in the swift running water, throw her arms and closed hands high up, (white hands and
35   bare forearms in the moonlight like a flash,) and then she sank. (I found
out afterwards that this young fellow had promptly jump'd in, swam after
the poor creature, and made, though unsuccessfully, the bravest efforts to
rescue her; but he didn't mention that part at all in telling me the story.)

Swallows on the River.

Sept. 3.—Cloudy and wet, and wind due east; air without palpable
fog, but very heavy with moisture—welcome for a change. Forenoon,
crossing the Delaware, I noticed unusual numbers of swallows in flight,
circling, darting, graceful beyond description, close to the water. Thick,
5   around the bows of the ferry-boat as she lay tied in her slip, they flew;
and as we went out I watch'd beyond the pier-heads, and across the broad
stream, their swift-winding loop-ribands of motion, down close to it, cutting and intersecting. Though I had seen swallows all my life, seem'd as
though I never before realized their peculiar beauty and character in the
10   landscape. (Some time ago, for an hour, in a huge old country barn, watching these birds flying, recall'd the 22d book of the Odyssey, where Ulysses
slays the suitors, bringing things to *eclaircissement*, and Minerva, swal-
low-bodied, darts up through the spaces of the hall, sits high on a beam,

Swallows on the River.
Printed from an autograph MS.

Begin a Long Jaunt West.
This section and the following twenty-eight (through "Upon Our Own Land")
were printed in SDC, with two exceptions, wholly from manuscripts written by Whitman at various times and on various kinds of paper, though mostly on gray sheets,
sometimes in dark ink, sometimes in light ink, and sometimes in pencil; the sheets
cut, pasted, and rearranged in ways too complex to be described in detail. Subtitles,
as a rule, are inserted in red ink. Together they constitute Whitman's record of his
journey from Philadelphia to Denver and return in the autumn of 1879, in the company of Colonel John W. Forney, publisher of the Philadelphia *Press*, who had been
invited to speak at the Old Settlers celebration at Bismarck Grove, near Lawrence,
Kansas, September 16. Whitman was also invited to be guest of honor and visiting
poet. No attempt is made to collate fully the printed text with the existing MSS,
but a few passages of special significance will be noted, particularly when they assist
in understanding the contents and arrangement of the materials as printed in SDC.
Many of the original notes, made on the spot, were rewritten later for SDC, usually in

looks complacently on the show of slaughter, and feels in her element, exulting, joyous.) 15

Begin a Long Jaunt West.

The following three or four months (Sept. to Dec. '79) I made quite a western journey, fetching up at Denver, Colorado, and penetrating the Rocky Mountain region enough to get a good notion of it all. Left West Philadelphia after 9 o'clock one night, middle of September, in a comfortable sleeper. Oblivious of the two or three hundred miles across 5 Pennsylvania; at Pittsburgh in the morning to breakfast. Pretty good view of the city and Birmingham—fog and damp, smoke, coke-furnaces, flames, discolor'd wooden houses, and vast collections of coal-barges. Presently a bit of fine region, West Virginia, the Panhandle, and crossing the river, the Ohio. By day through the latter State—then Indiana—and 10 so rock'd to slumber for a second night, flying like lightning through Illinois.

In the Sleeper.

What a fierce weird pleasure to lie in my berth at night in the luxurious palace-car, drawn by the mighty Baldwin—embodying, and filling me, too, full of the swiftest motion, and most resistless strength! It is late, perhaps midnight or after—distances join'd like magic—as we speed through Harrisburg, Columbus, Indianapolis. The element of danger 5

black ink on gray paper, but others may have been kept and extensively revised, or cut and pieced together, with linking passages of new or rewritten notes. Revisions may be in black or red ink, or in pencil. Sometimes a page will consist of as many as half a dozen strips of paper pasted on a large base sheet.

10. It is evident that the original notes for "Begin a Long Jaunt West" and the section following were made at the same time, perhaps on Whitman's arrival in St. Louis after his second night on the sleeper. After "Indiana—" the original MS continued: "(I reserve for another occasion all this portion of my notes)—then pass over our flight through Illinois a second night, rocked". This he crosses out in black ink, inserts "—and so," also in black ink, and draws a line in red ink from "Indiana—" down the page to the passage beginning: "—and so rock'd". The reserved notes were used, in part at least, in the following section.

In the Sleeper.
Printed from the autograph MS.
4–5. Obviously he did not pass through Harrisburg, Columbus, and Indianapolis the same night, since, as stated in the preceding section, he ate breakfast in Pittsburgh. See also note to line 10 of the preceding section.

adds zest to it all. On we go, rumbling and flashing, with our loud whin-
nies thrown out from time to time, or trumpet-blasts, into the darkness.
Passing the homes of men, the farms, barns, cattle—the silent villages.
And the car itself, the sleeper, with curtains drawn and lights turn'd down
10 —in the berths the slumberers, many of them women and children—as on,
on, on, we fly like lightning through the night—how strangely sound
and sweet they sleep! (They say the French Voltaire in his time designated the grand opera and a ship of war the most signal illustrations of
the growth of humanity's and art's advance beyond primitive barbarism.
15 Perhaps if the witty philosopher were here these days, and went in the
same car with perfect bedding and feed from New York to San Francisco,
he would shift his type and sample to one of our American sleepers.)

Missouri State.

We should have made the run of 960 miles from Philadelphia to St.
Louis in thirty-six hours, but we had a collision and bad locomotive smash
about two-thirds of the way, which set us back. So merely stopping over
night that time in St. Louis, I sped on westward. As I cross'd Missouri
5 State the whole distance by the St. Louis and Kansas City Northern Railroad, a fine early autumn day, I thought my eyes had never looked on
scenes of greater pastoral beauty. For over two hundred miles successive
rolling prairies, agriculturally perfect view'd by Pennsylvania and New
Jersey eyes, and dotted here and there with fine timber. Yet fine as the
10 land is, it isn't the finest portion; (there is a bed of impervious clay and
hard-pan beneath this section that holds water too firmly, "drowns the
land in wet weather, and bakes it in dry," as a cynical farmer told me.)
South are some richer tracts, though perhaps the beauty-spots of the State
are the northwestern counties. Altogether, I am clear, (now, and from
15 what I have seen and learn'd since,) that Missouri, in climate, soil, relative
situation, wheat, grass, mines, railroads, and every important materialistic
respect, stands in the front rank of the Union. Of Missouri averaged po-

Missouri State.

Printed from two autograph pages. The first page is composed of two strips
of white paper pasted on a gray base sheet with space between, on which is written
the sentence (lines 3–4) beginning "So merely". The second page is white like the
strips above mentioned.

Lawrence and Topeka, Kansas.

Printed from three strips of ruled white paper, the last two cut so as to allow
the insertion, on the base sheet to which they are pasted, of: "my RR. friends there,
and the city and State officials." (Lines 6–7.)

litically and socially I have heard all sorts of talk, some pretty severe—but I should have no fear myself of getting along safely and comfortably anywhere among the Missourians. They raise a good deal of tobacco. You see at this time quantities of the light greenish-gray leaves pulled and hanging out to dry on temporary frameworks or rows of sticks. Looks much like the mullein familiar to eastern eyes.

Lawrence and Topeka, Kansas.

We thought of stopping in Kansas City, but when we got there we found a train ready and a crowd of hospitable Kansians to take us on to Lawrence, to which I proceeded. I shall not soon forget my good days in L., in company with Judge Usher and his sons, (especially John and Linton,) true westerners of the noblest type. Nor the similar days in Topeka. Nor the brotherly kindness of my RR. friends there, and the city and State officials. Lawrence and Topeka are large, bustling, half-rural, handsome cities. I took two or three long drives about the latter, drawn by a spirited team over smooth roads.

The Prairies.
And an Undeliver'd Speech.

At a large popular meeting at Topeka—the Kansas State Silver Wedding, fifteen or twenty thousand people—I had been erroneously bill'd to deliver a poem. As I seem'd to be made much of, and wanted to be good-natured, I hastily pencill'd out the following little speech. Unfortunately, (or fortunately,) I had such a good time and rest, and talk and dinner, with the U. boys, that I let the hours slip away and didn't drive over to the meeting and speak my piece. But here it is just the same:

"My friends, your bills announce me as giving a poem; but I have no poem—have composed none for this occasion. And I can honestly say I am now

The Prairies.
And an Undeliver'd Speech.

Printed from several pages of autograph MS. The introductory part, lines 1–7, was originally written on ruled white paper, but part of this was cut away and rewritten on the gray sheet above the white paper pasted on it. All of the speech is written in heavy black ink on small white sheets, about 4½ by 6½ inches, except the last paragraph, lines 37–44, which is on a much larger ruled white sheet. The speech has been considerably revised in black and red ink, probably after the time it was intended for delivery.

10   glad of it. Under these skies resplendent in September beauty—amid the
peculiar landscape you are used to, but which is new to me—these interminable
and stately prairies—in the freedom and vigor and sane enthusiasm of this
perfect western air and autumn sunshine—it seems to me a poem would be
almost an impertinence. But if you care to have a word from me, I should speak

15   it about these very prairies; they impress me most, of all the objective shows I
see or have seen on this, my first real visit to the West. As I have roll'd rapidly
hither for more than a thousand miles, through fair Ohio, through bread-
raising Indiana and Illinois—through ample Missouri, that contains and raises
everything; as I have partially explor'd your charming city during the last two

20   days, and, standing on Oread hill, by the university, have launch'd my view
across broad expanses of living green, in every direction—I have again been
most impress'd, I say, and shall remain for the rest of my life most impress'd,
with that feature of the topography of your western central world—that vast
Something, stretching out on its own unbounded scale, unconfined, which there

25   is in these prairies, combining the real and ideal, and beautiful as dreams.

"I wonder indeed if the people of this continental inland West know how
much of first-class *art* they have in these prairies—how original and all your
own—how much of the influences of a character for your future humanity,
broad, patriotic, heroic and new? how entirely they tally on land the grandeur

30   and superb monotony of the skies of heaven, and the ocean with its waters? how
freeing, soothing, nourishing they are to the soul?

"Then is it not subtly they who have given us our leading modern Americans,
Lincoln and Grant?—vast-spread, average men—their foregrounds of character
altogether practical and real, yet (to those who have eyes to see) with finest

35   backgrounds of the ideal, towering high as any. And do we not see, in them,
foreshadowings of the future races that shall fill these prairies?

"Not but what the Yankee and Atlantic States, and every other part—
Texas, and the States flanking the south-east and the Gulf of Mexico—the
Pacific shore empire—the Territories and Lakes, and the Canada line (the day

40   is not yet, but it will come, including Canada entire)—are equally and inte-
grally and indissolubly this Nation, the *sine qua non* of the human, political and
commercial New World. But this favor'd central area of (in round numbers)
two thousand miles square seems fated to be the home both of what I would call
America's distinctive ideas and distinctive realities."

25. After "beautiful as dreams." the following paragraph in the MS was deleted,
perhaps because it did not express the sentiments he came to hold after he had seen
the Rocky Mountains, or because he eulogized the plains more fully later in "America's Characteristic Landscape" (*q.v.*).

"Let those who will laud the specially picturesque—the chasm, the cliff, the
mountain-peak;—henceforth, for me, these grander manifestations of God's geology
to man, for they are not divine only, they seem more human.—I don't want to be
awed only by the shows of Nature—not merely to admire,—I want to be dilated,
strengthened & soothed, not kept at a distance."

On to Denver—a Frontier Incident.

Printed from two pages of autograph MS. The first page, on ruled white paper, was evidently written as an introduction to the narrative of the "frontier incident,"

On to Denver—a Frontier Incident.

The jaunt of five or six hundred miles from Topeka to Denver took
me through a variety of country, but all unmistakably prolific, western,
American, and on the largest scale. For a long distance we follow the line
of the Kansas river, (I like better the old name, Kaw,) a stretch of very
rich, dark soil, famed for its wheat, and call'd the Golden Belt—then
plains and plains, hour after hour—Ellsworth county, the centre of the
State—where I must stop a moment to tell a characteristic story of early
days—scene the very spot where I am passing—time 1868. In a scrimmage at some public gathering in the town, A. had shot B. quite badly,
but had not kill'd him. The sober men of Ellsworth conferr'd with one another and decided that A. deserv'd punishment. As they wished to set a
good example and establish their reputation the reverse of a Lynching
town, they open an informal court and bring both men before them for deliberate trial. Soon as this trial begins the wounded man is led forward to
give his testimony. Seeing his enemy in durance and unarm'd, B. walks
suddenly up in a fury and shoots A. through the head—shoots him dead.
The court is instantly adjourn'd, and its unanimous members, without a
word of debate, walk the murderer B. out, wounded as he is, and hang
him.

In due time we reach Denver, which city I fall in love with from the
first, and have that feeling confirm'd, the longer I stay there. One of my
pleasantest days was a jaunt, via Platte cañon, to Leadville.

5

10

15

20

for only about half the page is used and the writing breaks off there in the middle of
a sentence. The second page is unruled white paper pasted on a sheet of ruled white
paper.

3. American] SDA: America
7. The first MS page concludes with the words "to tell a" and the second page
originally began "Here is a characteristic," but Whitman deleted "Here is a". Apparently the story of the incident existed previously to its incorporation in the copy
for SDC. It is written in pencil, lines 8–21.
20–22. This paragraph is written in black ink at the bottom of the second page.
20. According to one investigator, Whitman arrived in Denver Sept. 20, 1879.
[Robert R. Hubach, "Walt Whitman in Kansas," *Kansas Historical Quarterly*,
X (May, 1941), 153. Yet see "Denver Impressions," lines 36–37 and note, and
"I Turn South—and Then East Again," note.]

An Hour on Kenosha Summit.

Jottings from the Rocky Mountains, mostly pencill'd during a day's trip over the South Park RR., returning from Leadville, and especially the hour we were detain'd, (much to my satisfaction,) at Kenosha summit. As afternoon advances, novelties, far-reaching splendors, accumulate under the bright sun in this pure air. But I had better commence with the day.

The confronting of Platte cañon just at dawn, after a ten miles' ride in early darkness on the rail from Denver—the seasonable stoppage at the entrance of the cañon, and good breakfast of eggs, trout, and nice griddle-cakes—then as we travel on, and get well in the gorge, all the wonders, beauty, savage power of the scene—the wild stream of water, from sources of snows, brawling continually in sight one side—the dazzling sun, and the morning lights on the rocks—such turns and grades in the track, squirming around corners, or up and down hills—far glimpses of a hundred peaks, titanic necklaces, stretching north and south—the huge rightly-named Dome-rock—and as we dash along, others similar, simple, monolithic, elephantine.

An Egotistical "Find."

"I have found the law of my own poems," was the unspoken but more-and-more decided feeling that came to me as I pass'd, hour after hour, amid all this grim yet joyous elemental abandon—this plenitude of material, entire absence of art, untrammel'd play of primitive Nature— the chasm, the gorge, the crystal mountain stream, repeated scores, hundreds of miles—the broad handling and absolute uncrampedness—the fantastic forms, bathed in transparent browns, faint reds and grays, towering sometimes a thousand, sometimes two or three thousand feet high—

An Hour on Kenosha Summit.

Printed from four pieces of gray paper, written in ink; obviously copied from an earlier MS since the original notes were in pencil. At the top of the first piece is the date "Oct. 79" crossed out. This section and the following sections through "Denver Impressions" (with the exception of "New Senses—New Joys" and "Steam Power, Telegraphs, &c.," which were later insertions) were originally numbered pages 1–12, with Whitman's signature at the end, as if these pages had been intended for separate publication.

An Egotistical "Find."

Printed from an autograph MS page, black ink on gray paper, subtitle in-at their tops now and then huge masses pois'd, and mixing with the clouds, with only their outlines, hazed in misty lilac, visible. ("In Nature's grand- 10 est shows," says an old Dutch writer, an ecclesiastic, "amid the ocean's depth, if so might be, or countless worlds rolling above at night, a man thinks of them, weighs all, not for themselves or the abstract, but with reference to his own personality, and how they may affect him or color his destinies.") 15

New Senses—New Joys.

We follow the stream of amber and bronze brawling along its bed, with its frequent cascades and snow-white foam. Through the cañon we fly—mountains not only each side, but seemingly, till we get near, right in front of us—every rood a new view flashing, and each flash defying de- scription—on the almost perpendicular sides, clinging pines, cedars, 5 spruces, crimson sumach bushes, spots of wild grass—but dominating all, those towering rocks, rocks, rocks, bathed in delicate vari-colors, with the clear sky of autumn overhead. New senses, new joys, seem develop'd. Talk as you like, a typical Rocky Mountain cañon, or a limitless sea-like stretch of the great Kansas or Colorado plains, under favoring circum- 10 stances, tallies, perhaps expresses, certainly awakes, those grandest and subtlest element-emotions in the human soul, that all the marble temples and sculptures from Phidias to Thorwaldsen—all paintings, poems, remi- niscences, or even music, probably never can.

Steam-Power, Telegraphs, &c.

I get out on a ten minutes' stoppage at Deer creek, to enjoy the un- equal'd combination of hill, stone and wood. As we speed again, the yel- low granite in the sunshine, with natural spires, minarets, castellated

serted in red ink.

11. Whitman originally wrote "old Swiss writer," but crossed out "Swiss" and wrote "Dutch" in red ink above it. Source not identified.

New Senses—New Joys.

Printed from an autograph MS page consisting of a ruled white sheet, part of which is cut away, pasted on a gray sheet, apparently with revisions, fitted to it.

Steam-Power, Telegraphs, &c.

Printed from an autograph MS, black ink on gray paper.

perches far aloft—then long stretches of straight-upright palisades, rhi-
noceros color—then gamboge and tinted chromos. Ever the best of my
pleasures the cool-fresh Colorado atmosphere, yet sufficiently warm. Signs
of man's restless advent and pioneerage, hard as Nature's face is—deserted dug-outs by dozens in the side-hills—the scantling-hut, the tele-
graph-pole, the smoke of some impromptu chimney or outdoor fire—at
intervals little settlements of log-houses, or parties of surveyors or tele-
graph builders, with their comfortable tents. Once, a canvas office where
you could send a message by electricity anywhere around the world! Yes,
pronounc'd signs of the man of latest dates, dauntlessly grappling with
these grisliest shows of the old kosmos. At several places steam saw-mills,
with their piles of logs and boards, and the pipes puffing. Occasionally
Platte cañon expanding into a grassy flat of a few acres. At one such
place, toward the end, where we stop, and I get out to stretch my legs, as
I look skyward, or rather mountain-topward, a huge hawk or eagle (a
rare sight here) is idly soaring, balancing along the ether, now sinking
low and coming quite near, and then up again in stately-languid circles—
then higher, higher, slanting to the north, and gradually out of sight.

America's Back-Bone.

I jot these lines literally at Kenosha summit, where we return, afternoon, and take a long rest, 10,000 feet above sea-level. At this immense
height the South Park stretches fifty miles before me. Mountainous chains
and peaks in every variety of perspective, every hue of vista, fringe the
view, in nearer, or middle, or far-dim distance, or fade on the horizon. We
have now reach'd, penetrated the Rockies, (Hayden calls it the Front
Range,) for a hundred miles or so; and though these chains spread away
in every direction, specially north and south, thousands and thousands farther, I have seen specimens of the utmost of them, and know henceforth at
least what they are, and what they look like. Not themselves alone, for
they typify stretches and areas of half the globe—are, in fact, the verte-

America's Back-Bone.
Printed from two pages of autograph MS, with ink and paper like that of the
preceding section. Subtitle inserted in red ink between lines regularly spaced.
2. After the first sentence, the following passage in the MS, originally part of that
sentence, is deleted: "the view, revelations, astounding novelties, though a strangely
calm feeling pervades me, and I am enjoying it all as if some old story, altogether
too tumultuous for putting in literary order."
11–12. "verteber" in the MS remains unchanged, but must have been altered to
"vertebræ" in proof.

bræ or back-bone of our hemisphere. As the anatomists say a man is only a spine, topp'd, footed, breasted and radiated, so the whole Western world is, in a sense, but an expansion of these mountains. In South America they are the Andes, in Central America and Mexico the Cordilleras, and in our   15
States they go under different names—in California the Coast and Cascade ranges—thence more eastwardly the Sierra Nevadas—but mainly and more centrally here the Rocky Mountains proper, with many an elevation such as Lincoln's, Grey's, Harvard's, Yale's, Long's and Pike's peaks, all over 14,000 feet high. (East, the highest peaks of the Alleghanies, the   20
Adirondacks, the Cattskills, and the White Mountains, range from 2000 to 5500 feet—only Mount Washington, in the latter, 6300 feet.)

The Parks.

In the midst of all here, lie such beautiful contrasts as the sunken basins of the North, Middle, and South Parks, (the latter I am now on one side of, and overlooking,) each the size of a large, level, almost quadrangular, grassy, western county, wall'd in by walls of hills, and each park the source of a river. The ones I specify are the largest in Colorado,   5
but the whole of that State, and of Wyoming, Utah, Nevada and western California, through their sierras and ravines, are copiously mark'd by similar spreads and openings, many of the small ones of paradisiac loveliness and perfection, with their offsets of mountains, streams, atmosphere and hues beyond compare.   10

Art Features.

Talk, I say again, of going to Europe, of visiting the ruins of feudal castles, or Coliseum remains, or kings' palaces—when you can come *here*. The alternations one gets, too; after the Illinois and Kansas prairies of a thousand miles—smooth and easy areas of the corn and wheat of ten mil-

The Parks.
   Printed from a single gray sheet of autograph MS, unfilled. The original subtitle was "The Parks—the Streams," but in revision evidently all but the first paragraph was withdrawn from this section and given a new subtitle "Art Features."
   8. paradisiac] MS: paradisaic

Art Features.
   Printed from three pages of autograph MS, ink and paper like the preceding.
   The italicized sideheadings, *"Mountain streams"* in line 11 and *"Aerial effects"* in line 18 were inserted in black ink in the completed MS.

5   lion democratic farms in the future—here start up in every conceivable
presentation of shape, these non-utilitarian piles, coping the skies, emanating a beauty, terror, power, more than Dante or Angelo ever knew. Yes, I
think the chyle of not only poetry and painting, but oratory, and even the
metaphysics and music fit for the New World, before being finally assimi-
10   lated, need first and feeding visits here.

Mountain streams.—The spiritual contrast and etheriality of the
whole region consist largely to me in its never-absent peculiar streams—
the snows of inaccessible upper areas melting and running down
through the gorges continually. Nothing like the water of pastoral plains,
15   or creeks with wooded banks and turf, or anything of the kind elsewhere.
The shapes that element takes in the shows of the globe cannot be fully
understood by an artist until he has studied these unique rivulets.

Aerial effects.—But perhaps as I gaze around me the rarest sight
of all is in atmospheric hues. The prairies—as I cross'd them in my jour-
20   ney hither—and these mountains and parks, seem to me to afford new
lights and shades. Everywhere the aerial gradations and sky-effects inimitable; nowhere else such perspectives, such transparent lilacs and
grays. I can conceive of some superior landscape painter, some fine
colorist, after sketching awhile out here, discarding all his previous work,
25   delightful to stock exhibition amateurs, as muddy, raw and artificial.
Near one's eye ranges an infinite variety; high up, the bare whitey-brown,
above timber line; in certain spots afar patches of snow any time of year;
(no trees, no flowers, no birds, at those chilling altitudes.) As I write I see
the Snowy Range through the blue mist, beautiful and far off. I plainly
30   see the patches of snow.

Denver Impressions.

Through the long-lingering half-light of the most superb of evenings
we return'd to Denver, where I staid several days leisurely exploring,

Denver Impressions.

Printed from three pages of autograph MS, black ink on gray paper, subtitle
inserted in red ink, and a clipping from the Denver *Daily Tribune.* Apparently the
issue containing the interview quoted in the clipping, probably the issue of Sunday,
September 21, has not survived. A clipping of that paper containing all of the interview exists in the Trent Collection of the Duke University Library. It has the heading: "Walt Whitman's Impressions of Denver and the West. What He Says of its
Present, its People and its Future." This clipping bears the endorsement in Whitman's
autograph: "From the *Denver* (Colorado) *Tribune* Sept: 12 1879." The date is an
error, since Whitman's party did not leave Philadelphia until September 10, and
could not have left Topeka, Kansas, until after the Old Settlers' celebration of September 15 and 16. He probably arrived in Denver on the afternoon of September 18 or
19, and the interview was pretty certainly published Sunday, September 21. [See

receiving impressions, with which I may as well taper off this memorandum, itemizing what I saw there. The best was the men, three-fourths of them large, able, calm, alert, American. And cash! why they create it here. Out in the smelting works, (the biggest and most improv'd ones, for the precious metals, in the world,) I saw long rows of vats, pans, cover'd by bubbling-boiling water, and fill'd with pure silver, four or five inches thick, many thousand dollars' worth in a pan. The foreman who was showing me shovel'd it carelessly up with a little wooden shovel, as one might toss beans. Then large silver bricks, worth $2000 a brick, dozens of piles, twenty in a pile. In one place in the mountains, at a mining camp, I had a few days before seen rough bullion on the ground in the open air, like the confectioner's pyramids at some swell dinner in New York. (Such a sweet morsel to roll over with a poor author's pen and ink—and appropriate to slip in here—that the silver product of Colorado and Utah, with the gold product of California, New Mexico, Nevada and Dakota, foots up an addition to the world's coin of considerably over a hundred millions every year.)

A city, this Denver, well-laid out—Laramie street, and 15th and 16th and Champa streets, with others, particularly fine—some with tall storehouses of stone or iron, and windows of plate-glass—all the streets with little canals of mountain water running along the sides—plenty of people, "business," modernness—yet not without a certain racy wild smack, all its own. A place of fast horses, (many mares with their colts,) and I saw lots of big greyhounds for antelope hunting. Now and then groups of miners, some just come in, some starting out, very picturesque.

One of the papers here interview'd me, and reported me as saying off-hand: "I have lived in or visited all the great cities on the Atlantic third of the republic—Boston, Brooklyn with its hills, New Orleans, Baltimore, stately Washington, broad Philadelphia, teeming Cincinnati and Chicago, and for thirty years in that wonder, wash'd by hurried and glittering tides, my own New York, not only the New World's but the

---

notes to "I Turn South—and Then East Again" and also Appendix XXII.] Professor Rollo G. Silver published the interview from a surviving manuscript in *American Literature*, X (March, 1938), 84–87. That manuscript is collated with the Duke clipping in Appendix XXII.

    1–27. Printed from MS as revised in black ink.
    18. of considerably over a] *SDA:* of perhaps towards a
    25. smack] *SDA:* snack
    28–29. This introductory sentence is written in ink above the clipping.
    29–45. Printed from the clipping, with revisions as indicated.
    30. republic] Clip.: Republic
    30–31. New Orleans, Baltimore, stately] Clip.: New Orleans, stately
    32. wash'd] Clip.: washed

world's city—but, newcomer to Denver as I am, and threading its streets,
breathing its air, warm'd by its sunshine, and having what there is of its
human as well as aerial ozone flash'd upon me now for only three or four
days, I am very much like a man feels sometimes toward certain people he
meets with, and warms to, and hardly knows why. I, too, can hardly tell
why, but as I enter'd the city in the slight haze of a late September afternoon, and have breath'd its air, and slept well o' nights, and have roam'd
or rode leisurely, and watch'd the comers and goers at the hotels, and
absorb'd the climatic magnetism of this curiously attractive region, there
has steadily grown upon me a feeling of affection for the spot, which,
sudden as it is, has become so definite and strong that I must put it on
record."

So much for my feeling toward the Queen city of the plains and peaks,
where she sits in her delicious rare atmosphere, over 5000 feet above sea-
level, irrigated by mountain streams, one way looking east over the
prairies for a thousand miles, and having the other, westward, in constant
view by day, draped in their violet haze, mountain tops innumerable. Yes,
I fell in love with Denver, and even felt a wish to spend my declining and
dying days there.

I Turn South—and Then East Again.

Leave Denver at 8 A.M. by the Rio Grande RR. going south.
Mountains constantly in sight in the apparently near distance, veil'd

34. world's city] Clip.: World's city
34. newcomer] Clip.: new-comer
35. warm'd] Clip.: warmed
35–36. of its human] Clip.: of its people, its idiocrasy, and its human
36. aerial ozone] Clip.: æreal *ozone*
36–37. three or four days] Clip.: a couple of days
38. with, and warms to, and] Clip.: with and warms to, and suddenly, passionately loves, and
38. why. I, too, can] Clip.: why. Here in this very Denver, if it might be so, I
should like to cast my lot, above all other spots, all other cities. I honestly confess
I can
39. enter'd] Clip.: entered
40. its air] Clip.: its delicious air
41. leisurely, and watch'd] Clip.: leisurely through Latimer and Fourteenth
and Fifteenth and Sixteenth and Twenty-third streets, and have watched
42. the climatic] Clip.: the human as well as climatic
42. region] Clip.: city
44–45. must put it on record."] Clip.: must express it."
46–52. Printed from the autograph MS of *SDC*, with Whitman's signature.
50–52. In the MS this sentence is a separate paragraph.
Below the signature, which is lined out with blue pencil, he later added in black

slightly, but still clear and very grand—their cones, colors, sides, distinct against the sky—hundreds, it seem'd thousands, interminable necklaces of them, their tops and slopes hazed more or less slightly in that blue-gray, 5 under the autumn sun, for over a hundred miles—the most spiritual show of objective Nature I ever beheld, or ever thought possible. Occasionally the light strengthens, making a contrast of yellow-tinged silver on one side, with dark and shaded gray on the other. I took a long look at Pike's peak, and was a little disappointed. (I suppose I had expected something 10 stunning.) Our view over plains to the left stretches amply, with corrals here and there, the frequent cactus and wild sage, and herds of cattle feeding. Thus about 120 miles to Pueblo. At that town we board the comfortable and well-equipt Atchison, Topeka and Santa Fe RR., now striking east. 15

Unfulfill'd Wants—the Arkansas River.

I had wanted to go to the Yellowstone river region—wanted specially to see the National Park, and the geysers and the "hoodoo" or goblin land of that country; indeed, hesitated a little at Pueblo, the turning point—wanted to thread the Veta pass—wanted to go over the Santa Fe trail away southwestward to New Mexico—but turn'd and set my face 5 eastward—leaving behind me whetting glimpse-tastes of southeastern Colorado, Pueblo, Bald mountain, the Spanish peaks, Sangre de Christos, Mile-Shoe-curve (which my veteran friend on the locomotive told me was

ink and then crossed out the following sentence: "Returned east last of the year, and resume my occasional visits to the Jersey ponds and woods."

I Turn South—and Then East Again.
Printed from a page of autograph MS of irregular size, consisting of a large sheet with two narrow strips pasted on the lower part. On the second strip, written in blue pencil and crossed out in black ink, is the notation: "Take in Sept 23 '79. Evening on the Plains. Twilight hours." It seems probable that Whitman arrived in Denver Friday, September 19, was interviewed (or wrote an article purporting to be be an interview) Saturday, September 20 (see notes to "Denver Impressions," and to lines 28–29 and 36–37), made his trip to the mountains Monday, the 22nd, and left by train Tuesday, the 23rd, as indicated in the last paragraph (Appendix XXII) of the MS "Walt Whitman in Denver." (See also "A Silent Little Follower—the Coreopsis," line 16 and note.) The interview most likely was published in the Sunday issue of the *Daily Tribune*, September 21.

Unfulfill'd Wants—the Arkansas River.
Printed from two autograph pages, one gray, the other composed of two white strips pasted together.
8. Mile-Shoe-curve] [Possibly an error for "Mule-Shoe-curve." ED.]

"the boss railroad curve of the universe,") fort Garland on the plains,
Veta, and the three great peaks of the Sierra Blancas.

The Arkansas river plays quite a part in the whole of this region—I
see it, or its high-cut rocky northern shore, for miles, and cross and recross
it frequently, as it winds and squirms like a snake. The plains vary here
even more than usual—sometimes a long sterile stretch of scores of miles
—then green, fertile and grassy, an equal length. Some very large herds
of sheep. (One wants new words in writing about these plains, and all the
inland American West—the terms, *far*, *large*, *vast*, &c., are insufficient.)

A Silent Little Follower—the Coreopsis.

Here I must say a word about a little follower, present even now
before my eyes. I have been accompanied on my whole journey from
Barnegat to Pike's Peak by a pleasant floricultural friend, or rather millions of friends—nothing more or less than a hardy little yellow five-
petal'd September and October wild flower, growing I think everywhere in
the middle and northern United States. I had seen it on the Hudson and
over Long Island, and along the banks of the Delaware and through New
Jersey, (as years ago up the Connecticut, and one fall by Lake Cham-
plain.) This trip it follow'd me regularly, with its slender stem and eyes of
gold, from Cape May to the Kaw valley, and so through the cañons and to
these plains. In Missouri I saw immense fields all bright with it. Toward
western Illinois I woke up one morning in the sleeper and the first thing
when I drew the curtain of my berth and look'd out was its pretty countenance and bending neck.

Sept. 25th.—Early morning—still going east after we leave
Sterling, Kansas, where I stopp'd a day and night. The sun up about half
an hour; nothing can be fresher or more beautiful than this time, this
region. I see quite a field of my yellow flower in full bloom. At intervals
dots of nice two-story houses, as we ride swiftly by. Over the immense
area, flat as a floor, visible for twenty miles in every direction in the clear

A Silent Little Follower—the Coreopsis.
Printed from two autograph pages, each made up of strips of different kinds
of paper, with revisions, perhaps later, in heavier ink than the original.
16. The words "where I stopp'd a day and night" are written in the heavier, revising ink between the lines. This statement, together with the date, seems to confirm
the conjectural chronology. Whitman left Denver early the 23rd, arrived in Sterling,
Kansas, early the 24th, spent the day and night there, and so continued on the 25th.
24. E. L.] MS before revision: Ed. Lindsey

air, a prevalence of autumn-drab and reddish-tawny herbage—sparse stacks of hay and enclosures, breaking the landscape—as we rumble by, flocks of prairie-hens starting up. Between Sterling and Florence a fine country. (Remembrances to E. L., my old-young soldier friend of war times, and his wife and boy at S.)   25

The Prairies and Great Plains in Poetry.
(*After traveling Illinois, Missouri, Kansas and Colorado.*)

Grand as the thought that doubtless the child is already born who will see a hundred millions of people, the most prosperous and advanc'd of the world, inhabiting these Prairies, the great Plains, and the valley of the Mississippi, I could not help thinking it would be grander still to see all those inimitable American areas fused in the alembic of a perfect poem, or   5
other esthetic work, entirely western, fresh and limitless—altogether our own, without a trace or taste of Europe's soil, reminiscence, technical letter or spirit. My days and nights, as I travel here—what an exhilaration!—not the air alone, and the sense of vastness, but every local sight and feature. Everywhere something characteristic—the cactuses, pinks,   10
buffalo grass, wild sage—the receding perspective, and the far circle-line of the horizon all times of day, especially forenoon—the clear, pure, cool, rarefied nutriment for the lungs, previously quite unknown—the black patches and streaks left by surface-conflagrations—the deep-plough'd furrow of the "fire-guard"—the slanting snow-racks built all along to   15
shield the railroad from winter drifts—the prairie-dogs and the herds of antelope—the curious "dry rivers"—occasionally a "dug-out" or corral—Fort Riley and Fort Wallace—those towns of the northern plains, (like ships on the sea,) Eagle-Tail, Coyotè, Cheyenne, Agate, Monotony, Kit Carson—with ever the ant-hill and the buffalo-wallow—ever the herds of   20
cattle and the cow-boys ("cow-punchers") to me a strangely interesting class, bright-eyed as hawks, with their swarthy complexions and their broad-brimm'd hats—apparently always on horseback, with loose arms slightly raised and swinging as they ride.

The Prairies and Great Plains in Poetry.

Printed from two autograph pages, the first composed of three strips of paper cut and pasted together after they were filled with writing, and part of the writing cut away. This section and the following sections subtitled "The Spanish Peaks—Evening on the Plains," "America's Characteristic Landscape," "Earth's Most Important Stream," "Prairie Analogies—the Tree Question," and "Mississippi Valley Literature" were arranged as a unit, perhaps with the idea of separate publication. This conjecture is supported by the fact that all the pages, except the first, numbered

The Spanish Peaks—Evening on the Plains.

Between Pueblo and Bent's fort, southward, in a clear afternoon
sun-spell I catch exceptionally good glimpses of the Spanish peaks. We are
in southeastern Colorado—pass immense herds of cattle as our first-class
locomotive rushes us along—two or three times crossing the Arkansas,
5 which we follow many miles, and of which river I get fine views, sometimes for quite a distance, its stony, upright, not very high, palisade banks,
and then its muddy flats. We pass Fort Lyon—lots of adobie houses—
limitless pasturage, appropriately fleck'd with those herds of cattle—in
due time the declining sun in the west—a sky of limpid pearl over all—
10 and so evening on the great plains. A calm, pensive, boundless landscape
—the perpendicular rocks of the north Arkansas, hued in twilight—a thin
line of violet on the southwestern horizon—the palpable coolness and
slight aroma—a belated cow-boy with some unruly member of his herd—
an emigrant wagon toiling yet a little further, the horses slow and tired—
15 two men, apparently father and son, jogging along on foot—and around
all the indescribable *chiaroscuro* and sentiment, (profounder than anything at sea,) athwart these endless wilds.

America's Characteristic Landscape.

Speaking generally as to the capacity and sure future destiny of that
plain and prairie area (larger than any European kingdom) it is the inexhaustible land of wheat, maize, wool, flax, coal, iron, beef and pork,
butter and cheese, apples and grapes—land of ten million virgin farms—
5 to the eye at present wild and unproductive—yet experts say that upon it
when irrigated may easily be grown enough wheat to feed the world. Then

208–218 in the MS, were originally numbered as a unit, 2 to 11. The part of the first
page with the number was cut away and a new subtitle in red ink inserted on a
strip pasted at the top of the page. Moreover, all the titles, except that of the first
section of the group, were written in between regular lines, where obviously they were
an afterthought, and all are in red ink. The section titled "The Prairies and Great
Plains in Poetry" describes scenes which Whitman saw between Kansas City and
Denver on his trip west, and may have been partly written at that time.

The Spanish Peaks—Evening on the Plains.
Printed from an autograph page (3), paper and ink of the type of all the
pages numbered 2–11. Chronologically, this section precedes "A Silent Little Follower—the Coreopsis."

as to scenery (giving my own thought and feeling,) while I know the standard claim is that Yosemite, Niagara falls, the upper Yellowstone and the like, afford the greatest natural shows, I am not so sure but the Prairies and Plains, while less stunning at first sight, last longer, fill the esthetic sense fuller, precede all the rest, and make North America's characteristic landscape.

Indeed through the whole of this journey, with all its shows and varieties, what most impress'd me, and will longest remain with me, are these same prairies. Day after day, and night after night, to my eyes, to all my senses—the esthetic one most of all—they silently and broadly unfolded. Even their simplest statistics are sublime.

Earth's Most Important Stream.

The valley of the Mississippi river and its tributaries, (this stream and its adjuncts involve a big part of the question,) comprehends more than twelve hundred thousand square miles, the greater part prairies. It is by far the most important stream on the globe, and would seem to have been marked out by design, slow-flowing from north to south, through a dozen climates, all fitted for man's healthy occupancy, its outlet unfrozen all the year, and its line forming a safe, cheap continental avenue for commerce and passage from the north temperate to the torrid zone. Not even the mighty Amazon (though larger in volume) on its line of east and west—not the Nile in Africa, nor the Danube in Europe, nor the three great rivers of China, compare with it. Only the Mediterranean sea has play'd some such part in history, and all through the past, as the Mississippi is destined to play in the future. By its demesnes, water'd and welded by its branches, the Missouri, the Ohio, the Arkansas, the Red, the Yazoo, the St. Francis and others, it already compacts twenty-five millions of people, not merely the most peaceful and money-making, but the

America's Characteristic Landscape.
Printed from an autograph MS, including page 4 and part of 5, in this series. The earlier title "These Inland Plains" has been crossed out and the present title written in a cramped space in the upper left corner of the page. The revision of line 14 suggests that the original was written, perhaps before he started east, with reference only to his journey west.
14. varieties, what] MS before revision: varieties, from Barnegat to Pike's Peak, what

Earth's Most Important Stream.
Printed from the lower part of the autograph page numbered 5, all of 6, and the upper part of 7.

most restless and warlike on earth. Its valley, or reach, is rapidly concentrating the political power of the American Union. One almost thinks it
is the Union—or soon will be. Take it out, with its radiations, and what
20   would be left? From the car windows through Indiana, Illinois, Missouri,
or stopping some days along the Topeka and Santa Fe road, in southern
Kansas, and indeed wherever I went, hundreds and thousands of miles
through this region, my eyes feasted on primitive and rich meadows, some
of them partially inhabited, but far, immensely far more untouch'd, un-
25   broken—and much of it more lovely and fertile in its unplough'd innocence than the fair and valuable fields of New York's, Pennsylvania's,
Maryland's or Virginia's richest farms.

Prairie Analogies—the Tree Question.

The word Prairie is French, and means literally meadow. The
cosmical analogies of our North American plains are the Steppes of Asia,
the Pampas and Llanos of South America, and perhaps the Saharas of
Africa. Some think the plains have been originally lake-beds; others
5   attribute the absence of forests to the fires that almost annually sweep over
them—(the cause, in vulgar estimation, of Indian summer.) The tree
question will soon become a grave one. Although the Atlantic slope, the
Rocky mountain region, and the southern portion of the Mississippi valley,
are well wooded, there are here stretches of hundreds and thousands of
10   miles where either not a tree grows, or often useless destruction has
prevail'd; and the matter of the cultivation and spread of forests may
well be press'd upon thinkers who look to the coming generations of the
prairie States.

Mississippi Valley Literature.

Lying by one rainy day in Missouri to rest after quite a long exploration—first trying a big volume I found there of "Milton, Young, Gray,
Beattie and Collins," but giving it up for a bad job—enjoying however

---

21. some days along the Topeka and Santa Fe] MS before revision: some days
east of Pueblo, on the Santa Fe
[Compare the "stopping some days" of this line with the "where I stopp'd a
day and night" of line 16 of "A Silent Little Follower—The Coreopsis." Both,
presumably, refer to the same period, his stopover at Sterling, Kansas, Sept. 24.
—ED.]

for awhile, as often before, the reading of Walter Scott's poems, "Lay of the Last Minstrel," "Marmion," and so on—I stopp'd and laid down the book, and ponder'd the thought of a poetry that should in due time express and supply the teeming region I was in the midst of, and have briefly touch'd upon. One's mind needs but a moment's deliberation anywhere in the United States to see clearly enough that all the prevalent book and library poets, either as imported from Great Britain, or follow'd and *doppel-gang'd* here, are foreign to our States, copiously as they are read by us all. But to fully understand not only how absolutely in opposition to our times and lands, and how little and cramp'd, and what anachronisms and absurdities many of their pages are, for American purposes, one must dwell or travel awhile in Missouri, Kansas and Colorado, and get rapport with their people and country.

Will the day ever come—no matter how long deferr'd—when those models and lay-figures from the British islands—and even the precious traditions of the classics—will be reminiscences, studies only? The pure breath, primitiveness, boundless prodigality and amplitude, strange mixture of delicacy and power, of continence, of real and ideal, and of all original and first-class elements, of these prairies, the Rocky mountains, and of the Mississippi and Missouri rivers—will they ever appear in, and in some sort form a standard for our poetry and art? (I sometimes think that even the ambition of my friend Joaquin Miller to put them in, and illustrate them, places him ahead of the whole crowd.)

Not long ago I was down New York bay, on a steamer, watching the sunset over the dark green heights of Navesink, and viewing all that inimitable spread of shore, shipping and sea, around Sandy hook. But an intervening week or two, and my eyes catch the shadowy outlines of the Spanish peaks. In the more than two thousand miles between, though of infinite and paradoxical variety, a curious and absolute fusion is doubtless steadily annealing, compacting, identifying all. But subtler and wider and more solid, (to produce such compaction,) than the laws of the States, or the common ground of Congress or the Supreme Court, or the grim welding of our national wars, or the steel ties of railroads, or all the kneading and fusing processes of our material and business history, past or present, would in my opinion be a great throbbing, vital, imaginative

Prairie Analogies—the Tree Question.
Printed from the autograph MS, page 7 and the upper part of 8.

Mississippi Valley Literature.
Printed from MS, pages 8–11. The last page of this section (11) is not full, is much revised, and has Whitman's signature at the end.

40 work, or series of works, or literature, in constructing which the Plains, the Prairies, and the Mississippi river, with the demesnes of its varied and ample valley, should be the concrete background, and America's human-ity, passions, struggles, hopes, there and now—an *eclaircissement* as it is and is to be, on the stage of the New World, of all Time's hitherto drama of war, romance and evolution—should furnish the lambent fire, the ideal.

An Interviewer's Item.

Oct. 17, '79.—To-day one of the newspapers of St. Louis prints the following informal remarks of mine on American, especially Western literature: "We called on Mr. Whitman yesterday and after a somewhat desultory conversation abruptly asked him: 'Do you think we are to have a
5 distinctively American literature?' 'It seems to me,' said he, 'that our work at present is to lay the foundations of a great nation in products, in agriculture, in commerce, in networks of intercommunication, and in all that relates to the comforts of vast masses of men and families, with freedom of speech, ecclesiasticism, &c. These we have founded and are
10 carrying out on a grander scale than ever hitherto, and Ohio, Illinois, Indiana, Missouri, Kansas and Colorado, seem to me to be the seat and field of these very facts and ideas. Materialistic prosperity in all its varied forms, with those other points that I mentioned, intercommunication and

An Interviewer's Item.

Printed almost wholly from two newspaper clippings of the St. Louis *Post-Dispatch*, Oct. 17, 1879. This interview, together with two others from which Whitman did not quote in SDC, can be read in Robert R. Hubach's "Three Uncol-lected St. Louis Interviews of Walt Whitman," *American Literature*, XIV (May, 1942), 141–147.

1–3. These lines, through the word "yesterday" are prefixed in Whitman's hand-writing to the clipping.

4–5. The clipping indents the question beginning "Do you" and also the first line of Whitman's answer beginning "It seems".

6. present is] Clip.: present, and for a long time to come, is

6. the foundations] Clip.: the materialistic foundations

6–7. products, . . . in networks] Clip.: products, in commerce, in vast net-works

8. comforts of] Clip.: comforts and supplies of

8. families, with] Clip.: families, on a very grand scale, and those with

9. speech, . . . we] Clip.: speech and ecclesiasticism. This we] [The word "ecclesiasticism" is in capitals, in the clipping, in the center of the page.]

10. hitherto, and Ohio] Clip.: hitherto, and it seems to me that those great central States from Ohio to Colorado, and from Lake Superior down to Tennessee, the prairie States, will be the theater of our great future. Ohio

12. very . . . ideas. Materialistic] Clip.: very ideas. They seem to be carrying them out. Materialistic

freedom, are first to be attended to. When those have their results and get settled, then a literature worthy of us will begin to be defined. Our American superiority and vitality are in the bulk of our people, not in a gentry like the old world. The greatness of our army during the secession war, was in the rank and file, and so with the nation. Other lands have their vitality in a few, a class, but we have it in the bulk of the people. Our leading men are not of much account and never have been, but the average of the people is immense, beyond all history. Sometimes I think in all departments, literature and art included, that will be the way our superiority will exhibit itself. We will not have great individuals or great leaders, but a great average bulk, unprecedentedly great.' "

The Women of the West.

Kansas City.—I am not so well satisfied with what I see of the women of the prairie cities. I am writing this where I sit leisurely in a store in Main street, Kansas city, a streaming crowd on the sidewalks flowing by. The ladies (and the same in Denver) are all fashionably drest, and have the look of "gentility" in face, manner and action, but they do *not* have, either in physique or the mentality appropriate to them, any high native originality of spirit or body, (as the men certainly have, appropriate to them.) They are "intellectual" and fashionable, but dyspeptic-looking

12. Clipping begins a new paragraph with "Materialistic".
13. forms, with] Clip.: forms and on the grand scale of our times, with
15. defined.] Clip.: defined from our nebulous conditions. [End of first clipping. Second clipping cut from the end of the article, including the last two paragraphs.]
16. superiority] Clip.: greatness
17. like the] Clip.: like in the
17–18. army . . . was] Clip.: army was
18–19. Other . . . their] Clip.: Other nations had their
18–19. Hubach omits this entire sentence.
21. history. . . . in] Clip.: history. Lincoln seems to me to be our greatest specimen personality. Sometimes I think that in
21. Clipping begins a new paragraph with "Lincoln".
22. superiority] Clip.: greatness
24. great average bulk] Clip.: great bulk
[Whitman's other statements in answer to questions in this review, as well as in the others, are not included in this edition because he did not make them indisputably his own by incorporating them in a publication definitely edited by himself.—ED.]

The Women of the West.
Printed from an autograph page composed of two strips of unruled white paper pasted on a gray base sheet; original notes in pencil, revised in black ink. The subtitle is in red ink, and the sideheading "*Kansas City*" is in black ink. The first sentence and the first two words of the second are also in black ink, the first words, in pencil, on the first white strip being "writing this," etc.

10 and generally doll-like; their ambition evidently is to copy their eastern sisters. Something far different and in advance must appear, to tally and complete the superb masculinity of the West, and maintain and continue it.

The Silent General.

Sept. 28, '79.—So General Grant, after circumambiating the world, has arrived home again—landed in San Francisco yesterday, from the ship City of Tokio from Japan. What a man he is! what a history! what an illustration—his life—of the capacities of that American individuality
5 common to us all. Cynical critics are wondering "what the people can see in Grant" to make such a hubbub about. They aver (and it is no doubt true) that he has hardly the average of our day's literary and scholastic culture, and absolutely no pronounc'd genius or conventional eminence of any sort. Correct: but he proves how an average western farmer, me-
10 chanic, boatman, carried by tides of circumstances, perhaps caprices, into a position of incredible military or civic responsibilities, (history has presented none more trying, no born monarch's, no mark more shining for attack or envy,) may steer his way fitly and steadily through them all, carrying the country and himself with credit year after year—command over
15 a million armed men—fight more than fifty pitch'd battles—rule for eight years a land larger than all the kingdoms of Europe combined—and then, retiring, quietly (with a cigar in his mouth) make the promenade of the whole world, through its courts and coteries, and kings and czars and mikados, and splendidest glitters and etiquettes, as phlegmatically as
20 he ever walk'd the portico of a Missouri hotel after dinner. I say all this is what people like—and I am sure I like it. Seems to me it transcends Plutarch. How those old Greeks, indeed, would have seized on him! A mere plain man—no art, no poetry—only practical sense, ability to do, or

The Silent General.

Printed from two autograph pages, all written in pencil with revisions in black and red ink. The first page is composed of two strips of ruled white paper of the same type and width pasted together. The upper sheet of white paper shows the printed letterhead of the Water Commissioner of St. Louis. At the upper left corner of this sheet are the words "Kansas City" in pencil, crossed out in ink. The title of this section was first, in red ink, "A Very Utilitarian Hero," but this was crossed out and the present title substituted, also in red ink. The date in the first line is in black ink. The second page under this title is composed of five pieces of white paper of different sizes pasted together. If these penciled notes were made on the white paper in Kansas City on his return journey from Denver, as seems probable, he must have

try his best to do, what devolv'd upon him. A common trader, money-
maker, tanner, farmer of Illinois—general for the republic, in its terrific 25
struggle with itself, in the war of attempted secession—President following, (a task of peace, more difficult than the war itself)—nothing
heroic, as the authorities put it—and yet the greatest hero. The gods, the
destinies, seem to have concentrated upon him.

President Hayes's Speeches.

Sept. 30.—I see President Hayes has come out West, passing quite
informally from point to point, with his wife and a small cortege of big
officers, receiving ovations, and making daily and sometimes double-daily
addresses to the people. To these addresses—all impromptu, and some
would call them ephemeral—I feel to devote a memorandum. They are 5
shrewd, good-natur'd, face-to-face speeches, on easy topics not too deep;
but they give me some revised ideas of oratory—of a new, opportune
theory and practice of that art, quite changed from the classic rules, and
adapted to our days, our occasions, to American democracy, and to the
swarming populations of the West. I hear them criticised as wanting in 10
dignity, but to me they are just what they should be, considering all the
circumstances, who they come from, and who they are address'd to.
Underneath, his objects are to compact and fraternize the States, encourage their materialistic and industrial development, soothe and ex-
pand their self-poise, and tie all and each with resistless double ties not 15
only of inter-trade barter, but human comradeship.

From Kansas city I went on to St. Louis, where I remain'd nearly
three months, with my brother T. J. W., and my dear nieces.

acquired the paper, obviously from his brother Jeff's office, in St. Louis on his way to
Denver.

President Hayes's Speeches.

Printed from an autograph page consisting of two wide strips of ruled white
paper of different sizes pasted on the lower part of a gray sheet. The gray sheet is
written in ink and ends with the word "memorandum." in line 5. The upper and
larger white strip, written in pencil, begins with the next sentence and ends with the
words "self-poise, and" in line 15. It is revised in black and red ink. The lower white
strip, concluding the section, is written in ink. Presumably the white strip in pencil
is part of the notes made in Kansas City, whereas the gray sheet and the white strip
written in ink were added in St. Louis, or after Whitman returned to Camden.

St. Louis Memoranda.

Oct., Nov., and Dec., '79.—The points of St. Louis are its position, its absolute wealth, (the long accumulations of time and trade, solid riches, probably a higher average thereof than any city,) the unrivall'd amplitude of its well-laid-out environage of broad plateaus, for future
5   expansion—and the great State of which it is the head. It fuses northern and southern qualities, perhaps native and foreign ones, to perfection, rendezvous the whole stretch of the Mississippi and Missouri rivers, and its American electricity goes well with its German phlegm. Fourth, Fifth and Third streets are store-streets, showy, modern, metropolitan, with
10   hurrying crowds, vehicles, horse-cars, hubbub, plenty of people, rich goods, plate-glass windows, iron fronts often five or six stories high. You can purchase anything in St. Louis (in most of the big western cities for the matter of that) just as readily and cheaply as in the Atlantic marts. Often in going about the town you see reminders of old, even decay'd
15   civilization. The water of the west, in some places, is not good, but they make it up here by plenty of very fair wine, and inexhaustible quantities of the best beer in the world. There are immense establishments for slaughtering beef and pork—and I saw flocks of sheep, 5000 in a flock. (In Kansas city I had visited a packing establishment that kills and packs an
20   average of 2500 hogs a day the whole year round, for export. Another in Atchison, Kansas, same extent; others nearly equal elsewhere. And just as big ones here.)

St. Louis Memoranda.

Printed from two autograph pages. The first is composed of three pieces of white paper. The top piece is unruled, written in ink. The other sheets appear to be cut from the Water Commissioner's stationery, without the printed letterhead, and are written in pencil. The original title was "St. Louis Notes." Later "Notes" was deleted and "Memoranda" inserted in red ink. The original date in the upper left corner of the top strip was revised from "Oct. & Nov., '79" to the present sidehead. The second page consists of a gray sheet like many used for copying earlier pencil notes, the upper half in ink with few revisions, the lower part covered with a small unruled white sheet, written in pencil and pasted on, but all crossed out.

4. well-laid-out] [Both SDC and CP have "well-laid out," but the second hyphen was probably omitted unintentionally.—ED.]

22. After this line the MS continues (partly on this page and partly on two additional small scraps, pasted on an unnumbered sheet) as follows (all crossed out): "I often stopt towards noon in a large drugstore, Fourth and Locust—partly to get a glass of Vichy & partly to sit down and rest myself, and most of all to see the oceanic crowd of humanity (in full currents) that rolled along. You might have easily fancied yourself in some busy part of New York, even Broadway. Plenty of well-drest, good-sized, good-looking men, mostly young and middle aged—better

Nights on the Mississippi.

Oct. 29th, 30th, and 31st.—Wonderfully fine, with the full harvest moon, dazzling and silvery. I have haunted the river every night lately, where I could get a look at the bridge by moonlight. It is indeed a structure of perfection and beauty unsurpassable, and I never tire of it. The river at present is very low; I noticed to-day it had much more of a blue-clear look than usual. I hear the slight ripples, the air is fresh and cool, and the view, up or down, wonderfully clear, in the moonlight. I am out pretty late: it is so fascinating, dreamy. The cool night-air, all the influences, the silence, with those far-off eternal stars, do me good. I have been quite ill of late. And so, well-near the centre of our national demesne, these night views of the Mississippi.

Upon Our Own Land.

"Always, after supper, take a walk half a mile long," says an old proverb, dryly adding, "and if convenient let it be upon your own land." I wonder does any other nation but ours afford opportunity for such a jaunt as this? Indeed has any previous period afforded it? No one, I discover, begins to know the real geographic, democratic, indissoluble American Union in the present, or suspect it in the future, until he explores these Central States, and dwells awhile observantly on their

clothes and a more prevailing American physiognomy than the Atlantic Cities—Missourians in from the country—Germans quite frequent. Westerners are a handsome, healthy, full-sized race of men even with all their tobacco, hot bread, ham & whiskey."

Nights on the Mississippi.
Printed from an autograph page composed of two strips of ruled white paper and part of a gray sheet. The upper white strip in light black ink, the lower in pencil, and the gray sheet in heavy black ink. Whitman numbered the page "226 & 227," suggesting that two pages were revised and reduced to one after numbering was completed.

Upon Our Own Land.
Printed from two autograph pages, the first composed of three pieces of white paper of different sizes pasted together, all written in light black ink and revised in heavy black ink. The second page is a single sheet written, with few revisions, in heavy black ink on gray paper, probably a copy of an earlier draft. The subtitle is in red ink.

prairies, or amid their busy towns, and the mighty father of waters. A
ride of two or three thousand miles, "on one's own land," with hardly a
disconnection, could certainly be had in no other place than the United
States, and at no period before this. If you want to see what the railroad is,
and how civilization and progress date from it—how it is the conqueror of
crude nature, which it turns to man's use, both on small scales and on the
largest—come hither to inland America.

I return'd home, east, Jan. 5, 1880, having travers'd, to and fro and
across, 10,000 miles and more. I soon resumed my seclusions down in the
woods, or by the creek, or gaddings about cities, and an occasional dis-
quisition, as will be seen following.

Edgar Poe's Significance.

Jan. 1, '80.—In diagnosing this disease called humanity—to assume for the nonce what seems a chief mood of the personality and writings of my subject—I have thought that poets, somewhere or other on the
list, present the most mark'd indications. Comprehending artists in a mass,
musicians, painters, actors, and so on, and considering each and all of
them as radiations or flanges of that furious whirling wheel, poetry, the
centre and axis of the whole, where else indeed may we so well investigate
the causes, growths, tally-marks of the time—the age's matter and
malady?

By common consent there is nothing better for man or woman than a
perfect and noble life, morally without flaw, happily balanced in activity,
physically sound and pure, giving its due proportion, and no more, to the
sympathetic, the human emotional element—a life, in all these, unhasting,
unresting, untiring to the end. And yet there is another shape of personality dearer far to the artist-sense, (which likes the play of strongest lights

Edgar Poe's Significance.

Printed from clippings of the *Critic* for June 3, 1882. The collation includes,
besides printed texts, the clipping from CR, revised by Whitman in red ink, the
autograph MS submitted to CR, now in the Feinberg Collection, and two paragraphs
from the Washington *Star*, November 18, 1875.

1. The date is inserted in black ink on the clipping. Earlier dates have been
deleted, as follows: in black ink "Jan. 1 1878"; in red ink "April," "June 31 '82,"
and "Jan. 1 80."

13. human emotional] FMS: human-emotional
13. life, in] CR and FMS: life in
15. the play] CR and FMS: the lambent play
19. the power] CR and FMS: the wondrous power
21–24. The sentence in parentheses not in CR or FMS; written in red ink on the

and shades,) where the perfect character, the good, the heroic, although never attain'd, is never lost sight of, but through failures, sorrows, temporary downfalls, is return'd to again and again, and while often violated, is passionately adhered to as long as mind, muscles, voice, obey the power we call volition. This sort of personality we see more or less in Burns,   20
Byron, Schiller, and George Sand. But we do not see it in Edgar Poe. (All this is the result of reading at intervals the last three days a new volume of his poems—I took it on my rambles down by the pond, and by degrees read it all through there.) While to the character first outlined the service Poe renders is certainly that entire contrast and contradiction which is   25
next best to fully exemplifying it.

Almost without the first sign of moral principle, or of the concrete or its heroisms, or the simpler affections of the heart, Poe's verses illustrate an intense faculty for technical and abstract beauty, with the rhyming art to excess, an incorrigible propensity toward nocturnal themes, a demoniac   30
undertone behind every page—and, by final judgment, probably belong among the electric lights of imaginative literature, brilliant and dazzling, but with no heat. There is an indescribable magnetism about the poet's life and reminiscences, as well as the poems. To one who could work out their subtle retracing and retrospect, the latter would make a close tally   35
no doubt between the author's birth and antecedents, his childhood and youth, his physique, his so-call'd education, his studies and associates, the literary and social Baltimore, Richmond, Philadelphia and New York, of those times—not only the places and circumstances in themselves, but often, very often, in a strange spurning of, and reaction from them all.   40

The following from a report in the Washington "Star" of November 16, 1875, may afford those who care for it something further of my point of view toward this interesting figure and influence of our era. There occurr'd about that date in Baltimore a public reburial of Poe's remains, and dedication of a monument over the grave: 45

clipping.
    24. outlined the] FMS: outlined, the
    27. concrete or] FMS: concrete, or
    31. page—and] CR and FMS: page, and
    33. There is an] FMS: Then an
    41–42. "Star"] CR and FMS: Star [The quotation is, in fact, from the issue of November 18, 1875.]
    44. Baltimore a] FMS: Baltimore, a
    44. reburial] CR and FMS: re-burial
    45. Before the quotation, the Star has the following lines to begin the article headed "Walt Whitman at the Poe Funeral—Conspicuous *Absence of the Popular Poets.*—"; crossed out in FMS and omitted in CR: "About the most significant part of the Poe re-burial ceremonies yesterday—which only a crowded and remarkably magnetic audience of the very best class of young people, women preponderating,

"Being in Washington on a visit at the time, 'the old gray' went over to Baltimore, and though ill from paralysis, consented to hobble up and silently take a seat on the platform, but refused to make any speech, saying, 'I have felt a strong impulse to come over and be here to-day myself in memory of Poe, which I have obey'd, but not the slightest impulse to make a speech, which, my dear friends, must also be obeyed.' In an informal circle, however, in conversation after the ceremonies, Whitman said: 'For a long while, and until lately, I had a distaste for Poe's writings. I wanted, and still want for poetry, the clear sun shining, and fresh air blowing—the strength and power of health, not of delirium, even amid the stormiest passions—with always the background of the eternal moralities. Non-complying with these requirements, Poe's genius has yet conquer'd a special recognition for itself, and I too have come to fully admit it, and appreciate it and him.

" 'In a dream I once had, I saw a vessel on the sea, at midnight, in a storm. It was no great full-rigg'd ship, nor majestic steamer, steering firmly through the gale, but seem'd one of those superb little schooner yachts I had often seen lying anchor'd, rocking so jauntily, in the waters around New York, or up Long Island sound—now flying uncontroll'd with torn sails and broken spars through the wild sleet and winds and waves of the night. On the deck was a slender, slight, beautiful figure, a dim man, apparently enjoying all the terror, the murk, and the dislocation of which he was the centre and the victim. That figure of my lurid dream might stand for Edgar Poe, his spirit, his fortunes, and his poems—themselves all lurid dreams.' "

Much more may be said, but I most desired to exploit the idea put at the beginning. By its popular poets the calibres of an age, the weak spots of its embankments, its sub-currents, (often more significant than the biggest surface ones,) are unerringly indicated. The lush and the weird that have taken such extraordinary possession of Nineteenth century verse-lovers—what mean they? The inevitable tendency of poetic culture to morbidity, abnormal beauty—the sickliness of all technical thought or refinement in itself—the abnegation of the perennial and democratic concretes at first hand, the body, the earth and sea, sex and the like—and

prevented from growing tedious—was the marked absence from the spot of every popular poet and author, American and foreign. Only Walt Whitman was present." In the margin opposite this passage in FMS the date "Nov. 17, 1875" is crossed out.

51. *CR*, FMS, and *Star* begin a new paragraph with "In an informal".

58. After "it and him." *CR* and FMS have the following sentence, crossed out in red ink on the clipping: "Even my own objections draw me to him at last, and those very points, with his sad fate, will doubtless always make him dearer to young and fervid minds." The *Star* is the same as *CR* and FMS except that the words "doubtless always" do not appear.

61. schooner yachts] [With a hyphen in FMS and in the *Star*, but without it in *CR*. Whitman inserts the hyphen in revising the clipping, but it was either not printed or removed in the proof.]

63. sound—now] *CR* and FMS: Sound; now] *Star:* sound; now

64. On the deck] FMS and *Star:* On deck

66. murk, and the] *Star:* murk, the weirdness, and the

68. After "lurid dreams." the words "*Washington Star.*" are deleted in FMS.

the substitution of something for them at second or third hand—what bearings have they on current pathological study?

Beethoven's Septette.

Feb. 11, '80.—At a good concert to-night in the foyer of the opera house, Philadelphia—the band a small but first-rate one. Never did music more sink into and soothe and fill me—never so prove its soul-rousing power, its impossibility of statement. Especially in the rendering of one of Beethoven's master septettes by the well-chosen and perfectly-combined instruments (violins, viola, clarionet, horn, 'cello and contrabass,) was I carried away, seeing, absorbing many wonders. Dainty abandon, sometimes as if Nature laughing on a hillside in the sunshine; serious and firm monotonies, as of winds; a horn sounding through the tangle of the forest, and the dying echoes; soothing floating of waves, but presently rising in surges, angrily lashing, muttering, heavy; piercing peals of laughter, for interstices; now and then weird, as Nature herself is in certain moods— but mainly spontaneous, easy, careless—often the sentiment of the postures of naked children playing or sleeping. It did me good even to watch the violinists drawing their bows so masterly—every motion a study. I allow'd myself, as I sometimes do, to wander out of myself. The conceit came to me of a copious grove of singing birds, and in their midst a simple harmonic duo, two human souls, steadily asserting their own pensiveness, joyousness.

A Hint of Wild Nature.

Feb. 13.—As I was crossing the Delaware to-day, saw a large flock of wild geese, right overhead, not very high up, ranged in V-shape, in

69. said, but I] CR and FMS: said with considerations I have not touched upon. I
79. FMS is signed "Walt Whitman." Name deleted in clipping.

Beethoven's Septette.

Printed from a clipping of the *Critic*, paragraphs 9 and 10 of the fourth number of "How I Get Around," July 16, 1881.
  2. Philadelphia—the] CR: Philadelphia; the
  3. me—never] CR: me—(is there any thing else, at one's best hours, so spiritual-real? Is it not beyond all poetry?)—never
  4. power, its] CR: power—its
  14. After "sleeping." CR begins a new paragraph.
  17. birds, and] CR: birds, showers of melody, and

A Hint of Wild Nature.

Printed from a clipping of the *Critic*, paragraphs 4 and 5 of the same number.
  1. *Feb. 13.*—As] CR: *Feb:* 13, '80.—As

relief against the noon clouds of light smoke-color. Had a capital though momentary view of them, and then of their course on and on southeast, till gradually fading—(my eyesight yet first rate for the open air and its distances, but I use glasses for reading.) Queer thoughts melted into me the two or three minutes, or less, seeing these creatures cleaving the sky—the spacious, airy realm—even the prevailing smoke-gray color everywhere, (no sun shining)—the waters below—the rapid flight of the birds, appearing just for a minute—flashing to me such a hint of the whole spread of Nature, with her eternal unsophisticated freshness, her never-visited recesses of sea, sky, shore—and then disappearing in the distance.

Loafing in the Woods.

March 8.—I write this down in the country again, but in a new spot, seated on a log in the woods, warm, sunny, midday. Have been loafing here deep among the trees, shafts of tall pines, oak, hickory, with a thick undergrowth of laurels and grapevines—the ground cover'd everywhere by debris, dead leaves, breakage, moss—everything solitary, ancient, grim. Paths (such as they are) leading hither and yon—(how made I know not, for nobody seems to come here, nor man nor cattle-kind.) Temperature to-day about 60, the wind through the pine-tops; I sit and listen to its hoarse sighing above (and to the *stillness*) long and long, varied by aimless rambles in the old roads and paths, and by exercise-pulls at the young saplings, to keep my joints from getting stiff. Blue-birds, robins, meadow-larks begin to appear.

Next day, 9th.—A snowstorm in the morning, and continuing most of the day. But I took a walk over two hours, the same woods and paths, amid the falling flakes. No wind, yet the musical low murmur through the pines, quite pronounced, curious, like waterfalls, now still'd, now pouring

3–4. capital . . . view] CR: capital, though momentary, view
5. fading—(my] CR: fading (my
6. After "reading.)" CR begins a new paragraph.

Loafing in the Woods.
Printed from clippings of the *Critic*, paragraphs 11 and 12 of the same number, concluding the article.
1–2. *March 8.*—I . . . seated] CR: *March 8, '80.*—I write this seated
2. midday] CR: mid-day
4. grapevines] CR: grape-vines
14. and paths] CR: and familiar paths
15. low] CR: hoarse
20. tall straight] CR: tall-straight

again. All the senses, sight, sound, smell, delicately gratified. Every snowflake lay where it fell on the evergreens, holly-trees, laurels, &c., the multitudinous leaves and branches piled, bulging-white, defined by edge-lines of emerald—the tall straight columns of the plentiful bronze-topt 20 pines—a slight resinous odor blending with that of the snow. (For there is a scent to everything, even the snow, if you can only detect it—no two places, hardly any two hours, anywhere, exactly alike. How different the odor of noon from midnight, or winter from summer, or a windy spell from a still one.) 25

A Contralto Voice.

May 9, Sunday.—Visit this evening to my friends the J.'s—good supper, to which I did justice—lively chat with Mrs. J. and I. and J. As I sat out front on the walk afterward, in the evening air, the church-choir and organ on the corner opposite gave Luther's hymn, *Ein feste berg*, very finely. The air was borne by a rich contralto. For nearly half an hour 5 there in the dark, (there was a good string of English stanzas,) came the music, firm and unhurried, with long pauses. The full silver star-beams of Lyra rose silently over the church's dim roof-ridge. Vari-color'd lights from the stain'd glass windows broke through the tree-shadows. And under all—under the Northern Crown up there, and in the fresh breeze 10 below, and the *chiaroscuro* of the night, that liquid-full contralto.

20. bronze-topt] *CR:* browze-topt
21. pines—a] *CR:* pines—and a
21-22. is a scent] *CR:* is scent
25. The name "Walt Whitman." deleted at the end.
     A Contralto Voice.
        Printed from an autograph sheet of gray paper; black ink except subtitle in red ink. Since this page is numbered 234 and 235, it is probably a revised copy after the pages were assembled.
        11. After "contralto." MS has the following, crossed out: "(This kind of voice has always to me the sense of young maternity—the last art-sense of all. Alboni was its fruition and apex. I wonder if the lady will ever know that her singing, her method, gave the foundation, the start, thirty years ago, to all my poetic literary effort since?)"

Seeing Niagara to Advantage.

June 4, '80.—For really seizing a great picture or book, or piece of
music, or architecture, or grand scenery—or perhaps for the first time
even the common sunshine, or landscape, or may-be even the mystery of
identity, most curious mystery of all—there comes some lucky five minutes
of a man's life, set amid a fortuitous concurrence of circumstances, and
bringing in a brief flash the culmination of years of reading and travel
and thought. The present case about two o'clock this afternoon, gave me
Niagara, its superb severity of action and color and majestic grouping, in
one short, indescribable show. We were very slowly crossing the Sus-
pension bridge—not a full stop anywhere, but next to it—the day clear,
sunny, still—and I out on the platform. The falls were in plain view about
a mile off, but very distinct, and no roar—hardly a murmur. The river
tumbling green and white, far below me; the dark high banks, the plentiful umbrage, many bronze cedars, in shadow; and tempering and arching
all the immense materiality, a clear sky overhead, with a few white
clouds, limpid, spiritual, silent. Brief, and as quiet as brief, that picture—
a remembrance always afterwards. Such are the things, indeed, I lay
away with my life's rare and blessed bits of hours, reminiscent, past—the
wild sea-storm I once saw one winter day, off Fire island—the elder
Booth in Richard, that famous night forty years ago in the old Bowery—
or Alboni in the children's scene in Norma—or night-views, I remember,
on the field, after battles in Virginia—or the peculiar sentiment of moon-

Seeing Niagara to Advantage.

Printed from a clipping of the London *Advertiser* (Ontario, Canada) for
June 22, 1880, paragraphs 3 and 4 of an article entitled "Summer Days in Canada"
describing some of Whitman's experiences while visiting Dr. R. M. Bucke, superintendent of the asylum for the insane in London, Ontario.

    1. *June 4*, '80.—For] *LA: June 4*.—For
    3. may-be even the] *LA:* maybe the
    4. comes some] *LA:* comes now and then some
    8. majestic grouping, in] *LA:* majestic grouping, (like some colossal cluster
of Greek statuary), in] *SDA:* majesty grouping, in
      9–10. crossing the Suspension] *LA:* crossing Suspension
    15. all the immense] *LA:* all this immense
    16–17. picture—a] *LA:* picture—yet a
    17. After "afterwards." *LA* begins a new paragraph.
    18. "hits" corrected to "bits" on the clipping of *LA.*
    18. hours, reminiscent] *LA:* hours, mostly reminiscent
    21. The words "or Alboni in the children's scene in Norma" are crossed out on
the clipping in black ink but marked "stet" in the margin in red ink.

Jaunting to Canada.

Printed from paragraphs 5 and 6 of the same clipping. The title of this

light and stars over the great Plains, western Kansas—or scooting up
New York bay, with a stiff breeze and a good yacht, off Navesink. With
these, I say, I henceforth place that view, that afternoon, that combination   25
complete, that five minutes' perfect absorption of Niagara—not the great
majestic gem alone by itself, but set complete in all its varied, full, indispensable surroundings.

Jaunting to Canada.

To go back a little, I left Philadelphia, 9th and Green streets, at
8 o'clock P.M., June 3, on a first-class sleeper, by the Lehigh Valley
(North Pennsylvania) route, through Bethlehem, Wilkesbarre, Waverly,
and so (by Erie) on through Corning to Hornellsville, where we arrived
at 8, morning, and had a bounteous breakfast. I must say I never put in   5
such a good night on any railroad track—smooth, firm, the minimum of
jolting, and all the swiftness compatible with safety. So without change to
Buffalo, and thence to Clifton, where we arrived early afternoon; then on
to London, Ontario, Canada, in four more—less than twenty-two hours
altogether. I am domiciled at the hospitable house of my friends Dr. and   10
Mrs. Bucke, in the ample and charming garden and lawns of the asylum.

Sunday with the Insane.

June 6.—Went over to the religious services (Episcopal) main
Insane asylum, held in a lofty, good-sized hall, third story. Plain boards,

section in *LA* was "A Good Route to Canada" but on the clipping, in red ink, it
was first changed to "How I Got Here" and then to the present title. Revisions are
mostly in black ink.

2. first-class] *LA:* first-rate

6. railroad] *LA:* R R

8. Clifton, where] *LA:* Clifton, Canada, where

8–9. afternoon; then . . . Canada, in] *LA:* afternoon. (When I recommend this
route to Niagara either from New York, Philadelphia or Washington, let no suspicious
reader nose a puff, for I paid my honest fare, and here give these lines for pure
satisfaction and love.)
So we came through from Philadelphia to Clifton in seventeen hours without
change, and then on to this city in

9. After "and love.)" *LA* begins a new paragraph.

10. of my friends Dr.] *LA:* of Dr.

11. asylum.] *LA:* Asylum for the Insane. Besides the extensive ornamental
grounds, there is a vast farm.

Sunday with the Insane.

Printed from clippings of paragraphs 7–11 of *LA*, same article. Most of the
revisions are in black ink.

whitewash, plenty of cheap chairs, no ornament or color, yet all scru-
pulously clean and sweet. Some three hundred persons present, mostly
patients. Everything, the prayers, a short sermon, the firm, orotund voice
of the minister, and most of all, beyond any portraying or suggesting,
that audience, deeply impress'd me. I was furnish'd with an arm-chair
near the pulpit, and sat facing the motley, yet perfectly well-behaved and
orderly congregation. The quaint dresses and bonnets of some of the
women, several very old and gray, here and there like the heads in old
pictures. O the looks that came from those faces! There were two or three
I shall probably never forget. Nothing at all markedly repulsive or
hideous—strange enough I did not see one such. Our common humanity,
mine and yours, everywhere:

"The same old blood—the same red, running blood;"

yet behind most, an inferr'd arriere of such storms, such wrecks, such
mysteries, fires, love, wrong, greed for wealth, religious problems, crosses
—mirror'd from those crazed faces (yet now temporarily so calm, like
still waters,) all the woes and sad happenings of life and death—now
from every one the devotional element radiating—was it not, indeed, *the
peace of God that passeth all understanding*, strange as it may sound? I
can only say that I took long and searching eye-sweeps as I sat there, and
it seem'd so, rousing unprecedented thoughts, problems unanswerable. A
very fair choir, and melodeon accompaniment. They sang "Lead, kindly
light," after the sermon. Many join'd in the beautiful hymn, to which the
minister read the introductory text, *"In the daytime also He led them
with a cloud, and all the night with a light of fire."* Then the words:

Lead, kindly light, amid the encircling gloom,
    Lead thou me on.
The night is dark, and I am far from home;
    Lead thou me on.
Keep thou my feet; I do not ask to see
The distant scene; one step enough for me.

4. Some . . . present] *LA:* Some 200 or more present
8. motley, yet] *LA:* motley, eager, pitiful, huddled, yet
9. After "congregation." *LA* begins a new paragraph.
10. women, several very] *LA:* women, some of them girls, some very
18. (yet now temporarily] *LA:* (yet temporarily
20–21. *the peace*] *LA: that peace*
23. unanswerable. A] *LA:* unanswerable. (How, sometimes, a flash of the living
sight, magnetic, confounds all previous statements, and reams, folios of arguments.) A
23. After "arguments.)" *LA* begins a new paragraph.
24–25. "Lead, kindly light"] *LA:* "Lead, Kindly Light"
26–27. In *LA* the Bible quotation is set in roman letters.
28. kindly light] *LA:* kindly Light

I was not ever thus, nor pray'd that thou
    Should'st lead me on;
I lov'd to choose and see my path; but now   35
    Lead thou me on.
I loved the garish day, and spite of fears
Pride ruled my will; remember not past years.

A couple of days after, I went to the "Refractory building," under   40
special charge of Dr. Beemer, and through the wards pretty thoroughly,
both the men's and women's. I have since made many other visits of the
kind through the asylum, and around among the detach'd cottages. As far
as I could see, this is among the most advanced, perfected, and kindly
and rationally carried on, of all its kind in America. It is a town in itself,   45
with many buildings and a thousand inhabitants.

    I learn that Canada, and especially this ample and populous province,
Ontario, has the very best and plentiest benevolent institutions in all departments.

Reminiscence of Elias Hicks.

    June 8.—To-day a letter from Mrs. E. S. L., Detroit, accompanied
in a little post-office roll by a rare old engraved head of Elias Hicks,
(from a portrait in oil by Henry Inman, painted for J. V. S., must have
been 60 years or more ago, in New York)—among the rest the following
excerpt about E. H. in the letter: 5

    "I have listen'd to his preaching so often when a child, and sat with my
mother at social gatherings where he was the centre, and every one so pleas'd
and stirr'd by his conversation. I hear that you contemplate writing or speaking
about him, and I wonder'd whether you had a picture of him. As I am the
owner of two, I send you one."   10

    39. After the song the following paragraph in *LA* is deleted:
"I felt as I came out in the verdant June forenoon that the hour and scene had
roused reverences, sanctity, deepest emotions, of which the stateliest churches I had
ever seen, with all their ceremonies, stained glass, pealing organs, and velvet and
sumptuousness, gave me no reminiscence."
    42. have . . . other] *LA:* have made other
    45. in America] *LA:* in all America
    46. After "inhabitants." *LA* continues the same paragraph through the next
sentence.
    Reminiscence of Elias Hicks.
    Printed from a clipping of paragraph 13 of the same article.
    1. Mrs. E. S. L.] *LA:* Mrs. E. L. L.

Grand Native Growth.

In a few days I go to lake Huron, and may have something to say of
that region and people. From what I already see, I should say the young
native population of Canada was growing up, forming a hardy, democratic, intelligent, radically sound, and just as American, good-natured
and *individualistic* race, as the average range of best specimens among
us. As among us, too, I please myself by considering that this element,
though it may not be the majority, promises to be the leaven which must
eventually leaven the whole lump.

A Zollverein Between the U. S. and Canada.

Some of the more liberal of the presses here are discussing the
question of a zollverein between the United States and Canada. It is proposed to form a union for commercial purposes—to altogether abolish the
frontier tariff line, with its double sets of custom house officials now
existing between the two countries, and to agree upon one tariff for both,
the proceeds of this tariff to be divided between the two governments on
the basis of population. It is said that a large proportion of the merchants
of Canada are in favor of this step, as they believe it would materially add
to the business of the country, by removing the restrictions that now exist
on trade between Canada and the States. Those persons who are op-

Grand Native Growth.
Printed from a clipping of paragraph 14, the last of the article, subtitled "A
Grand Native Growth in Canada."
  7. though . . . be] *LA:* though may be not
  8. whole lump.] *SDA:* whole being.

A Zollverein Between the U. S. and Canada.
Printed from a clipping of paragraph 12 of the same article, with revisions in
black ink. The words "United States" in the clipping are deleted and "U. S." written in.
  10. Those] *LA:* Many of those
  14. sentiment can] *LA:* sentiment in question can
  18–22. The clipping ends with "United States." The next two sentences, in
parentheses, were written in ink below the clipping.
  22. In the autograph revision, undeleted, the word "artery" appears between the
word "interior" and the word "or". The probable original of this sentence is here
quoted from the MS of Whitman's *Diary in Canada* in the Feinberg Collection,
where it appears following the date August 14, London, after his return from the
Saguenay trip, on a page headed "Canada? for lecture for conclusion": "No stream

posed to the measure believe that it would increase the material welfare of the country, but it would loosen the bonds between Canada and England; and this sentiment overrides the desire for commercial prosperity. Whether the sentiment can continue to bear the strain put upon it is a question. It is thought by many that commercial considerations must in the end prevail. It seems also to be generally agreed that such a zollverein, or common customs union, would bring practically more benefits to the Canadian provinces than to the United States. (It seems to me a certainty of time, sooner or later, that Canada shall form two or three grand States, equal and independent, with the rest of the American Union. The St. Lawrence and lakes are not for a frontier line, but a grand interior or mid-channel.)

The St. Lawrence Line.

August 20.—Premising that my three or four months in Canada were intended, among the rest, as an exploration of the line of the St. Lawrence, from lake Superior to the sea, (the engineers here insist upon considering it as one stream, over 2000 miles long, including lakes and Niagara and all)—that I have only partially carried out my programme; but for the seven or eight hundred miles so far fulfill'd, I find that the *Canada question* is absolutely control'd by this vast water line, with its first-class features and points of trade, humanity, and many more —here I am writing this nearly a thousand miles north of my Philadelphia starting-point (by way of Montreal and Quebec) in the midst of regions

this for side *frontier*—stream rather for the great central current, the glorious mid-artery, of the great Free Pluribus Unum of America, the solid Nationality of the present and the future the home of an improved grand race of men & women, not of some select class only, but of larger, saner, better masses." (Cf. W. S. Kennedy's edition of the *Diary in Canada*, 1904, p. 41.)

For the first and second paragraphs of "Summer Days in Canada," omitted in SDC, see Appendix XXIII, *1*.

The St. Lawrence Line.

Printed from a clipping of the first paragraph of an article titled simply "Letter from Walt Whitman" in the London (Ont.) *Advertiser* for August 26, 1880. The place and date are cut away: "Ha Ha Bay, Saguenay River, Aug. 20."

1. The subtitle and the date, and all revisions, are inserted in black ink on the clipping.

2. the line] *LA:* the whole line

3. sea, (the engineers] *LA:* sea, (for the great engineers

7. *Canada question* is] *LA: Canada question* (of which more anon, perhaps an informal lecture) is

8. trade, humanity] *LA:* trade, art, humanity

9. am writing this nearly] *LA:* am nearly

that go to a further extreme of grimness, wildness of beauty, and a sort of still and pagan *scaredness*, while yet Christian, inhabitable, and partially fertile, than perhaps any other on earth. The weather remains perfect; some might call it a little cool, but I wear my old gray overcoat and find it 15 just right. The days are full of sunbeams and oxygen. Most of the forenoons and afternoons I am on the forward deck of the steamer.

The Savage Saguenay.

Up these black waters, over a hundred miles—always strong, deep, (hundreds of feet, sometimes thousands,) ever with high, rocky hills for banks, green and gray—at times a little like some parts of the Hudson, but much more pronounc'd and defiant. The hills rise higher—keep their 5 ranks more unbroken. The river is straighter and of more resolute flow, and its hue, though dark as ink, exquisitely polish'd and sheeny under the August sun. Different, indeed, this Saguenay from all other rivers— different effects—a bolder, more vehement play of lights and shades. Of a rare charm of singleness and simplicity. (Like the organ-chant at mid- 10 night from the old Spanish convent, in "Favorita"—one strain only, simple and monotonous and unornamented—but indescribably penetrating and grand and masterful.) Great place for echoes: while our steamer was tied at the wharf at Tadousac (taj-oo-sac) waiting, the escape-pipe letting off steam, I was sure I heard a band at the hotel up in the rocks—could 15 even make out some of the tunes. Only when our pipe stopp'd, I knew

13. After "on earth." the following sentence in *LA* is deleted: "This is one of the countless feeders of the mighty St. Lawrence."

13–14. perfect; some] *LA:* perfect. Some

16. the steamer.] *LA:* our steamer.

9–16. With these lines, and with the first lines of "The Savage Saguenay," compare the following passages in Whitman's MS of *Diary in Canada* (cf. also Kennedy's edition, pp. 30–31):

"Aug 6th night—we are steaming up the Saguenay from Quebec to Chicou 235

"I am here nearly 1000 miles slightly east of due north from my Phil. se. starting point by way of Montreal & Quebec, in the strangest country

"Cold—overcoat—had a good night's sleep—but up before sunrise—northern lights every night as with overcoat on, or wrapt in my blanket I plant myself on the forward deck—

"Aug. 6 and 7, Ha-ha bay. Up the black Saguenay river, a hundred or so miles —dashes of the grimmest, wildest, savagest scenery on the planet, I guess—a strong, deep, (always hundreds of feet, sometimes thousands) dark-water'd river, very dark, with high, rocky hills—green and gray-edged banks in all directions—no flowers, no fruits (plenty of delicious wild blue-berries and raspberries though) up at Chicoutimy and Ha-ha bay"

The Savage Saguenay.

Printed from a clipping of paragraph 2 of the same article. The title on the

what caused it. Then at cape Eternity and Trinity rock, the pilot with his whistle producing similar marvellous results, echoes indescribably weird, as we lay off in the still bay under their shadows.

Capes Eternity and Trinity.

But the great, haughty, silent capes themselves; I doubt if any crack points, or hills, or historic places of note, or anything of the kind elsewhere in the world, outvies these objects—(I write while I am before them face to face.) They are very simple, they do not startle—at least they did not me—but they linger in one's memory forever. They are placed 5 very near each other, side by side, each a mountain rising flush out of the Saguenay. A good thrower could throw a stone on each in passing—at least it seems so. Then they are as distinct in form as a perfect physical man or a perfect physical woman. Cape Eternity is bare, rising, as just said, sheer out of the water, rugged and grim (yet with an indescribable 10 beauty) nearly two thousand feet high. Trinity rock, even a little higher, also rising flush, top-rounded like a great head with close-cut verdure of hair. I consider myself well repaid for coming my thousand miles to get the sight and memory of the unrivall'd duo. They have stirr'd me more profoundly than anything of the kind I have yet seen. If Europe or Asia 15 had them, we should certainly hear of them in all sorts of sent-back poems, rhapsodies, &c., a dozen times a year through our papers and magazines.

clipping, "The River Itself," is crossed out and "The Saguenay Itself" is written in; this is changed to "Up the Saguenay," and then to the present title. These changes were made in red ink; other revisions were in black ink.

    3. gray—at] *LA:* gray—no flowers or fruits (plenty of delicious wild blueberries and raspberries though.) At] [Cf. the last passage quoted from the MS of *Diary in Canada.*]

    6–7. the August] *LA:* this August

    10. "Favorita"] *LA: Favorita*

    12–13. while . . . tied] *LA:* while tied

    13. waiting, . . . letting] *LA:* waiting, letting

    15. our pipe] *LA:* our pipes

Capes Eternity and Trinity.

    Printed from a clipping of paragraphs 3 and 4 of the same article, subtitle as in SDC. Revisions in black ink chiefly.

    1–2. silent capes . . . crack] *LA:* silent, savage Capes themselves! I doubt if any of the crack

    5. in one's memory] *LA:* in my memory

    8. so. Then they] *LA:* so. Yet they

    9. man or a] *LA:* man and a

    13. After "of hair." *LA* begins a new paragraph.

    14. sight and memory] *LA:* sight or memory

Chicoutimi and Ha-Ha Bay.

No indeed—life and travel and memory have offer'd and will preserve to me no deeper-cut incidents, panorama, or sights to cheer my soul, than these at Chicoutimi and Ha-ha bay, and my days and nights up and down this fascinating savage river—the rounded mountains, some
5   bare and gray, some dull red, some draped close all over with matted green verdure or vines—the ample, calm, eternal rocks everywhere—the long streaks of motley foam, a milk-white curd on the glistening breast of the stream—the little two-masted schooner, dingy yellow, with patch'd sails, set wing-and-wing, nearing us, coming saucily up the water with a
10   couple of swarthy, black-hair'd men aboard—the strong shades falling on the light gray or yellow outlines of the hills all through the forenoon, as we steam within gunshot of them—while ever the pure and delicate sky spreads over all. And the splendid sunsets, and the sights of evening— the same old stars, (relatively a little different, I see, so far north) Arctu-
15   rus and Lyra, and the Eagle, and great Jupiter like a silver globe, and the constellation of the Scorpion. Then northern lights nearly every night.

The Inhabitants—Good Living.

Grim and rocky and black-water'd as the demesne hereabout is, however, you must not think genial humanity, and comfort, and good-

Chicoutimi and Ha-Ha Bay.
Printed from a clipping of paragraph 5 of the same article. The subtitle, "Ha-Ha Bay," changed in red ink on the clipping. Revisions in black and red ink.
     4. the rounded mountains] *LA:* the countless mountains
     9. water with] *LA:* water (like a bit from the Mediterranean) with
     11. light gray or] *SDA:* light or
     13. And the] *LA:* And then the

The Inhabitants—Good Living.
Printed from a clipping of paragraph 6 of the same article. The subtitle, "The Inhabitants," changed on the clipping by adding "—*good living*" in red ink. Revisions mostly in black ink.
     3. met.] *LA:* met here.
     3. After "met here." *LA* has the following two sentences, deleted on the clipping: "I find hardly anybody who can speak English but I can testify to the just-mentioned points. There are villages and hotels and boarders."
     3. this memorandum] *LA:* this letter
     7. the province] *LA:* the great French province
     14. After the paragraph ending with this line, the remaining lines of the clipping, under the heading "Description of the Saguenay by a Canadian Friend—A Fellow

living are not to be met. Before I began this memorandum I made a first-rate breakfast of sea-trout, finishing off with wild raspberries. I find smiles and courtesy everywhere—physiognomies in general curiously like those in the United States—(I was astonish'd to find the same resemblance all through the province of Quebec.) In general the inhabitants of this rugged country (Charlevoix, Chicoutimi and Tadousac counties, and lake St. John region) a simple, hardy population, lumbering, trapping furs, boating, fishing, berry-picking and a little farming. I was watching a group of young boatmen eating their early dinner—nothing but an immense loaf of bread, had apparently been the size of a bushel measure, from which they cut chunks with a jack-knife. Must be a tremendous winter country this, when the solid frost and ice fully set in.

Cedar-Plums Like—Names.
(Back again in Camden and down in Jersey.)

One time I thought of naming this collection "Cedar-Plums Like" (which I still fancy wouldn't have been a bad name, nor inappropriate.) A melange of loafing, looking, hobbling, sitting, traveling—a little thinking thrown in for salt, but very little—not only summer but all seasons—not only days but nights—some literary meditations—books, authors examined, Carlyle, Poe, Emerson tried, (always under my cedar-tree, in the open air, and never in the library)—mostly the scenes everybody sees, but some of my own caprices, meditations, egotism—truly an open air and

Voyager," are crossed out. This section, which was written by Dr. R. M. Bucke, is partly cut away. Besides the prose description, it includes a poem of twenty lines, unrhymed and metrically irregular. This material is omitted because it is not Whitman's.

After the poem, two paragraphs (9 and 10) by Whitman, omitted from SDC, complete the article. See Appendix XXIV, 1.

Cedar-Plums Like—Names.

Printed for SDC from clipped proof sheets; not previously published. Whitman numbered the first page of his MS 242–246, probably because it was first printed from autograph pages with these numbers; the second page is numbered 247. At the end of this page the note "next 248, 249, 251 & 252 on one page" is crossed out. The footnote, on two pages unnumbered, is in ink. The title is written above the clipping in red ink. The italicized line is in black ink. Revisions all in black.

1. One time I . . . "Cedar-Plums Like"] Proof: I thought of naming my book *Cedar-Plums Like*

3. hobbling, sitting, traveling] Proof: hobbling, traveling

5–7. These lines, beginning with "—some" and ending with "library)—" were inserted in ink in a marginal note.

8. meditations, egotism] Proof: meditations—jottings and gaddings—some egotism

mainly summer formation—singly, or in clusters—wild and free and
somewhat acrid—indeed more like cedar-plums than you might guess at
first glance.

But do you know what they are? (To city man, or some sweet parlor
lady, I now talk.) As you go along roads, or barrens, or across country,
anywhere through these States, middle, eastern, western, or southern, you
will see, certain seasons of the year, the thick woolly tufts of the cedar
mottled with bunches of china-blue berries, about as big as fox-grapes. But
first a special word for the tree itself: everybody knows that the cedar is a
healthy, cheap, democratic wood, streak'd red and white—an evergreen
—that it is not a *cultivated* tree—that it keeps away moths—that it grows
inland or seaboard, all climates, hot or cold, any soil—in fact rather
prefers sand and bleak side spots—content if the plough, the fertilizer
and the trimming-axe, will but keep away and let it alone. After a long
rain, when everything looks bright, often have I stopt in my wood-
saunters, south or north, or far west, to take in its dusky green, wash'd
clean and sweet, and speck'd copiously with its fruit of clear, hardy blue.
The wood of the cedar is of use—but what profit on earth are those sprigs
of acrid plums? A question impossible to answer satisfactorily. True,
some of the herb doctors give them for stomachic affections, but the
remedy is as bad as the disease. Then in my rambles down in Camden
county I once found an old crazy woman gathering the clusters with zeal
and joy. She show'd, as I was told afterward, a sort of infatuation for
them, and every year placed and kept profuse bunches high and low
about her room. They had a strange charm on her uneasy head, and
effected docility and peace. (She was harmless, and lived near by with her
well-off married daughter.) Whether there is any connection between
those bunches, and being out of one's wits, I cannot say, but I myself
entertain a weakness for them. Indeed, I love the cedar, anyhow—its
naked ruggedness, its just palpable odor, (so different from the per-

---

9. summer] Proof: autumn
15–16. cedar mottled] Proof: Cedar tree mottled
17. itself: everybody] Proof: itself.
17. After "itself." Proof begins a new paragraph.
29. is as bad] Proof: is bad
30. county I] Proof: County, New Jersey, I
33. charm on] Proof: charm (of course it just happen'd so—gave her occupation) on
36. those bunches] Proof: those weird bunches
37. After "weakness for them." Proof begins a new paragraph.
39. best,) its] Proof: best)—its
43. collection] Proof: Book

fumer's best,) its silence, its equable acceptance of winter's cold and summer's heat, of rain or drouth—its shelter to me from those, at times—its 40
associations—(well, I never could explain *why* I love anybody, or anything.) The service I now specially owe to the cedar is, while I cast
around for a name for my proposed collection, hesitating, puzzled—after
rejecting a long, long string, I lift my eyes, and lo! the very term I want.
At any rate, I go no further—I tire in the search. I take what some 45
invisible kind spirit has put before me. Besides, who shall say there is not
affinity enough between (at least the bundle of sticks that produced) many
of these pieces, or granulations, and those blue berries? their uselessness
growing wild—a certain aroma of Nature I would so like to have in my
pages—the thin soil whence they come—their content in being let alone 50
—their stolid and deaf repugnance to answering questions, (this latter
the nearest, dearest trait affinity of all.)

Then reader dear, in conclusion, as to the point of the name for the
present collection, let us be satisfied to *have* a name—something to identify
and bind it together, to concrete all its vegetable, mineral, personal 55
memoranda, abrupt raids of criticism, crude gossip of philosophy, varied
sands and clumps—without bothering ourselves because certain pages do
not present themselves to you or me as coming under their own name with
entire fitness or amiability. (It is a profound, vexatious, never-explicable
matter—this of names. I have been exercised deeply about it my whole 60
life.*)

After all of which the name "Cedar-Plums Like" got its nose put out of
joint; but I cannot afford to throw away what I pencill'd down the lane
there, under the shelter of my old friend, one warm October noon. Besides, it wouldn't be civil to the cedar tree. 65

* In the pocket of my receptacle-book I find a list of suggested and rejected
names for this volume, or parts of it—such as the following:

43. puzzled—after] Proof: puzzled; after
44–45. want. At] Proof: want (I am writing in the open air). At
45. After "open air)." Proof begins a new paragraph.
48. these pieces, . . . and] Proof: the following pieces, or parts of them, and
50. their content] Proof: their great content
54. present collection, let] Proof: present Book—collection: let
54–55. identify and] Proof: identify it and
55. its vegetable] Proof: its gossip, its vegetable
56. memoranda, . . . varied] Proof: memoranda, thoughts, varied
59. After "amiability." Proof begins a new paragraph.
62. "Cedar-Plums Like"] Proof: *Cedar-Plums Like*
66–89. This note is written in black ink on two autograph pages.
67. Before "names" the words "by now quite forgotten" are crossed out.

> *As the wild bee hums in May,*
> *& August mulleins grow,*
> *& Winter snow-flakes fall,*
> *& stars in the sky roll round.*

70

> *Away from Books—away from Art,*
> *Now for the Day and Night—the lesson done,*
> *Now for the Sun and Stars.*

75

Notes of a half-Paralytic,	*As Voices in the Dusk, from Speakers*
Week in and Week out,	*far or hid,*
Embers of Ending Days,	*Autochthons.....Embryons,*
Ducks and Drakes,	*Wing-and-Wing,*
Flood Tide and Ebb,	*Notes and Recallés,*
Gossip at Early Candle-light,	*Only Mulleins and Bumble-Bees,*
Echoes and Escapades,	*Pond-Babble.....Tête-a-Têtes,*
Such as I.....Evening Dews,	*Echoes of a Life in the 19th Century in*
Notes after Writing a Book,	*the New World,*
Far and Near at 63,	*Flanges of Fifty Years,*
Drifts and Cumulus,	*Abandons.....Hurry Notes,*
Maize-Tassels.....Kindlings,	*A Life-Mosaic.....Native Moments,*
Fore and Aft.....Vestibules,	*Types and Semi-Tones,*
Scintilla at 60 and after,	*Oddments.....Sand-Drifts,*
Sands on the Shores of 64,	*Again and Again.*

Death of Thomas Carlyle.

Feb. 10, '81.—And so the flame of the lamp, after long wasting and flickering, has gone out entirely.

---

76. *in and Week*] SDC: *in ana Week*] MS: *in and Week*] [Printer's error corrected in SDC Glasgow and all later texts.]

Death of Thomas Carlyle.
Printed from clippings of proof sheets of the article "Death of Carlyle," CR, Feb. 12, 1881, and from clippings of proof sheets of the article "The Dead Carlyle" in BLW, the same date. The *Critic* article was reprinted in *Essays from "The Critic,"* Boston, 1882, without revision except two or three very minor changes in punctuation. The following versions are included in the collation in addition to the honored text of CPW and SDC: CR and BLW, the proof clippings (referred to as "Proof") from which SDC was printed, and an autograph rough draft of the *Critic* MS in the collection of Charles E. Feinberg (here referred to as FMS) bearing the date "Feb. 6, '81."
1–26. Printed from the first clipping. The word "Thomas" in the title was inserted in red ink. The inserted date and the revisions are in black ink.
2. has gone] FMS: has at last gone
3–7. In place of these first two sentences FMS has three: "As an author, a figure, no man else more significant of our stormy age, its paradoxes, its din, the terrible parturition period that it is, than Carlyle. He belongs to our stock too. Neither Latin or Greek, but essentially Gothic."
7. more a] FMS: more of a
8. than any of his] FMS: than his

As a representative author, a literary figure, no man else will bequeath to the future more significant hints of our stormy era, its fierce paradoxes, its din, and its struggling parturition periods, than Carlyle. He belongs to our own branch of the stock too; neither Latin nor Greek, but altogether Gothic. Rugged, mountainous, volcanic, he was himself more a French revolution than any of his volumes. In some respects, so far in the Nineteenth century, the best equipt, keenest mind, even from the college point of view, of all Britain; only he had an ailing body. Dyspepsia is to be traced in every page, and now and then fills the page. One may include among the lessons of his life—even though that life stretch'd to amazing length—how behind the tally of genius and morals stands the stomach, and gives a sort of casting vote.

Two conflicting agonistic elements seem to have contended in the man, sometimes pulling him different ways like wild horses. He was a cautious, conservative Scotchman, fully aware what a fœtid gas-bag much of modern radicalism is; but then his great heart demanded reform, demanded change—often terribly at odds with his scornful brain. No author ever put so much wailing and despair into his books, sometimes palpable, oftener latent. He reminds me of that passage in Young's poems where as death presses closer and closer for his prey, the soul rushes hither and thither, appealing, shrieking, berating, to escape the general doom.

Of short-comings, even positive blur-spots, from an American point of view, he had serious share.

8. After "volumes." Proof and FMS begin a new paragraph.

9–10. century, . . . of all] FMS: Century, the sturdiest and best equipt mind of all

11–14. In place of the last sentence of the paragraph, FMS has this: "One would include among others how behind the tally of genius and morals stands the stomach, and gives a sort of casting vote."

15. conflicting . . . to] FMS: conflicting almost agonistic elements seen indeed to

18. is; but then] FMS: is; and then

18–19. heart . . . brain.] CR and Proof: heart demanded reform, demanded change—an always sympathetic, always human heart—often terribly at odds with his scornful brain.] FMS: heart demanding reform was fully sympathetic, fully human. It was thus evidently at terrible odds with his brain.

19. After "scornful brain." CR, Proof, and FMS begin a new paragraph.

20–21. books, . . . He] FMS: books. He

21. me of] FMS: me at times of

22–23. soul rushes hither] FMS: soul runs hither

23–24. shrieking, . . . doom.] FMS: shrieking, storming, berating, and finds no escape, no resort from the general doom.

26. After "share" CR and Proof have a semicolon and complete the paragraph as follows: "but this is no time for specifying them. When we think how great changes never go by jumps in any department of our universe, but that long preparations,

Not for his merely literary merit, (though that was great)—not as "maker of books," but as launching into the self-complacent atmosphere of our days a rasping, questioning, dislocating agitation and shock, is
30 Carlyle's final value. It is time the English-speaking peoples had some true idea about the verteber of genius, namely power. As if they must always have it cut and bias'd to the fashion, like a lady's cloak! What a needed service he performs! How he shakes our comfortable reading circles with a touch of the old Hebraic anger and prophecy—and indeed it
35 is just the same. Not Isaiah himself more scornful, more threatening: "The crown of pride, the drunkards of Ephraim, shall be trodden under feet: And the glorious beauty which is on the head of the fat valley shall be a fading flower." (The word prophecy is much misused; it seems narrow'd to prediction merely. That is not the main sense of the Hebrew
40 word translated "prophet;" it means one whose mind bubbles up and pours forth as a fountain, from inner, divine spontaneities revealing God. Prediction is a very minor part of prophecy. The great matter is to reveal and outpour the God-like suggestions pressing for birth in the soul. This is briefly the doctrine of the Friends or Quakers.)

45 Then the simplicity and amid ostensible frailty the towering strength of this man—a hardy oak knot, you could never wear out—an old farmer dress'd in brown clothes, and not handsome—his very foibles fascinating. Who cares that he wrote about Dr. Francia, and "Shooting Niagara" and "the Nigger Question,"—and didn't at all admire our United States?

processes, awakenings, are indispensable, Carlyle was the most serviceable democrat of the age."
  25–26. In place of this sentence paragraph, FMS has:
"Of short-comings, positive blur-spots from our American and Democratic point of view, he had serious share; but this is no time for specifying them. Great changes do not go by jumps in the universe. Long preparations, processes, break ground. Viewed that way he was the most serviceable democrat of the century."
  27–51. Printed from two clippings pasted on separate MS pages prepared for the printer; they are proof sheets of the article published in the *Literary World*. Not in FMS.
  29–30. is Carlyle's final] BLW and Proof: is the man's final
  32. After "cloak!" BLW and Proof begin a new paragraph. This is the end of the first clipping.
  38–39. it seems narrow'd] BLW and Proof: it is narrowed
  40. "prophet;"] BLW and Proof: prophet;
  46. of this man] BLW and Proof: of the man
  51. The second clipping ends and concludes the paragraph with "we deserve.)"
  51–63. Printed from a second clipping of proof of the *Critic* article, the two paragraphs next following the CR proof clipping collated above. A version of these lines appears also in FMS.
  51. of modern literature] FMS: of literature
  52. After "politics!" FMS begins a new paragraph.
  52–53. Doubtless, . . . observation, the] FMS: Doubtless one needs respecting the latter to realize the

(I doubt if he ever thought or said half as bad words about us as we de- 50
serve.) How he splashes like leviathan in the seas of modern literature
and politics! Doubtless, respecting the latter, one needs first to realize,
from actual observation, the squalor, vice and doggedness ingrain'd in the
bulk-population of the British Islands, with the red tape, the fatuity, the
flunkeyism everywhere, to understand the last meaning in his pages. Ac- 55
cordingly, though he was no chartist or radical, I consider Carlyle's by far
the most indignant comment or protest anent the fruits of feudalism to-day
in Great Britain—the increasing poverty and degradation of the homeless,
landless twenty millions, while a few thousands, or rather a few hundreds,
possess the entire soil, the money, and the fat berths. Trade and shipping, 60
and clubs and culture, and prestige, and guns, and a fine select class of
gentry and aristocracy, with every modern improvement, cannot begin to
salve or defend such stupendous hoggishness.

The way to test how much he has left his country were to consider, or
try to consider, for a moment, the array of British thought, the resultant 65
ensemble of the last fifty years, as existing to-day, *but with Carlyle left
out*. It would be like an army with no artillery. The show were still a gay
and rich one—Byron, Scott, Tennyson, and many more—horsemen and
rapid infantry, and banners flying—but the last heavy roar so dear to the
ear of the train'd soldier, and that settles fate and victory, would be 70
lacking.

For the last three years we in America have had transmitted glimpses

55–56. understand . . . though] FMS: understand much that is in his books.
Though
55. After "his pages." CR and Proof begin a new paragraph.
56–58. consider . . . Britain—the] FMS: consider his books by far the most
indignant protest against the continuation of Feudalism to-day—the
58. of the homeless] FMS: of a homeless
59. millions, while] FMS: millions in Old England—while
60. the entire soil] FMS: the soil
60–63. In place of this sentence FMS has the following: "Cash and trade and
shipping, and 'culture,' and clubs, and sure payment of dividends, and literature and
guns and prestige, with every modern improvement cannot salve or defend the stupendous hoggishness."
64–71. Printed from a third clipping of proof of the BLW article. Not in FMS.
64. left his country were] BLW and Proof: left us all were
65–66. resultant *ensemble*] BLW and Proof: resultant and *ensemble*
71. After "lacking." BLW has the following concluding paragraph, cut from the
clipping and omitted in SDC:
"His mantle is unfallen. We certainly have no one left like him. I doubt if any
nation of the world has. Walt Whitman."
72–110. Printed from two clippings of proof sheets of the *Critic*, four paragraphs
next following the two collated above, lines 51–63. A version of these lines appears
in FMS.
72–73. glimpses . . . very old] CR: glimpses of Carlyle's prostration and
bodily decay—pictures [Proof: decay, pictures] of a thin-bodied, lonesome, wifeless,

of a thin-bodied, lonesome, wifeless, childless, very old man, lying on a sofa, kept out of bed by indomitable will, but, of late, never well enough 75 to take the open air. I have noted this news from time to time in brief descriptions in the papers. A week ago I read such an item just before I started out for my customary evening stroll between eight and nine. In the fine cold night, unusually clear, (Feb. 5, '81,) as I walk'd some open grounds adjacent, the condition of Carlyle, and his approaching—perhaps 80 even then actual—death, filled me with thoughts eluding statement, and curiously blending with the scene. The planet Venus, an hour high in the west, with all her volume and lustre recover'd, (she has been shorn and languid for nearly a year,) including an additional sentiment I never noticed before—not merely voluptuous, Paphian, steeping, fascinating— 85 now with calm commanding seriousness and hauteur—the Milo Venus now. Upward to the zenith, Jupiter, Saturn, and the moon past her quarter, trailing in procession, with the Pleiades following, and the constellation Taurus, and red Aldebaran. Not a cloud in heaven. Orion strode through the southeast, with his glittering belt—and a trifle below hung 90 the sun of the night, Sirius. Every star dilated, more vitreous, nearer than usual. Not as in some clear nights when the larger stars entirely outshine

childless, very old] FMS: glimpses of Carlyle's prostration & bodily decay—pictures of a thin-bodied lonesome, wifeless, childless, pain-suffering, old

74–75. but, of late, never well enough to] FMS: but never well enough even to

75. open air. . . . from] CR and Proof: open air. News of this sort was brought us last fall by the sick man's neighbor, Moncure Conway; and I have noted it from

75–76. In place of this sentence FMS has: "News of this sort came in the talk of the old man's neighbor and occasional crony, Moncure Conway, lately visiting us; sometimes in brief items in the papers."

76–77. In place of this sentence FMS has: "I read one of these items one evening lately, just before I started out for my usual evening stroll, between 8 and 9."

77. After "eight or nine." CR and Proof begin a new paragraph. FMS continues.

78. night, . . . (Feb. 5, '81,)] FMS: night (Feb. 5, '81,)

79–81. approaching . . . the scene.] FMS: approaching death fill'd me with speculations, thoughts, that curiously blended with my observation of the heavens.

81. After "heavens." FMS begins a new paragraph.

81. The planet Venus,] FMS: Venus,

82. her volume and lustre] FMS: her old volume of lustre

82–83. and languid . . . additional] FMS: and dim for a year) and a new additional

84. before—not merely voluptuous] FMS: before—no mere voluptuous

84–85. fascinating . . . seriousness] CR and Proof: fascinating—now with calm, commanding, dazzling seriousness] FMS: fascinating star, now—but a calm, commanding, dazzling seriousness

86. After "Venus now." FMS begins a new paragraph.

86–88. In place of this sentence FMS has (beginning a new paragraph): "Jupiter, Saturn, and the half-Moon trailing, in procession above her, and close after in the arch of space, the Pleiades and the constellation Taurus, and Bright Aldebaran."

88–89. Orion . . . his] CR and Proof: Orion strode through the south-east, with his] FMS: Every star of Orion to the south east, and his

the rest. Every little star or cluster just as distinctly visible, and just as nigh. Berenice's hair showing every gem, and new ones. To the northeast and north the Sickle, the Goat and kids, Cassiopea, Castor and Pollux, and the two Dippers. While through the whole of this silent indescribable 95 show, inclosing and bathing my whole receptivity, ran the thought of Carlyle dying. (To soothe and spiritualize, and, as far as may be, solve the mysteries of death and genius, consider them under the stars at midnight.)

And now that he has gone hence, can it be that Thomas Carlyle, soon 100 to chemically dissolve in ashes and by winds, remains an identity still? In ways perhaps eluding all the statements, lore and speculations of ten thousand years—eluding all possible statements to mortal sense—does he yet exist, a definite, vital being, a spirit, an individual—perhaps now wafted in space among those stellar systems, which, suggestive and 105 limitless as they are, merely edge more limitless, far more suggestive systems? I have no doubt of it. In silence, of a fine night, such questions are answer'd to the soul, the best answers that can be given. With me, too, when depress'd by some specially sad event, or tearing problem, I wait till I go out under the stars for the last voiceless satisfaction. 110

89–90. below . . . than] FMS: below the sun of suns, Sirius—all dilated, nearer, more vitreous than
91. larger stars entirely] FMS: larger orbs entirely
92. cluster just] FMS: cluster of the myriads, just
93–94. northeast and north] CR and Proof: north-east and north] FMS: north east or north
95. the two Dippers.] FMS: the Great Dipper.
95. After "two Dippers." CR and Proof begin a new paragraph.
95–97. In place of this sentence FMS has (continuing the paragraph): "And through this silent, far-off indescribable show, ran the thought of Carlyle dying as started by the picture I had absorbed."
97–99. FMS omits the marks of parenthesis and indents this sentence as a paragraph.
97. and, . . . the] FMS: and average the
100. can . . . Thomas] FMS: can Thomas
101. winds, . . . identity] FMS: winds remain an essential identity
102. ways . . . statements] FMS: ways eluding the statement
102. speculations] FMS: speculation
103. years . . . does] FMS: years, but simple to all-enclosing spiritual law, does
104. definite, . . . perhaps] FMS: definite a vital being, an individual, a spirit—perhaps
105–107. among . . . systems?] FMS: among those systems, so indescribably suggestive & grand yet are merely the edge of other and more limitless systems?
107. After "systems?" CR, Proof, and FMS begin a new paragraph.
107. The sentence, "I have no doubt of it." is the last of FMS. There is no signature.
110. The name "Walt Whitman." appears in CR and the Proof; deleted in the Proof. At one time Whitman thought of adding a footnote at this point, but changed his mind. In the Feinberg Collection is an autograph MS written in pencil on two pages of small notebook paper, as follows:

Later Thoughts and Jottings.
Carlyle from American Points of View.

There is surely at present an inexplicable *rapport* (all the more piquant from its contradictoriness) between that deceas'd author and our United States of America—no matter whether it lasts or not.* As we Westerners assume definite shape, and result in formations and fruitage
5   unknown before, it is curious with what a new sense our eyes turn to representative outgrowths of crises and personages in the Old World. Beyond question, since Carlyle's death, and the publication of Froude's memoirs, not only the interest in his books, but every personal bit regarding the famous Scotchman—his dyspepsia, his buffetings, his parentage,
10   his paragon of a wife, his career in Edinburgh, in the lonesome nest on Craigenputtock moor, and then so many years in London—is probably wider and livelier to-day in this country than in his own land. Whether I succeed or no, I, too, reaching across the Atlantic and taking the man's dark fortune-telling of humanity and politics, would offset it all, (such is
15   the fancy that comes to me,) by a far more profound horoscope-casting of those themes—G. F. Hegel's.†

First, about a chance, a never-fulfill'd vacuity of this pale cast of thought—this British Hamlet from Cheyne row, more puzzling than the Danish one, with his contrivances for settling the broken and spavin'd
20   joints of the world's government, especially its democratic dislocation. Carlyle's grim fate was cast to live and dwell in, and largely embody, the parturition agony and qualms of the old order, amid crowded accumulations of ghastly morbidity, giving birth to the new. But conceive of him (or his parents before him) coming to America, recuperated by the cheering
25   realities and activity of our people and country—growing up and delving face-to-face resolutely among us here, especially at the West—inhaling

"Modify the Carlyle article? put in a note*
"His eternal snarling at people—always something bitter and contemptuous about his fellow authors—and fault-finding never a good word towards every thing and every body; In his autobiography he continually praises beyond measure his father & mother & his wife Janet; but from all that is said, first and last, they appear to be the only two human beings out of the thousand millions inhabiting this globe whose characters in TC's opinion were not a mass of distortion, defection & offensiveness. What I have written in the foregoing obituary I shall let stand as it is—a man deserving to be judged by his best and not his worst; but there are moments in reading & estimating Carlyle when you see very clearly for all the loud and fierce blasts of invective he is so fond of, there is nothing more deserving of them at their loudest and fiercest than Carlyles own narrowness uppishness & unequalled malignance. No

and exhaling our limitless air and eligibilities—devoting his mind to the theories and developments of this Republic amid its practical facts as exemplified in Kansas, Missouri, Illinois, Tennessee, or Louisiana. I say *facts*, and face-to-face confrontings—so different from books, and all those quiddities and mere reports in the libraries, upon which the man (it was wittily said of him at the age of thirty, that there was no one in Scotland who had glean'd so much and seen so little,) almost wholly fed, and which even his sturdy and vital mind but reflected at best. 30

Something of the sort narrowly escaped happening. In 1835, after more than a dozen years of trial and non-success, the author of "Sartor Resartus" removing to London, very poor, a confirmed hypochondriac, "Sartor" universally scoffed at, no literary prospects ahead, deliberately settled on one last casting-throw of the literary dice—resolv'd to compose and launch forth a book on the subject of *the French Revolution*—and if that won no higher guerdon or prize than hitherto, to sternly abandon the trade of author forever, and emigrate for good to America. But the venture turn'd out a lucky one, and there was no emigration. 35 40

Carlyle's work in the sphere of literature as he commenced and carried it out, is the same in one or two leading respects that Immanuel Kant's was in speculative philosophy. But the Scotchman had none of the stomachic phlegm and never-perturb'd placidity of the Konigsberg sage, and did not, like the latter, understand his own limits, and stop when he got to the end of them. He clears away jungle and poison-vines and underbrush—at any rate hacks valiantly at them, smiting hip and thigh. Kant did the like in his sphere, and it was all he profess'd to do; his labors have left the ground fully prepared ever since—and greater service was probably never perform'd by mortal man. But the pang and hiatus of Carlyle seem to me to consist in the evidence everywhere that amid a whirl of fog and fury and cross-purposes, he firmly believ'd he had a clue to the medication of the world's ills, and that his bounden mission was to exploit it.‡ 45 50 55

doubt he had at least two natures (like most of us)—and a sketch of him would be thoroughly unfair that did not give full prominence to these traits also."

Carlyle from American Points of View.

Printed, except for one short clipping, from 29 pages of autograph MS in black ink on gray paper, most of the pages consisting of from two to six separate slips of paper pasted together. Some of the "jottings" were made, apparently, while the *Critic* article was in preparation, though most of them were probably made afterwards but designed for collation and eventual publication. Revisions in the MS are mostly minor. Originally the pages were separately numbered 1–25, with four pages of footnotes not numbered. The page number was cut away from the first three pages. Presumably, Whitman once intended to publish this essay separately.

There were two anchors, or sheet-anchors, for steadying, as a last resort, the Carlylean ship. One will be specified presently. The other, perhaps the main, was only to be found in some mark'd form of personal force, an extreme degree of competent urge and will, a man or men "born to command." Probably there ran through every vein and current of the Scotchman's blood something that warm'd up to this kind of trait and character above aught else in the world, and which makes him in my opinion the chief celebrater and promulger of it in literature—more than Plutarch, more than Shakspere. The great masses of humanity stand for nothing—at least nothing but nebulous raw material; only the big planets and shining suns for him. To ideas almost invariably languid or cold, a number-one forceful personality was sure to rouse his eulogistic passion and savage joy. In such case, even the standard of duty hereinafter rais'd, was to be instantly lower'd and vail'd. All that is comprehended under the terms republicanism and democracy were distasteful to him from the first, and as he grew older they became hateful and contemptible. For an undoubtedly candid and penetrating faculty such as his, the bearings he persistently ignored were marvellous. For instance, the promise, nay certainty of the democratic principle, to each and every State of the current world, not so much of helping it to perfect legislators and executives, but as the only effectual method for surely, however slowly, training people on a large scale toward voluntarily ruling and managing themselves (the ultimate aim of political and all other development)—to gradually reduce the fact of *governing* to its minimum, and to subject all its staffs and their doings to the telescopes and microscopes of committees and parties—and greatest of all, to afford (not stagnation and obedient content, which went well enough with the feudalism and ecclesiasticism of the antique and medieval world, but) a vast and sane and recurrent ebb and tide action for those floods of the great deep that have henceforth palpably burst forever their old bounds—seem never to have enter'd Carlyle's thought. It was splendid how he refus'd any compromise to the last. He was curiously antique. In that harsh, picturesque, most potent voice and figure, one seems to be carried back from the present of the British islands more than two thousand years, to the range between Jerusalem and Tarsus. His fullest best biographer justly says of him:

"He was a teacher and a prophet, in the Jewish sense of the word. The prophecies of Isaiah and Jeremiah have become a part of the permanent spiritual

66. Shakspere] MS before revision: Shakespeare
93–108. This quotation is from the Preface to J. A. Froude's *Thomas Carlyle: a History of the First Forty Years of His Life, 1795–1835* (New York, 1882). The clipping used by Whitman is probably from a review, but the source has not been

inheritance of mankind, because events proved that they had interpreted cor- 95
rectly the signs of their own times, and their prophecies were fulfill'd. Carlyle,
like them, believ'd that he had a special message to deliver to the present age.
Whether he was correct in that belief, and whether his message was a true
message, remains to be seen. He has told us that our most cherish'd ideas of
political liberty, with their kindred corollaries, are mere illusions, and that the 100
progress which has seem'd to go along with them is a progress towards
anarchy and social dissolution. If he was wrong, he has misused his powers.
The principles of his teachings are false. He has offer'd himself as a guide upon
a road of which he had no knowledge; and his own desire for himself would be
the speediest oblivion both of his person and his works. If, on the other hand, he 105
has been right; if, like his great predecessors, he has read truly the tendencies of
this modern age of ours, and his teaching is authenticated by facts, then
Carlyle, too, will take his place among the inspired seers."

To which I add an amendment that under no circumstances, and no
matter how completely time and events disprove his lurid vaticinations, 110
should the English-speaking world forget this man, nor fail to hold in
honor his unsurpass'd conscience, his unique method, and his honest fame.
Never were convictions more earnest and genuine. Never was there less of
a flunkey or temporizer. Never had political progressivism a foe it could
more heartily respect. 115

The second main point of Carlyle's utterance was the idea of *duty
being done*. (It is simply a new codicil—if it be particularly new, which is
by no means certain—on the time-honor'd bequest of dynasticism, the
mould-eaten rules of legitimacy and kings.) He seems to have been impatient sometimes to madness when reminded by persons who thought at 120
least as deeply as himself, that this formula, though precious, is rather a
vague one, and that there are many other considerations to a philosophical
estimate of each and every department either in general history or individual affairs.

Altogether, I don't know anything more amazing than these persistent 125
strides and throbbings so far through our Nineteenth century of perhaps
its biggest, sharpest, and most erudite brain, in defiance and discontent
with everything; contemptuously ignoring, (either from constitutional
inaptitude, ignorance itself, or more likely because he demanded a definite
cure-all here and now,) the only solace and solvent to be had. 130

There is, apart from mere intellect, in the make-up of every superior
human identity, (in its moral completeness, considered as *ensemble*, not

identified. The text of Froude is collated here as well as that of the clipping.
   103. teachings] Clip. and Froude: teaching
   108. inspired seers.] Clip. and Froude: inspired seers, and he will shine on, another
fixed star in the intellectual sky.

for that moral alone, but for the whole being, including physique,) a
wondrous something that realizes without argument, frequently without
135 what is called education, (though I think it the goal and apex of all education deserving the name)—an intuition of the absolute balance, in time
and space, of the whole of this multifarious, mad chaos of fraud, frivolity,
hoggishness—this revel of fools, and incredible make-believe and general
unsettledness, we call *the world;* a soul-sight of that divine clue and un-
140 seen thread which holds the whole congeries of things, all history and
time, and all events, however trivial, however momentous, like a leash'd
dog in the hand of the hunter. Such soul-sight and root-centre for the
mind—mere optimism explains only the surface or fringe of it—Carlyle
was mostly, perhaps entirely without. He seems instead to have been
145 haunted in the play of his mental action by a spectre, never entirely laid
from first to last, (Greek scholars, I believe, find the same mocking and
fantastic apparition attending Aristophanes, his comedies,)—the spectre
of world-destruction.

How largest triumph or failure in human life, in war or peace, may
150 depend on some little hidden centrality, hardly more than a drop of
blood, a pulse-beat, or a breath of air! It is certain that all these weighty
matters, democracy in America, Carlyleism, and the temperament for
deepest political or literary exploration, turn on a simple point in speculative philosophy.

155 The most profound theme that can occupy the mind of man—the
problem on whose solution science, art, the bases and pursuits of nations,
and everything else, including intelligent human happiness, (here to-day,
1882, New York, Texas, California, the same as all times, all lands,)
subtly and finally resting, depends for competent outset and argument, is
160 doubtless involved in the query: What is the fusing explanation and tie—
what the relation between the (radical, democratic) Me, the human
identity of understanding, emotions, spirit, &c., on the one side, of and
with the (conservative) Not Me, the whole of the material objective universe and laws, with what is behind them in time and space, on the other
165 side? Immanuel Kant, though he explain'd, or partially explain'd, as may
be said, the laws of the human understanding, left this question an open
one. Schelling's answer, or suggestion of answer, is (and very valuable
and important, as far as it goes,) that the same general and particular

177. scheme just epitomized] MS: schema just epitomised
182. reconstruct, at any] SDC: reconstruct it, any] MS: reconstruct it, at any]
[Corrected in Whitman's paperbound copy of SDC, in the Feinberg Collection.
The corrected reading appears in SDC Glasgow and in all later texts.]
185. After this paragraph MS has several lines intended for a footnote. They were

intelligence, passion, even the standards of right and wrong, which exist in a conscious and formulated state in man, exist in an unconscious state, or in perceptible analogies, throughout the entire universe of external Nature, in all its objects large or small, and all its movements and processes—thus making the impalpable human mind, and concrete Nature, notwithstanding their duality and separation, convertible, and in centrality and essence one. But G. F. Hegel's fuller statement of the matter probably remains the last best word that has been said upon it, up to date. Substantially adopting the scheme just epitomized, he so carries it out and fortifies it and merges everything in it, with certain serious gaps now for the first time fill'd, that it becomes a coherent metaphysical system, and substantial answer (as far as there can be any answer) to the foregoing question—a system which, while I distinctly admit that the brain of the future may add to, revise, and even entirely reconstruct, at any rate beams forth to-day, in its entirety, illuminating the thought of the universe, and satisfying the mystery thereof to the human mind, with a more consoling scientific assurance than any yet.

According to Hegel the whole earth, (an old nucleus-thought, as in the Vedas, and no doubt before, but never hitherto brought so absolutely to the front, fully surcharged with modern scientism and facts, and made the sole entrance to each and all,) with its infinite variety, the past, the surroundings of to-day, or what may happen in the future, the contrarieties of material with spiritual, and of natural with artificial, are all, to the eye of the *ensemblist*, but necessary sides and unfoldings, different steps or links, in the endless process of Creative thought, which, amid numberless apparent failures and contradictions, is held together by central and never-broken unity—not contradictions or failures at all, but radiations of one consistent and eternal purpose; the whole mass of everything steadily, unerringly tending and flowing toward the permanent *utile* and *morale*, as rivers to oceans. As life is the whole law and incessant effort of the visible universe, and death only the other or invisible side of the same, so the *utile*, so truth, so health, are the continuous-immutable laws of the moral universe, and vice and disease, with all their perturbations, are but transient, even if ever so prevalent expressions.

To politics throughout, Hegel applies the like catholic standard and faith. Not any one party, or any one form of government, is absolutely and

apparently cancelled at the time they were written, and in fact make no coherent statement, but seem to support the argument for Hegel as opposed to Carlyle.

200. the continuous-immutable] SDC and MS: the unseen but immutable] [This change was made in Whitman's paperbound copy and retained in SDC Glasgow and all later texts.]

204. party, or any] MS (unrevised): party, nor any

205   exclusively true. Truth consists in the just relations of objects to each other. A majority or democracy may rule as outrageously and do as great harm as an oligarchy or despotism—though far less likely to do so. But the great evil is either a violation of the relations just referr'd to, or of the moral law. The specious, the unjust, the cruel, and what is called the

210   unnatural, though not only permitted but in a certain sense, (like shade to light,) inevitable in the divine scheme, are by the whole constitution of that scheme, partial, inconsistent, temporary, and though having ever so great an ostensible majority, are certainly destin'd to failure, after causing great suffering.

215   Theology, Hegel translates into science.†† All apparent contradictions in the statement of the Deific nature by different ages, nations, churches, points of view, are but fractional and imperfect expressions of one essential unity, from which they all proceed—crude endeavors or distorted parts, to be regarded both as distinct and united. In short (to put it in our own

220   form, or summing up,) that thinker or analyzer or overlooker who by an inscrutable combination of train'd wisdom and natural intuition most fully accepts in perfect faith the moral unity and sanity of the creative scheme, in history, science, and all life and time, present and future, is both the truest cosmical devotee or religioso, and the profoundest philosopher.

225   While he who, by the spell of himself and his circumstance, sees darkness and despair in the sum of the workings of God's providence, and who, in that, denies or prevaricates, is, no matter how much piety plays on his lips, the most radical sinner and infidel.

I am the more assured in recounting Hegel a little freely here,‡‡ not

230   only for offsetting the Carlylean letter and spirit—cutting it out all and several from the very roots, and below the roots—but to counterpoise, since the late death and deserv'd apotheosis of Darwin, the tenets of the evolutionists. Unspeakably precious as those are to biology, and henceforth indispensable to a right aim and estimate in study, they neither

235   comprise or explain everything—and the last word or whisper still remains to be breathed, after the utmost of those claims, floating high and forever above them all, and above technical metaphysics. While the contributions which German Kant and Fichte and Schelling and Hegel have bequeath'd to humanity—and which English Darwin has also in his field—are in-

240   dispensable to the erudition of America's future, I should say that in all of

235. comprise or explain] MS (unrevised): comprise nor explain
250. era—and with Emerson and] MS before revision: era—with Kant, Hegel, Darwin, Emerson, and
264. After "America?" MS has (crossed out): "No such influence had yet appeared

them, and the best of them, when compared with the lightning flashes and
flights of the old prophets and *exaltés*, the spiritual poets and poetry of all
lands, (as in the Hebrew Bible,) there seems to be, nay certainly is, something lacking—something cold, a failure to satisfy the deepest emotions of
the soul—a want of living glow, fondness, warmth, which the old *exaltés*   245
and poets supply, and which the keenest modern philosophers so far do
not.

Upon the whole, and for our purposes, this man's name certainly belongs on the list with the just-specified, first-class moral physicians of
our current era—and with Emerson and two or three others—though his   250
prescription is drastic, and perhaps destructive, while theirs is assimilat-
ing, normal and tonic. Feudal at the core, and mental offspring and radia-
tion of feudalism as are his books, they afford ever-valuable lessons and
affinities to democratic America. Nations or individuals, we surely learn
deepest from unlikeness, from a sincere opponent, from the light thrown   255
even scornfully on dangerous spots and liabilities. (Michel Angelo in-
voked heaven's special protection against his friends and affectionate
flatterers; palpable foes he could manage for himself.) In many particulars Carlyle was indeed, as Froude terms him, one of those far-off Hebraic
utterers, a new Micah or Habbakuk. His words at times bubble forth with   260
abysmic inspiration. Always precious, such men; as precious now as any
time. His rude, rasping, taunting, contradictory tones—what ones are
more wanted amid the supple, polish'd, money-worshipping, Jesus-and-
Judas-equalizing, suffrage-sovereignty echoes of current America? He has
lit up our Nineteenth century with the light of a powerful, penetrating,   265
and perfectly honest intellect of the first-class, turn'd on British and
European politics, social life, literature, and representative personages—
thoroughly dissatisfied with all, and mercilessly exposing the illness of all.
But while he announces the malady, and scolds and raves about it, he himself, born and bred in the same atmosphere, is a mark'd illustration of it.   270

* It will be difficult for the future—judging by his books, personal dis-
sympathies, &c.,—to account for the deep hold this author has taken on the
present age, and the way he has color'd its method and thought. I am certainly at a loss to account for it all as affecting myself. But there could be no
view, or even partial picture, of the middle and latter part of our Nineteenth   275
century, that did not markedly include Thomas Carlyle. In his case (as so many

in English literature, almost announcing a new order of power."
 270. At the end of the last page the signature "Walt Whitman." is crossed out.
The presence of this signature and the separate numbering of the pages through 25
(several unnumbered pages added later) suggest that Whitman had intended this
article for periodical publication.

others, literary productions, works of art, personal identities, events,) there has been an impalpable something more effective than the palpable. Then I find no better text, (it is always important to have a definite, special, even oppositional, living man to start from,) for sending out certain speculations and comparisons for home use. Let us see what they amount to—those reactionary doctrines, fears, scornful analyses of democracy—even from the most erudite and sincere mind of Europe.

† Not the least mentionable part of the case, (a streak, it may be, of that humor with which history and fate love to contrast their gravity,) is that although neither of my great authorities during their lives consider'd the United States worthy of serious mention, all the principal works of both might not inappropriately be this day collected and bound up under the conspicuous title: *"Speculations for the use of North America, and Democracy there, with the relations of the same to Metaphysics, including Lessons and Warnings (encouragements too, and of the vastest,) from the Old World to the New."*

‡ I hope I shall not myself fall into the error I charge upon him, of prescribing a specific for indispensable evils. My utmost pretension is probably but to offset that old claim of the exclusively curative power of first-class individual men, as leaders and rulers, by the claims, and general movement and result, of ideas. Something of the latter kind seems to me the distinctive theory of America, of democracy, and of the modern—or rather, I should say, it *is* democracy, and *is* the modern.

†† I am much indebted to J. Gostick's abstract.

‡‡ I have deliberately repeated it all, not only in offset to Carlyle's ever-lurking pessimism and world-decadence, but as presenting the most thoroughly *American points of view* I know. In my opinion the above formulas of Hegel are an essential and crowning justification of New World democracy in the creative realms of time and space. There is that about them which only the vastness, the multiplicity and the vitality of America would seem able to comprehend, to give scope and illustration to, or to be fit for, or even originate. It is strange to me that they were born in Germany, or in the old world at all. While a Carlyle, I should say, is quite the legitimate European product to be expected.

293. indispensable] MS: indispensible
299. Joseph Gostwick's *German Literature*, 1854.

A Couple of Old Friends—a Coleridge Bit.

Printed from a clipping of the Philadelphia *American*, paragraphs 5 and 6 of the article "Bumble-Bees and Bird Music," May 14, 1881, with introductory and closing additions in Whitman's autograph. Subtitle inserted in red ink.

1–2. The sidehead, in italics, and the first sentence are written in black ink above the clipping. The first sentence of the paragraph in *PA*, not reprinted, reads: "Then an item of two special favorites."

3. here (but only one—the mate not here yet.) This] *PA:* here—but only one—(for there are two, I have noticed three summers past). This

A Couple of Old Friends—a Coleridge Bit.

Latter April.—Have run down in my country haunt for a couple of
days, and am spending them by the pond. I had already discover'd my
kingfisher here (but only one—the mate not here yet.) This fine bright
morning, down by the creek, he has come out for a spree, circling, flirting,
chirping at a round rate. While I am writing these lines he is disporting   5
himself in scoots and rings over the wider parts of the pond, into whose
surface he dashes, once or twice making a loud *souse*—the spray flying in
the sun—beautiful! I see his white and dark-gray plumage and peculiar
shape plainly, as he has deign'd to come very near me. The noble, graceful bird! Now he is sitting on the limb of an old tree, high up, bending   10
over the water—seems to be looking at me while I memorandize. I almost
fancy he knows me. *Three days later.*—My second kingfisher is here with
his (or her) mate. I saw the two together flying and whirling around. I
had heard, in the distance, what I thought was the clear rasping staccato
of the birds several times already—but I couldn't be sure the notes came   15
from both until I saw them together. To-day at noon they appear'd, but
apparently either on business, or for a little limited exercise only. No wild
frolic now, full of free fun and motion, up and down for an hour.
Doubtless, now they have cares, duties, incubation responsibilities. The
frolics are deferr'd till summer-close.   20
 I don't know as I can finish to-day's memorandum better than with
Coleridge's lines, curiously appropriate in more ways than one:

> "All Nature seems at work—slugs leave their lair,
> The bees are stirring—birds are on the wing,
> And winter, slumbering in the open air,   25
> Wears on his smiling face a dream of spring;
> And I, the while, the sole unbusy thing,
> Nor honey make, nor pair, nor build, nor sing."

 4. morning, down] *PA:* morning, as I am down
 8. I see his] *SDC:* I saw his] *PA:* I saw his] [Revised in the paperbound copy.
Revision in *SDC* Glasgow and in all later texts.]
 12. After "knows me." *PA* begins a new paragraph.
 20. Clipping ends with "summer-close."
 21–28. These lines added in pencil on two strips of ruled white paper. The verses
are from Coleridge's "Work Without Hope." They are collated here with the text of
W. G. T. Shedd's edition of the *Complete Works* (New York, 1871), VII, 281.
 23. work—slugs leave their lair,] Shedd: work. Slugs leave their lair—
 24. wing,] Shedd: wing—
 25. winter, slumbering] Shedd: Winter slumbering
 26. spring;] Shedd: Spring!

A Week's Visit to Boston.

May 1, '81.—Seems as if all the ways and means of American travel
to-day had been settled, not only with reference to speed and directness,
but for the comfort of women, children, invalids, and old fellows like me.
I went on by a through train that runs daily from Washington to the
Yankee metropolis without change. You get in a sleeping-car soon after
dark in Philadelphia, and after ruminating an hour or two, have your
bed made up if you like, draw the curtains, and go to sleep in it—fly
on through Jersey to New York—hear in your half-slumbers a dull jolting
and bumping sound or two—are unconsciously toted from Jersey city by a
midnight steamer around the Battery and under the big bridge to the
track of the New Haven road—resume your flight eastward, and early the
next morning you wake up in Boston. All of which was my experience. I
wanted to go to the Revere house. A tall unknown gentleman, (a fellow-
passenger on his way to Newport he told me, I had just chatted a few moments before with him,) assisted me out through the depot crowd, procured a hack, put me in it with my traveling bag, saying smilingly and
quietly, "Now I want you to let this be *my* ride," paid the driver, and before I could remonstrate bow'd himself off.

The occasion of my jaunt, I suppose I had better say here, was for a
public reading of "the death of Abraham Lincoln" essay, on the sixteenth
anniversary of that tragedy; which reading duly came off, night of
April 15. Then I linger'd a week in Boston—felt pretty well (the mood
propitious, my paralysis lull'd)—went around everywhere, and saw all
that was to be seen, especially human beings. Boston's immense material
growth—commerce, finance, commission stores, the plethora of goods, the
crowded streets and sidewalks—made of course the first surprising show.

A Week's Visit to Boston.

Printed from a clipping of the *Critic*, the first four paragraphs of the third
number of "How I Get Around," May 7, 1881. The *CR* title of this article was "My
Late Visit to Boston." New title was inserted in red ink.

1. Date inserted in black ink.

12. After "experience." *CR* begins a new paragraph.

19–39. These lines have the subtitle in *CR*: "But Why Do I Go So Far From
Home?"

22. After "April 15." *CR* begins a new paragraph.

24. beings. Boston's immense] *CR*: beings. It is a theory of mine that occasionally there is vouchsafed to us one sudden hour, day, moment (opens quietly like
a bud or pod) when we clearly *see things*, perhaps the people and places familiar
for years, now realized for the first. I apply this to scenery, persons, works of art,

In my trip out West, last year, I thought the wand of future prosperity, future empire, must soon surely be wielded by St. Louis, Chicago, beautiful Denver, perhaps San Francisco; but I see the said wand stretch'd out just as decidedly in Boston, with just as much certainty of staying; 30 evidences of copious capital—indeed no centre of the New World ahead of it, (half the big railroads in the West are built with Yankees' money, and they take the dividends.) Old Boston with its zigzag streets and multitudinous angles, (crush up a sheet of letter-paper in your hand, throw it down, stamp it flat, and that is a map of old Boston)—new Boston with its 35 miles upon miles of large and costly houses—Beacon street, Commonwealth avenue, and a hundred others. But the best new departures and expansions of Boston, and of all the cities of New England, are in another direction.

The Boston of To-Day.

In the letters we get from Dr. Schliemann (interesting but fishy) about his excavations there in the far-off Homeric area, I notice cities, ruins, &c., as he digs them out of their graves, are certain to be in layers— that is to say, upon the foundation of an old concern, very far down indeed, is always another city or set of ruins, and upon that another super- 5 added—and sometimes upon that still another—each representing either a long or rapid stage of growth and development, different from its predecessor, but unerringly growing out of and resting on it. In the moral, emotional, heroic, and human growths, (the main of a race in my opinion,) something of this kind has certainly taken place in Boston. The New Eng- 10 land metropolis of to-day may be described as sunny, (there is something else that makes warmth, mastering even winds and meteorologies, though those are not to be sneez'd at,) joyous, receptive, full of ardor,

and all. This time my theory had its day in Boston. The immense
    27. West, last year, I] *CR:* West not long since, I
    29. wand stretch'd] *CR:* wand invisibly stretched
    30–31. staying; . . . capital—] *CR: staying;* evidences of copious "capital"—
    33. dividends.) Old] *CR:* dividends)—old
    37. the best new] *CR:* the real new

    The Boston of To-Day.
    Printed from clippings of *CR,* same article, paragraph 5; subtitle as in *SDC.*
    2. excavations . . . Homeric] *CR:* excavations off there in the Homeric
    3–4. layers—that] *CR:* layers; that
    18. in *the race*] *SDC* and later texts: in the *the race*] *CR:* in *the race*] [obviously a printer's error in *SDC;* here corrected.]

sparkle, a certain element of yearning, magnificently tolerant, yet not to be
fool'd; fond of good eating and drinking—costly in costume as its purse
can buy; and all through its best average of houses, streets, people, that
subtle something (generally thought to be climate, but it is not—it is something indefinable in *the race*, the turn of its development) which ef-
fuses behind the whirl of animation, study, business, a happy and joyous
public spirit, as distinguish'd from a sluggish and saturnine one. Makes
me think of the glints we get (as in Symonds's books) of the jolly old
Greek cities. Indeed there is a good deal of the Hellenic in B., and the
people are getting handsomer too—padded out, with freer motions, and
with color in their faces. I never saw (although this is not Greek) so many
fine-looking gray hair'd women. At my lecture I caught myself pausing
more than once to look at them, plentiful everywhere through the audience
—healthy and wifely and motherly, and wonderfully charming and beautiful—I think such as no time or land but ours could show.

My Tribute to Four Poets.

April 16.—A short but pleasant visit to Longfellow. I am not one
of the calling kind, but as the author of "Evangeline" kindly took the
trouble to come and see me three years ago in Camden, where I was ill, I
felt not only the impulse of my own pleasure on that occasion, but a duty.
He was the only particular eminence I called on in Boston, and I shall not
soon forget his lit-up face and glowing warmth and courtesy, in the modes
of what is called the old school.

And now just here I feel the impulse to interpolate something about
the mighty four who stamp this first American century with its birth-
marks of poetic literature. In a late magazine one of my reviewers, who
ought to know better, speaks of my "attitude of contempt and scorn and
intolerance" toward the leading poets—of my "deriding" them, and
preaching their "uselessness." If anybody cares to know what I think—

My Tribute to Four Poets.

Printed from clippings of CR, same article, paragraphs 6–10, under the subtitle (deleted) "I Call on Longfellow"; new subtitle inserted in red ink.

1. After "Longfellow." CR begins a new paragraph.
2. "Evangeline"] CR: Evangeline
7. After "old school." CR continues with the lines, deleted: "I did not see
Emerson, and have never seen Whittier.
"I found Mr. Longfellow troubled by neuralgia, but free from it just at the hour
of my visit. The good, gentle, handsome old man—the true poet!"
15. After "propound." CR begins a new paragraph.
15. these States] CR: the United States

and have long thought and avow'd—about them, I am entirely willing to propound. I can't imagine any better luck befalling these States for a   15
poetical beginning and initiation than has come from Emerson, Long-fellow, Bryant, and Whittier. Emerson, to me, stands unmistakably at the head, but for the others I am at a loss where to give any precedence. Each illustrious, each rounded, each distinctive. Emerson for his sweet, vital-tasting melody, rhym'd philosophy, and poems as amber-clear as the   20
honey of the wild bee he loves to sing. Longfellow for rich color, graceful forms and incidents—all that makes life beautiful and love refined—competing with the singers of Europe on their own ground, and, with one exception, better and finer work than that of any of them. Bryant pulsing the first interior verse-throbs of a mighty world—bard of the river and   25
the wood, ever conveying a taste of open air, with scents as from hayfields, grapes, birch-borders—always lurkingly fond of threnodies—beginning and ending his long career with chants of death, with here and there through all, poems, or passages of poems, touching the highest universal truths, enthusiasms, duties—morals as grim and eternal, if not as stormy   30
and fateful, as anything in Eschylus. While in Whittier, with his special themes—(his outcropping love of heroism and war, for all his Quakerdom, his verses at times like the measur'd step of Cromwell's old veterans)—in Whittier lives the zeal, the moral energy, that founded New England—the splendid rectitude and ardor of Luther, Milton, George Fox—I must   35
not, dare not, say the wilfulness and narrowness—though doubtless the world needs now, and always will need, almost above all, just such nar-rowness and wilfulness.

Millet's Pictures—Last Items.

April 18.—Went out three or four miles to the house of Quincy Shaw, to see a collection of J. F. Millet's pictures. Two rapt hours. Never before have I been so penetrated by this kind of expression. I stood long

17. After "Whittier." CR has the following sentence, deleted: "One of the four has already finished his noble career, and it cannot be very long before the lives of the other three must, in the nature of things, be closed."
32–33. Marks of parenthesis inserted on the clipping.

Millet's Pictures—Last Items.
Printed from clippings of CR, same article, paragraphs 11–15, subtitled "Millet's Pictures—New Suggestions, Awakenings," the first (16) of four paragraphs subtitled "Amid the Tablets," and the last paragraph (19) of the article. Whitman's subtitle is inserted in red ink.
1–2. Quincy Shaw] CR: Mr. Quincy A. Shaw

and long before "the Sower." I believe what the picture-men designate
"the first Sower," as the artist executed a second copy, and a third, and,
some think, improved in each. But I doubt it. There is something in this
that could hardly be caught again—a sublime murkiness and original
pent fury. Besides this masterpiece, there were many others, (I shall never
forget the simple evening scene, "Watering the Cow,") all inimitable, all
perfect as pictures, works of mere art; and then it seem'd to me, with that
last impalpable ethic purpose from the artist (most likely unconscious to
himself) which I am always looking for. To me all of them told the full
story of what went before and necessitated the great French revolution—
the long precedent crushing of the masses of a heroic people into the
earth, in abject poverty, hunger—every right denied, humanity attempted
to be put back for generations—yet Nature's force, titanic here, the
stronger and hardier for that repression—waiting terribly to break forth,
revengeful—the pressure on the dykes, and the bursting at last—the
storming of the Bastile—the execution of the king and queen—the tempest
of massacres and blood. Yet who can wonder?

> Could we wish humanity different?
> Could we wish the people made of wood or stone?
> Or that there be no justice in destiny or time?

The true France, base of all the rest, is certainly in these pictures. I
comprehend "Field-People Reposing," "the Diggers," and "the Angelus"
in this opinion. Some folks always think of the French as a small race,
five or five and a half feet high, and ever frivolous and smirking. Nothing
of the sort. The bulk of the personnel of France, before the revolution,
was large-sized, serious, industrious as now, and simple. The revolution
and Napoleon's wars dwarf'd the standard of human size, but it will come
up again. If for nothing else, I should dwell on my brief Boston visit for

4. "the Sower." I] CR: "the Sower" (see frontispiece in Scribner's of last November). This particular painting is, I
8. After "pent fury." CR begins a new paragraph.
21–23. From Whitman's poem "France: The 18th Year of these States," lines
9–11, slightly altered.
21. Could . . . different?] L of G: Could I wish humanity different?] SDA:
Could we wish humanity indifferent?
22. Could we . . . or stone] L of G: Could I wish the people made of wood
and stone?
26. After "opinion." CR begins a new paragraph.
31. After "up again." CR begins a new paragraph.
31. my brief Boston] CR: my Boston
34. Sunday, April 17.—An] CR: Sunday, April 17.—There are little episodes
in life's experience which you cannot define, or say how it is they do affect you;
yet they filter into one's heart, and tinge its blood forever. Such was an

opening to me the new world of Millet's pictures. Will America ever have such an artist out of her own gestation, body, soul?

Sunday, April 17.—An hour and a half, late this afternoon, in silence and half light, in the great nave of Memorial hall, Cambridge, the walls thickly cover'd with mural tablets, bearing the names of students and graduates of the university who fell in the secession war.

April 23.—It was well I got away in fair order, for if I had staid another week I should have been killed with kindness, and with eating and drinking.

Birds—and a Caution.

May 14.—Home again; down temporarily in the Jersey woods. Between 8 and 9 A.M. a full concert of birds, from different quarters, in keeping with the fresh scent, the peace, the naturalness all around me. I am lately noticing the russet-back, size of the robin or a trifle less, light breast and shoulders, with irregular dark stripes—tail long—sits hunch'd up by the hour these days, top of a tall bush, or some tree, singing blithely. I often get near and listen, as he seems tame; I like to watch the working of his bill and throat, the quaint sidle of his body, and flex of his long tail. I hear the woodpecker, and night and early morning the shuttle of the whip-poor-will—noons, the gurgle of thrush delicious, and *meo-o-ow* of the cat-bird. Many I cannot name; but I do not very particularly seek information. (You must not know too much, or be too precise or scientific about birds and trees and flowers and water-craft; a certain free margin, and even vagueness—perhaps ignorance, credulity—helps your enjoyment of these things, and of the sentiment of feather'd, wooded, river, or marine Nature generally. I repeat it—don't want to know too exactly, or the reasons why. My own notes have been written off-hand in the latitude

37. After "secession war." CR has two paragraphs (17 and 18) omitted from SDC. See Appendix XXVII, 1.
38–40. These lines, paragraph 19, end the article in CR.
38. April 23.—It . . . in] CR: It was well I got away (April 23) in
40. Whitman's name at the end deleted on the clipping.

Birds—and a Caution.

Printed from an autograph MS consisting of three gray sheets (in black ink) on which several strips of white paper (pencil, corrected in ink) are pasted at intervals. A small clipping of the Philadelphia *American*, May 14, 1881, pasted on the third gray sheet, is the last paragraph of "Bumble-Bees and Bird-Music."
17–20. This excerpt from PA is made a part of the parenthesis beginning in line 12.
17. My . . . written] PA: My notes are written

of middle New Jersey. Though they describe what I saw—what appear'd
to me—I dare say the expert ornithologist, botanist or entomologist will
20 detect more than one slip in them.)

Samples of My Common-Place Book.

I ought not to offer a record of these days, interests, recuperations,
without including a certain old, well-thumb'd common-place book,* filled
with favorite excerpts, I carried in my pocket for three summers, and
absorb'd over and over again, when the mood invited. I find so much in
5   having a poem or fine suggestion sink into me (a little then goes a great
ways) prepar'd by these vacant-sane and natural influences.

* *Samples of my common-place book down at the creek:*
I have—says old Pindar—many swift arrows in my quiver which speak to
the wise, though they need an interpreter to the thoughtless.

10 Such a man as it takes ages to make, and ages to understand.
                                                            H. D. Thoreau.

If you hate a man, don't kill him, but let him live.—*Buddhistic.*

Famous swords are made of refuse scraps, thought worthless.

Poetry is the only verity—the expression of a sound mind speaking after the
15 ideal—and not after the apparent.—*Emerson.*

The form of oath among the Shoshone Indians is, "The earth hears me. The
sun hears me. Shall I lie?"

The true test of civilization is not the census, nor the size of cities, nor the
crops—no, but the kind of a man the country turns out.—*Emerson.*

20   The whole wide ether is the eagle's sway:
                The whole earth is a brave man's fatherland.—*Euripides.*

                Spices crush'd, their pungence yield,
                   Trodden scents their sweets respire;
                Would you have its strength reveal'd?
25   Cast the incense in the fire.

18–19. I . . . to] *PA:* I see—what appears to
19. ornithologist, botanist or] *PA:* ornithologist or

Samples of My Common-Place Book.
Printed from five pages, including half a page (lines 1–7) in black ink; the
footnote consists of scraps of quotations copied in ink or pencil, interspersed with short
printed clippings, apparently from newspapers, all pasted on the larger gray sheets.

Matthew Arnold speaks of "the huge Mississippi of falsehood called History."

> The wind blows north, the wind blows south,
> The wind blows east and west;
> No matter how the free wind blows,   30
> Some ship will find it best.

Preach not to others what they should eat, but eat as becomes you, and be silent.—*Epictetus.*

Victor Hugo makes a donkey meditate and apostrophize thus:

> My brother, man, if you would know the truth,   35
> We both are by the same dull walls shut in;
> The gate is massive and the dungeon strong.
> But you look through the key-hole out beyond,
> And call this knowledge; yet have not at hand
> The key wherein to turn the fatal lock.   40

"William Cullen Bryant surprised me once," relates a writer in a New York paper, "by saying that prose was the natural language of composition, and he wonder'd how anybody came to write poetry."

> Farewell! I did not know thy worth;
> But thou art gone, and now 'tis prized: 45
> So angels walk'd unknown on earth,
> But when they flew were recognized.—*Hood.*

John Burroughs, writing of Thoreau, says: "He improves with age—in fact requires age to take off a little of his asperity, and fully ripen him. The world likes a good hater and refuser almost as well as it likes a good lover and accepter—only it likes him farther off."   50

Louise Michel at the burial of Blanqui, (*1881.*)
Blanqui drill'd his body to subjection to his grand conscience and his noble passions, and commencing as a young man, broke with all that is sybaritish in modern civilization. Without the power to sacrifice self, great ideas will never   55
bear fruit.

> Out of the leaping furnace flame
> A mass of molten silver came;
> Then, beaten into pieces three,
> Went forth to meet its destiny.   60
> The first a crucifix was made,
> Within a soldier's knapsack laid;

No attempt is made to discover the exact source of the quotation or clipping.
    16–17. From a clipping; "only" deleted before "form".
    28–31. From a clipping; "blow" changed to "blows" in line 30.
    35–40. From a clipping, to which line 40, in ink, is introductory.
    41–43. From a clipping, after Bryant's name, which read as follows before revisions: surprised me once," says Stoddard, "by saying that prose was the natural language of composition, and he wondered how anybody came to write poetry."
    57–66. From a clipping, where the lines are arranged in couplets.

The second was a locket fair,
  Where a mother kept her dead child's hair;
65 The third—a bangle, bright and warm,
  Around a faithless woman's arm.

A mighty pain to love it is,
  And 'tis a pain that pain to miss;
But of all pain the greatest pain,
70 It is to love, but love in vain.

                Maurice F. Egan on De Guérin.
  A pagan heart, a Christian soul had he,
    He follow'd Christ, yet for dead Pan he sigh'd,
    Till earth and heaven met within his breast:
75 As if Theocritus in Sicily
    Had come upon the Figure crucified,
    And lost his gods in deep, Christ-given rest.

And if I pray, the only prayer
  That moves my lips for me,
80 Is, leave the mind that now I bear,
  And give me Liberty.—*Emily Brontë.*

I travel on not knowing,
  I would not if I might;
I would rather walk with God in the dark,
85 Than go alone in the light;
I would rather walk with Him by faith
  Than pick my way by sight.

Prof. Huxley in a late lecture.
  I myself agree with the sentiment of Thomas Hobbes, of Malmesbury, that
90 "the scope of all speculation is the performance of some action or thing to be
done." I have not any very great respect for, or interest in, mere "knowing," as
such.
Prince Metternich.
  Napoleon was of all men in the world the one who most profoundly despised
95 the race. He had a marvellous insight into the weaker sides of human nature,
(and all our passions are either foibles themselves, or the cause of foibles.) He
was a very small man of imposing character. He was ignorant, as a sub-
lieutenant generally is: a remarkable instinct supplied the lack of knowledge.
From his mean opinion of men, he never had any anxiety lest he should go

  72-77. From a clipping, preceded, in ink, by the line printed in italics.
  94-103. From a clipping, with the words "*Prince Metternich*" written in ink
above it.
  95. the race] Clip.: the human race
  96. Whitman inserts the marks of parenthesis before "and" and after "foibles."
  96-97. foibles.) He was] Clip.: foibles. He had a habit of telling me the most
tremendous whoppers. I always let him go to the end and contented myself when he
got through with saying, "that is not so!" He would look steadily at me, burst out
laughing and turn off, saying, "Sono fugie per i Parigini"—they are bams for the
Parisians.
  All may be said in two words: Napoleon was

wrong. He ventur'd everything, and gain'd thereby an immense step toward   100
success. Throwing himself upon a prodigious arena, he amaz'd the world,
and made himself master of it, while others cannot even get so far as being
masters of their own hearth. Then he went on and on, until he broke his neck.

My Native Sand and Salt Once More.

*July 25, '81.—Far Rockaway, L. I.—*A good day here, on a jaunt,
amid the sand and salt, a steady breeze setting in from the sea, the sun
shining, the sedge-odor, the noise of the surf, a mixture of hissing and
booming, the milk-white crests curling over. I had a leisurely bath and
naked ramble as of old, on the warm-gray shore-sands, my companions off   5
in a boat in deeper water—(I shouting to them Jupiter's menaces against
the gods, from Pope's Homer.)

*July 28—to Long Branch.—*8½ A.M., on the steamer "Plymouth
Rock," foot of 23d street, New York, for Long Branch. Another fine day,
fine sights, the shores, the shipping and bay—everything comforting to the   10
body and spirit of me. (I find the human and objective atmosphere of New
York city and Brooklyn more affiliative to me than any other.) *An hour
later—*Still on the steamer, now sniffing the salt very plainly—the long
pulsating *swash* as our boat steams seaward—the hills of Navesink and
many passing vessels—the air the best part of all. At Long Branch the bulk   15
of the day, stopt at a good hotel, took all very leisurely, had an excellent
dinner, and then drove for over two hours about the place, especially Ocean
avenue, the finest drive one can imagine, seven or eight miles right along
the beach. In all directions costly villas, palaces, millionaires—(but few
among them I opine like my friend George W. Childs, whose personal in-   20
tegrity, generosity, unaffected simplicity, go beyond all worldly wealth.)

Hot Weather New York.

*August.—*In the big city awhile. Even the height of the dog-days,
there is a good deal of fun about New York, if you only avoid fluster, and

My Native Sand and Salt Once More.
Printed from two autograph pages written in black ink on gray paper. The
original title, written and revised in red ink, was "Off to My Native Shores Once
More."

Hot Weather New York.
Printed from clippings of NYTR, the first five paragraphs of the article "City
Notes in August," August 15, 1881. Subtitle inserted in red ink; date and the first
line in black ink; other revisions in black and red ink.
    1. *August. . . . height*] NYTR: Sir: Even in the height

take all the buoyant wholesomeness that offers. More comfort, too, than most folks think. A middle-aged man, with plenty of money in his pocket, tells me that he has been off for a month to all the swell places, has disburs'd a small fortune, has been hot and out of kilter everywhere, and has return'd home and lived in New York city the last two weeks quite contented and happy. People forget when it is hot here, it is generally hotter still in other places. New York is so situated, with the great ozonic brine on both sides, it comprises the most favorable health-chances in the world. (If only the suffocating crowding of some of its tenement houses could be broken up.) I find I never sufficiently realized how beautiful are the upper two-thirds of Manhattan island. I am stopping at Mott Haven, and have been familiar now for ten days with the region above One-hundredth street, and along the Harlem river and Washington heights. Am dwelling a few days with my friends, Mr. and Mrs. J. H. J., and a merry housefull of young ladies. Am putting the last touches on the printer's copy of my new volume of "Leaves of Grass"—the completed book at last. Work at it two or three hours, and then go down and loaf along the Harlem river; have just had a good spell of this recreation. The sun sufficiently veil'd, a soft south breeze, the river full of small or large shells (light taper boats) darting up and down, some singly, now and then long ones with six or eight young fellows practicing—very inspiriting sights. Two fine yachts lie anchor'd off the shore. I linger long, enjoying the sundown, the glow, the streak'd sky, the heights, distances, shadows.

Aug. 10.—As I haltingly ramble an hour or two this forenoon by the more secluded parts of the shore, or sit under an old cedar half way up the hill, the city near in view, many young parties gather to bathe or swim, squads of boys, generally twos or threes, some larger ones, along the sand-bottom, or off an old pier close by. A peculiar and pretty carnival—at its

7. New York city the] *NYTR:* New-York the
8. here, it] *NYTR:* here in the city it
10–12. world. . . . I find] *NYTR:* world, if only the suffocating crowding of some of its living quarters and of the tenement houses could be broken up. Go through those East Side streets that intersect the Bowery, or along Centre-st., any hot evening, and see the swarms and sweat interminably covering the stoops and curbstone. And yet they seem to be curiously jolly and hearty. I find
12. After "hearty." *NYTR* begins a new paragraph, the first of two subtitled "Upper Two-Thirds of New-York."
14–15. One-hundredth street, and] *NYTR:* One-hundredth-st., especially Mott-ave. and
15. After the sentence ending "Washington heights." *NYTR* continues with the last part of this paragraph (2) and all the next (3), omitted in *SDC*. See Appendix XXXV, 1.
15–25. These lines, beginning with "Am dwelling," are a separate paragraph in *NYTR* subtitled "Harlem River at Sunset." The date "Aug. 8." is at the beginning

height a hundred lads or young men, very democratic, but all decent be-
having. The laughter, voices, calls, responses—the springing and diving
of the bathers from the great string-piece of the decay'd pier, where climb
or stand long ranks of them, naked, rose-color'd, with movements, postures ahead of any sculpture. To all this, the sun, so bright, the dark-   35
green shadow of the hills the other side, the amber-rolling waves, changing as the tide comes in to a transparent tea-color—the frequent splash of
the playful boys, sousing—the glittering drops sparkling, and the good
western breeze blowing.

"Custer's Last Rally."

Went to-day to see this just-finish'd painting by John Mulvany, who
has been out in far Dakota, on the spot, at the forts, and among the
frontiersmen, soldiers and Indians, for the last two years, on purpose to
sketch it in from reality, or the best that could be got of it. Sat for over an
hour before the picture, completely absorb'd in the first view. A vast can-   5
vas, I should say twenty or twenty-two feet by twelve, all crowded, and
yet not crowded, conveying such a vivid play of color, it takes a little
time to get used to it. There are no tricks; there is no throwing of
shades in masses; it is all at first painfully real, overwhelming, needs good
nerves to look at it. Forty or fifty figures, perhaps more, in full finish and   10
detail in the mid-ground, with three times that number, or more, through
the rest—swarms upon swarms of savage Sioux, in their war-bonnets,
frantic, mostly on ponies, driving through the background, through the
smoke, like a hurricane of demons. A dozen of the figures are wonderful.
Altogether a western, autochthonic phase of America, the frontiers, culmi-   15

of the first line in *NYTR;* deleted in *SDC.*
 17. of young ladies] *NYTR:* of young young ladies
 18. of "Leaves of Grass"—the] *NYTR:* of poems—the
 20. a good spell of] *NYTR:* a half-afternoon of
 26–39. This paragraph in *NYTR* is subtitled "Forenoon River Scene."
 28. city near in] *NYTR:* city in

"Custer's Last Rally."
 Printed from clippings of *NYTR*, paragraphs 6–9 of the same article; subtitle
unchanged; revisions in black and red ink.
 1. Went] *NYTR:* I went
 2. far Dakota, on] *NYTR:* far Montana on
 3. two years] *NYTR:* two or three years
 4. Sat] *NYTR:* I sat
 11. detail in] *NYTR:* detail, life-size, in

nating, typical, deadly, heroic to the uttermost—nothing in the books like it, nothing in Homer, nothing in Shakspere; more grim and sublime than either, all native, all our own, and all a fact. A great lot of muscular, tan-faced men, brought to bay under terrible circumstances—death ahold of
20   them, yet every man undaunted, not one losing his head, wringing out every cent of the pay before they sell their lives. Custer (his hair cut short) stands in the middle, with dilated eye and extended arm, aiming a huge cavalry pistol. Captain Cook is there, partially wounded, blood on the white handkerchief around his head, aiming his carbine coolly, half kneel-
25   ing—(his body was afterwards found close by Custer's.) The slaughter'd or half-slaughter'd horses, for breastworks, make a peculiar feature. Two dead Indians, herculean, lie in the foreground, clutching their Winchester rifles, very characteristic. The many soldiers, their faces and attitudes, the carbines, the broad-brimm'd western hats, the powder-smoke in
30   puffs, the dying horses with their rolling eyes almost human in their agony, the clouds of war-bonneted Sioux in the background, the figures of Custer and Cook—with indeed the whole scene, dreadful, yet with an attraction and beauty that will remain in my memory. With all its color and fierce action, a certain Greek continence pervades it. A sunny sky and clear light
35   envelop all. There is an almost entire absence of the stock traits of European war pictures. The physiognomy of the work is realistic and Western. I only saw it for an hour or so; but it needs to be seen many times—needs to be studied over and over again. I could look on such a work at brief intervals all my life without tiring; it is very tonic to me; then it has
40   an ethic purpose below all, as all great art must have. The artist said the sending of the picture abroad, probably to London, had been talk'd of. I advised him if it went abroad to take it to Paris. I think they might appreciate it there—nay, they certainly would. Then I would like to show Messieur Crapeau that some things can be done in America as well as
45   others.

16. uttermost—nothing] *NYTR:* uttermost; nothing
17. Shakspere] *NYTR:* Shakespeare
19. circumstances—death] *NYTR:* circumstances. Death
21. After the sentence ending "their lives." *NYTR* begins a new paragraph.
24. head, aiming] *NYTR:* head, but aiming
24–25. kneeling—(his] *NYTR:* kneeling (his
32. Cook . . . dreadful,] *NYTR:* Cook, with, indeed, the whole scene, inexpressible, dreadful,
33. remain in] *NYTR:* remain forever in
36–37. After "Western." *NYTR* begins a new paragraph.
39. *NYTR* has periods instead of semicolons.
40. After "must have." *NYTR* begins a new paragraph.

Some Old Acquaintances—Memories.

Aug. 16.—"Chalk a big mark for to-day," was one of the sayings of an old sportsman-friend of mine, when he had had unusually good luck—come home thoroughly tired, but with satisfactory results of fish or birds. Well, to-day might warrant such a mark for me. Everything propitious from the start. An hour's fresh stimulation, coming down ten miles of Manhattan island by railroad and 8 o'clock stage. Then an excellent breakfast at Pfaff's restaurant, 24th street. Our host himself, an old friend of mine, quickly appear'd on the scene to welcome me and bring up the news, and, first opening a big fat bottle of the best wine in the cellar, talk about ante-bellum times, '59 and '60, and the jovial suppers at his then Broadway place, near Bleecker street. Ah, the friends and names and frequenters, those times, that place. Most are dead—Ada Clare, Wilkins, Daisy Sheppard, O'Brien, Henry Clapp, Stanley, Mullin, Wood, Brougham, Arnold—all gone. And there Pfaff and I, sitting opposite each other at the little table, gave a remembrance to them in a style they would have themselves fully confirm'd, namely, big, brimming, fill'd-up champagne-glasses, drain'd in abstracted silence, very leisurely, to the last drop. (Pfaff is a generous German *restaurateur*, silent, stout, jolly, and I should say the best selecter of champagne in America.)

A Discovery of Old Age.

Perhaps the best is always cumulative. One's eating and drinking one wants fresh, and for the nonce, right off, and have done with it—but I would not give a straw for that person or poem, or friend, or city, or

---

45. For the last two paragraphs of NYTR (10–11), omitted in SDC, see Appendix XXXV, 2.

Some Old Acquaintances—Memories.
    Printed from an autograph page consisting of two small sheets of white paper pasted together, written in black ink, and much revised. Subtitle in red ink on a strip pasted at the top.
    13. Stanley] MS (unrevised): Shanley

A Discovery of Old Age.
    Printed from an autograph page consisting of a gray sheet (in black ink) of regular size with a smaller white sheet (in pencil) pasted in the middle. Subtitle in red ink.

work of art, that was not more grateful the second time than the first—
and more still the third. Nay, I do not believe any grandest eligibility
ever comes forth at first. In my own experience, (persons, poems, places,
characters,) I discover the best hardly ever at first, (no absolute rule
about it, however,) sometimes suddenly bursting forth, or stealthily opening to me, perhaps after years of unwitting familiarity, unappreciation,
usage.

A Visit, at the Last, to R. W. Emerson.

Concord, Mass.—Out here on a visit—elastic, mellow, Indian-sum-
mery weather. Came to-day from Boston, (a pleasant ride of 40 minutes
by steam, through Somerville, Belmont, Waltham, Stony Brook, and
other lively towns,) convoy'd by my friend F. B. Sanborn, and to his
ample house, and the kindness and hospitality of Mrs. S. and their fine
family. Am writing this under the shade of some old hickories and elms,
just after 4 P.M., on the porch, within a stone's throw of the Concord
river. Off against me, across stream, on a meadow and side-hill, hay-
makers are gathering and wagoning-in probably their second or third crop.
The spread of emerald-green and brown, the knolls, the score or two of
little haycocks dotting the meadow, the loaded-up wagons, the patient
horses, the slow-strong action of the men and pitch-forks—all in the just-
waning afternoon, with patches of yellow sun-sheen, mottled by long
shadows—a cricket shrilly chirping, herald of the dusk—a boat with two
figures noiselessly gliding along the little river, passing under the stone
bridge-arch—the slight settling haze of aerial moisture, the sky and the
peacefulness expanding in all directions and overhead—fill and soothe me.

Same evening.—Never had I a better piece of luck befall me: a long
and blessed evening with Emerson, in a way I couldn't have wish'd better
or different. For nearly two hours he has been placidly sitting where I

A Visit, at the Last, to R. W. Emerson.
Printed from clippings of the *Critic*, paragraphs 2–5 of the fifth number of
"How I Get Around," December 3, 1881. The title and most of the revisions are in
black ink.
For the first paragraph of the article, omitted in SDC, see Appendix XXIX, 1.
1–17. This paragraph in CR subtitled "An Early Autumn Side-Bit."
1. *Concord, Mass.*—Out] CR: Concord, Mass., Sept. 17.—Out
7. within a stone's] CR: within stone's
18–38. These lines in CR are subtitled "Emerson As He Looks To-Day," and are
divided into two paragraphs.
33. briefly and] CR: briefly, easily and

could see his face in the best light, near me. Mrs. S.'s back-parlor well
fill'd with people, neighbors, many fresh and charming faces, women,
mostly young, but some old. My friend A. B. Alcott and his daughter
Louisa were there early. A good deal of talk, the subject Henry Thoreau—
some new glints of his life and fortunes, with letters to and from him—   25
one of the best by Margaret Fuller, others by Horace Greeley, Channing,
&c.—one from Thoreau himself, most quaint and interesting. (No doubt I
seem'd very stupid to the room-full of company, taking hardly any part
in the conversation; but I had "my own pail to milk in," as the Swiss proverb puts it.) My seat and the relative arrangement were such that, with-   30
out being rude, or anything of the kind, I could just look squarely at E.,
which I did a good part of the two hours. On entering, he had spoken
very briefly and politely to several of the company, then settled himself in
his chair, a trifle push'd back, and, though a listener and apparently an
alert one, remain'd silent through the whole talk and discussion. A   35
lady friend quietly took a seat next him, to give special attention. A good
color in his face, eyes clear, with the well-known expression of sweetness,
and the old clear-peering aspect quite the same.

Next Day.—Several hours at E.'s house, and dinner there. An old
familiar house, (he has been in it thirty-five years,) with surroundings,   40
furnishment, roominess, and plain elegance and fullness, signifying
democratic ease, sufficient opulence, and an admirable old-fashioned simplicity—modern luxury, with its mere sumptuousness and affectation,
either touch'd lightly upon or ignored altogether. Dinner the same. Of
course the best of the occasion (Sunday, September 18, '81) was the sight   45
of E. himself. As just said, a healthy color in the cheeks, and good light in
the eyes, cheery expression, and just the amount of talking that best suited,
namely, a word or short phrase only where needed, and almost always
with a smile. Besides Emerson himself, Mrs. E., with their daughter
Ellen, the son Edward and his wife, with my friend F. S. and Mrs. S.,   50
and others, relatives and intimates. Mrs. Emerson, resuming the subject
of the evening before, (I sat next to her,) gave me further and fuller in-

36. After "attention." *CR* begins a new paragraph, the first sentence of which,
omitted in *SDC*, is as follows:
"And so, there Emerson sat, and I looking at him."
44. the same. Of] *CR:* the same. (It was not my first dinner with Emerson.
In 1857, and along there, when he came to New York to lecture, we two would dine
together at the Astor House. And some years after, I living for a while in Boston,
we would occasionally meet for the same purpose at the American or Parker's. Before
I get through these notes I will allude to one of our dinners, following a pretty vehement discussion.) Of
44. After "discussion.)" *CR* begins a new paragraph.
45. the occasion] *CR:* the present occasion

formation about Thoreau, who, years ago, during Mr. E.'s absence in Europe, had lived for some time in the family, by invitation.

Other Concord Notations.

Though the evening at Mr. and Mrs. Sanborn's, and the memorable family dinner at Mr. and Mrs. Emerson's, have most pleasantly and permanently fill'd my memory, I must not slight other notations of Concord. I went to the old Manse, walk'd through the ancient garden, enter'd the
5   rooms, noted the quaintness, the unkempt grass and bushes, the little panes in the windows, the low ceilings, the spicy smell, the creepers embowering the light. Went to the Concord battle ground, which is close by, scann'd French's statue, "the Minute Man," read Emerson's poetic inscription on the base, linger'd a long while on the bridge, and stopp'd by the
10   grave of the unnamed British soldiers buried there the day after the fight in April '75. Then riding on, (thanks to my friend Miss M. and her spirited white ponies, she driving them,) a half hour at Hawthorne's and Thoreau's graves. I got out and went up of course on foot, and stood a long while and ponder'd. They lie close together in a pleasant wooded spot well
15   up the cemetery hill, "Sleepy Hollow." The flat surface of the first was densely cover'd by myrtle, with a border of arbor-vitæ, and the other had a brown headstone, moderately elaborate, with inscriptions. By Henry's side lies his brother John, of whom much was expected, but he died young. Then to Walden pond, that beautifully embower'd sheet of water, and
20   spent over an hour there. On the spot in the woods where Thoreau had his solitary house is now quite a cairn of stones, to mark the place; I too carried one and deposited on the heap. As we drove back, saw the "School of Philosophy," but it was shut up, and I would not have it open'd for me.

54. After "by invitation." CR has six paragraphs (6–11) omitted in SDC. See Appendix XXIX, 2.

Other Concord Notations.
Printed from a clipping of paragraphs 12–15 and the first part of 16 of the same article in the *Critic.* Revised in black ink.
5. rooms, . . . quaintness] Clip. after revision: rooms—noted the quaintness] CR: rooms. Here Emerson wrote his principal poems. (The spot, I see as I look around, serves the understanding of them like a frame does a picture. The same of Hawthorne's "Mosses".) One notes the quaintness
7. light. Went] CR: light, a certain severity, precision, and melancholy, even a *twist* to all, notwithstanding the pervading calmness and normality of the scene. The house, too, gives out the aroma of generations of buried New England Puritanism and its ministers. I went
7. After "ministers." CR begins a new paragraph.

Near by stopp'd at the house of W. T. Harris, the Hegelian, who came
out, and we had a pleasant chat while I sat in the wagon. I shall not soon   25
forget those Concord drives, and especially that charming Sunday forenoon one with my friend Miss M., and the white ponies.

Boston Common—More of Emerson.

Oct. 10–13.—I spend a good deal of time on the Common, these
delicious days and nights—every mid-day from 11.30 to about 1—and
almost every sunset another hour. I know all the big trees, especially the
old elms along Tremont and Beacon streets, and have come to a sociable-
silent understanding with most of them, in the sunlit air, (yet crispy-cool   5
enough,) as I saunter along the wide unpaved walks. Up and down this
breadth by Beacon street, between these same old elms, I walk'd for two
hours, of a bright sharp February mid-day twenty-one years ago, with
Emerson, then in his prime, keen, physically and morally magnetic, arm'd
at every point, and when he chose, wielding the emotional just as well as   10
the intellectual. During those two hours he was the talker and I the listener. It was an argument-statement, reconnoitring, review, attack, and
pressing home, (like an army corps in order, artillery, cavalry, infantry,)
of all that could be said against that part (and a main part) in the con-
struction of my poems, "Children of Adam." More precious than gold to   15
me that dissertation—it afforded me, ever after, this strange and paradoxical lesson; each point of E.'s statement was unanswerable, no judge's
charge ever more complete or convincing, I could never hear the points
better put—and then I felt down in my soul the clear and unmistakable
conviction to disobey all, and pursue my own way. "What have you to say   20
then to such things?" said E., pausing in conclusion. "Only that while I

9. stopp'd] *CR:* stopt
11. After "April '75." *CR* begins a new paragraph.
14. lie] *CR:* lay
18. After "died young." *CR* begins a new paragraph.
19. Then to] *CR:* Also to
25. After "the wagon." *CR* begins a new paragraph.
27. After "white ponies." the rest of the paragraph in *CR* was cut away and
omitted in *SDC.* For these lines see Appendix XXIX, 3.

Boston Common—More of Emerson.

Printed from clippings of the *Critic*, same article, paragraphs 17–19; subtitle
unchanged; revised in red ink.
1. *Oct. 10–13.*—I] *CR:* Oct. 10–13, '81.—I
6. After "walks." *CR* begins a new paragraph.
16. dissertation—it] *CR:* dissertation—(I only wish I had it now, verbatim). It

can't answer them at all, I feel more settled than ever to adhere to my own
theory, and exemplify it," was my candid response. Whereupon we went
and had a good dinner at the American House. And thenceforward I
25   never waver'd or was touch'd with qualms, (as I confess I had been two or
three times before).

An Ossianic Night—Dearest Friends.

Nov., '81.—Again back in Camden. As I cross the Delaware in
long trips to-night, between 9 and 11, the scene overhead is a peculiar one
—swift sheets of flitting vapor-gauze, follow'd by dense clouds throwing
an inky pall on everything. Then a spell of that transparent steel-gray
5   black sky I have noticed under similar circumstances, on which the moon
would beam for a few moments with calm lustre, throwing down a broad
dazzle of highway on the waters; then the mists careering again. All silently, yet driven as if by the furies they sweep along, sometimes quite
thin, sometimes thicker—a real Ossianic night—amid the whirl, absent
10   or dead friends, the old, the past, somehow tenderly suggested—while
the Gael-strains chant themselves from the mists—["Be thy soul blest, O
Carril! in the midst of thy eddying winds. O that thou woulds't come to
my hall when I am alone by night! And thou dost come, my friend. I hear
often thy light hand on my harp, when it hangs on the distant wall, and
15   the feeble sound touches my ear. Why dost thou not speak to me in my
grief, and tell me when I shall behold my friends? But thou passest away
in thy murmuring blast; the wind whistles through the gray hairs of
Ossian."]
But most of all, those changes of moon and sheets of hurrying vapor
20   and black clouds, with the sense of rapid action in weird silence, recall the

24. After "American House." CR begins a new paragraph, which contains only
the one sentence.
26. For paragraph 20, the last of the article, omitted from SDC, see Appendix
XXIX, 4.
An Ossianic Night—Dearest Friends.
Printed from five gray sheets of autograph MS; the third sheet is mostly covered by two smaller white sheets pasted on. Subtitle in red ink but the rest in black.
The lines from *Ossian*, partly on the white sheets, had been previously copied and
were adapted to this section at the time the material was assembled for printing.
11–18. This quotation is from "Fingal," Book VI, *Poems of Ossian*.
16. tell me when] *Ossian:* tell when
18. At this point on the third page the following words are written but crossed
out: "Like the ghost of a giant in some dream after reading the wild rhythm—['Who
comes with the locks of age? It is the son of song. Hail, Carril of other times! Thy
voice is like the harp in the halls of Tura. Thy words are the shower that falls on
the sunny fields.']" This is a quotation, slightly altered, from near the end of

far-back Erse belief that such above were the preparations for receiving the wraiths of just-slain warriors—["We sat that night in Selma, round the strength of the shell. The wind was abroad in the oaks. The spirit of the mountain roar'd. The blast came rustling through the hall, and gently touch'd my harp. The sound was mournful and low, like the song of the   25 tomb. Fingal heard it the first. The crowded sighs of his bosom rose. Some of my heroes are low, said the gray-hair'd king of Morven. I hear the sound of death on the harp. Ossian, touch the trembling string. Bid the sorrow rise, that their spirits may fly with joy to Morven's woody hills. I touch'd the harp before the king; the sound was mournful and low. Bend   30 forward from your clouds, I said, ghosts of my fathers! bend. Lay by the red terror of your course. Receive the falling chief; whether he comes from a distant land, or rises from the rolling sea. Let his robe of mist be near; his spear that is form'd of a cloud. Place a half-extinguish'd meteor by his side, in the form of a hero's sword. And oh! let his countenance be lovely,   35 that his friends may delight in his presence. Bend from your clouds, I said, ghosts of my fathers, bend. Such was my song in Selma, to the lightly trembling harp."]

How or why I know not, just at the moment, but I too muse and think of my best friends in their distant homes—of William O'Connor, of   40 Maurice Bucke, of John Burroughs, and of Mrs. Gilchrist—friends of my soul—stanchest friends of my other soul, my poems.

Only a New Ferry Boat.

Jan. 12, '82.—Such a show as the Delaware presented an hour before sundown yesterday evening, all along between Philadelphia and

---

"Fingal," preceding by one page the quotation in lines 11–18. In *Ossian* the last sentence quoted above reads: "Thy words are pleasant as the shower which falls on the sunny field."

19–38. This quotation, beginning on the second white sheet and continued on the fourth gray sheet, is from "Dar-Thula," *Poems of Ossian*, the second poem following "Fingal." Whitman quotes accurately except that he omits quotation marks from the reported speeches of Fingal and Ossian (lines 27–29 and 30–37), and that the last sentence of the quotation, which begins a new paragraph in *Ossian*, is shifted.

Only a New Ferry Boat.
Printed from two newspaper clippings. The first clipping contains only the title; it is probable therefore that part of the story was cut away when the clippings were pasted on the base sheet. The change from "this city" in the clipping to "Camden" in SDC suggests that the clipping was from a Camden newspaper, perhaps the *Courier*, where he published "Starting Newspapers" originally. Files of this paper for 1882 are no longer available.

Camden, is worth weaving into an item. It was full tide, a fair breeze
from the southwest, the water of a pale tawny color, and just enough motion to make things frolicsome and lively. Add to these an approaching
sunset of unusual splendor, a broad tumble of clouds, with much golden
haze and profusion of beaming shaft and dazzle. In the midst of all, in the
clear drab of the afternoon light, there steam'd up the river the large, new
boat, "the Wenonah," as pretty an object as you could wish to see, lightly
and swiftly skimming along, all trim and white, cover'd with flags, transparent red and blue, streaming out in the breeze. Only a new ferry-boat,
and yet in its fitness comparable with the prettiest product of Nature's
cunning, and rivaling it. High up in the transparent ether gracefully balanced and circled four or five great sea hawks, while here below, amid the
pomp and picturesqueness of sky and river, swam this creation of artificial beauty and motion and power, in its way no less perfect.

Death of Longfellow.

Camden, April 3, '82.—I have just return'd from an old forest
haunt, where I love to go occasionally away from parlors, pavements,
and the newspapers and magazines—and where, of a clear forenoon, deep
in the shade of pines and cedars and a tangle of old laurel-trees and vines,
the news of Longfellow's death first reach'd me. For want of anything better, let me lightly twine a sprig of the sweet ground-ivy trailing so
plentifully through the dead leaves at my feet, with reflections of that
half hour alone, there in the silence, and lay it as my contribution on the
dead bard's grave.

Longfellow in his voluminous works seems to me not only to be emi-
nent in the style and forms of poetical expression that mark the present
age, (an idiosyncrasy, almost a sickness, of verbal melody,) but to bring
what is always dearest as poetry to the general human heart and taste, and

---

3. Camden] Clip.: this city
3. an item] Clip.: an impromptu item
7. After "and dazzle." Clipping begins a new paragraph.
7. all, in] Clip.: all this, in
8–9. new . . . as] Clip.: new Camden ferry boat, the Wenonah, as
11. breeze. Only] Clip.: breeze.
Indeed the boat and the scene made a picture worth contemplating. Only

Death of Longfellow.
Printed from clippings of the *Critic*, Whitman's article with the same title,
April 8, 1882. Revised in black and red ink.

probably must be so in the nature of things. He is certainly the sort of
bard and counteractant most needed for our materialistic, self-assertive,
money-worshipping, Anglo-Saxon races, and especially for the present age
in America—an age tyrannically regulated with reference to the manu-
facturer, the merchant, the financier, the politician and the day workman
—for whom and among whom he comes as the poet of melody, courtesy,
deference—poet of the mellow twilight of the past in Italy, Germany,
Spain, and in Northern Europe—poet of all sympathetic gentleness—and
universal poet of women and young people. I should have to think long
if I were ask'd to name the man who has done more, and in more valuable
directions, for America.

I doubt if there ever was before such a fine intuitive judge and selecter
of poems. His translations of many German and Scandinavian pieces are
said to be better than the vernaculars. He does not urge or lash. His influence is like good drink or air. He is not tepid either, but always vital, with
flavor, motion, grace. He strikes a splendid average, and does not sing
exceptional passions, or humanity's jagged escapades. He is not revolutionary, brings nothing offensive or new, does not deal hard blows. On the
contrary, his songs soothe and heal, or if they excite, it is a healthy and
agreeable excitement. His very anger is gentle, is at second hand, (as in
the "Quadroon Girl" and the "Witnesses.")

There is no undue element of pensiveness in Longfellow's strains.
Even in the early translation, the Manrique, the movement is as of strong
and steady wind or tide, holding up and buoying. Death is not avoided
through his many themes, but there is something almost winning in his
original verses and renderings on that dread subject—as, closing "the
Happiest Land" dispute,

> And then the landlord's daughter
> Up to heaven rais'd her hand,
> And said, "Ye may no more contend,
> There lies the happiest land."

1–2. *Camden*, . . . where I] CR: *Camden, N. J., April* 3, '82.—I have just
returned from a couple of weeks down in some primitive woods w[h]ere I [MS:
where I]

3–4. where, . . . in] MS: where, in

8. silence, and lay] CR: silence, the mottled light, 'mid those earth-smells [MS:
with the spring smells] of the Jersey woods in spring, and lay

11. the style and forms] MS: the forms

12. idiosyncrasy] MS: idiocracy

36. the Manrique] CR: "the Manrique"

41–44. Quoted from Longfellow's poem, "The Happiest Land: from the German." Whitman quotes correctly except that he omits the dash after the comma in
the third line and substitutes a period for the exclamation point after the fourth line.

45   To the ungracious complaint-charge of his want of racy nativity and
special originality, I shall only say that America and the world may well
be reverently thankful—can never be thankful enough—for any such
singing-bird vouchsafed out of the centuries, without asking that the notes
be different from those of other songsters; adding what I have heard

50   Longfellow himself say, that ere the New World can be worthily original,
and announce herself and her own heroes, she must be well saturated with
the originality of others, and respectfully consider the heroes that lived
before Agamemnon.

Starting Newspapers.

Reminiscences—(*From the "Camden Courier."*)—As I sat taking
my evening sail across the Delaware in the staunch ferryboat "Beverly,"
a night or two ago, I was join'd by two young reporter friends. "I have
a message for you," said one of them; "the C. folks told me to say they

5   would like a piece sign'd by your name, to go in their first number. Can
you do it for them?" "I guess so," said I; "what might it be about?" "Well,
anything on newspapers, or perhaps what you've done yourself, starting
them." And off the boys went, for we had reach'd the Philadelphia side.
The hour was fine and mild, the bright half-moon shining; Venus, with ex-

10   cess of splendor, just setting in the west, and the great Scorpion rearing its
length more than half up in the southeast. As I cross'd leisurely for an
hour in the pleasant night-scene, my young friend's words brought up
quite a string of reminiscences.
I commenced when I was but a boy of eleven or twelve writing senti-

---

45. complaint-charge of] CR: complaint-charge—(as by Margaret Fuller many
years ago, and several times since)—of
53. After "Agamemnon." CR has two paragraphs (6 and 7) omitted in SDC.
See Appendix XXXVI, 1.

Starting Newspapers.
Printed from two clippings of the Camden *Courier*, first issue, June 1, 1882;
reprinted in the New York *World*, Sunday, June 11, 1882. This issue of the *Courier*
has not, apparently, been preserved. The title, including the sideheading in italics, is
inserted in black ink above the clipping, from which the headline is clipped away. The
date "June 1, '82" is inserted in black ink, but crossed out. The headlines in the
NYW are as follows: "Walt Whitman: His Several Ventures as a Journalist as
Described by Himself. [*From the First Number of the Camden Courier.*]"
2. "Beverly,"] NYW: Beverly,] *Courier: Beverly*
4. the C. folks] NYW and *Courier:* the *Courier* folks
8. After "Philadelphia side." NYW and *Courier* begin a new paragraph.
15. old "Long Island Patriot," in] NYW and *Courier:* old *Patriot* in

mental bits for the old "Long Island Patriot," in Brooklyn; this was about   15
1832. Soon after, I had a piece or two in George P. Morris's then celebrated and fashionable "Mirror," of New York city. I remember with
what half-suppress'd excitement I used to watch for the big, fat, red-faced,
slow-moving, very old English carrier who distributed the "Mirror" in
Brooklyn; and when I got one, opening and cutting the leaves with   20
trembling fingers. How it made my heart double-beat to see *my piece*
on the pretty white paper, in nice type.

My first real venture was the "Long Islander," in my own beautiful
town of Huntington, in 1839. I was about twenty years old. I had been
teaching country school for two or three years in various parts of Suffolk   25
and Queens counties, but liked printing; had been at it while a lad, learn'd
the trade of compositor, and was encouraged to start a paper in the region
where I was born. I went to New York, bought a press and types, hired
some little help, but did most of the work myself, including the press-
work. Everything seem'd turning out well; (only my own restlessness pre-   30
vented me gradually establishing a permanent property there.) I bought
a good horse, and every week went all round the country serving my
papers, devoting one day and night to it. I never had happier jaunts—going over to south side, to Babylon, down the south road, across to Smith-
town and Comac, and back home. The experiences of those jaunts, the   35
dear old-fashion'd farmers and their wives, the stops by the hay-fields, the
hospitality, nice dinners, occasional evenings, the girls, the rides through
the brush, come up in my memory to this day.

I next went to the "Aurora" daily in New York city—a sort of free
lance. Also wrote regularly for the "Tattler," an evening paper. With   40
these and a little outside work I was occupied off and on, until I went to

15–16. about 1832.] *SDA:* about 1831.
17. "Mirror,"] *NYW* and *Courier: Mirror,*
19. "Mirror"] *NYW* and *Courier: Mirror*
21. *my piece*] *NYW* and *Courier:* my piece
23. "Long Islander,"] *NYW* and *Courier: Long-Islander*
24. Huntington, in 1839.] *NYW* and *Courier:* Huntington, Long Island, New
York, in 1839.
26. printing; had] *NYW* and *Courier:* printing. I had
26. lad, learn'd] *NYW* and *Courier:* lad, and learned
30. well; (only] *NYW:* well (only
31. me] *NYW* and *Courier:* my
38. brush, . . . day.] *NYW* and *Courier:* brush and the smell from the salt of
the South roads come up in my memory to this day, after more than forty years.
The *Long Islander* has stuck it out ever since—is now in the hands of Charles E.
Shephard, who was born to the brevier, the chase and the ink-block, and prints the
best country weekly for local news I know of anywhere.
39. "Aurora"] *NYW* and *Courier: Aurora*
40. "Tatler,"] *NYW* and *Courier: Tatler,*

edit the "Brooklyn Eagle," where for two years I had one of the pleasantest
sits of my life—a good owner, good pay, and easy work and hours. The
troubles in the Democratic party broke forth about those times (1848–'49)
45 and I split off with the radicals, which led to rows with the boss and "the
party," and I lost my place.

Being now out of a job, I was offer'd impromptu, (it happen'd between the acts one night in the lobby of the old Broadway theatre near
Pearl street, New York city,) a good chance to go down to New Orleans
50 on the staff of the "Crescent," a daily to be started there with plenty of
capital behind it. One of the owners, who was north buying material, met
me walking in the lobby, and though that was our first acquaintance, after
fifteen minutes' talk (and a drink) we made a formal bargain, and he paid
me two hundred dollars down to bind the contract and bear my expenses
55 to New Orleans. I started two days afterwards; had a good leisurely time,
as the paper wasn't to be out in three weeks. I enjoy'd my journey and
Louisiana life much. Returning to Brooklyn a year or two afterward I
started the "Freeman," first as a weekly, then daily. Pretty soon the secession war broke out, and I, too, got drawn in the current southward, and
60 spent the following three years there, (as memorandized preceding.)

Besides starting them as aforementioned, I have had to do, one time
or another, during my life, with a long list of papers, at divers places,
sometimes under queer circumstances. During the war, the hospitals at
Washington, among other means of amusement, printed a little sheet
65 among themselves, surrounded by wounds and death, the "Armory Square
Gazette," to which I contributed. The same long afterward, casually, to a
paper—I think it was call'd the "Jimplecute"—out in Colorado where I
stopp'd at the time. When I was in Quebec province, in Canada, in 1880,
I went into the queerest little old French printing office near Tadousac.
70 It was far more primitive and ancient than my Camden friend William

42. "Brooklyn Eagle,"] *NYW* and *Courier: Brooklyn Eagle,*
43. hours. The] *NYW* and *Courier:* hours (it came out about 3 o'clock every
afternoon). The
50. "Crescent,"] *NYW* and *Courier: Crescent,*
51. it. One] *NYW* and *Courier:* it, in opposition to the *Picayune.* One
51. owners, who] *NYW* and *Courier:* owners, Mr. McClure, who
53–54. and he . . . down] *NYW* and *Courier:* and McClure paid me $200 down
56. three weeks.] *NYW* and *Courier:* three or four weeks.
57. Louisiana life much.] *NYW* and *Courier:* Louisiana venture very much. I believe the *Crescent* is an institution there yet.
57. *NYW* and *Courier* begin a new paragraph with "Returning".
58. "Freeman,"] *NYW* and *Courier: Freeman,*
60. there, . . . preceding.)] *NYW* and *Courier:* there.
62. another, . . . with] *NYW* and *Courier:* another, with
65–66. "Armory Square Gazette,"] *NYW* and *Courier: Armory Square Gazette,*

Kurtz's place up on Federal street. I remember, as a youngster, several characteristic old printers of a kind hard to be seen these days.

The Great Unrest of Which We Are Part.

My thoughts went floating on vast and mystic currents as I sat to-day in solitude and half-shade by the creek—returning mainly to two principal centres. One of my cherish'd themes for a never-achiev'd poem has been the two impetuses of man and the universe—in the latter, creation's incessant unrest,* exfoliation, (Darwin's evolution, I suppose.) Indeed,   5
what is Nature but change, in all its visible, and still more its invisible processes? Or what is humanity in its faith, love, heroism, poetry, even morals, but *emotion?*

* "Fifty thousand years ago the constellation of the Great Bear or Dipper was a starry cross; a hundred thousand years hence the imaginary Dipper will   10
be upside down, and the stars which form the bowl and handle will have changed places. The misty nebulæ are moving, and besides are whirling around in great spirals, some one way, some another. Every molecule of matter in the whole universe is swinging to and fro; every particle of ether which fills space is in jelly-like vibration. Light is one kind of motion, heat another,   15
electricity another, magnetism another, sound another. Every human sense is the result of motion; every perception, every thought is but motion of the molecules of the brain translated by that incomprehensible thing we call mind. The processes of growth, of existence, of decay, whether in worlds, or in the minutest organisms, are but motion."   20

67. "Jimplecute"] *NYW* and *Courier: Jimplecute*
68. After "at the time." *NYW* and *Courier* begin a new paragraph.
71. After "Federal street." *NYW* and *Courier* began a new paragraph.
72. After "these days." the clipping is cut away, but the remaining part, as given in *NYW*, is as follows: "If my space were not exhausted I should like to say something about those quaint old characters.
"So, my dear old friends, and typos, if these impromptu yarns will do, you are welcome to them.

Walt Whitman."

The Great Unrest of Which We Are Part.
Printed from a page of autograph MS in black ink on gray paper. The note is a clipping from an unidentified newspaper, which Whitman encloses in quotation marks. The first eight lines of the clipping are crossed out.

By Emerson's Grave.

May 6, '82.—We stand by Emerson's new-made grave without sadness—indeed a solemn joy and faith, almost hauteur—our soul-benison no mere

"Warrior, rest, thy task is done,"

5 for one beyond the warriors of the world lies surely symboll'd here. A just man, poised on himself, all-loving, all-inclosing, and sane and clear as the sun. Nor does it seem so much Emerson himself we are here to honor—it is conscience, simplicity, culture, humanity's attributes at their best, yet applicable if need be to average affairs, and eligible to all. So used are we

10 to suppose a heroic death can only come from out of battle or storm, or mighty personal contest, or amid dramatic incidents or danger, (have we not been taught so for ages by all the plays and poems?) that few even of those who most sympathizingly mourn Emerson's late departure will fully appreciate the ripen'd grandeur of that event, with its play of calm and

15 fitness, like evening light on the sea.

How I shall henceforth dwell on the blessed hours when, not long since, I saw that benignant face, the clear eyes, the silently smiling mouth, the form yet upright in its great age—to the very last, with so much spring and cheeriness, and such an absence of decrepitude, that even

20 the term *venerable* hardly seem'd fitting.

Perhaps the life now rounded and completed in its mortal development, and which nothing can change or harm more, has its most illustrious halo, not in its splendid intellectual or esthetic products, but as form-

---

By Emerson's Grave.

Printed from a clipping of the *Critic*, Whitman's article of the same title, May 6, 1882. A much revised autograph MS in the Feinberg Collection (not the printer's copy) is here collated with the printed texts, referred to as FMS. At the upper left side of FMS the endorsement: "Pub in N Y *Critic* about May 4, '82"; at upper right side: "Emerson died April 27 '82".

　1. The date in italics was inserted on the clipping in ink.
　4. In the quotation FMS has a semicolon at the end and no comma before "rest".
　5. for one . . . world lies] FMS: for beyond all the warriors of the earth lies
　6. all-inclosing] CR and FMS: all-enclosing
　7. we . . . honor] FMS: we honor
　8. best, . . . if] FMS: best, applied, if
　9. After "eligible to all." CR and FMS begin a new paragraph.
　10–11. death . . . or mighty] FMS: death means only one from out of war or some mighty
　11–12. (have we not been] FMS: (we seem to have been

ing in its entirety one of the few, (alas! how few!) perfect and flawless
excuses for being, of the entire literary class.   25

We can say, as Abraham Lincoln at Gettysburg, It is not we who
come to consecrate the dead—we reverently come to receive, if so it may
be, some consecration to ourselves and daily work from him.

At Present Writing—Personal.
A letter to a German friend—extract.

May 31, '82.—"From to-day I enter upon my 64th year. The
paralysis that first affected me nearly ten years ago, has since remain'd,
with varying course—seems to have settled quietly down, and will probably continue. I easily tire, am very clumsy, cannot walk far; but my
spirits are first-rate. I go around in public almost every day—now and   5
then take long trips, by railroad or boat, hundreds of miles—live largely
in the open air—am sunburnt and stout, (weigh 190)—keep up my activity and interest in life, people, progress, and the questions of the day.
About two-thirds of the time I am quite comfortable. What mentality I
ever had remains entirely unaffected; though physically I am a half-   10
paralytic, and likely to be so, long as I live. But the principal object of
my life seems to have been accomplish'd—I have the most devoted and
ardent of friends, and affectionate relatives—and of enemies I really
make no account."

12. poems?)] FMS: poems)

13. mourn . . . will] *CR:* mourn Emerson's departure will] FMS: mourn the
departure of Emerson will

14–15. calm and fitness] FMS: calm fitness

16–17. hours . . . saw] FMS: hours I saw

18. form . . . to] FMS: form in its upright old age! To

19. an absence of decrepitude, that even] FMS: an entire absence of decrepitude,
even

21–22. Perhaps . . . and] FMS: The best life here rounded and completed,
and

24. (alas! how few!)] FMS: (alas! too few!)

At Present Writing—Personal.

Printed from a page of autograph MS made up of a main gray sheet and two
strips, pasted on top and bottom, all written in black ink except the subtitle, which is
in red ink.

After Trying a Certain Book.

I tried to read a beautifully printed and scholarly volume on "the Theory of Poetry," received by mail this morning from England—but gave it up at last for a bad job. Here are some capricious pencillings that follow'd, as I find them in my notes:

5 In youth and maturity Poems are charged with sunshine and varied pomp of day; but as the soul more and more takes precedence, (the sensuous still included,) the Dusk becomes the poet's atmosphere. I too have sought, and ever seek, the brilliant sun, and make my songs according. But as I grow old, the half-lights of evening are far more to me.

10 The play of Imagination, with the sensuous objects of Nature for symbols, and Faith—with Love and Pride as the unseen impetus and moving-power of all, make up the curious chess-game of a poem.

Common teachers or critics are always asking "What does it mean?" Symphony of fine musician, or sunset, or sea-waves rolling up the beach—
15 what do they mean? Undoubtedly in the most subtle-elusive sense they mean something—as love does, and religion does, and the best poem;— but who shall fathom and define those meanings? (I do not intend this as a warrant for wildness and frantic escapades—but to justify the soul's frequent joy in what cannot be defined to the intellectual part, or to calcu-
20 lation.)

At its best, poetic lore is like what may be heard of conversation in the dusk, from speakers far or hid, of which we get only a few broken murmurs. What is not gather'd is far more—perhaps the main thing.

Grandest poetic passages are only to be taken at free removes, as we
25 sometimes look for stars at night, not by gazing directly toward them, but off one side.

(*To a poetic student and friend.*)—I only seek to put you in rapport. Your own brain, heart, evolution, must not only understand the matter, but largely supply it.

After Trying a Certain Book.

Printed from four pages of autograph MS. The introductory paragraph, evidently recopied from an earlier draft, is written on the upper half of a gray sheet. The other three pages, constituting Whitman's notes on the book he was reading, are on white paper and were not recopied. The book cannot be certainly identified, but it may have been J. C. Sharp's *Aspects of Poetry*, which was published in England late in 1881. The Boston edition was dated 1882. It seems probable that Whitman's notes were made sometime before he thought of assembling them for publication in SDC, in spite of the reference to the mail "this morning," otherwise he would not have needed to "find them" in his notes.

Final Confessions—Literary Tests.

So draw near their end these garrulous notes. There have doubtless occurr'd some repetitions, technical errors in the consecutiveness of dates, in the minutiæ of botanical, astronomical, &c., exactness, and perhaps else-where;—for in gathering up, writing, peremptorily dispatching copy, this hot weather, (last of July and through August, '82,) and delaying not the printers, I have had to hurry along, no time to spare. But in the deepest veracity of all—in reflections of objects, scenes, Nature's outpourings, to my senses and receptivity, as they seem'd to me—in the work of giving those who care for it, some authentic glints, specimen-days of my life—and in the *bona fide* spirit and relations, from author to reader, on all the subjects design'd, and as far as they go, I feel to make unmitigated claims.

The synopsis of my early life, Long Island, New York city, and so forth, and the diary-jottings in the Secession war, tell their own story. My plan in starting what constitutes most of the middle of the book, was originally for hints and data of a Nature-poem that should carry one's experiences a few hours, commencing at noon-flush, and so through the after-part of the day—I suppose led to such idea by my own life-afternoon now arrived. But I soon found I could move at more ease, by giving the narrative at first hand. (Then there is a humiliating lesson one learns, in serene hours, of a fine day or night. Nature seems to look on all fixed-up poetry and art as something almost impertinent.)

Thus I went on, years following, various seasons and areas, spinning forth my thought beneath the night and stars, (or as I was confined to my room by half-sickness,) or at midday looking out upon the sea, or far north steaming over the Saguenay's black breast, jotting all down in the loosest sort of chronological order, and here printing from my impromptu notes, hardly even the seasons group'd together, or anything corrected—so afraid of dropping what smack of outdoors or sun or starlight might cling to the lines, I dared not try to meddle with or smooth them. Every

30   now and then, (not often, but for a foil,) I carried a book in my pocket—
or perhaps tore out from some broken or cheap edition a bunch of loose
leaves; most always had something of the sort ready, but only took it out
when the mood demanded. In that way, utterly out of reach of literary
conventions, I re-read many authors.

35   I cannot divest my appetite of literature, yet I find myself eventually
trying it all by Nature—*first premises* many call it, but really the crowning results of all, laws, tallies and proofs. (Has it never occurr'd to any
one how the last deciding tests applicable to a book are entirely outside of
technical and grammatical ones, and that any truly first-class production
40   has little or nothing to do with the rules and calibres of ordinary critics?
or the bloodless chalk of Allibone's Dictionary? I have fancied the ocean
and the daylight, the mountain and the forest, putting their spirit in a
judgment on our books. I have fancied some disembodied human soul giving its verdict.)

Nature and Democracy—Morality.

Democracy most of all affiliates with the open air, is sunny and hardy
and sane only with Nature—just as much as Art is. Something is required
to temper both—to check them, restrain them from excess, morbidity. I
have wanted, before departure, to bear special testimony to a very old
5   lesson and requisite. American Democracy, in its myriad personalities, in
factories, work-shops, stores, offices—through the dense streets and
houses of cities, and all their manifold sophisticated life—must either be
fibred, vitalized, by regular contact with out-door light and air and
growths, farm-scenes, animals, fields, trees, birds, sun-warmth and free
10   skies, or it will certainly dwindle and pale. We cannot have grand races

the MS are crossed out: "Memoranda of casual days here and there—now in New
York, now railroad traveling, now in some solitary recess of the woods—no order, or
finish, capricious, jumping backward or forward,—only tied together by all being
from the same identity, drops from the same one-flowing stream, different moods,
lights, shades, under no law, no rule—system."
    35–44. These lines were printed from a clipping from Whitman's article "A
Christmas Garland," in the Christmas number, 1874, of the New York *Daily
Graphic*, where they are not enclosed in parentheses. This number cannot be located
and may be lost. The collation here is made from the clipping. Professor Emory
Holloway published this paragraph in his UPP (II, 55–56), thinking it had not
been included by Whitman in SDC or CPW. In NYDG it was the second paragraph
following a section of "A Christmas Garland" subtitled "A Dialogue," which was reprinted in SDC as the first item of "Ventures, on an Old Theme." (See the notes on
that section in *Prose 1892*, II.)
    38. one how the] Clip.: one that the

of mechanics, work people, and commonalty, (the only specific purpose of America,) on any less terms. I conceive of no flourishing and heroic elements of Democracy in the United States, or of Democracy maintaining itself at all, without the Nature-element forming a main part—to be its health-element and beauty-element—to really underlie the whole politics, sanity, religion and art of the New World. 15

Finally, the morality: "Virtue," said Marcus Aurelius, "what is it, only a living and enthusiastic sympathy with Nature?" Perhaps indeed the efforts of the true poets, founders, religions, literatures, all ages, have been, and ever will be, our time and times to come, essentially the same—to bring people back from their persistent strayings and sickly abstractions, to the costless average, divine, original concrete. 20

38–39. are . . . ones, and] Clip.: are indeed entirely outside of literary taste and

Nature and Democracy—Morality.

Printed from two pages of autograph MS, in black ink, each page consisting of several small strips pasted together. The subtitle is in red ink.

10. will certainly dwindle] SDC: will morbidly dwindle] [The revision was made in the paperbound copy. The present reading first appeared in the text of SDC Glasgow, 1883.]

In the upper left corner of the second page of the MS of this section, Whitman has written in pencil: "Last page Specimen Days Collect comes now same type—same arrangement."

[This concludes Specimen Days. All of Collect, except Whitman's appendix containing "Pieces in Early Youth," appears in the present edition of Whitman's writings in Prose 1892, II.—ED.]

Appendix A

[When Whitman prepared the printer's copy of *SDC* he incorporated as clippings, with revisions, the greater part of his earlier publications that he wished to preserve. All omitted passages not incorporated at the appropriate places in the textual notes are printed here. For convenience of reference, each separate publication, book or periodical, is here given a Roman numeral, and each continuous quoted passage is given an Arabic numeral.—ED.]

I   *"The Great Army of the Sick."*
        NYT, February 26, 1863.
        [Reprinted with the title "The Great Army of the Wounded" in *The Wound Dresser*, 1898, edited by Richard M. Bucke. No part of this article was used in *SDC* except the sixth paragraph, subtitled "The Patent Office," which was incorporated in "The Patent-Office Hospital," *q.v.*]

1

The military hospitals, convalescent camps, etc. in Washington and its neighborhood sometimes contain over fifty thousand sick and wounded men. Every form of wound, (the mere sight of some of them having been known to make a tolerably hardy visitor faint away,) every kind of malady, like a long procession, with typhoid fever and diarrhœa at the head as leaders, are here in steady motion. The soldier's hospital! how many sleepless nights [,] how many woman's tears, how many long and aching hours and days of suspense, from every one of the Middle, Eastern, and Western States, have concentrated here! Our own New-York, in the form of hundreds and thousands of her young men, may consider herself here— Pennsylvania, Ohio, Indiana and all the West and Northwest the same— and all the New-England States the same.

Upon a few of these hospitals I have been almost daily calling as a missionary, on my own account, for the sustenance and consolation of some of the most needy cases of sick and dying men, for the last two months. One has much to learn in order to do good in these places. Great tact is required. These are not like other hospitals. By far the greatest proportion (I should say five sixth) of the patients are American young men, intelligent, of independent spirit, tender feelings, used to a hardy and healthy life; largely the farmers are represented by their sons—largely the mechanics and workingmen of the cities. Then they are *soldiers*. All these points must be borne in mind.

People through our Northern cities have little or no idea of the great and prominent feature which these military hospitals and convalescent camps make in and around Washington. There are not merely two or three or a dozen, but some fifty of them, of different degrees of capacity. The newspapers here find it necessary to print every day a directory of the hospitals; a long list, something like what a directory of the churches would be in New-York, Philadelphia, or Boston.

BARRACKS ADOPTED BY GOVERNMENT

The Government, (which really tries, I think, to do the best and quickest it can for these sad necessities,) is gradually settling down to adopt the plan of placing the hospitals in clusters of one-story wooden barracks, with their accompanying tents and sheds for cooking and all needed purposes. Taking all things into consideration, no doubt these are best adapted to the purpose; better than using churches and large public buildings like the Patent Office. These sheds now adopted are long, one-story edifices, sometimes ranged along in a row, with their heads to the street, and numbered either alphabetically, Wards A or B, C, D, and so on; or Wards 1, 2, 3, &c. The middle one will be marked by a flagstaff, and is the office of the establishment, with rooms for the Ward Surgeons, &c. One of these sheds or wards, will contain sixty cots—sometimes, on an emergency, they move them close together, and crowd in more. Some of the barracks are larger, with, of course [,] more inmates. Frequently, there are tents, more comfortable here than one might think, whatever they may be down in the army.

Each ward has a Ward-master, and generally a nurse for every ten or twelve men. A Ward Surgeon has, generally, two wards—although this varies. Some of the wards have a woman nurse; the Armory-square wards have some very good ones. The one in Ward E is one of the best.

.   .   .

[The paragraph omitted here is incorporated in "Patent-Office Hospital" and is collated in the textual notes, *q.v.*]

2

Of course there are among these thousands of prostrated soldiers in hospital here, all sorts of individual cases. On recurring to my note-book, I am puzzled which cases to select to illustrate the average of these young men and their experiences. I may here say, too, in general terms, that I could not wish for more candor and manliness, among all their sufferings, than I find among them.

CASE OF J.A.H., OF COMPANY C., TWENTY-NINTH MASSACHUSETTS

Take this case in Ward 6, Campbell Hospital—a young man from Plymouth County, Massachusetts; a farmer's son, aged about 20 or 21, a soldierly American young fellow, but with sensitive and tender feelings. Most of December and January last, he lay very low, and for quite a while I never expected he would recover. He had become prostrated with an obstinate diarrhœa; his stomach would hardly keep the least thing down, he was vomiting half the time. But that was hardly the worst of it. Let me tell his story—it is but one of thousands.

He had been some time sick with his regiment in the field, in front, but did his duty as long as he could—was in the battle of Fredericksburgh—soon after was put in the regimental hospital. He kept getting worse—could not eat anything they had there—the doctor told him nothing could be done for him there—the poor fellow had fever also—received (perhaps it could not be helped) little or no attention—lay on the ground getting worse. Toward the latter part of December, very much enfeebled, he was sent up from the front, from Falmouth Station, in an open platform car; (such as hogs are transported upon north,) and dumped with a crowd of others on the boat at Aquia Creek, falling down like a rag where they deposited him, too weak and sick to sit up or help himself at all. No one spoke to him or assisted him—he had nothing to eat or drink—was used (amid the great crowds of sick) either with perfect indifference, or, as in two or three instances, with heartless brutality.

On the boat, when night came and the air grew chilly, he tried a long time to undo the blankets he had in his knapsack, but was too feeble. He asked one of the employees, who was moving around deck, for a moment's assistance, to get the blankets. The man asked him back if he could not get them himself? He answered no, he had been trying for more than half an hour, and found himself too weak. The man rejoined, he might then go without them, and walked off. So H. lay chilled and damp, on deck, all night, without anything under or over him, while two good blankets were within reach. It caused him a great injury—nearly cost him his life.

Arrived at Washington, he was brought ashore and again left on the wharf, or above it, amid the great crowds, as before, without any nourishment—not a drink for his parched mouth—no kind hand offered to cover his face from the forenoon sun. Conveyed at last some two miles by the ambulance to the hospital, and assigned a bed, (bed 49, ward 6, Campbell Hospital, January and February, 1863,) he fell down exhausted upon the bed; but the Ward-master (he has since been changed) came to him with a growling order to get up—the rules, he said, permitted no man to lie down in that way with his old clothes on; he must sit up—must first go to the bath-room, be washed, and have his clothes completely changed. (A very good rule, properly applied.) He was taken to the bath-room and scrubbed well with cold water. The attendants, callous for a while, were soon alarmed, for suddenly the half-frozen and lifeless body fell limpsy in their hands, and they hurried it back to the cot, plainly insensible, perhaps dying.

Poor boy! the long train of exhaustion, deprivation, rudeness, no food, no friendly word or deed, but all kinds of upstart airs and impudent, unfeeling speeches and deeds, from all kinds of small officials, (and some big ones,) cutting like razors into that sensitive heart, had at last done the job. He now lay, at times out of his head but quite silent, asking nothing of any one, for some days, with death getting a closer and surer grip upon him—he cared not, or rather he welcomed death. His heart was broken. He felt the struggle to keep up any longer to be useless. God, the world, humanity—all had abandoned him. It would feel so good to shut his eyes forever on the cruel things around him and toward him.

As luck would have it, at this time, I found him. I was passing down Ward No. 6 one day, about dusk (4th of January, I think,) and noticed his glassy eyes, with a look of despair and hopelessness, sunk low in his thin, pallid-brown young face. One learns to divine quickly in the hospital, and as I stopped by him and spoke some commonplace remark, (to which he made no reply,) I saw as I looked that it was a case for ministering to the affection first, and other nourishment and medicines afterward. I sat down by him without any fuss—talked a little—soon saw that it did him good —led him to talk a little himself—got him somewhat interested—wrote a letter for him to his folks in Massachusetts, (to L. H. Campbell, Plymouth County,) soothed him down as I saw he was getting a little too much agitated, and tears in his eyes—gave him some small gifts, and told him I should come again soon. (He has told me since that this little visit, at that hour, just saved him—a day more, and it would have been perhaps too late.)

Of course I did not forget him, for he was a young fellow to interest any one. He remained very sick—vomiting much every day, frequent diarrhœa, and also something like bronchitis, the doctor said. For a while I visited him almost every day—cheered him up—took him some little gifts, and gave him small sums of money, (he relished a drink of new milk, when it was brought through the ward for sale). For a couple of weeks his condition was uncertain—sometimes I thought there was no chance for him at all. But of late he is doing better—is up and dressed, and goes around more and more (Feb. 21) every day. He will not die, but will recover.

The other evening, passing through the ward, he called me—he wanted to say a few words, particular. I sat down by his side on the cot, in the dimness of the long ward, with the wounded soldiers there in their beds, ranging up and down. H. told me I had saved his life. He was in the deepest earnest about it. It was one of those things that repay a soldiers' hospital missionary a thousand-fold—one of the hours he never forgets.

THE FIELD IS LARGE, THE REAPERS FEW

A benevolent person with the right qualities and tact, cannot perhaps make a better investment of himself, at present, anywhere upon the varied surface of the whole of this big world, than in these same military hospitals, among such thousands of most interesting young men. The army is very young—and so much more American than I supposed. Reader, how can I describe to you the mute appealing look that rolls and moves from many a manly eye, from many a sick cot, following you as you walk slowly down one of these wards? To see these, and to be incapable of responding to them, except in a few cases, (so very few compared to the whole of the suffering men,) is enough to make one's heart crack. I go through in some cases cheering up the men; distributing now and then little sums of money—and, regularly, letter-paper and envelopes, oranges, tobacco, jellies, &c., &c.

OFFICIAL AIRS AND HARSHNESS

Many things invite comment, and some of them sharp criticism, in these hospitals. The Government, as I said, is anxious and liberal in its practice toward its sick; but the work has to be left, in its personal application to the men, to hundreds of officials of one grade or another about the hospitals, who are sometimes entirely lacking in the right qualities. There are tyrants and shysters in all positions, and especially those dressed in subordinate authority. Some of the ward doctors are careless, rude, capricious, needlessly strict. One I found who prohibited the men from all enlivening amusements; I found him sending men to the guard-house for the most trifling offence. In general, perhaps, the officials—especially the new ones, with their straps or badges—put on too many airs. Of all places in the world, the hospitals of American young men and soldiers, wounded in the volunteer service of their country, ought to be exempt from mere conventional military airs and etiquette of shoulder-straps. But they are not exempt. W. W.

II   *"Washington in the Hot Season."*

NYT, August 16, 1863.

[The first four paragraphs of this article were reprinted in *MDW*, pages 22–24, under the date *"Aug.* 12," and in *SDC* under the subtitle "Abraham Lincoln," *q.v.;* paragraphs 8–9 were reprinted in *MDW* and *SDC* under the subtitle "Heated Term," and in the present edition in that section and the notes thereto; paragraphs 10–14 were reprinted in *MDW*, pages 21–22, under the date *"Aug.* 8" and in *SDC* under the subtitle "Home-Made Music," and in the present edition in that section and the notes thereto; and paragraphs 15–17, the last of the article, in *MDW* and *SDC* under the subtitle "Soldiers and Talks."]

1 (Paragraphs 5–7)

ONE THING HERE UNRIVALED

Washington is unrivaled for fine healthy shade trees. They come in very good this weather, and indeed go far toward making the place and time endurable. I often retreat to the Capitol grounds, west side. (I should advise that just as soon as the Capitol front is finished, with the splendid entrances to the Senate and Representative wings, the city railroad track on the east side, intersecting the grounds there, be removed to some street further east, and the fine flat space on that side too, be preserved and improved unimpaired.)

As folks know, the back or west side of the Capitol is practically the front of that edifice. Every one goes and comes that way. The grounds on that side are not large, but kept in perfection. I go there occasionally of an afternoon. The dense shade is a great help. The trees are plenty, some of them large, some of them giving out aromatic smells. I find there, (I think the light is extra-powerful here,) besides a large effect of green, varied with the white of the Capitol, fountains playing, locusts whirring, the grass-cutters whetting their scythes, the chirp of robins, the tinkling of the Georgetown and Navy-yard cars as they wind the hill, a few lazy promenaders, soldiers, some with crutches or one-armed, come to take a look, and lots of loungers on the iron settees, completely sheltered from the sun by the dense umbrage.

OUR DRAFT, ETC.

We have put the draft through, have conscribed a goodly lot of whites, blacks and Secessionists; and it is the height of the Summer interregnum of Congress, and there is a lull in the war, and we are having an unprecedented heated term. Men and horses suffer fearfully. The army off at Warrenton, or beyond, bakes in its tents or melts under the march.

In the huge Government hospitals here the poor sick and wounded lie languishing in their cots; and many an old bad wound I find now taking an irrevocable turn for the worst from this cruel heat.

III   *"Our Wounded and Sick Soldiers."*

NYT, Dec. 11, 1864.

[This article consists of fifty-nine paragraphs, most of which were incorporated in *SDC*, to wit: paragraphs 3–5 in "Down at the Front"; 6–8 in "After First Fredericksburg," and 9 in the textual notes to that section; 10–11 and 13–15 in "Back to Washington" and 12 in the textual notes to that section; 16–18 in "Fifty Hours Left Wounded on the Field"; 20 in the textual notes to "Hospital Scenes and Persons"; 21–23 in "The Wounded from Chancellorsville"; 24 in "Bad Wounds—the Young"; 27 in "Ambulance Processions"; 28 in "A New York Soldier"; 34 and the first five lines of 35 in the first part of "Hospitals Ensemble"; 40, in part, in "Army Surgeons—Aid Deficiencies"; 43–44 in "Hospital Scenes.—Incidents"; 45 in "A Case from Second Bull Run"; 54 in "Gifts—Money—Discrimination"; 55 in "Wounds and Diseases"; 56 in "Army Surgeons—Aid Deficiencies." For reprintings before *SDC*, see the textual notes to the sections named above. Other paragraphs are printed below, with proper identification and variants in later reprintings (if any) before *SDC* inserted in brackets.]

1 (Paragraphs 1–2)

As this tremendous war goes on, the public interest becomes more general and gathers more and more closely about the wounded, the sick, the great Government Hospitals, the Surgeons, and all appertaining to the medical department of the army. Up to the date of this writing, (Dec. 9, 1864,) there have been, as I estimate, near 400,000 cases under treatment, and there are to-day, probably, taking the whole service of the United States, 200,000, or an approximation of that number, on the doctors' lists. Half of these are comparatively slight ailments or hurts. Every family has directly or indirectly some representative among this vast army of the wounded and sick.

The following sketch is made to gratify the general interest in this field of the war, and also for a few special persons through whose means alone I have aided the men. It extends over a period of two years, coming down to the present hour, and exhibits the army hospitals at Washington, the camp hospitals in the field, &c. A very few cases are given as specimens of the thousands. The account may be relied upon as faithful, though rapidly thrown together. It will put the reader in as direct contact as may be, with scenes, sights, and cases of these immense hospitals. As will be seen, it begins back two years since, at a very gloomy period of the contest.

2 (*Paragraph 19*)

METHODS OF VISITS, ENLIVENING, ETC.

I continue among the hospitals during March, April, &c., without intermission. My custom is to go through a ward, or collection of wards, endeavoring to give some trifle to each, without missing any. Even a sweet biscuit, a sheet of paper, or a passing word of friendliness, or but a look or nod, if no more. In this way I go through large numbers, without delaying, yet do not hurry. I find out the general mood of the ward at the time; sometimes see that there is a heavy weight of listlessness prevailing, and the whole ward wants cheering up. I, perhaps, read to the men, to break the spell; calling them around me, careful to sit away from the cot of any one who is very bad with sickness or wounds. Also, I find out, by going through in this way, the cases that need special attention, and can then devote proper time to them. Of course, I am very cautious among the patients, in giving them food. I always confer with the doctor, or find out from the nurse or ward-master, about a new case. But I soon get sufficiently familiar with what is to be avoided, and learn also to judge almost intuitively what is best.

3 (*Paragraphs 25–26*)

I buy, during the hot weather, boxes of oranges from time to time, and distribute them among the men; also preserved peaches and other fruits. Also lemons and sugar, for lemonade. Tobacco is also much in demand. Large numbers of the men come up, as usual, without a cent of money. Through the assistance of friends in Brooklyn and Boston, I am again able to help many of those that fall in my way. It is only a small sum in each case, but it is much to them. As before, I go around daily and talk with the men, to cheer them up.

My note books are full of memoranda of the cases of this Summer, and the wounded from Chancellorsville, but space forbids my transcribing them.

4 (*Paragraphs 29–33*)

VISITS CONTINUED—HOSPITAL WISDOM

August, September, October, &c.—I continue among the hospitals in the same manner, getting still more experience, and daily and nightly meeting with most interesting cases. Through the winter of 1863–4, the same. The work of the Army Hospital Visitor is indeed a trade, an art, requiring both experience and natural gifts, and the greatest judgment. A large number of the visitors go from curiosity—as to a show of animals. Others give the men improper things. Then there are always some poor fellows in the cases of sickness or wounds, that imperatively need perfect quiet—not to be talked to by strangers. Few realize that it is not the mere giving of gifts that does good: it is the proper adaptation. Nothing is of any avail among the soldiers except conscientious personal investigation of cases, each one for itself; with sharp, critical faculties, but in the fullest spirit of human sympathy and boundless love. The men feel such love, always, more than anything else. I have met very few persons who realize the importance of humoring the yearnings for love and friendship of these American young men, prostrated by sickness and wounds.

CULPEPPER AND BRANDY STATION

February, 1864.—I am down at Culpepper and Brandy Station, among the camps of the First, Second and Third Corps, and going through the division hospitals. The condition of the camps here this Winter is immensely improved from last Winter near Falmouth. All the army is now in huts of logs and mud, with fireplaces: and the food is plentiful and deposited in the Washington hospitals, mostly but to linger awhile and die, after being kept at the front too long.
and tolerably good. In the camp hospitals I find diarrhœa more and more prevalent, and in chronic form. It is at present the great disease of the army. I think the doctors generally give too much medicine, oftener making things worse. Then they hold on to the cases in camp too long. When the disease is almost fixed beyond remedy, they send it up to Washington. Alas! how many such wrecks have I seen landed from boat and railroad,
The hospitals in front, this Winter, are also much improved. The men have cots and often wooden floors, and the tents are well warmed.

MARCH AND APRIL, 1864

Back again in Washington. They are breaking up the camp hospitals in Meade's army, preparing for a move. As I write this in March, there are all the signs. Yesterday and last night the sick were arriving here in long trains, all day and night. I was among the new comers most of the night. One train of a thousand came into the depot, and others followed. The ambulances were going all night, distributing them to the various hospitals here. When they come in, some literally in a dying condition, you may well imagine it is a lamentable sight. I hardly know which is worse, to see the wounded after a battle, or these wasted wrecks.

I remain in capital health and strength, and go every day, as before, among the men, in my own way, enjoying my life and occupation more than I can tell.

5 (*Last part of paragraph 35 and paragraphs 36–42*)

Any one of these hospitals is a little city in itself. Take, for instance, the Carver Hospital, out a couple of miles, on a hill, northern part of Fourteenth-street. It has more inmates than an ordinary country town. The same with the Lincoln Hospital, east of the Capitol, or the Finley Hospital, on high grounds northeast of the city; both large establishments. Armory-square Hospital, under Dr. Bliss, in Seventh-street, (one of the best anywhere,) is also temporarily enlarged this Summer, with additional tents, sheds, &c. It must have nearly a hundred tents, wards, sheds, and structures of one kind and another. The worst cases are always to be found here.

A wanderer like me about Washington, pauses on some high land which commands the sweep of the city, (one never tires of the noble and ample views presented here, in the generally fine, soft, peculiar air and light,) and has his eyes attracted by these white clusters of barracks in almost every direction. They make a great show in the landscape, and I often use them as landmarks.

Some of these clusters are very full of inmates. Counting the whole, with the convalescent camps, (whose inmates are often worse off than the sick in the hospitals,) they have numbered, in this quarter and just down the Potomac, as high as fifty thousand invalid, disabled, or sick and dying men.

WOUNDED FROM WILDERNESS, SPOTTSYLVANIA, ETC.

My sketch has already filled up so much room that I shall have to omit any detailed account of the wounded of May and June, 1864, from the battles of the Wilderness, Spottsylvania, etc. That would be a long history in itself. The arrivals, the numbers, and the severity of the wounds, outvied anything that we had seen before. For days and weeks the melancholy tide set in upon us. The weather was very hot; the wounded had been delayed in coming, and much neglected. Very many of the wounds had worms in them. An unusual proportion mortified. It was among these that, for the first time in my life, I began to be prostrated with real sickness, and was, before the close of the Summer, imperatively ordered North by the physicians, to recuperate and have an entire change of air.

LAMENTABLE DEFICIENCIES AFTER HEAVY BATTLES

What I know of first Fredericksburgh, Chancellorsville, Wilderness, &c., makes clear to me that there has been, and is yet, a total lack of science in elastic adaptation to the needs of the wounded, after a battle. The hospitals are long afterward filled with proofs of this.

I have seen many battles, their results, but never one where there was not, during the first few days, an unaccountable and almost total deficiency of everything for the wounded, appropriate sustenance—nursing, cleansing, medicines, stores, &c.

．　．　．

[The rest of paragraph 40 was used in the section "Army Surgeons—Aid Deficiencies," *q.v.*]

ASSISTANCE—MORE ABOUT HOSPITAL VISITING AS AN ART

The reader has doubtless inferred the fact that my visits among the wounded and sick have been as an Independent Missionary, in my own style, and not as agent for any commission. Several noble women and men of Brooklyn, Boston, Salem and Providence have voluntarily supplied funds at times. I only wish they could see a tithe of the actual work performed by their generous and benevolent assistance, among these suffering men.

He who goes among the soldiers with gifts, &c., must beware how he proceeds. It is much more of an art than one would imagine. They are not charity-patients, but American young men, of pride and independence. The spirit in which you treat them, and bestow your donations, is just as important as the gifts themselves; sometimes more so. Then there is continual [*NYWG*, Sixth Paper: continual hygienic] discrimination necessary. Each [*NYWG*, Sixth Paper: Besides, each] case requires some peculiar adaptation to itself. It is very important to slight nobody—not a single case. Some hospital visitors, especially the women, pick out the handsomest looking soldiers, or have a few for their pets. Of course some will attract you more than others, and some will need more attention than others; but be careful not to ignore any patient. A word, a friendly turn of the eye, or touch of the hand in passing, if nothing more.

6 (*Paragraphs 46–53*)

CONVALESCENT CAMP

Through Fourteenth-street to the river, and then over Long [*NYWG*, Sixth Paper: over the Long] Bridge, and some three miles beyond, is the huge collection called the Convalescent Camp. It is a respectable sized army in itself, for these hospitals, tents, sheds, &c., at times contain from five to ten thousand men. Of course, there are continual changes. Large squads are sent off to their regiments or elsewhere, and new men received. Sometimes I found large numbers of paroled returned prisoners here.

LATTER PART OF 1864 IN NEW-YORK

During October, November and December, 1864, I have visited the military hospitals about New-York City, but have not room in this article to describe these visits.

I have lately been (Nov. 25) in the Central Park Hospital, near One Hundred and Fourth-street. It seems to be a well-managed institution.

During September, and previously, went many times to the Brooklyn City Hospital, in Raymond-street, where I found (taken in by contract) a number of wounded and sick from the army. Most of the men were badly off, and without a cent of money, many wanting tobacco. I supplied them, and a few special cases with delicacies, also repeatedly with letter-paper, stamps, envelopes, &c., writing the addresses myself plainly, (a pleased crowd gathering around me, as I directed for each one in turn.) This Brooklyn hospital is a bad place for soldiers, or anybody else. Cleanliness, proper nursing, watching, &c., are more deficient than in any hospital I know. For dinner on Sundays, I invariably found nothing but rice and molasses. The men all speak well of Drs. Yale and Kissam for kindness, patience, &c., and I think, from what I saw, they are also skillful young medical men. But in its management otherwise, this is the poorest hospital I have yet been in, out of many hundreds.

HOSPITAL, ASYLUM, ETC., AT FLATBUSH, L.I.

Among places, apart from soldiers', visited lately, (Dec. 7,) I must specially mention the great Brooklyn General Hospital and other public institutions at Flatbush, including the extensive Lunatic Asylum, under charge of Drs. Chapin and Reynolds. Of the latter (and I presume I might include these county establishments generally) I have deliberately to put on record about the profoundest satisfaction with professional capacity, completeness of house arrangements to ends required, and the right vital spirit animating all, that I have yet found in any public curative institution among civilians.

READING, INTERESTING THE MEN, ETC.

In Washington, in camp, and everywhere, I was in the habit of reading to the men. They were very fond of it, and like declamatory poetical pieces. Miles O'Reilly's pieces were also great favorites. I have had many

happy evenings with the men. We would gather in a large group by ourselves, after supper, and spend the time in such readings, or in talking, and
occasionally by an amusing game called the game of Twenty Questions.

WOMEN NURSES

Middle-aged women and mothers of families are best. I am com-
pelled to say young ladies, however refined, educated and benevolent,
do not succeed as army nurses, though their motives are noble; neither do
the Catholic nuns. Mothers, full of motherly feeling, and however illiterate, but bringing reminiscences of home, and with the magnetic touch
of hands, are the true women nurses. Many of the wounded are between 15
and 20 years of age.

GOVERNMENT CARE FOR WOUNDED

I should say that the Government, from my observation, is always
full of anxiety and liberality toward the sick and wounded. The system in
operation in the permanent hospitals is good, and the money flows without
stint. But the details have to be left to hundreds and thousands of subordinate officials. Among these, laziness, heartlessness, gouging and incom-
petency are more or less prevalent. Still, I consider the permanent hospitals, generally, well conducted.

7 (Paragraphs 57–59)

AMOUNT OF THE TWO YEARS' VISITS

During my two years in the hospitals and upon the field, I have
made over 600 visits, and have been, as I estimate, among from 80,000
to 100,000 of the wounded and sick, as sustainer of spirit and body in
some slight degree, in their time of need. These visits varied from an
hour or two, to all day or night; for with dear or critical cases I watched
all night. Sometimes I took up my quarters in the hospital, and slept or
watched there several nights in succession. I may add that I am now
just resuming my occupation in the hospitals and camps for the winter of
1864–5, and probably to continue the seasons ensuing.

HUMAN MAGNETISM AS A MEDICAL AGENT

To many of the wounded and sick, especially the youngsters, there
is something in personal love, caresses and the magnetic flood of [*NYWG,
Sixth Paper:* something in the magnetism of] sympathy and friendship,
that does, in its way, more good than all the medicine in the world. I have
spoken of my regular gifts of delicacies, money, tobacco, special articles of

food, nick-nacks, [*NYWG*, Sixth Paper: knick-knacks,] &c., &c. But I steadily found more and more, that I could help and turn [*NYWG*, Sixth Paper: could turn] the balance in favor of cure, by the means here alluded to, in a curiously large proportion of cases. The American soldier is full of affection, [*NYWG*, Sixth Paper: The average American soldier is full not only of pride but of affection,] and the yearning for affection. And it comes wonderfully grateful to him to have this yearning gratified when he is laid up with painful wounds or illness, far away from home, among strangers. Many will think this merely sentimentalism, [*NYWG*, Sixth Paper: merely imaginary,] but I know it is the most solid of facts. I believe that even [*NYWG*, Sixth Paper: facts. Even] the moving around among the men, or through the ward, of a hearty, healthy, clean, strong, generous-souled person, man or woman, full of humanity and love, sending out invisible, constant currents thereof, does immense good to the sick and wounded.

CONCLUSION

To those who might be interested in knowing it, I must add, in conclusion, that I have tried to do justice to all the suffering that fell in my way. While I have been with wounded and sick in thousands of cases from the New-England States, and from New-York, New-Jersey and Pennsylvania, and from Michigan, Wisconsin, Indiana, Illinois and the Western States, I have been with more or less from all the States North and South, without exception. I have been with many from the border States, especially from Maryland and Virginia, and found far more Union Southerners than is supposed. I have been with many rebel officers and men among our wounded, and given them always what I had, and tried to cheer them the same as any. I have been among the army teamsters considerably, and indeed always find myself drawn to them. Among the black soldiers, wounded or sick, and in the contraband camps, I also took my way whenever in their neighborhood, and did what I could for them.

Walt Whitman.

IV   *"The Soldiers."*

NYT, March 6, 1865.

[This article was almost all used in *SDC*: paragraphs 1–2 in "The Blue Everywhere," 3 in "A Yankee Soldier," 4 in "A Model Hospital," 5–7 in "Boys in the Army," 8 in "Burial of a Lady Nurse," 9 in "Female Nurses for Soldiers," and 10, out of sequence, in "A Secesh Brave." For reprintings before *SDC*, see the textual notes to the sections named. The postscript, following the tenth paragraph and Whitman's name, omitted in *SDC*, is printed in the textual notes to "A Secesh Brave," *q.v.*]

v   *" 'Tis But Ten Years Since," First Paper.*

NYWG, January 24, 1874.

[Of the twenty-four paragraphs of this article, the following were reprinted: paragraphs 5–6 in *MDW*, pp. 3–4, and in *SDC* in "A Happy Hour's Command" and the textual notes to that section; 9 in *MDW*, p. 65, "Notes," and in *SDC* in "Origins of Attempted Secession" and the textual notes to that section in *Prose 1892,* II; 12 and 15–20 in *SDC* in "Death of Abraham Lincoln" and the textual notes to that section in *Prose 1892,* II, and 16–18 previously in the footnote, pp. 22–23 of *MDW; 21* in *MDW,* p. 60, "Notes," and *SDC* in "Opening of the Secession War." The remaining paragraphs of *NYWG,* First Paper, are printed in this appendix.]

1 (Paragraphs 1–2)

[These paragraphs were reprinted in *MDW,* p. 65, "Notes."]

Already, the events of 1863 and '4, and the reasons that immediately preceded, as well as those that closely followed them, have quite lost their direct personal impression, and the living heat and excitement of their own time, and are being marshalled for casting, or getting ready to be cast, into the cold and bloodless electrotype plates of History.

Or if we admit that the savage temper and wide differences of opinion, and feelings of wrongs, and mutual recriminations, that led to the Secession War and flamed in its mortal conflagration, may not have yet entirely burnt themselves out, still, all will acknowledge that the embers of them are already dying embers, and a few more winters and summers, a few more rains and snows, will surely quench their fires, and leave them only as a far off memory.

2 (Paragraphs 3–4)

Different indeed our America of the present, and its position and prospects, from those murky clouds and storms, and weeks of suspense, and mortal doubt and dismay, of But 10 Years Since, reddened with gouts of blood, and pallid with wholesale death.

The present! Our great Centennial of 1876 nigher and nigher at hand —the abandonment, by tacit consent, of dead issues—the general readjustment and rehabilitation, at least by intention and beginning, South and North, to the exigencies of the Present and Future—the momentous nebulæ left by the convulsions of the previous thirty years definitely considered and settled by the re-election of Gen. Grant—the Twenty-second Presidentiad well-sped on its course—the inevitable unfolding and development of this tremendous complexity we call the United States—our Union with restored, doubled, trebled solidity seems to vault unmistakably to dominant position among the governments of the world in extent, population, products, and in the permanent sources of naval and military power.

3 (*Paragraphs 7–11*)

A THOUGHT OR SO, UPON THE THRESHOLD

But before entering on my personal memoranda of the war, I have one or two thoughts to ventilate before they are entirely out of date. Strange, that those months and years, and all that marked them, with the vividest of their experiences and impressions, should so soon pass away— as they seem already to have passed—like a dream!

Everything indeed moves in our lands and age, with such a velocity, on such a large scale, and such resistless force (altogether regardless of, and unmeasured by, the old standards, other lands, former times,) that I have to stop a moment as I now write out—January, 1874—these opening lines to some of my memoranda, and ask myself whether it is indeed so lately since we were in the midst of that thunder-roll of fratricidal fights—that deluge of ruin and death, threatening to submerge the whole Union.

·   ·   ·

SOLID LAND APPEARING—THE PEAKS OF THE FUTURE

[For paragraph 9, under this subtitle, see "Origins of Attempted Secession" and the textual notes to that section, *Prose 1892*, II.]

·   ·   ·

POINTS OF RELIEF ALREADY

Already points of good unerringly begin, and will in due time overbalance the losses. Among the rest, two cases of relief are even now particularly welcome. In the Southern States, riddance of that special class forever blowing about "the South." The North and West have had, and still have, their full share of bladder humanity, but in the old Slave States there seemed to exist no end of blusterers, braggarts, windy, melodramatic, continually screaming in falsetto, a nuisance to the States, their own just as much as any; altogether the most impudent persons that have yet appeared in the history of lands, and, up to 1860, with the most incredible successes, having pistol'd, bludgeoned, yelled and threatened America into one long train of cowardly concessions.

The North, too, has now eliminated, or is fast eliminating from itself, a fierce, unreasoning squad of men and women, quite insane, concentrating their thoughts upon a single fact and idea—(in the land, of all the world the land of all facts, all ideas)—full as welcome a release here as the riddance there. By that war, *exit* Fire-Eaters—*exit* Abolitionists.

4 (*Paragraphs 13–14, the last two under the subtitle "Our Surging Politics from 1840–'60."*)

(What would have been the condition of things in the United States—and what would it be now—if the secession quarrel had been compromised? which was the other name, of course, for yielding substantially to all the demands of the planters and their satellites).

It is difficult enough now to resume the anxieties and fears which at that period, amid all our material prosperity, spread like a lowering horizon over the whole land. In Europe, too, were everywhere heard underground rumblings, that died out, only to again surely return. While in the New World, the volcano, though civic yet, continued to grow more and more convulsive—more and more lurid, stormy and seething.

5 (*Paragraphs 22–23, the last two under the subtitle "Night of April 13," etc., and paragraph 24, concluding the First Paper.*)

The ball had been opened, then! Not only the *first gun* had been fired—and as if to show that it was no mere freak of passion, deliberately by an aged, highly educated, and wealthy Southerner—but continued rounds from well-organized batteries.

(Said first gun was fired by Edmund Ruffin, a prominent Virginian, seventy years of age. To anticipate a little I will give the gloomy conclusion of this enthusiastic personal episode, as it took place in less than five years. Soon after the surrender of General Lee and the collapse of the rebellion Mr. Ruffin committed suicide, June, '65, at his residence in Amelia county, Virginia, near Mattaox. He was seventy-four years old. The Richmond *Whig*, a couple of days after, gave the following account: "It is now said that Mr. Ruffin's mind had been very perceptibly affected since the evacuation of Richmond and the surrender of the Confederate armies. For a week previous to terminating his life, Mr. Ruffin kept his chamber, busily employed in writing what subsequently turned out to be a history of his political life. He also wrote letters, and in one of them he left directions as to the disposal of his body. He bathed himself, put on clean under and outer clothing, and directed that his body should be buried in the habiliments he had put on, without shroud or coffin. He then seated himself in a chair, put a loaded musket to his mouth, and, leaning back, struck the trigger with his hickory stick. The first cap did not explode, and he replaced it by another, which discharged the musket, the charge of ball and buck blowing off the crown of the venerable old gentleman's head, and scattering his brains and snowy hair against the ceiling of the room. When the family, alarmed by the report, reached Mr. Ruffin's room he was found lying back in his chair, the gun leaning against him, and life gone. A paragraph in the letter left for the perusal of family and friends, explained the tragic deed. It reads: 'I cannot survive the loss of the liberties of my country.' ")

THE EVE OF A LONG WAR

I have now given out of my memoranda what may be called the overtures of the war—the first appearance of Lincoln on the scene, the firing of the first rounds by the Disunionists at Charleston, and the reception of the news in the Free States. In my next paper, after itemizing the prompt uprisal at the North, I shall bring back First Bull Run, and describe what ensued immediately and for several days in Washington City, after the shock and humiliation of that unlooked-for-defeat.

(TO BE CONTINUED)

VI " '*Tis But Ten Years Since*," *Second Paper.*

NYWG, February 7, 1874.

[This article contains twenty-four paragraphs, of which the following were reprinted: paragraphs 1–3 in MDW, p. 60 and in SDC "National Uprising and Volunteering"; 5–6 in MDW, p. 60 and SDC "Contemptuous Feeling"; 7 and 10–18 in MDW, pp. 60–62 and SDC "Battle of Bull Run, July, 1861"; 8–9 and 19–20 in MDW, p. 62 and SDC "The Stupor Passes—Something Else Begins"; 22 in MDW, pp. 5–6 and SDC, the last paragraph of "The Real War Will Never Get in the Books"; and 23 in MDW, p. 65 and in SDC, near the end of "Origins of Attempted Secession," to be included in *Prose 1892*, II. The remaining paragraphs of the Second Paper are printed below.]

1 (*Paragraph 4, the last under the subtitle "National Uprising and Enthusiasm, [Yet with a Drawback],*" *and paragraphs 21 and 24, concluding the Second Paper.*)

But while the Nationalists were arming in an undoubted majority, and exhibiting a spirit that made it madness to oppose them, there was still a wide secession affiliation and sympathy at the North, especially in New York City and Philadelphia—indeed, everywhere at the North, much more than was shown or spoken outright, and continued through the whole war, waiting always for a good chance to make a sortie in any way that would tell best; but it was at first utterly cowed by the general and sudden rising, and though afterward a source of great anxiety to the Government, it never got the coveted chance of successfully showing its treachery, and eventually went under.

.   .   .

THE INNER POINTS OF THE WAR CAN NEVER BE WRITTEN

For the remaining part of my sketches I shall adopt the diary form, in chronological order. The events of the remainder of '61, and most of those of '62, were not of momentous interest North and East, though exciting the West—the bloody battle of Shiloh, the surrender of Island No. 10, the lower Mississippi occupied, and New Orleans taken by Farragut.

.   .   .

ITEMS OF MY NEXT

In my next paper I shall come to the battle of First Fredericksburg, and shall enter on my experiences among the wounded in the Army Hospitals, which latter rapidly became a large feature in the war. I shall also give a brief, hitherto unpublished account of the actual particulars of the capture of the United States vessel Hatteras by the Alabama, in the Gulf of Mexico, at the commencement of 1863.

(TO BE CONTINUED)

VII   *" 'Tis But Ten Years Since," Third Paper.*
NYWG, February 14, 1874.
[This article contains twenty-five paragraphs, of which paragraphs 1–3, 7–9, and 15–23 had previously been published in the NYT article, Dec. 11, 1864. Paragraphs 1–3, 7–9, and 15–23 were reprinted in both MDW and SDC; paragraph 4 was reprinted only in MDW, and 5–6 and 10–14 were not reprinted. The paragraphs that were not reprinted in SDC are printed below, with the exception of paragraph 4, which is printed in Appendix XI, 2.]

1   (Paragraphs 5–6; which with 4, have the subtitle "An Artillery Storm.")

The battle comprised December 12, 13, 14 and 15. On the 11th the engineers succeeded in bridging the Rappahannock with pontoons and keeping their integrity; and on that day and the 12th, (though troubled by the rebel sharp-shooters,) our men crossed over, and did pretty much what they pleased in Fredericksburgh.

Saturday, 13th, was the main battle. Our troops, with a courage and coolness, taken in the whole, never excelled anywhere, advanced upon some of the strongest natural positions in the world, receding and rising terraces, fortified tier upon tier with well-handled batteries, protected by covers of swarming rebel sharp-shooters, superb marksmen, in impromptu rifle-pits wherein they concealed themselves. Sunday, 14th, we lay upon the contested field. That night and the next day we recrossed the river in good order to our old camp on the Falmouth side. But our losses in killed and wounded had been fearful.

> 2 (*Paragraphs 10–14, under the subtitle "The Scene Shifted from Land—Specimen Case of a Rebel Capture at Sea."*)

1863—Sunday, January 11.—This evening occurred one of the first of those captures, afterwards so common, by rebel privateers at sea. It was about thirty miles off the coast of Galveston, Texas. (I am able to give here an exact account, hitherto unpublished.) It is a specimen of many cases of the kind, and was the entrapping by the Alabama of the United States steamer Hatteras. The latter had been signalled from Galveston to pursue a doubtful-looking steamer, a stranger—went on and on several hours—it got to be towards evening—came up—the stranger showed English colors. Captain Blake, of the Hatteras, hailed her—asked who she was. She answered, "We are Her Britannic Majesty's steamer Vixen." Captain Blake rejoined, "Then lay to, and I will send a boat aboard," (intending to send his compliments, &c.) The two vessels, in the half-dusk, lay less than 200 feet apart. The boat was lowered—had just touched the water, when a voice (Captain Semmes) sang out from the stranger, "You needn't come —I am the Confederate vessel Alabama,"—and instantly, without a moment's intermission or warning, sent a full broadside into the unsuspecting Hatteras.

The engagement then commenced. It is a mistake to suppose, as has been asserted and published, that there was no fight. There was a fierce one of half an hour's duration—two men killed and eighteen wounded. The effort of the Hatteras was to board the Alabama; and she would have done so—was on the move and was likely to do it—when a shot from the Alabama went into her steam chamber, and she lay at once helpless, in full control of the rebel cruiser. The crew and officers of the Hatteras were transferred rapidly in boats to the Alabama, and as soon as they touched the decks were paroled—not a moment's delay.

(Out of the 158 men of the Alabama only eight were Americans—and five of these eight were a family of brothers, Southern pilots of the name of

King. Nearly all the hands were English; there were no Irish in the rebel crew, or very few indeed; there were two or three Austrians, and one Italian.)

The Alabama immediately sailed for Kingston, into which port she made a gala-entrance with her prize. Bands on the English vessels and ashore played "Dixie," and all Kingston went to hurrahing and treating and shaking hands in great glee.

The officers and crew of the Hatteras came on to Key West in the Borodino, and thence to New York in a Government vessel.

[Whitman received an account of this incident from a young man who had been an officer on the *Hatteras*. See the letter to his mother March 31, 1863.]

3 (*Paragraphs 24–25, subtitled "The Army Wounded," concluding the Third Paper.*)

In my Fourth Paper, next week, I shall give a fuller description of the immense army hospitals, with characteristic cases.

[Though following and running into the others, each paper is, for the reader's purposes, complete in itself. It but makes almost random selections out of a vast mass of contemporaneous memoranda. Of those notes of Soldiers, Hospitals, Battles, President Lincoln, &c., I collate some of them now to occupy and while away the tedium of a strange illness, paralysis disabling me bodily, temporarily. They are significant, if at all, of the vast and interesting, indescribable *arriere*—the graves of the past, nearly obliterated, though but ten years have intervened. Phantoms now, yet terribly real then—a countless crowd, still fading, still receding—of which each here, flashed from life, is but a rapid suggestion-sketch.—W. W. Camden, N.J., February 5, 1874.]

(TO BE CONTINUED)

VIII   *" 'Tis But Ten Years Since," Fourth Paper.*

NYWG, February 21, 1874.

[This article contains eighteen paragraphs, none of which had been previously published. The following paragraphs were reprinted: Paragraph 2 in MDW, p. 28, and in SDC in "Hospital Perplexity"; 4 in MDW, p. 9, and in SDC, the first paragraph of "Hospital Scenes and Persons"; 5–6 in MDW, pp. 11–12, and SDC, "An Army Hospital Ward"; 7–9 in MDW, p. 12, and SDC, "A Connecticut Case"; 10 in MDW, p. 12, and SDC, "Two Brooklyn Boys"; 14–15 in MDW, pp. 26–27, and SDC, the latter part of "Hospitals Ensemble"; 17 in MDW, p. 31, and SDC, lines 8–13 of "Summer of 1864"; and 18 in MDW, p. 36, and SDC (in part), "Gifts—Money—Discrimination." The rest of the Fourth Paper is printed below.]

1 (Paragraph 1, the first under the subtitle "Fifty Army Hospitals Here—1863—Spring.")

You will easily judge that one of the greatest institutions of Washington and its neighborhood this current time is the Hospital. I don't mean by that any particular hospital, for I think there are about fifty such establishments. There is a regular directory of them printed in most of the papers here in alphabetical order, and it has a dreary significance. Now, such a list makes a Washington journal much more called for, and is an indispensable part of the intelligence sought here.

2 (Paragraph 3, with the subtitle "My Visits and Distributions.")

I now regularly devote from four to five hours every day or evening going among the sick and wounded. I have not yet been to all the Washington establishments; to visit them effectually would be next to impossible for one visitor. I keep going a good deal to Campbell and Armory squares, and Judiciary and Emory Hospitals, and occasionally to that at the Patent Office (now broken up), and once or twice to others. There is plenty to do, and one soon falls in the way of putting his means where it will do the most good. Tobacco I buy by the quantity, and cut it up in small plugs. Then I buy now and then a box of oranges. Everything at retail is dear here in Washington (and wholesale, too, for that matter).

3 (Paragraphs 11–12, under the subtitle "About Mules.")

One hardly supposed there were so many mules in the Western world as you see these times about Washington and everywhere in the military camps, little and large, through Virginia. Saturday forenoon last on K street, moving up, I saw an immense drove of mules, I should think towards two thousand, and most of them very fine animals. Three or four horsemen went just ahead, with peculiar cries that seemed to have a kind of charm over the creatures, for those along the front part of the drove followed the shouting horsemen implicitly, and thus the great mass were drawn resistlessly on. Other horsemen—a score of them—dashed athwart the sides, whipping in the stragglers; but it was remarkable to me how such a great mule army in motion kept together with so little perversity and off-shooting. The charm was the magnetic shouting of the men on the lead, and the keeping of the mass in pretty good headway all the time.

But there was one obstinate fellow that redeemed the mulish reputation. Some two or three minutes after the mass entire had passed along, followed two horsemen having a sullen, laggard skedaddler under their charge. He had evidently deserted a while before, and made them a good deal of trouble. It was quite fresh and nomadic, the way these two primal cavaliers, well mounted as they were on expert nags, turned short and halted, and veered and sped on, and turned again, and surrounded and cut off the persistent efforts of muley to get away.

4 (*Paragraph 13, the first under the subtitle "Still More of the Hospitals."*)

Washington, 1863—Summer.—Great as the Army Hospitals already are, they are rapidly growing greater and greater. I have heard that the number of our army sick regularly under treatment now exceeds three hundred and fifty thousand. They are spread everywhere. Here and in the cities of the Middle and Northeastern States, they are collected in establishments already assuming special character, with much that is novel and national.

5 (*Paragraph 16, the first under the subtitle "Long One-Story Wooden Barracks."*)

In general terms a hospital in and around Washington is a cluster of long one-story wooden buildings for the sick wards, and lots of other edifices and large and small tents. There will be ten or twelve wards grouped together, named A, B, C, &c., or numerically 1, 2, or 3, &c. One of these wards will be a hundred to a hundred and fifty feet long, twenty-five or thirty feet wide, and eighteen or twenty feet high, well-windowed, white-washed inside and out, and kept very clean. It will contain from sixty to a hundred cots, a row on each side, and a space down the middle. In summer the cots often have musquito-curtains, and look airy and nice. Nearly all the wards are ornamented with evergreens, cheap pictures, &c.

IX   " '*Tis But Ten Years Since,*" *Fifth Paper.*

NYWG, February 28, 1874.

[This article contains seventeen paragraphs; of these, paragraphs 4–6, 8–10, and 15 had been published previously in NYT, Dec. 11, 1864, and paragraphs 8 and 16–17 had been published in NYT, March 6, 1865. Paragraph 1 is in MDW, p. 30, and SDC, in the first paragraph of "Summer of 1864"; 3 (in part) in MDW, p. 31, and in SDC, lines 14–20 of "Summer of 1864"; 4–6 in MDW, p. 13, and in SDC, "The Wounded from Chancellorsville"; 7 in MDW, pp. 12–13, and in SDC, "A Secesh Brave"; 8 in MDW, p. 33, and in SDC, "A

Yankee Soldier"; 9 in *MDW*, p. 18, and in *SDC*, "Ambulance Processions"; 10 in *MDW*, pp. 18–19, and in *SDC*, "Bad Wounds—the Young"; 11 in *MDW*, pp. 39–40, and *SDC*, "Female Nurses for Soldiers"; 12 in *MDW*, p. 39, and *SDC*, "Burial of a Lady Nurse"; 15 in *MDW*, p. 21, and *SDC*, in "A New York Soldier"; and 16–17 in *MDW*, p. 38, and *SDC*, in "The Blue Everywhere." For variant texts of all paragraphs reprinted in *SDC*, see the textual notes to the sections named. The rest of the Fifth Paper is printed below.]

1 (*Paragraph 2*)

I distribute tobacco in small plugs, with clay pipes, and so on. I think smoking ought not only to be allowed, but rather encouraged, among the men in every ward. I myself never used a pinch of tobacco in any way, but I am clear that in soldiers' hospitals, in barracks, it would be good for the men and neutralize exhalations.

2 (*Paragraphs 13–14: "Abraham Lincoln Again."*)

Monday, June 29.—To-day, about half-past six P.M., I saw the President going by in his two-horse barouche toward his nightly retreat, the Soldiers' Home. He was guarded by about twenty-five cavalry. The barouche goes on the lead under a slow trot, driven by one man on the box and no servant or footman beside; the cavalry all follow closely two and two with a lieutenant at their head, riding at the side of the carriage. I had a good view of the President. He looks more careworn even than usual, his face with deep lines and his complexion a kind of gray through his dark brown swarthy skin. I said to a lady who was looking with me, "Who can see that man without losing all disposition to be sharp upon him personally? He has certainly a good soul." The lady assented, although she condemns the course of the President as not pronounced enough.

The equipage is far from showy; indeed, rather shabby; the horses second-rate. The President dresses in plain black clothes, wears what is called the dress hat (the cylinder with a rim). He first drove over to the house of Secretary of War Mr. Stanton, on K Street, where, in a couple of minutes, Mr. S. came out, and the two had a talk of several minutes, when the Presidential equipage drove off.

x " *'Tis But Ten Years Since,*" *Sixth Paper.*

NYWG, March 7, 1874.

[This article contains twenty paragraphs, of which paragraphs 6, 10, and 13–15 had been previously published in *NYT*, Dec. 11, 1864. Paragraphs 1–5 were reprinted in *MDW*, pp. 25–26, and in *SDC*, "Death of a Wisconsin Officer"; 7–8 in *MDW*, p. 31, and in *SDC*, latter part of "Summer of 1864"; 10 in

MDW, p. 46, and in *SDC*, "Wounds and Diseases"; 11–12 in *MDW*, p. 36, and in *SDC*, "Gifts—Money—Discrimination"; 14–15 in *MDW*, pp. 32–33, and in *SDC*, "Hospital Scenes.—Incidents"; 16 in *MDW*, pp. 54–55, and in *SDC*, "Calhoun's Real Monument"; 17–18 in *MDW*, pp. 52–53, and in *SDC*, "Western Soldiers"; and 19–20 in *MDW*, pp. 55–56, and in *SDC*, "Three Years Summ'd Up." The rest of the Sixth Paper is printed elsewhere in the Appendix as indicated below.]

1 *(Paragraph 6. See Appendix III, 7, second paragraph.)*

2 *(Paragraph 9: "Convalescent Camp." See Appendix III, 6.)*

3 *(Paragraph 13. See Appendix III, 5, last paragraph.)*

XI *Memoranda During the War, 1875–76.*

[All of *MDW*, including the "Notes" at the end, pp. 59–68, was reprinted in *Two Rivulets* from the same plates without change, and with the same pagination. Those parts of *MDW* not included in *SDC* are printed below in the Appendix, with variant readings of earlier printings, if any, inserted in brackets or otherwise clearly indicated. Each continuous passage, as elsewhere in the Appendix, is given an Arabic numeral, and its place in *MDW* identified.]

1

[The last half of p. 3 and most of p. 4 of *MDW;* the first part, through the sentence ending "meditation.)", had been previously published in paragraphs 5 and 6 of the First Paper of "Ten Years," *NYWG*, and variants in that text are inserted in brackets.]

Even these days, at the lapse of many years, I [*NYWG:* days I] can never turn [*NYWG:* never take them up or turn] their tiny leaves, or even take one in my hand, without [*NYWG:* leaves, without] the actual army sights and hot emotions of the time rushing [*NYWG:* actual camp and hospital and army sights from '62 to '5 rushing] like a river in full tide through me. Each line, each scrawl, each memorandum, has [*NYWG:* Each page, nay each line, has] its history. Some pang of anguish—some tragedy, [*NYWG:* some heroic life, or more heroic death, is in every one; some tragedy,] profounder than ever poet wrote. Out [*NYWG:* wrote. To me, the war, abdicating all its grand historical aspects, and entirely untouched by the Slavery question, revolves around these miniature pages, and what is designated by them. They are the closest; they are not words, but magic spells. Out] of them arise active [*NYWG:* arise yet active] and breathing forms. They summon up, even in this silent and vacant room as I write, not only the sinewy regiments and brigades, marching or in camp, but the countless phantoms of those who fell and were hastily buried by wholesale in the battle-pits, or whose dust and bones have been since removed to the National Cemeteries of the land, especially through [*NYWG*: Cemeteries, all through] Virginia and Tennessee. (Not [*NYWG* begins a new paragraph with "Not" and omits the mark of parenthesis.— ED.] Northern soldiers only—many indeed the Carolinian, Georgian, Alabamian, Louisianian, Virginian—many a Southern face and form, pale, emaciated, with that strange tie of confidence [*NYWG*: of subtlest confidence] and love between us, welded by sickness, pain of wounds, and little daily, nightly offices of nursing and friendly words and visits, comes up amid the rest, and does not mar, but rounds and gives a finish to the meditation.) [Here ends the part published in *NYWG*, where the final mark of parenthesis is omitted. The rest of the passage first appeared in *MDW*.— ED.] Vivid as life, they recall and identify the long Hospital Wards, with their myriad-varied scenes of day or night—the graphic incidents of field or camp—the night before the battle, with many solemn yet cool preparations —the changeful exaltations and depressions of those four years, North and South—the convulsive memories, (let but a word, a broken sentence, serve to recall them)—the clues already quite vanish'd, like some old dream, and yet the list significant enough to soldiers—the scrawl'd, worn slips of paper that came up by bushels from the Southern prisons, Salisbury or Andersonville, by the hands of exchanged prisoners—the clank of crutches on the pavements or floors of Washington, or up and down the stairs of the Paymasters' offices—the Grand Review of homebound veterans at the close of the War, cheerily marching day after day by the President's house, one brigade succeeding another until it seem'd as if they would never end—the strange squads of Southern deserters, (*escapees*, I call'd them;)—that little *genre* group, unreck'd amid the mighty whirl, I remember passing in a hospital corner, of a dying Irish boy, a Catholic priest, and an improvised altar—Four years compressing centuries of native passion, first-class pictures, tempests of life and death—an inexhaustible mine for the Histories, Drama, Romance and even Philosophy of centuries to come—indeed the Verteber of Poetry and Art, (of personal character too,) for all future America, (far more grand, in my opinion, to the hands capable of it, than Homer's siege of Troy, or the French wars to Shakspere;)—and looking over all, in my remembrance, the tall form of President Lincoln, with his face of deep-cut lines, with the large, kind, canny eyes, the complexion of dark brown, and the tinge of wierd melancholy saturating all.

More and more, in my recollections of that period, and through its varied, multitudinous oceans and murky whirls, appear the central resolution and sternness of the bulk of the average American People, animated in Soul by a definite purpose, though sweeping and fluid as some great storm—the Common People, emblemised in thousands of specimens of first-class Heroism, steadily accumulating, (no regiment, no company, hardly a file of men, North or South, the last three years, without such first-class specimens.)

[In the Feinberg Collection there is a clipping of the lower part of page 3 of MDW (beginning "Even these days . . .") with autograph revisions and the penciled note in the margin: "Would not all this come in for a long note at the end of the War mem.?]

2

[MDW, p. 6, second paragraph; this paragraph was previously published, without the enclosing parentheses, as the first paragraph under the subtitle "An Artillery Storm," the fourth of the Third Paper of "Ten Years," NYWG. The NYWG variants are inserted in brackets.]

(Everything is quiet now, here about Falmouth and the Rappahannock, but [NYWG: now, but] there was noise enough a week or so ago. Probably the earth never shook by artificial means, nor the air reverberated, more than on that winter daybreak of eight or nine days since, when Gen. Burnside [NYWG: when Burnside] order'd all the batteries of the army to combine for the bombardment of Fredericksburgh. It was in its way the most magnificent and terrible spectacle, with all the adjunct of sound, throughout the War. The perfect hush of the just-ending night was suddenly broken by the first gun, and in an instant all the thunderers, big and little, were in full chorus, which they kept up without intermission for several hours.) [NYWG: Few know, by experience, the grandeur of immense sound; but it was here then in all its sublimity. Storm-symphonies, or battle-compositions, or Wagner's or Beethoven's, were a mere impertinence to it.]

3

[MDW, pp. 57–58, the last two paragraphs of the main part of the book, preceding the "Notes"; not previously published.]

As I write this conclusion—in the open air, latter part of June, 1875, a delicious forenoon, everything rich and fresh from last night's copious rain—ten years and more have pass'd away since that War, and its wholesale deaths, burials, graves. (*They* make indeed the true Memoranda of the War—mute, subtle, immortal.) From ten years' rain and snow, in their seasons—grass, clover, pine trees, orchards, forests—from all the noiseless miracles of soil and sun and running streams—how peaceful and how beautiful appear to-day even the Battle-Trenches, and the many hundred thousand Cemetery mounds! Even at Andersonville, to-day, innocence and a smile. (A late account says, 'The stockade has fallen to decay, is grown upon, and a season more will efface it entirely, except from our hearts and memories. The *dead line*, over which so many brave soldiers pass'd to the freedom of eternity rather than endure the misery of life, can only be traced here and there, for most of the old marks the last ten years have obliterated. The thirty-five wells, which the prisoners dug with cups and spoons, remain just as they were left. And the wonderful spring which was discover'd one morning, after a thunder storm, flowing down the hillside, still yields its sweet, pure water as freely now as then. The Cemetery, with its thirteen thousand graves, is on the slope of a beautiful hill. Over the quiet spot already trees give the cool shade which would have been so gratefully sought by the poor fellows whose lives were ended under the scorching sun.')

And now, to thought of these—on these graves of the dead of the War, as on an altar—to memory of these, or North or South, I close and dedicate my book.

4

[Two paragraphs of MDW, pp. 59–60, "Notes"; not previously published.]

Before I went down to the Field, and among the Hospitals, I had my hours of doubt about These States; but not since. The bulk of the Army, to me, develop'd, transcended, in personal qualities—and, radically, in moral ones—all that the most enthusiastic Democratic-Republican ever fancied, idealized in loftiest dreams. And curious as it may seem, the War, to me, *proved* Humanity, and proved America and the Modern.

(I think I am perfectly well aware of the corruption and wickedness of my lands and days—the general political, business and social shams and shysterisms, everywhere. Heaven knows, I see enough of them—running foul of them continually! But I also see the noblest elements in society— and not in specimens only, but vast, enduring, inexhaustible strata of them —ruggedness, simplicity, courage, love, wit, health, liberty, patriotism— all the virtues, the main bulk, public and private.)

5

[*MDW*, p. 63, "Notes"; paragraph not previously published.]

No good Portrait of Abraham Lincoln.—Probably the reader has seen physiognomies (often old farmers, sea-captains, and such) that, behind their homeliness, or even ugliness, held superior points so subtle, yet so palpable, defying the lines of art, making the real life of their faces almost as impossible to depict as a wild perfume or fruit-taste, or a passionate tone of the living voice. . . . .and such was Lincoln's face, the peculiar color, the lines of it, the eyes, mouth, expression, &c. Of technical *beauty* it had nothing—but to the eye of a great artist it furnished a rare study, a feast and fascination. . . . . . .The current portraits are all failures—most of them caricatures.

6

[*MDW*, pp. 63–65, beginning with the paragraph with sidehead *"The War, though with two sides,"* etc., and including the second paragraph on p. 65. This material was used in "Origins of Attempted Secession," a part of "Collect." See *Prose 1892*, II.]

7

[*MDW*, p. 65, the third paragraph on the page; not previously published. It was included as paragraph 10 in the article "Walt Whitman on the American War," published in the London *Examiner* without change, March 18, 1876.]

Then another fact, never hitherto broach'd, Nationally—probably several facts, perhaps paradoxical—needing rectification—(for the whole sense and justice of the War must not be supposed to be confined to the Northern point of view.) Is there not some side from which the Secession cause itself has its justification? Was there ever a great popular movement, or revolt, or revolution, or attempt at revolution, without some solid basis interwoven with it, and supporting it? at least something that could be said in behalf of it?. . . . . .We are apt to confine our view to the few more glaring and more atrocious Southern features—the arrogance of most of the leading men and politicians—the fearful crime of Slavery itself —But the time will come—perhaps has come—to begin to take a Philosophical view of the whole affair.

8

[*MDW*, p. 65, the fourth paragraph on the page; the second and third sentences had been previously published in *NYWG* as the first two paragraphs of the First Paper of "Ten Years." Variants in the text of *NYWG* are inserted in brackets. This paragraph was printed unchanged as paragraph 11 in "Walt Whitman on the American War," London *Examiner*, March 18, 1876.]

Already, as I write this concluding Note to my Memoranda, (Summer, 1875,) a new, maturing generation has swept in, obliterating with oceanic currents the worst reminiscences of the War; and the passage of time has heal'd over at least its deepest scars. Already, the events of 1861–65, and [*NYWG*: of 1863 and '4, and] the seasons that immediately preceded, as well as those that closely follow'd them, have lost [*NYWG*: have quite lost] their direct personal impression, and the living heat and excitement of their own time, and are being marshall'd for casting, or getting ready to be cast, into the cold and bloodless electrotype plates of History. Or, if [*NYWG* begins a new paragraph with "Or if"] we admit that the savage temper and wide differences of opinion, and feelings of wrongs, and mutual recriminations, that led to the War, [*NYWG*: the Secession War] and flamed in its mortal conflagration, may not have yet entirely burnt themselves out, the embers [*NYWG*: out, still, all will acknowledge that the embers] of them are dying [*NYWG*: are already dying] embers, and a few more winters and summers, a few more rains and snows, will surely quench their fires, and leave them only as a far off memory. Already the War of Attempted Secession has become a thing of the past.

9

[*MDW*, pp. 65–66, "Notes"; the last two paragraphs of p. 65 and the first of p. 66. These had not previously been published. The first has some resemblance to the first four or five lines of "Origins of Attempted Secession." See *Prose 1892*, II. It was included without change as paragraph 12, the last, of the article "Walt Whitman on the American War" in the London *Examiner*, March 18, 1876.]

And now I have myself, in my thought, deliberately come to unite the whole conflict, both sides, the South and North, really into One, and to view it as a struggle going on within One Identity. Like any of Nature's great convulsions, wars going on within herself—not from separated sets of laws and influences, but the same—really, efforts, conflicts, most violent ones, for deeper harmony, freer and larger scope, completer homogeneousness and power.

What is any Nation, after all—and what is a human being—but a struggle between conflicting, paradoxical, opposing elements—and they themselves and their most violent contests, important parts of that One Identity, and of its development?

Results South—Now and Hence.—The present condition of things (1875) in South Carolina, Mississippi, Louisiana, and other parts of the former Slave States—the utter change and overthrow of their whole social, and the greatest coloring feature of their political institutions—a horror and dismay, as of limitless sea and fire, sweeping over them, and substituting the confusion, chaos, and measureless degradation and insult of the present—the black domination, but little above the beasts—viewed as a temporary, deserv'd punishment for their Slavery and Secession sins, may perhaps be admissible; but as a permanency of course is not to be consider'd for a moment. (Did the vast mass of the blacks, in Slavery in the United States, present a terrible and deeply complicated problem through the just ending century? But how if the mass of the blacks in freedom in the U. S. all through the ensuing century, should present a yet more terrible and more deeply complicated problem?)

10

[*MDW*, p. 66, "Notes"; four paragraphs in the middle of the page, not previously published.]

Extricating one's-self from the temporary gaucheries of the hour, can there be anything more certain than the rehabilitated prosperity of the Southern States, all and several, if their growing generations, refusing to be dismay'd by present embarrassments and darkness, accept their position in the Union as an immutable fact, and like the Middle and Western States, "fly the flag of practical industry and business, and adopting the great ideas of America with faith and courage, developing their resources, providing for education, abandoning old fictions, leave the Secession war and its bygones behind, and resolutely draw a curtain over the past"?

I want to see the Southern States, in a better sense than ever, and under the new dispensation, again take a leading part in what is emphatically *their* Nationality as much as anybody's. Soon, soon, it will begin to be realized that out of the War, after all, *they* have gained a more substantial victory than anybody.

Future History of the United States, growing out of the War—(My Speculations.) Our Nation's ending Century, thus far—even with the great struggle of 1861-'65—I do not so much call the History of the United States. Rather, our preparation, or preface. As the chief and

permanent result of those four years, and the signal triumph of National-
ism at the end of them, we now commence that History of the United
States, which, grandly developing, exfoliating, stretching through the
future, is yet to be enacted, and is only to be really written hundreds of
years hence.

And of the events of that Future—as well as the Present and the Past,
or war or peace—have they been, and will they continue to be, (does any
one suppose?) a series of *accidents*, depending on either good luck or bad
luck, as may chance to turn out? Rather, is there not, behind all, some vast
average, sufficiently definite, uniform and unswervable Purpose, in the
development of America, (may I not say divine purpose? only all is divine
purpose,) which pursues its own will, maybe unconscious of itself—of
which the puerilities often called history, are merely crude and temporary
emanations, rather than influences or causes? and of which the justification is only to be look'd for in the formulations of centuries to come? (Let
us not be deceiv'd by flatulent fleeting notorieties, political, official, literary
and other. In any profound, philosophical consideration of our politics,
literature &c., the best-known leaders—even the Presidents, Congresses,
Governors, &c.—are only so many passing spears or patches of grass on
which the cow feeds.)

11

[*MDW*, pp. 66–68, "Notes": the last paragraph on page 66, all of page 67
except the entire paragraph in the middle of the page (printed below) and
the last two lines on the page, and the two short paragraphs on page 68 that
conclude the "Notes" were included in the long footnote near the end of
"Poetry To-Day in America—Shakspere—the Future." See *Prose 1892*, II.]

The old theory of a given country or age, or people, as something
isolated and standing by itself—something which only fulfills its luck,
eventful or uneventful—or perhaps some meteor, brilliantly flashing on
the background or foreground of Time—is indeed no longer advanced
among competent minds, as a theory for History—has been supplanted
by theories far wider and higher. . . . . . .The development of a Nation—of the American Republic, for instance, with all its episodes of
peace and war—the events of the past, and the facts of the present—aye,
the entire political and intellectual processes of our common race—if beheld from a point of view sufficiently comprehensive, would doubtless exhibit the same regularity of order and exactness, and the same plan of
cause and effect, as the crops in the ground, or the rising and setting of
the stars.

12

[*MDW*, pp. 67–68, "Notes": two paragraphs beginning with the last two lines of page 67; not previously published.]

Are not these—or something like these—the simple, perennial Truths now present to the Future of the United States, out of all its Past, of war and peace? Has not the time come for working them in the tissues of the coming History and Politics of The States? And, (as gold and silver are cast into small coin,) are not, for their elucidation, entirely new classes of men, uncommitted to the past, fusing The Whole Country, adjusted to its conditions, present and to come, imperatively required, Seaboard and Interior, North and South? and must not such classes begin to arise, and be emblematic of our New Politics and our real Nationality?

Now, and henceforth, and out of the conditions, the results of the War, of all the experiences of the past—demanding to be rigidly construed with reference to the whole Union, not for a week or year, but immense cycles of time, come crowding and gathering in presence of America, like veil'd giants, original, native, larger questions, possibilities, problems, than ever before. To-day, I say, the evolution of The United States, (South, and Atlantic Seaboard, and especially of the Mississippi Valley, and the Pacific slope,) coincident with these thoughts and problems, and their own vitality and amplitude, and winding steadily along through the unseen vistas of the future, affords the greatest moral and political work in all the so-far progress of Humanity. And fortunately, to-day, after the experiments and warnings of a hundred years, we can pause and consider and provide for these problems, under more propitious circumstances, and new and native lights, and precious even if costly experiences—with more political and material advantages to illumine and solve them—than were ever hitherto possess'd by a Nation.

XII   *"Death of a Fireman."*
New Republic, Camden, N.J., November 14, 1874.

"Three Young Men's Deaths."
Cope's Tobacco Plant, April, 1879.
[The brief article "Death of a Fireman" was reprinted with other items under the title of "Three Young Men's Deaths" in *Cope's Tobacco Plant*, II (April, 1879), 318–319, and under the same title in *SDC*.]

XIII   *"Abraham Lincoln's Death."*
New York *Sun*, February 12, 1876.
[This was incorporated in large part in "A Poet on the Platform," *NYTR*,

April 15, 1879, and in the section "Death of Abraham Lincoln." For collation, see the textual notes to that section, *Prose 1892*, II.]

XIV *"In Memory of Thomas Paine."*

NYTR, January 29, 1877.
[For collation see the textual notes to the section by the same title.]

XV *"A Poet's Recreation."*

NYTR, July 4, 1878.
[This article contains seventeen paragraphs, most of which were included in
SDC: paragraphs 2–4 in "Death of William Cullen Bryant," 8 in "Jaunt Up
the Hudson," 9 in "Happiness and Raspberries," 10–11 in "A Specimen Tramp
Family," 12–13 and the first part of 14 in "Manhattan from the Bay," and
16–17 in "Human and Heroic New York." The remaining portions are
printed below.]

1 (Paragraph 1)

New-York, *July 3, 1878.*—Just closing a three weeks' visit to New-
York, with fuller personal observations in and around the city, and with
that sense of getting the true inwardness of many things and characters,
long, long familiar, but never before so declared, and never before assuming such definite purpose, which strangely comes to one sometimes after
long delay—I give the following diary-jottings, or notes, (the ruling passion strong in—But I must not say it yet,)—just as rapidly written down
of late from day to day.

2 (Paragraphs 5–7)

EVENING, SAME DAY

A pleasant hour at the reception and tea of young Watson Gilder
and Mrs. G.; everything charming and informal; met Modjeska, the ac-
tress, Wyatt Eaton, the artist, Miss Jenny Gilder, and Charles De Kay,
and had off-hand talks.

UP THE HUDSON

Sunday, 16th—Steamboat jaunt in the Plymouth Rock up the river
to West Point, to Mr. and Mrs. John Bigelow's hospitable house to dinner.
Three hours spent in the good old way, sitting, eating and drinking, sauntering around, chatting, &c. The grounds a wonderful fine, high situation,
secluded enough, yet expanded, most picturesque—river, sky, wood and
mountain views.

We came down on the same boat, through a stiff breeze, latter part
of the afternoon. The kindness, both up and down on the boat, of Mr. Jar-

rett, Mr. Russell, Commodore Tooker, and the Captain and Pilot—real gentlemanly, brotherly, old-fashioned hearty kindness—was not the least part of the pleasure of this trip.

3 (Paragraph 15)

I say, moreover, the highest scenic picturesquenesses, beauties and varieties of the world are illustrated, (of the sort, of course, not the Caucasus, not mid-ocean, not Yellowstone or Yosemite), by three days' exploration of the bay of New-York, the stretch through the East River and Sound, and a hundred miles up the Hudson. Any season, these demesnes are unsurpassable; but if one time is to be pick'd out more than another it is just this time of matured June.

XVI   "Winter Sunshine. A Trip from Camden to the Coast."
Philadelphia *Times*, January 26, 1879.
[This article contains sixty paragraphs, mostly short. The following paragraphs were included, in whole or in part, in *SDC*, and are collated in the textual notes on the sections where they are used: 1–2 in "A Winter Day on the Sea-Beach"; 9 in Whitman's note to "A Happy Hour's Command"; 10 in "An Interregnum Paragraph"; 12–22, the first eleven of the "Jottings at Timber Creek" inserted in the article, in "February Days"; 25, the fourteenth of "Jottings," in "Sundown Lights"; 26–28, the fifteenth to seventeenth of "Jottings," in "Thoughts Under an Oak—a Dream"; 31, the twentieth of "Jottings," in "A July Afternoon by the Pond"; and 42–45 and 47 in "A Winter Day on the Sea-Beach." The remaining thirty-five paragraphs are printed below.]

1 (Paragraphs 3–8)

Walking slowly, or rather hobbling (my paralysis, though partial, seems permanent), the hundred rods to the little platform and shanty bearing the big name of "Pennsylvania Junction," were not without enjoyment to me, in this pleasant mixture of cold and sunbeams. While I waited outside the yet unopened hut, two good-looking middle-aged men, also journey-bound, held animated talk on gunning, ducks, the shore, the woods, the best places for sport, etc. Each had a long story to tell about "his gun," its properties, price and history generally. Their anecdotes of wonderful shots, bird events, and such—all with many idioms, and great volubility. (Have you ever heard two sportsmen recounting their opinions and experience that way? To me it is not lacking in interest or amusement for a change. And perhaps there is no more innocent style of blowing.)

From the car-windows a good view of the country, in its winter garb.

These farms are mostly devoted to market truck, and are generally well cultivated. Passing the little stations of Glenwood and Collingswood— then stopping at old, beautiful, rich and quite populous Haddonfield, with its fine tree-lined, main street (Revolutionary, military reminiscences too— a tradition that the Continental Congress itself held a session here).

OLD SPORTING TIMES IN JERSEY

This quarter of the State has an old sporting history, not without interest, as a reminiscence. Hereabouts lived many of the Jersey members of the once famous (fifty, eighty, even a hundred years ago) Gloucester Fox Hunting Club, which, though long deceased, has left its records in an ancient history, or memorial, in my possession and from which I now quote. The club was formed in October, 1766, by twenty-seven gentlemen of Philadelphia, who were subsequently joined by several Jerseymen. They used to meet once a week or oftener for hunting—their most favorite fields for action being along the banks of Cooper's creek, four or five miles from Camden, or at the Horseheads, two or three miles from Woodbury, in Deptford, at Chew's Landing, Blackwoodtown, Heston's Glass-works, now Glassboro', and Thomson's Point on the Delaware. The kennel of the club, which was kept at the Point by an old negro named Natty, contained twenty-two excellent dogs, whose names the eloquent and enthusiastic memorialist of the club has with due solemnity preserved. During the Revolution, many of the members of the club were in their country's service. The association, however, was reorganized after the war, and continued in existence down to 1818, when the death of Captain Ross, the boldest rider and best hunter of the company, caused it to languish and die. The chase generally lasted only for a few hours; but once Raynard carried the pack in full cry to Salem. It was a point of honor not to give up until the bush was taken; after which there ensued a banquet, whereat he who was first in at the death was, for the time being, the lion.

The farmers, who suffered much in those days from the great number of foxes with which the county still abounded, were always glad to hear the sound of the horns and hounds. From the tenth of October to the tenth of April, the club had the entire freedom of their fields and woods, and often on catching the music of the approaching pack, the sturdy husbandman bridled his best horse, and joined the merry dashing train, drinking as deep as any the excitement of the royal sport.

There were many distinguished men connected with the Gloucester Club. But none is more deserving immortality than Jonas Cattell, for twenty years grand guide and whipper-in to the hunters, "always at his post," says the memorialist, "whether at setting out with the company, leading off, at fault, or at the death." While all the rest rode, he traveled on foot with his gun and tomahawk, and was always on hand for any emergency, before half the riders came in sight. His physical strength and activity were almost incredible. When about fifty years of age he ran a foot race from Mount Holly to Woodbury with an Indian runner of great celebrity, and came off victor. About the same time he won a wager by going on foot from Woodbury to Cape Island in one day, delivering a letter, and returning in the same manner, with an answer, on the day following. He accomplished this extraordinary feat with ease, and was willing to repeat it the same week on the same terms. (Jonas lived to be over ninety years of age, and it is only a couple of years ago that a daughter of his, a very old lady, died at Haddonfield.)

KIRKWOOD—(WHITE HORSE)

Some four or five miles south of Haddonfield we come to the handsome railroad station of Kirkwood. (This place looks to me like home— but I am not intending to stop now.) Here is a beautiful broad pond or lake. They are getting the ice from it, and a good sight it is to see the great thick, pure, silvery cakes cut and hauled. In summer the pond, with its young groves and adjacent handsome pavilion, form a favorite destination for Philadelphia and Camden picnics.

2 (Paragraph 11)

THUMB-NAIL JOTTINGS AT TIMBER CREEK

From impromptu notes and scribblings at this spot at different times, let me excerpt the following, to show you how idle and happy and contented even a half-paralytic can be—if he has a mind to—in the country:

> [Here follow, in the article, twenty paragraphs in a smaller type than the rest.]

3 (Paragraphs 23–24, the 12th and 13th of "Jottings.")

Authors, Etc.—When I feel in the mood (which is only at wide intervals), I read and filter some book or piece or page or author through my mind, amid these influences, in these surroundings. Queer, how new and different the books and authors appear in open air, with wind blowing and birds calling in the bushes and you on the rude banks of the negligent pond.

I get some old edition of no pecuniary value, and take portions in my pocket. In this way I have dislocated the principal American writers of my time—Emerson, Longfellow, Whittier and the rest—with translations of the French Madame Dudevant (always good to me), the German metaphysician Hegel, and nearly all the current foreign poets.

4 (*Paragraphs 29–30, the 18th and 19th of "Jottings."*)

June 10.—The mulleins are here again, more vigorous, more plentiful, more eloquent than ever. The thick-studded knobs on their erect stems are beginning to unfold in flowers of clear bright yellow. The mullein—nothing but a weed, a stalk, three or four (sometimes five or even six) feet high, growing singularly plumb and upright, with large velvety palm-shaped leaves of greenish drab, very large near the ground and smaller as they ascend, and just now the upper part of the stalk bossed thickly with close-adhering bean-shaped buds, breaking out in the brightest golden blossoms. Nothing but this, and yet inimitable, innocent, fresh—especially in early morning, when the large drab leaves are thick with dew diamonds.

How much those sturdy-graceful stalks and broad leaves and yellow flowers are to me!

5 (*Paragraphs 32–41*)

So much for musings and observations summer and winter along my West Jersey creek. But we will resume our jaunt on the Camden and Atlantic.

LONG-A-COMING—ATCO—THE DIVIDE

Five miles from Kirkwood we strike the thrifty town of Berlin (old name Long-a-Coming, which they had much better kept). We reach Atco, three miles further on—quite a brisk settlement in the brush, with a newspaper, some stores, and a little branch railroad to Williamstown. At the eighteen-mile post the grade of the railroad reaches its highest point, being one hundred and eighty feet above the level of the sea. Here is what is called by the engineer, "the divide," the water on the west flowing to the Delaware, and on the east to the ocean.

The soil has now become sandy and thin, and continues so for the ensuing forty miles; flat, thin, bare gray-white, yet not without agreeable features—pines, cedars, scrub oaks plenty—patches of clear fields, but much larger patches of pines and sand.

I must not forget to mention that there are some manufactories both off and on the line of the road. At Williamstown, Tansboro', Waterford and Winslow junction are glassworks, and at Gibsboro', two miles west of Kirkwood station the white lead, zinc and color works of John Lucas & Co. and the pleasant country-seat of Mr. and Mrs. L. and their large family. Beside a few cloth and cotton mills through these counties, working in ice, charcoal, pottery, wine, etc., give a little variety to agriculture, which is of course the vastly preponderating occupation.

MANUFACTORIES AND PRODUCTS ELSEWHERE

In other parts of the State (remember, I am only jaunting through two counties) there is great manufacturing foundation and enterprise. In pottery, both for extent and finish, the Trenton establishments claim to stand in the front rank of the world—and it is not certain but their claim should be allowed. Essex County has zinc works; Morris, Sussex and Warren counties extensive iron works. There are sixteen blast furnaces in the State. The fertilizing marl beds of New Jersey are incalculable. It has also large quarries and mines, iron (a millions tons of ore a year), limestone, marble, slate, glass sand, black lead, etc. Middlesex county is full of brick-kilns, tiles, etc.

New Jersey stands sixth in the list of manufacturing States. Her leading products in this department are leather, iron (and metals other than iron), cotton, wool, glass, silk, jewelry, pottery, rubber, fire-brick and carriages. Her area is not quite eight thousand square miles—not quite five million acres—two-thirds in cultivated farms. The solid-rugged, ever fast foundation of the State consists in its farm lands and in its mines, its marl, clay, etc. Its population to-day is a million and a quarter.

HAMMONTON—THE COUNTRY ALL ALONG

We steam rapidly on to Hammonton, about thirty miles from Philadelphia (half way on the route) and the liveliest looking town on this part of the road. Then, after touching at Da Costa, arrive at Elwood—rather pleasant appearing.

A thin-soiled, non-fertile country all along, yet as healthy and not so rocky and broken as New England. The fee-simple cheap, vines and small fruits eligible. The whole route (at any rate from Haddonfield to the seashore) has been literally made and opened up to growth by the Camden and Atlantic Railroad. That has furnished spine or verteber to a section previously without any.

It all reminds me much of my old native Long Island, N.Y., especially takes me back to the *plains* and *brush*—the same level stretch, thin soil—healthy but barren—pines, scrub oak, laurel, kill-calf, and splashes of white sand everywhere.

We come to Egg Harbor City, settled about twenty-five years ago by the Germans, and now with quite a reputation for grape culture and wine-making—scattered houses off in the brush in the distances, and a little branch railroad to May's Landing; then Pomona, and then another lively town, Absecon, an old and quite good-sized settlement, 52 miles from Philadelphia.

6 (*Paragraph 46*)

Then, after nearly two hours of this shore, we trotted rapidly around and through the city itself—capital good roads everywhere, hard, smooth, well-kept, a pleasure to drive on them. Atlantic avenue, the principal street; Pacific avenue, with its rows of choice private cottages, and many, many others. (I had the good fortune to be driven around by William Biddle, a young married man—a hackman by occupation—an excellent companion and *cicerone*—owner of his own good team and carriage.)

7 (*Paragraphs 48–60*)

Although it is not generally thought of, except in connection with hot weather, I am not sure but Atlantic City would suit me just as well, perhaps best, for winter quarters. As to bad weather, it is no worse here than anywhere else; and when fine, the pleasures and characteristic attractions are inimitable.

Cape May I must reserve for another screed, Gloucester, Salem, Cumberland and Cape May counties to the south—the whole line of the West Jersey Railroad, with its occasional fertile spots and the towns it reaches —Woodbury, Glassboro', Salem, Bridgeton, Vineland, Millville, and so to the staunch old (both popular and "aristocratic") summer resort and watering place, Cape May—surely, as soon as the spring opens, beginning the foundation of better attractions and accommodations even than before the terrible fire of three months ago. Bad as that disaster was, it may be, I say (out of the nettle danger plucking the flower safety) that Cape May, even from it, will start on a prosperity, popularity, attractiveness, beyond any and all of the past.

CIVILIZATION AND RAILROADS

What a place (is it not indeed the main place?) the railroad plays in modern democratic civilization! How indirectly, but surely, and beyond all other influences to-day in America, it thaws, ploughs up, prepares, and even fortifies the fallows of unnumbered counties and towns!—the tough sward of morals and manners of the low average (nine-tenths) of our vulgar humanity! Silently and surely and on a scale as large and genuine as Nature's, it sets in motion every indirect and many direct means of making a really substantial community—beginning at the bottom, subsoiling as it were—bringing information and light into dark places, opening up trade, markets, purchases, newspapers, fashions, visitors, etc.

All boys, and the young farmers like railroad life, I notice—want to be engineers, firemen, conductors. Then the swiftness, power, absolute *doing something* which it teaches!

The land that has plenty of railroads can never be an inferior land. An insensible multiform, progressive agitation (the very centre of all the laws of the universe), radiates constantly through it—of course, not all for good, not all in the pessimist sense, but perfect to the true philosopher, the optimist. While T. and W. P. and B. I. and all such are railing and sniveling and berating social evils with their purulent words, each one

> Falling to cursing like a very drab.

(As if a doctor should do nothing but blackguard and yell at the pimples and pallors that show disease, and its far-down, far-back causes) here is a vast series of institutes practically, scientifically introducing or laying the sure foundations for introducing modernness, strength, knowledge, development and religion—aye, religion—everywhere they go.

The vehement agrarians I notice (and some others) can find no words scalding enough for "railroad monopolies"—the wealth and profits they represent—their autocratic management, etc. But it is doubtful to me if democracy (in its bases, stimulants, educings, indirections) has had anywhere else so precious and potent an aid. Not sentimental aid—not mere words, or in the style of the goody-goody mush of the average reformers (I sometimes think I wouldn't give one cent for all the mere *talk* of temperance, morals, manners or political liberty either, for the last ten years), but strong, real, rank and practical, like Nature—doing just the thing that is needed without timid regard to nicety—with an opulence of power—just what is wanted for the case and conditions that need treatment—probably need ruthless breaking up.

What would all interior or central or sea coast New Jersey be—what the whole southern part of the State—if the Camden and Atlantic tracks were obliterated? Or if the West Jersey road and its branches were?

New Jersey has quite a warlike record—both ancient and modern. (From 1861 to 1865 it contributed 90,000 men to the National army). Of real *grit*, I think the bulk of Jerseymen have as much as any people anywhere. Their besetting sin is worldliness—and a pretty low average of it, too—which is probably, however, the besetting sin not only of every State, North and South, but of all of us, and of every civilized land under the sun.

GENERAL NEW JERSEY CHARACTER

Of course New Jersey character is in the main the same as all other human character. It must ever be borne in mind that the facts of resemblance between any people, place or time, and any other, however distant people, place or time, are far closer and more numerous than the facts of difference. Of course, too, in New Jersey humanity there are many phases or strata. Materialistic, very set and obstinate, but good sterling ore, native qualities—good material for the future. If we were asked to strike an average for the morality and intellectuality of the people, it would be neither the highest nor lowest. Thrift, wariness, stolidity prevail. The women are the best, as everywhere. There is a quality in the men analogous to open air, to barns and earth-fields and sea-shore—on a low plane, but real and breezy—most welcome and delightful to me. (I am speaking of Camden, Atlantic and Burlington counties, and the middle and southern parts more particularly.) The Jerseyite has neither the sharpness of the New Englander nor the enterprise of the West. From the situation of the State, not from any native impetus, it has been cut through by railroads and travel—forced into a connection with the busy, bustling world—yet the common ranges of the people are sluggish, content with little, and hard to rouse. With all this I like them much, and some of my best times of late years have been passed with them. Character is, indeed, on a low key, but it is fresh, independent and tough as a knot. Carlyle would find acceptable studies among them. In a good many points they are like the Scotch, only not so *canny*.

In these parts, more than anywhere else, yet linger the far-back tracts, ancient hymn-books, Doddridge's essays and the like. In one excellent family I found that ponderous and primitive work, "The Bible Looking-Glass," with its texts of hundreds of puerile conceits, illustrated by their hundreds of rawest of wood engravings—all quite curious as a study of the past, of crudeness, and how, seen through cheap and ignorant eyes, the grandest and sublimest become helplessly cheap and ignorant.

No doubt the nature of the soil has had to do with advancing certain personal traits and repressing others. Flat, much sand, few forests worthy the name, no natural wheat land, immense lines of sea-sand, vast wilds of dwarf pine and scrub oak, mostly describe it. The northern portion of the

State is hilly, even mountainous, with mines and furnaces, and doubtless would require a different portraiture. I hope to explore it one of these days and perhaps report.

But to me it is the sea-side region that gives stamp to Jersey, even in human character. I am counting with eagerness next summer (as the Yanks say, "make reckoning") on a special long-contemplated exploration of this creek-indented and sea-beat region from Cape May to Sandy Hook—100 miles—a stretch offering both the people and the places most interesting to my taste, in which salt and sedge are inborn.

W. W.

XVII *"The First Spring Day on Chestnut Street."*
Philadelphia *Progress*, March 8, 1879.
[This article was included in SDC. See the section by the same title in this edition.]

XVIII *"Only Crossing the Delaware."*
Philadelphia *Progress*, April 5, 1879.
[Most of this article was included in SDC, and all of it is printed in the present edition in the following sections and in the textual notes to them: "Delaware River—Days and Nights," "Scenes on Ferry and River—Last Winter's Nights."]

XIX *"Broadway Revisited."*
New York *Tribune*, May 10, 1879.
[This article containing twelve paragraphs was reprinted as follows: paragraphs 1–4 in GBF, "New York—the Bay—the Old Name," which is collated in *Prose 1892*, II; 7–8 in SDC, "Plays and Operas Too," the last part of 9 in SDC, "Broadway Sights," and 10–12 in SDC, "Omnibus Jaunts and Drivers." Paragraphs 5–6 and the first two sentences of 9, not reprinted by Whitman, are printed in the Appendix below.]

1 (Paragraphs 5–6)

THE BATTERY

April 19.—One fine day I devoted a good part of it, first to the Battery, and then a ride and partial walk (or hobble) nearly the whole distance up Broadway to Fourteenth-st. Everything looks yet familiar—the same old view from the Battery, with steamers plying constantly, vessels lying at anchor, and the vistas down the bay seaward, or over to Staten Island, or up the Hudson. The broad fan-shaped street-space at South Ferry now all covered over with its open-work roof, and ponderous netting of iron beams, rail-tracks, supports, etc., I can't get used to—(either here or Third-ave., or the Bowery, or anywhere—but doubtless would in time.)

The Battery—its past associations—what tales those trees and walks could tell! The old times—even twenty-five or thirty years ago. Who of my readers will recall the splendid seasons of Italian Opera, by the Havana troupe under Maretzek, in the old Building—the fine band and the cool breezes—Bettini, the tenor, Marini, the bass—the sopranos, Bosio, Truffi —"Marino Faliero"? No better playing or singing ever in New-York.

2 (*First two sentences of paragraph 9*)

JOHN JACOB ASTOR GOES SLEIGHRIDING

Still up Broadway and along the most crowded, glittering, showy, fashionable, bustling parts of it—the great stores, the panorama of the vehicles, the interminable streams of well-dressed men and women on the sidewalks—overhead the pure bright sky, the finest about the globe—the Flag Beautiful flaunting in the west wind—the interesting streets, Canal, Grand, Bleecker. But let me stop a moment opposite Metropolitan Hotel.

xx *"Real Summer Openings."*

New York *Tribune*, May 17, 1879.

[This article contains twenty-three paragraphs, most of which were included in SDC in whole or in part: paragraphs 2–4 in "Up the Hudson to Ulster County," 5–9 in "Days at J. B.'s—Turf-Fires—Spring Songs," 14–17 in "Hudson River Sights," 18 in "Meeting a Hermit," 21 in "An Ulster County Waterfall," and 22 in "Walter Dumont and His Medal." The remaining portions are printed below.]

1 (*Paragraph 1*)

Sir: As I sit down to-day (May 13,) to arrange the notes of a just-concluded trip up the Hudson, I look out of my window, at 1300 Fifth-ave., on Nature's real summer opening, in full flush, in beautiful Central Park. Tree-blossoms and verdure; and that sight I love best, the emerald carpet of the grass, now in its richest, freshest green, thick-spotted, over hundreds of acres, with myriads of golden-yellow dandelions. But to my memoranda:

2 (*Paragraphs 10–13*)

JOHN BURROUGHS'S BABY

I am having good times here with my friends Mr. and Mrs. Burroughs, at their hospitable house on the hill. Mr. B. works somewhat on his farm, takes matters easy, devoting his Winters to literary work. Nor must I forget the centre of the establishment—their magnificent year-old baby boy. From 10 to 11, forenoon, J. B., when home, faithfully devotes himself to pushing or drawing this youngster around in his carriage, especially up and down the grass-patch.

The baby—some fine specimen like this (but then are they not all fine specimens?) as a theme for poetry in its broader flights—is it not worth thinking about?

FROM MY BAY-WINDOW

I see my friend S. C. out in the raspberry field carefully ploughing with one horse between the rows. The strong, lithe, tan-faced, liquid-eyed young farmer! He makes quite a picture there, walking slowly and firmly along, holding the plough-handles, followed by his charming child-son, little blonde, sweet-voiced Channy. Then afterward S. and J. B. with scion, saw, clay and bandage, perform grafting operations on several young pear trees.

From my bay-window I sleepily yet so much enjoy everything—the place, the day, the Hudson of the bending curves! I have laid aside my books. (For the ten days of my visit here I re-read for a change Sainte-Beuve's "Portraits," Taine's "English Literature," and Addington Symonds' glowing resumé, the "Greek Poets." I have taken possession of a great south bay-window with wide ledges.)

3 (Paragraphs 19–20)

TWO CONFRONTING INSTITUTIONS

April 28.—Started after breakfast, driving down the west bank of the river six or seven miles, to Highland Village, where we crossed to Poughkeepsie. Explored that lively and handsome little city, especially Main and Hamilton-sts.; spent an hour or more at Vassar College (the Art Building and Hall), and had a chat with President Caldwell; received good impressions of this large school and the three or four hundred young women here studying to be "fully educated," so-called. The rest of the day had good talks, good lunch and a good time generally with our friends Professor and Mrs. Ritter.

As we had gone down on the West Side, Esopus, we passed the Catholic Institution, "Manresa," a large religious school and farm-rendezvous for students for the priesthood—men and young fellows, numbering many scores, perhaps, in the hundreds—exclusively males—not a woman about the premises. So that on one bank of the river are marshalled the masculines, in lofty towers looking to the East—and on the other side the broad grounds and red bricks of Vassar with their lovely feminine army. (But what should prevent an old man like me, who takes in everything, from having a capital good time in both places?)

4 (*Paragraph 23*)

CONCLUSION

As I conclude my memoranda, Summer has indeed opened around us, with orchard blossoms, chestnut foliage and May perfumes. I have let my pen run freely in the presence of waters, trees, skies, birds. As I age more and more, I like to abandon myself to this kind of outdoor gossip. Not only sane nourishment and content, but I sometimes fancy even real Morality, in deepest sense, comes from air, sun, space—from prairie, sea, mountains. Without these, all goodness educed of inside books, churches, abstract lore, seems—does it not?—mere statue-goodness—mere marble —without breath of life. ("Virtue," said Marcus Aurelius, "what is it, only a living and enthusiastic sympathy with Nature?")

W. W.

New-York, May 14, 1879.

xxi *"These May Afternoons."*

New York *Tribune*, May 24, 1879.

[This article contains sixteen paragraphs, most of which were included in *SDC*: paragraphs 1–2 in "Two City Areas, Certain Hours," 3–5 in "Central Park Walks and Talks," 6–8 in "A Fine Afternoon, 4 to 6," 9–11 in "Departing of the Big Steamers" and the textual notes to that section, and 12 in "Two Hours on the Minnesota." The remaining portions are printed in the Appendix below.]

1

Strolled leisurely and quite thoroughly over the Minnesota, convoyed part of the time by Lieutenant Little, and part by Lieutenant Murphy. Saw the black, sluggish guns everywhere. Saw the animated scene or call of piping to hammocks. The hammocks, scores of them, are rolled up, put outside above all day, covered with tarpaulin, and then about 8:30, at a signal, the deck swarms with the hurrying crowd of lads taking these great army-worm looking rolls and carrying them below.

I am markedly indebted to Captain Luce for a courteous reception— and to the kind cordiality of the before mentioned officers, with Engineer Moore, Dr. Sowerby, Mr. Pay Clerk Daley, and Mr. Till; but as I listened to the young crew and school singing, or went among them, or strolled on the berth-deck below, and then went above on the open deck among the crowds of blue-clads—or as I watched them, their brown faces confronting me, with muscular arms pulling their oars, as I was boated to or from the ship—I must confess my heart went out most to those specimens, among the best I have yet seen of the promise, the average, of the future manliness of America on sea and land.

PLAY-ACTORS STOOD UP FOR

One of my correspondents, A. J. B., takes me to task to-day for a side allusion, in my late lecture to the actors, whom he makes a very spirited defence of, as follows:

"I am not, never have been, and never expect to be, an actor, so I have no personal interest in the thing; but allow me to say that I don't like so well as I do the rest, what you say (according to your reporter) of stage-performers—though they really act very little more than most people off the stage. Why should you hold them up as a class to contempt, by speaking of them as 'human jackstraws, moving about with their silly little gestures, foreign spirit' (I read your Centennial poem, but I doubt if the American spirit is any better as a whole than almost any national one across the seas) 'and flatulent text'? Actors follow their trade exactly as omnibus drivers, kings, presidents, judges, generals, arch-bishops, physicians, farmers, poets, scientists, lecturers, mechanics, counter-jumpers, char-women and architects do theirs—namely, primarily and mainly, for the sake of getting their daily bread either on silver salvers or out of ash-barrels, and to scrape enough gold or copper together to have a good time with the other sex, and to pay for the children's school books and shoes, for church pews and theatre tickets. And if actors do their work well, they are just as useful and respectable as any of the others. There are always actors on the histrionic stage who are as great men in brain, heart, body and culture as any of the others—including President Lincoln—off it;—you and the late Judge Edmunds to the contrary notwithstanding. Mr. Lincoln I have no doubt from something Mr. Sumner once told me, probably fully realized this, and felt that in the recreation and reinvigoration he received from Mr. Sothern and Miss Laura Keene, he got full as much from them as they got from him."

W. W.

New York, May 23, 1879.

[The lecture referred to was "The Death of Abraham Lincoln," delivered at Steck Hall, April 14, 1879. It was printed under the same title in *SDC*, and the reference to actors was not changed. See *Prose 1892*, II.—ED.]

XXII *"Walt Whitman's Impressions of Denver and the West.
       What He Says of its Present, its People and its Future."*

Denver *Daily Tribune*, September 21 [?], 1879.

[Part of this article was used by Whitman in "Denver Impressions," *q.v.*
The entire article is here printed from a photographic copy of a complete
clipping in the Trent Collection of the Duke University Library, showing in
brackets the revisions on that clipping, presumably made by Whitman, and
the MS variations. The second line of the heading is deleted in the Duke
clipping. The title on the MS is "Walt Whitman in Denver."]

Hearing of the arrival of "the good Gray Poet" in the city on [MS: city,
on] a short week's visit, a TRIBUNE man was dispatched to see him, and
[MS: visit, we dispatched one of our staff to see & welcome him, and] get
his impressions of the West generally and [MS: generally, and] Colorado
in particular. At the American House, where Mr. Whitman is stopping,
was found, on [MS: stopping, on] entering the public reception room, a
[MS: we found a] large, tall, strongly-built [MS: strong-built] man, with a
tanned and scarlet face, plenteous white beard and hair and of a bodily
frame weighing about one hundred and ninety pounds. He was dressed
[MS: weighing 190. Dressed] in a complete suit of English gray, with a
wide, [MS: with wide] turned-over shirt-collar, unusually open at the neck,
and on his head he wore a [MS: head a] drab wool hat like a Southern
planter's. This was Walt Whitman, and he was apparently quite at ease
in his ample arm chair, and perfectly at home in the midst of the varied
and shifting crowd, not a face of which but seemed to be scanned by his
[MS: of whom seemed to escape his] rapid but silent and quiet glance.

He received THE TRIBUNE's man most [MS: received us most] pleasantly, as was to be expected from the avowed Poet of Comradeship, [the
words "as . . . Comradeship" deleted on the Duke clipping] and, at a
request, [MS: at our request,] readily gave his [MS: the] impressions of his
[MS: this] visit to Colorado. He talks in a clear tone, neither slowly nor
hurriedly. As was perhaps to be expected, what most struck him (born
and brought up on the seashore and [MS: &] used to New York, Philadelphia and [MS: &] Baltimore) with wonder and admiration, through
Kansas and all the way to Denver—as previously through the whole three
hundred miles [MS: previously, the whole 300 miles] across Missouri—
and, indeed, from the time he left Pittsburg, traversing Ohio, Indiana and
Illinois—but more especially over the immense area of the Great Plains,
was [MS: Plains—was] the Prairie character of these mighty central States,

forming, as he said, not the heart only but the *torso* of the geography of the Republic. A stupendous area of 1,500 square miles, and more, stretching from Manitoba to Texas one way, and from the Shenandoah to the Platte the other, an [MS: other; an] average soil of incredible fertility, not one-fifteenth of it waste, Missouri [MS: waste; Missouri] alone enough to feed the world with corn and wheat.

Mr. Whitman spoke of the Prairies (under which he grouped all the Central States) as a new and original influence in coloring humanity, and in art and in literature. [MS: art and literature.] "These limitless and beautiful landscapes," he said, "indeed fill me best and most, and will longest remain with me, of all the objective shows I see on this, my first visit to the Central States, [the words "the Central States," deleted on the Duke clipping] the grand interior. I wonder if the people of the Prairies know how much *art*, [MS: much of first-class *art*,] original and all their own, they have in those rolling and grassy plains—what a profound [MS: what profound] cast and bearing they have on [MS: bearing on] their coming populations and races, broader, newer, more patriotic, more heroic than ever before—better comrades than ever before—giving a racy flavor and stamp to the United States of the future, and encouraging [MS: averaging] and compacting all. [Note: A few words are uncertain because of a tear at the left margin of the clipping about the middle of the above sentence. The printer evidently misread Whitman's "averaging."—ED.] No wonder the Prairies have given the Nation its two leading modern typical men, Lincoln and Grant, of a vast average of [the words "a vast" and "of" are deleted on the Duke clipping] elements of characters altogether practical and real, yet to [MS: yet, to] subtler observation, with shaded backgrounds of the ideal, lofty and fervid as any.

"But I must say something of Denver," said Mr. Whitman. "I have lived in or visited all the great cities on the Atlantic third of the Republic—Boston, Brooklyn, with [MS: Brooklyn with] its hills, New Orleans, stately Washington, broad Philadelphia, teeming Cincinnati and Chicago, and for thirty years, in that wonder, washed by hurried and glittering tides, my own New York, not only the New World's, but the World's city—but, new-comer to Denver as [MS: new comer as] I am, and threading its streets, breathing its air, warmed by its sunshine, and having what there is of its [MS: is in its] people, its idiocrasy, and its human as well as aereal *ozone*, flashed upon me now for only a couple of days, I am very much like a man feels sometimes [MS: *feels sometimes*] toward certain people he [MS: people, he] meets with and [MS: with, and] warms to, and suddenly, passionately [MS: suddenly passionately] loves and [MS: loves, and] hardly knows why. Here in this very Denver, if it might be so, I should like to cast my lot, above all other spots, all other cities. I honestly confess I can hardly tell why, but as I entered the city in the slight haze of a late September afternoon, and have breathed its delicious air, and slept well o'nights, and have roamed or rode leisurely through Latimer and Fourteenth and Fifteenth and Sixteenth and Twenty-third streets and have watched [MS: through Laramer, and 15th and 16th and Champa and 23d streets and watched] the comers and goers at the hotels and [MS: hotels, and] absorbed the human as well as climatic magnetism of this curiously attractive city, there has steadily grown upon me a feeling of affection for the spot, which, sudden as it is, has become so definite and strong that I must express it. I count on coming again to Denver."

We understand that Mr. Whitman left Philadelphia September 10th with Colonel [MS: Col.] J. W. Forney, on the invitation of the Old Settlers' Kansas Committee, who had selected Colonel Forney [MS: Col. F.] as their chief orator at [MS: orator, at] the late Lawrence celebration. Mr. Whitman [MS: Mr W.] spent some days in St. Louis, and has explored Missouri and Kansas pretty thoroughly. He goes to the mountains by the South Park road to-morrow. Mr. Whitman calls [MS: road on Monday next. He calls] himself a half-paralytic and [MS: half-paralytic, and] gets around with difficulty but [MS: difficulty, but] he looks ruddy and in good flesh. He starts back from Denver for St. Louis next Tuesday to [MS: Tuesday, to] stay there on a visit of some weeks. [Throughout the MS "Mr" and "St" are without the period.]

XXIII *"Summer Days in Canada."*

The London (Ont.) *Advertiser*, June 22, 1880.

[This article consists of fourteen paragraphs, of which the following were reprinted in SDC: 3–4 in "Seeing Niagara to Advantage," 5–6 in "Jaunting to Canada," 7–11 in "Sunday with the Insane," 13 in "A Reminiscence of Elias Hicks," and 14 in "Grand Native Growth." Paragraph 12 is, in this edition, included in the textual notes on "Sunday with the Insane." The first two paragraphs are printed in the Appendix below.]

1 *(Paragraphs 1–2)*

London, Ontario, Canada, June 19.

I am here almost 600 miles west-by-north-west of New York City, in a beautiful country, ("the Dominion" they call it all—not that "Old Dominion" of Virginia I was years ago quite familiar with, but having its own charms and amplitudes). After crossing the Niagara river, the topography the whole way, 120 miles, is pleasantly broken, attractive and thrifty, seldom much woods, the usual farm-sights dotting the landscape from the car windows in every direction, and passing some handsome and busy towns, St. Catherine's, Hamilton, Paris and Woodstock. Take it throughout, I should be at a loss to mention any portions of the States, east or west, with a more prosperous show, and of fairer comfortable human living.

CROPS, THE SEASON, ETC.

The land, although not the best I have ever seen, seems generally good, not prairie, quite diversified, and fairly tilled, the grass and wheat looking well. The hay crop indeed promises to be tremendous, as in the States. I can testify (have been in Canada now two weeks) to the excellence and plenty of such nice things as asparagus, pie-plant, strawberries, etc., from our daily table. Potatoes, oats, rye, growing well; corn ditto, but late. No potato-bug or army-worm here, so far. Sorghum is beginning to be raised on trial. June 9th to 15th frequent rains. Upon the whole, the season delightful, and the weather more bracing than in our Middle United States. June 15, afternoon and evening, I had to put on my old thick overcoat. Folks here talked anticipatingly of frost—they told me its freezing touch often came in June; but it did not come this time. I find all our birds singing in the bush and woods, and all our flowers in the gardens. This seems to be the special country of gorgeous cream-colored or cardinal peonies; they flaunt their great blossoms in every door yard and along the road. Then as I go about, I am never without the scent of the hardy jessamine and seringa-bush. (Perhaps I may as well notify the reader that in the jottings following no attention is paid to the consecutiveness of dates. I am spending the season half-indolently in Canada, and these are some of my summer happenings, thoughts, and impressions, as I go about.)

XXIV *"Letter from Walt Whitman."*

The London (Ont.) *Advertiser*, August 26, 1880.

[This article contains ten paragraphs and a poem. Six of the paragraphs were included in SDC: paragraph 1 in "The St. Lawrence Line," 2 in "The Savage Saguenay," 3–4 in "Capes Eternity and Trinity," 5 in "Chicoutimi and Ha-Ha Bay," and 6 in "The Inhabitants—Good Living." Paragraphs 7–8 and the poem are credited by Whitman to his friend and fellow traveler, Dr. R. B. Bucke, and are not included in this edition; paragraphs 9–10, concluding the article, are printed in the Appendix below.]

1 *(Paragraphs 9–10)*

All of which, for the present, must do, with my best respects and love to the Stream of Savage Peaks and Inky waters—to Saguenay of the fathomless sounding. Shall soon go from Ha-ha to spend a while in the old French city of Quebec, from whence I may write you again.

W. W.

P.S.—But my head quarters and reliable mail address is London, Ontario, Canada. I shall continue on there (with one or two short excursions) for a good part of September, and then return to Camden, New Jersey.

xxv *"How I Get Around at Sixty and Take Notes."*

First Number. *Critic*. January 29, 1881.

[This article contains fifteen paragraphs, all included in SDC: paragraphs 1–2 in "New Themes Entered Upon," 3–5 in "A Winter Day on the Sea-Beach," 6–7 in "Sea-Shore Fancies," 8–12 in "Autumn Side-Bits," and 13–15 in "Spring Overtures—Recreations."]

xxvi *"How I Get Around at Sixty and Take Notes."*

Second Number. *Critic*, April 9, 1881.

[This article contains fourteen paragraphs, all except one included in SDC in whole or in part: the last part of paragraph 1 in lines 14–23 of "An Interregnum Paragraph"; the first part, omitted in SDC, in the textual notes to that section in the present edition; the first part of paragraph 2 in the second paragraph of Whitman's footnote to "A Happy Hour's Command"; the last part of paragraph 2, some of which had previously appeared as the tenth paragraph of "Winter Sunshine," PT, Jan. 26, 1879, in "An Interregnum Paragraph," lines 10–14; paragraph 3 in lines 17–21 of "An Early Summer Reveille"; paragraphs 4–5, the first two under the CR subtitle "By the Pond," in "Horse-Mint"; paragraphs 6–7 and 9, the third, fourth, and sixth under "By the Pond," in "Distant Sounds," and paragraph 8, omitted in SDC, in the textual notes to that section in the present edition; paragraph 10, the first of five under the CR subtitle "Convalescent Hours," in lines 1–15 of "A Sun-Bath—Nakedness"; paragraphs 11–12, the second and third under "Convalescent Hours," in "The Oaks and I"; and paragraphs 13–14, the fourth and fifth of "Convalescent Hours," concluding the second number, in "A Quintette."]

xxvii *"How I Get Around at Sixty and Take Notes."*

Third Number. *Critic*, May 7, 1881.

[This article consists of nineteen paragraphs, all but two of which were included in SDC: 1–4 in "A Week's Visit to Boston," 5 in "The Boston of To-Day," 6–10 in "My Tribute to Four Poets," and 11–16 and 19 in "Millet's Pictures—Last Items." Paragraphs 17–18 are printed in the Appendix below.]

1 *(Paragraphs 17–18)*

Guard the tablets well, New England—ay, America entire! They do not appear in your census returns, or statistics of products, yet all the cotton and wheat, and all the mines of California, cannot countervail what those little slabs stand for.

ACKNOWLEDGMENTS

Among many, I desire gratefully to specify a few Bostonians by name: G. P. Lathrop, Boyle O'Reilly of the *Pilot*, T. H. Bartlett, the sculptor; Frank Hill Smith, the artist, and Charles B. Ferrin, proprietor of the Revere House. Then for kindest visits and offered hospitalities from Col. and Mrs. Charles Fairchild, Mr. and Mrs. J. T. Trowbridge, Mr. and Mrs. Fields, Mrs. Ole Bull and Mrs. Mosher, F. B. Sanborn; and friendliest calls from W. D. Howells, General Banks, C. A. Bartol, T. B. Aldrich, and from my old friends George Clapp, and J. R. Newhall of Lynn. These and many others.

XXVIII *"How I Get Around at Sixty and Take Notes."*

Fourth Number. *Critic*, July 16, 1881. In the *Critic* this number was erroneously designated "No. 3."

[This article contains twelve paragraphs, all included in SDC, though not in the same order: 1 in "One of the Human Kinks," 2–3 in "An Afternoon Scene," 4–5 in "A Hint of Wild Nature," 6–8 in "A Two Hours' Ice-Sail," 9–10 in "Beethoven's Septette," and 11–12 in "Loafing in the Woods."]

XXIX *"How I Still Get Around at Sixty and Take Notes."*

Fifth Number. *Critic*, December 3, 1881. The word "still" is introduced into the general title in the fifth and sixth numbers where it had not appeared before, though the series is obviously the same.

[This article contains twenty paragraphs, of which thirteen were included in SDC in whole or in part: 2–5 in "A Visit, at the Last, to R. W. Emerson," 12–15 and the first part of 16 in "Other Concord Notations," and 17–19 in "Boston Common—More of Emerson." Paragraphs 1, 6–11, 20, and the last part of 16, omitted in SDC, are printed in the Appendix below.]

1 (Paragraph 1)

Camden, N.J., Dec. 1, '81.—During my late three or four months' jaunt to Boston and through New England, I spent such good days at Concord, and with Emerson, seeing him under such propitious circumstances, in the calm, peaceful, but most radiant, twilight of his old age (nothing in the height of his literary action and expression so becoming and impressive), that I must give a few impromptu notes of it all. So I devote this cluster entirely to the man, to the place, the past, and all leading up to, and forming, that memorable and peculiar Personality, now near his 80th year—as I have just seen him there, in his home, silent, sunny, surrounded by a beautiful family.

2 (*Paragraphs 6–11*)

But I suppose I must glide lightly over these interiors. (Some will say I ought to have skipped them entirely.) It is certain that E. does not like his friends to make him and his the subjects of publication-gossip. I write as I do because I feel that what I say is justified not only in itself, and my own respect and love, but by the fact that thousands of good men and women, here and abroad, have a right to know it, and that it will comfort them to know it. Besides, why should the finest critic of our land condemn the last best means and finish of criticism?

FINALES OF LITERATURE

If Taine, the French critic, had done no other good, it would be enough that he has brought to the fore the first, last, and all-illuminating point, with respect to any grand production of literature, that the only way to finally understand it is to minutely study the personality of the one who shaped it—his origin, times, surroundings, and his actual fortunes, life, and ways. All this supplies not only the glass through which to look, but is the atmosphere, the very light itself. Who can profoundly get at Byron or Burns without such help? Would I apply the rule to Shakspere? Yes, unhesitatingly; the plays of the great poet are not only the concentration of all that lambently played in the best fancies of those times—not only the gathered sunset of the stirring days of feudalism, but the particular life that the poet led, the kind of man he was, and what his individual experience absorbed. I don't wonder the theory is broached that other brains and fingers (Bacon's, Raleigh's, and more,) had to do with the Shaksperian work—planned main parts of it, and built it. The singular absence of information about the *person* Shakspere leaves unsolved many a riddle, and prevents the last and dearest descriptive touches and dicta of criticism.

Accordingly, I doubt whether general readers and students of Emerson will get the innermost flavor and appositeness of his utterances, as not only precious in the abstract, but needing (to scientific taste and inquiry, and complete appreciation), those hereditary, local, biographic, even domestic statements and items he is so shy of having any one print. Probably no man lives too, who could so well bear such inquiry and statement to the minutest and fullest degree. This is all just as it must be—and the paradox is that that is the worst of it.

A LIFE-OUTLINE

Emerson, born May 25, 1803, and now of course in his 79th year, is the native and raised fruit of New England Puritanism, and the fullest justification of it I know. His ancestry on both sides forms an indispensable explanation and background of every page of his writings. 'The Emerson family,' says his latest biographer, speaking of his father, 'were intellectual, eloquent, with a strong individuality of character, robust and vigorous in their thinking—practical and philanthropic. His mother (Ruth Haskins her maiden name) was a woman of great sensibility, modest, serene, and very devout. She was possessed of a thoroughly sincere nature, devoid of all sentimentalism, and of a temper the most even and placid—(one of her sons said that in his boyhood, when she came from her room in the morning, it seemed to him as if she always came from communion with God)—knew how to guide the affairs of her house, of the sweetest authority—always manners of natural grace and dignity. Her dark, liquid eyes, from which old age did not take away the expression, were among the remembrances of all on whom they ever rested.'

As lad and young man his teachers were Channing, Ticknor, Everett, President Kirkland of Harvard, and Caleb Cushing. His favorite study was Greek; and his chosen readings, as he grew to manhood, were Montaigne, Shakspere, and old poets and dramatists. He assisted his brother William at school-teaching. Soon he studied theology. In 1826 he was 'approbated to preach'—failed in strength and health—went south to Florida and South Carolina—preached in Charleston several times—returned to New England—seems to have had some pensive and even sombre times—wrote

'Good bye proud world, I'm going home,'
—in 1829 was married, ordained, and called to the Second Unitarian Church of Boston—was acceptable, yet in 1832 resigned his post (the immediate cause was his repugnance to serving the conventional communion service)—his wife died this year—he went off on an European tour, and saw Coleridge, Wordsworth, and Carlyle, the latter quite intimately—back home—in 1834 had a call to settle as pastor in New Bedford, but declined—in 1835 began lecturing in Boston (themes, Luther, Milton, Burke, Michel Angelo, and George Fox)—married the present Mrs. E. this year—absorbed Plotinus and the mystics and (under the influence of them, but living at the Old Manse, and in the midst of New England landscape and life), wrote and launched out 'Nature' as his formal entrance into highest authorship—(with poor publishing success, however, only about 500 copies being sold or got rid of in twelve years).

Soon afterward he entered the regular lecture field, and with speeches, poems, essays and books, began, matured, and duly maintained for forty years, and holds to this hour, and in my opinion, fully deserves, the first literary and critical reputation in America.

3 (*Last part of paragraph 16*)

The town deserves its name, has nothing stunning about it, no mountains, and I should think no malaria—ample in fields, grass, grain, orchards, shade trees—comfortable, roomy, opulent-enough houses in all directions—but I saw neither any thing very ambitious indeed, nor any low quarter; reminiscences of '76, the cemeteries, sturdy old names, brown and mossy stone fences, lanes and linings and clumps of oaks, sunny areas of land, everywhere signs of thrift, comfort, ease—with the locomotives and trains of the Fitchburg road rolling and piercingly whistling every hour through the whole scene. I dwell on it here because I couldn't better suggest the background atmospheres and influences of the Emerson cultus than by Concord town itself, its past for several generations, what it has been our time, and what it is to-day.

4 (*Paragraph 20*)

Which hurried notes, scribbled off here at the eleventh hour, let me conclude by the thought, after all the rest is said, that most impresses me about Emerson. Amid the utter delirium-disease called bookmaking, its feverish cohorts filling our world with every form of dislocation, morbidity, and special type of anemia or exceptionalism (with the propelling idea of getting the most possible money, first of all), how comforting to know of an author who has, through a long life, and in spirit, written as honestly, spontaneously and innocently, as the sun shines or the wheat grows—the truest, sanest, most moral, sweetest literary man on record—unsoiled by pecuniary or any other warp—ever teaching the law within—ever loyally out cropping his own self only—his own poetic and devout soul! If there be a Spirit above that looks down and scans authors, here is one at least in whom It might be well pleased.

Walt Whitman.

xxx *"How I Still Get Around at Sixty and Take Notes."*

Sixth Number. *Critic*, July 15, 1882.
[This entire article, except the first paragraph, was printed in SDC in the section "Hours for the Soul." The first paragraph, in the present edition, is included in the textual notes on "Hours for the Soul."]

xxxi *"Death of Carlyle."*

Critic, February 12, 1881.

[This article was all reprinted in SDC, in the section subtitled "Death of Thomas Carlyle." It constitutes all of that section except lines 29–57 and 72–80.]

xxxii *"The Dead Carlyle."*

Boston Literary World, February 12, 1881.

[This article was all reprinted in SDC as lines 29–57 and 72–80 of "Death of Thomas Carlyle."]

xxxiii *"Bumble-Bees and Bird-Music."*

The Philadelphia *American*, May 14, 1881.

[This article, consisting of eighteen paragraphs, was all reprinted in SDC except the last paragraph: paragraphs 1–3 in "Bumble-Bees," 4 in "Birds and Birds and Birds," 5–6 in "A Couple of Old Friends—A Coleridge Bit," 7 in "An Unknown," 8–10 in "Bird-Whistling," and 11–17 in "Bumble-Bees." Paragraph 18 is reprinted in the present edition in the textual notes on "Bumble-Bees."]

xxxiv *"A Week at West Hills."*

New York *Tribune*, August 4, 1881.

[This article contains fourteen paragraphs, of which the following were included in SDC: 2, 3, 6, and 9 in "The Old Whitman and Van Velsor Cemeteries," 7 in "Genealogy—Van Velsor and Whitman," and 10–12 in "The Maternal Homestead." The remainder of the article, paragraphs 1, 4, 5, 8, 13, and 14, omitted from SDC, are printed in the Appendix below.]

1 (Paragraph 1)

Sir: I have been for the last two weeks jaunting around Long Island, and now devote this letter to West Hills (Suffolk County, 30 miles from New-York), and the main purpose of a journey thither, to resume and identify my birth-spot, and that of my parents and their parents, and to explore the picturesque regions comprised in the townships of Huntington and Cold Spring Harbor. I shall just give my notes verbatim as I pencilled them.

2 (Paragraphs 4–5)

THE ACTUAL BIRTH-SPOT

Went down nearly a mile further to the house where I was born (May 31, 1819) in the fertile meadow land. As I paused and looked around I felt that any good farmer would have gloated over the scene. Rich corn in tassel, many fields; they had cradled their wheat and rye, and were cutting their oats. Everything had changed so much, and it looked so fine, I began to doubt about the house, and drove in and inquired, to be certain. I saw Mrs. J---, wife of the owner, (son of the J--- that bought the farm of my father 60 years ago). She was very courteous, and invited us in (Dr. Bucke, of Canada, with me), but we declined.

We drove back to the homestead, let down some bars at the foot of a slope, and ascended to a spot most interesting of all.

3 (*Paragraph 8*)

The Whitmans as originally spreading from this outset, were long-lived, most of them farmers, had big families, and were strenuous for the best education that could be obtained. One is mentioned as a great linguist, and sometimes acted in the courts as interpreter with the Indians; and down to the present date twelve of the name have graduated at Harvard, five at Yale and nine at other New-England colleges. There have been ministers and deacons and teachers by the dozen.

4 (*Paragraphs 13–14*)

JAYNE'S HILL

I write this back again at West Hills on the high elevation (the highest spot on Long Island?) of Jayne's Hill, which we have reached by a fascinating winding road. A view of thirty or forty, or even fifty or more miles, especially to the east and south and southwest; the Atlantic Ocean to the latter points in the distance—a glimpse or so of Long Island Sound to the north.

WHAT LINGERS PLEASANTEST IN MEMORY

Huntington, Aug. 1.—We are just leaving; a perfect day in sun, temperature, after the rain of yesterday and last night. I am indebted to Charles Velsor, Henry Lloyd, John Chichester, Lemuel Carll, Lawyer Street, Charles Shepard and other friends and relatives, for courtesies. Seems to me I have had the memorable though brief and quiet jaunt of my life. Every day a point attained; every day something refreshing, Nature's medicine. All about here, an area of many miles, Huntington, Cold Spring Harbor, East and West and Lloyd's Necks (to say nothing of the water views), the hundreds of tree-lined roads and lanes, with their turns and gentle slopes, the rows and groves of locusts, after the main objects of my jaunt, made the most attraction, as I rode around. I didn't know there was so much in mere lanes and trees. I believe they have done me more good than all the swell scenery I could find.

August 3, 1881.   W. W.

XXXV *"City Notes in August."*

New York *Tribune*, August 15, 1881.

[This article contains eleven paragraphs, of which the following were included in *SDC*: 1, the first two sentences of 2, and 4 and 5 in "Hot Weather New York," and 6–9 in "Custer's Last Rally." The remainder of the article, 3, 10, 11, and the last two sentences of 2, omitted in *SDC*, are printed below.]

1 (*Paragraph 3 and the last part of 2*)

You get here by steam from Forty-fourth-st. in fifteen minutes, and the fare is but six cents. Real estate is pretty high though; a nice corner plot, a hundred feet square, looking down on the river sixty rods off, they ask $11,000 for!

The city for miles is pleasantly varied and broken—the finest elms I have seen out of New-Haven, and many old oaks and other trees; nothing much of course in the farming line, but plenty of rural shows, gardens, flowers, lawns and small fruits. The August nights are cool and wonderfully bright here, with the harvest moon rising large and pale-yellow, and its plenteous sheen presently falling on water or shore, as we go out for an hour's rowing and floating in a boat.

2 (*Paragraphs 10–11*)

Altogether, "Custer's Last Rally" is one of the very few attempts at deliberate artistic expression for our land and people, on a pretty ambitious standard and programme, that impressed me as filling the bill.

COSMOPOLITANISM

I get around Manhattan Island more or less every day—get down in the city on Broadway or to the ferries—have gone once or twice to Brooklyn—wherever humanity is most copious and significant—let it all filter into me. The amelioration, superior growth, expansion, robustness, sympathy, good-natured universality, I noted two years ago as prevailing characteristics of average New-York everywhere are confirmed by this visit. New-York loves crowds—and I do, too. I can no more get along without houses, civilization, aggregations of humanity, meetings, hotels, theatres, than I can get along without food. Have I, too, somewhere in my writings been shallow enough to speak of living absolutely alone? of how good it were to hear nothing but silent Nature in woods, mountains far recesses? to see no tormenting sights, reeking presence of men, women, children? Ah, the permanent mood for one's clear and normal hours refuses such philosophy—such absence of philosophy rather.

W. W.

Mott Haven, Aug. 13, 1881

xxxvi *"Death of Longfellow."*

Critic, April 8, 1882.

[This article has seven paragraphs, the first five of which are included in SDC, "Death of Longfellow." The last two paragraphs, omitted in SDC, are printed in the Appendix below.]

1

Without jealousies, without mean passions, never did the personality character, daily and yearly life of a poet, more steadily and truly assimilate his own loving, cultured, guileless, courteous ideal, and exemplify it. In the world's arena, he had some special sorrows—but he had prizes, triumphs, recognitions, the grandest.

Extensive and heartfelt as is to-day, and has been for a long while, the fame of Longfellow, it is probable, nay certain, that years hence it will be wider and deeper. Walt Whitman.

xxxvii *"By Emerson's Grave."*

Critic, May 6, 1882.

[This article of five paragraphs was all included in SDC, "By Emerson's Grave."]

xxxviii *"Starting Newspapers."*

Camden *Courier*, first issue, June 1, 1882; reprinted in the New York *World*, June 11, 1882.

[This article of eleven paragraphs was all included in SDC except the eleventh paragraph and the last sentence of the tenth, which are quoted in the textual notes to this section.]

xxxix *"Edgar Poe's Significance."*

Critic, June 3, 1882. Two paragraphs are quoted in the *Critic* from the Washington *Star* of November 18, 1875.

[This article of eight paragraphs is all included in SDC, "Edgar Poe's Significance," except two or three sentences, which are quoted in the textual notes on "Edgar Poe's Significance" in the present edition.]

Appendix B

CHRONOLOGY
OF WALT WHITMAN'S LIFE AND WORK

1819	Born May 31 at West Hills, near Huntington, Long Island.
1823	May 27, Whitman family moves to Brooklyn.
1825 – 30	Attends public school in Brooklyn.
1830	Office boy for doctor, lawyer.
1830 – 34	Learns printing trade.
1835	Printer in New York City until great fire August 12.
1836 – 38	Summer of 1836, begins teaching at East Norwich, Long Island; by winter 1837 – 38 has taught at Hempstead, Babylon, Long Swamp, and Smithtown.
1838 – 39	Edits weekly newspaper, the *Long Islander*, at Huntington.
1840 – 41	Autumn 1840, campaigns for Van Buren; then teaches school at Trimming Square, Woodbury, Dix Hills, and Whitestone.
1841	May, goes to New York City to work as printer in *New World* office; begins writing for the *Democratic Review*.
1842	Spring, edits a daily newspaper in New York City, the *Aurora;* edits *Evening Tattler* for short time.
1845 – 46	August, returns to Brooklyn, writes for Brooklyn *Evening Star* (daily) and *Long Island Star* (weekly) until March, 1846.
1846 – 48	From March, 1846, until January, 1848, edits Brooklyn *Daily Eagle;* February, 1848, goes to New Orleans to work on the *Crescent;* leaves May 27 and returns via Mississippi and Great Lakes.
1848 – 49	September 9, 1848, to September 11, 1849, edits a "free soil" newspaper, the Brooklyn *Freeman*.
1850 – 54	Operates printing office and stationery store; does free-lance journalism; builds and speculates in houses.
1855	Early July, *Leaves of Grass* is printed by Rome Brothers in Brooklyn; father dies July 11.
1856	Writes for *Life Illustrated;* publishes second edition of *Leaves of Grass* in summer and writes "The Eighteenth Presidency!"
1857 – 59	From spring of 1857 until about summer of 1859 edits the Brooklyn *Times;* unemployed, winter of 1859–60, frequents Pfaff's bohemian restaurant.
1860	March, goes to Boston to see third edition of *Leaves of Grass* through the press.
1861	April 12, Civil War begins; George Whitman enlists.

1862	December, goes to Fredericksburg, Virginia, scene of recent battle in which George was wounded, stays in camp two weeks.
1863	Remains in Washington, D.C., working part time in Army Paymaster's Office, visits soldiers in hospitals.
1864	Mid-June, returns to Brooklyn because of illness.
1865	January 24, appointed clerk in Department of Interior, returns to Washington; meets Peter Doyle; witnesses Lincoln's second inauguration; Lincoln assassinated, April 14; May, *Drum-Taps* is printed; June 30, is discharged from position by Secretary James Harlan but reemployed next day in Attorney General's Office; autumn, prints *Drum-Taps and Sequel*, containing "When Lilacs Last in the Dooryard Bloom'd."
1866	William D. O'Connor publishes *The Good Gray Poet*.
1867	John Burroughs publishes *Notes on Walt Whitman as Poet and Person;* July 6, William Rossetti publishes article on Whitman's poetry in London *Chronicle;* "Democracy" (part of *Democratic Vistas*) published in December *Galaxy*.
1868	William Rossetti's *Poems of Walt Whitman* (selected and expurgated) published in England; "Personalism" (second part of *Democratic Vistas*) in May *Galaxy;* second issue of fourth edition of *Leaves of Grass*, with *Drum-Taps and Sequel* added.
1869	Mrs. Anne Gilchrist reads Rossetti edition and falls in love with the poet.
1870	July, is very depressed for unknown reasons; prints fifth edition of *Leaves of Grass*, and *Democratic Vistas* and *Passage to India*, all dated 1871.
1871	September 3, Mrs. Gilchrist's first love letter; September 7, reads "After All Not to Create Only" at opening of American Institute Exhibit in New York.
1872	June 26, reads "As a Strong Bird on Pinions Free" at Dartmouth College commencement.
1873	January 23, suffers paralytic stroke; mother dies May 23; unable to work, stays with brother George in Camden, New Jersey.
1874	"Song of the Redwood-Tree" and "Prayer of Columbus."
1875	Prepares Centennial Edition of *Leaves of Grass* and *Two Rivulets* (dated 1876).
1876	Controversy in British and American press over America's neglect of Whitman; spring, begins recuperation at Stafford Farm, at Timber Creek; September, Mrs. Gilchrist arrives and rents house in Philadelphia.
1877	January 28, gives lecture on Tom Paine in Philadelphia; during summer gains strength by sun-bathing at Timber Creek.
1878	Spring, too weak to give projected Lincoln lecture, but in June visits J. H. Johnson and John Burroughs in New York.
1879	April 14, first lecture on Lincoln in New York; September, makes trip to Colorado, long visit with brother Jeff in St. Louis.
1880	January, returns to Camden; summer, visits Dr. R. M. Bucke in London, Ontario.

1881   April 15, gives Lincoln lecture in Boston; returns to Boston in late summer to read proof of *Leaves of Grass*, being published by James R. Osgood; poems receive final arrangement in this edition.

1882   Osgood ceases to distribute *Leaves of Grass* because District Attorney threatens prosecution unless the book is expurgated; publication is resumed by Rees Welsh in Philadelphia, who also publishes *Specimen Days and Collect;* both books transferred to David McKay, Philadelphia.

1883   Dr. Bucke publishes *Walt Whitman*, biography written with poet's cooperation.

1884   Buys house on Mickle Street, Camden, New Jersey.

1885   In poor health; friends buy a horse and phaeton so that the poet will not be "house-tied"; November 29, Mrs. Gilchrist dies.

1886   Gives Lincoln lecture in Philadelphia.

1887   Gives Lincoln lecture in New York; is sculptured by Sidney Morse, painted by Herbert Gilchrist, J. W. Alexander, Thomas Eakins.

1888   Horace Traubel raises funds for doctors and nurses; *November Boughs* printed; money sent from England.

1889   Last birthday dinner, proceedings published in *Camden's Compliments*.

1890   Writes angry letter to J. A. Symonds, dated August 19, denouncing Symonds' interpretation of "Calamus" poems, claims six illegitimate children.

1891   *Good-Bye My Fancy* is printed, and the "death-bed edition" of *Leaves of Grass* (dated 1892).

1892   Dies March 26, buried in Harleigh Cemetery, Camden, New Jersey.